THE NON-COHERENCE THEORY OF DIGITAL HUMAN RIGHTS

Mart Susi offers a novel non-coherence theory of digital human rights to explain the change in meaning and scope of human rights rules, principles, ideas and concepts, and the interrelationships and related actors, when moving from the physical domain into the online domain. The transposition into the digital reality can alter the meaning of well-established offline human rights to a wider or narrower extent, impacting core concepts such as transparency, legal certainty and foreseeability. Susi analyses the 'loss in transposition' of some core features of the rights to privacy and freedom of expression. The non-coherence theory is used to explore key human rights theoretical concepts, such as the network society approach, the capabilities approach, transversality and self-normativity, and it is also applied to e-state and artificial intelligence, challenging the idea of the sameness of rights. This title is part of the Flip it Open Programme and may also be available Open Access. Check our website Cambridge Core for details.

Mart Susi is Professor of Human Rights Law at the School of Governance, Law and Society, Tallinn University. He has initiated several academic networks and projects involving more than 100 academics from around the world and is Chair of the Global Digital Human Rights Network.

The Non-coherence Theory of Digital Human Rights

MART SUSI
Tallinn University

CAMBRIDGE
UNIVERSITY PRESS

CAMBRIDGE
UNIVERSITY PRESS

Shaftesbury Road, Cambridge CB2 8EA, United Kingdom

One Liberty Plaza, 20th Floor, New York, NY 10006, USA

477 Williamstown Road, Port Melbourne, VIC 3207, Australia

314–321, 3rd Floor, Plot 3, Splendor Forum, Jasola District Centre, New Delhi – 110025, India

103 Penang Road, #05-06/07, Visioncrest Commercial, Singapore 238467

Cambridge University Press is part of Cambridge University Press & Assessment, a department of the University of Cambridge.

We share the University's mission to contribute to society through the pursuit of education, learning and research at the highest international levels of excellence.

www.cambridge.org
Information on this title: www.cambridge.org/9781009407700

DOI: 10.1017/9781009407717

First published 2024

A catalogue record for this publication is available from the British Library

Library of Congress Cataloging-in-Publication Data
NAMES: Susi, Mart, 1965- author.
TITLE: The non-coherence theory of digital human rights / Mart Susi, Tallinn University.
DESCRIPTION: Cambridge, United Kingdom ; New York, NY : Cambridge University Press, [2024] | Includes bibliographical references and index.
IDENTIFIERS: LCCN 2023038087 (print) | LCCN 2023038088 (ebook) | ISBN 9781009407700 (hardback) | ISBN 9781009407724 (paperback) | ISBN 9781009407717 (epub)
SUBJECTS: LCSH: Human rights. | Human rights–Data processing. | Internet–Law and legislation. | Technological innovations–Law and legislation. | Civil rights.
CLASSIFICATION: LCC K3240 .S859 2024 (print) | LCC K3240 (ebook) | DDC 342.08/5–dc23/eng/20231003
LC record available at https://lccn.loc.gov/2023038087
LC ebook record available at https://lccn.loc.gov/2023038088

ISBN 978-1-009-40770-0 Hardback

Contents

Acknowledgements

I would like to thank several colleagues for their invaluable assistance in preparing this manuscript. I am grateful to my PhD student Tomoe Watashiba for helping to bring the footnotes into proper order. I thank Michael Haagensen for language editing and keeping my original style as much as possible. Likewise, I express my gratitude to Kate McIntosh for her assistance with the preparation of the index. And I am thankful to Tobias Ginsberg and Gemma Smith from Cambridge University Press for their advice and availability during the preparation of this manuscript for print.

My special appreciation goes to dear colleague Robert Alexy for agreeing to have our exchange of views about the Internet Balancing Formula reprinted here. This exchange was first printed in the *European Law Journal* March 2019 'Special Issue on Internet and Human Rights Law'.

The graphic image illustrating the proportionality deficit paradox in Chapter 19 of the present volume first appeared in my article 'Digital Human Rights Proportionality during Global Crises' in the book *Pandemocracy in Europe: Power, Parliaments and People in Times of COVID-19*, edited by Matthias C. Kettemann and Konrad Lachmeyer and published in 2021 by Hart Publishing, an imprint of Bloomsbury Publishing Plc.

Finally, I wish to thank my family for patiently enabling me the 'magical three hours' each day to work on the manuscript. Not a single day without a word written, thank you.

Introduction

The Distorted Image

Finding simple words to describe a new theory – especially when it addresses somewhat complex matters – may be among the hardest of tasks, if not impossible. Since simplicity itself is a manifestation of non-coherence, its meaning being affected by a variety of properties – such as time, belonging to groups, understandings about idealism and practicalities – an attempt at a simple beginning has to be abandoned here. Yet, a soft start with some impressionistic brushstrokes can instead be chosen by presenting the image of the non-coherence theory of digital human rights through three non-legal lenses: Aristotelian logic, Plato's myth of the cave and Lewis Carroll's *Alice's Adventures in Wonderland*.

Most of us were taught that the following Aristotelian logic is independent of time and space: if all As are Bs, and all Bs are Cs, this means that all As are Cs. But what if we find a domain where this logic is precarious and we are faced with the following: if all As are Bs, and all Bs are Cs, it is not certain that all As are Cs. This would be a conclusion from observations of practice. A domain where the logic may not hold is that of digital human rights. And it calls for an explanation beyond the careful description of the non-reliability of a causal sequence. The Aristotelian logic may be upset because, while we established that all As have to be Cs, the meaning of some As changes and our initial statement that all As are Bs does not cover those As whose meaning altered in the meantime. In the alternative, and separately from time, we may have to conclude that the Aristotelian premise may turn into an invalid syllogism, and therefore it does not appear that all As are Cs, despite all As being Bs and all Bs being Cs. Various explanations are possible. The first is about Aristotelian logic being paradigm-centred; that is, it does not reach beyond the offline human rights paradigm to the online human rights domain. Another is that something happens during the transposition of As and Bs and Cs from the offline to the online domain. The meaning of these elements changes, and therefore the Aristotelian logic may still be valid in the online domain taken separately, but since offline As do not overlap with online As, the logical consequence cannot be validated. The variance from the initial Aristotelian logic is what reveals non-coherence theory.

Plato's myth of the cave is a perfect postulation of non-coherence theory. Plato put forward a description where the majority of people are living in a large cave, which has an opening to the outside world. Most people cannot or do not wish to exit into the sunlight. Near the cave outside are some individuals who carry objects, and the shadow of these objects is cast on the walls of the cave. Individuals inside look at these shadows, describe them to one another and debate who has the most accurate understanding about the reality of these objects. However, they never understand the true nature of all elements of these objects since they only discuss the shadows. People nowadays using digital tools and the Internet can be compared to those inside the cave from a digital human rights perspective. Offline human rights norms and procedures cast a shadow onto the walls inside – the digital walls – from the offline reality outside. We detect that here is a digital human rights norm, and there is a remedy, and over there is a principle, which might correspond to those outside. Debates assume that the shadow images are accurate duplications of the norms and remedies existing in the *real world*, but the fact remains that these are only shadows. We might ask about the rationality of such discourse. My response is: the *traditional* human rights paradigm is of such magnitude that replacement by a new paradigm seems formidable. The fact remains that content may be *lost in the shadows*. Non-coherence theory takes such loss as an assumption.

In 1871, Lewis Carroll published the novel *Through the Looking-Glass*, which was a sequel to *Alice's Adventures in Wonderland*. On entering a different world behind the looking glass, Alice is confronted with a reversal of the outside world. For example, the quicker you run away from something, the closer it gets to you. You may wish to move a chess figure in a game but you discover that this figure is alive and is already in a different place from where you thought it was standing. Alice now exists in two separate worlds, where identical words and actions exist, but their meaning and effects are different. That difference, as will be shown again and again in this monograph, is one of degree. Calling two different things using the same name is known as equivocation. Non-coherence theory argues that there is an equivocation of human rights law when we compare the offline and online domains. Privacy online is not the same as privacy offline. An effective remedy online is different from an effective remedy offline. Accepting such equivocation necessitates, from one angle, the abandonment of several key understandings about human rights law, such as the vertical governance model and the sameness of rights doctrine, and from another angle, justifying the normativity of equivocation. Non-coherence theory provides some key tools for such a justification.

For these reasons, I call this introduction an impression of the distorted image. Human rights online are distorted versions of human rights offline. This distortion appears in various formats and properties and will be the subject of this monograph.

PART I

The Contextual Challenges and Purpose of the Non-coherence Theory of Digital Human Rights

1

Horizontal and Vertical Governance Models and Normativity

1.1 THE IDEA OF NON-COHERENCE AND POTENTIAL OBJECTIONS

The idea of non-coherence theory originates from the distorted image of well-established human rights[1] in digital settings. This distorted image appears in various ontological and epistemic aspects. It reveals an absence of clarity on whether human rights rules and principles, the possibility of their realisation and related obligations and remedies against violations as established in the offline world (human rights law and practice *as we know it*) continue to exist online with or without variance. If variance exists between the two domains, the obvious matters of interest are the degree and consequences of such variance, whether it amounts to distortion, and, if distorted, whether its degree calls into question the feasibility or limits the scope of the transposability of offline human rights law and practice to online. For the purposes of this book, I bring the terms *variance* and *distortion* under a common denominator of *non-coherence*. There is no clear boundary to distinguish between them; the dividing line is whether the difference reflected after transposition from offline to online is narrow and concerns only some elements or whether the difference is more comprehensive. Every distorted image is at variance from the

[1] Referral to 'well-established human rights' maintains the focus while introducing the idea of non-coherence theory. These are rights which are recognised in various global human rights instruments as uncontested. This is a one-way street: the observer is interested in how element 'A' from the offline domain is transposable and reflected in the online domain. This is because the well-established human rights carry theoretical and practical offline history. In principle, the reverse is also possible. There are several new human rights which have emerged due to new technologies and whose cradle is online. The observer can now ask if and how these rights are transposable and reflected offline. Occasionally the monograph will observe this reversal also. See for reference A. von Arnauld, K. von der Decken, M. Susi (eds.), *Cambridge Handbook on New Human Rights: Recognition, Novelty, and Rhetoric* (Cambridge: Cambridge University Press, 2020).

original meaning and scope of the reflected element. But not every image at variance from the original can be labelled a distortion.

Numerous potential objections[2] can be raised against the idea of non-coherence theory – these are related to theoretical justifiability and the availability of evidence from practice. This book will address these potential objections in detail as it progresses. Here I raise the potential objection from normativity, in which it can be said that the main premise of non-coherence theory – the consistent condition of the unpredictability of human rights law and practice in the digital domain – remains speculative since normative regulation and policies do exist vis-à-vis human rights online. An objector could simply point to the vast body of norms and policies towards online human rights and certainly the related academic discourse. This argument can continue by highlighting that vertical and horizontal internet governance models, despite their mutual co-existence leading to a withering of the claim to exclusiveness against one another, as a sole source of online regulation, accomplish what normative structures are called to do – provide a rational basis for governance. At this point we have to note the focus of the discussion – governance models do not concern the content of rights but rather only concern formal questions about the processes by which the rights are defined – who are the relevant actors, how can the rights be enforced and what are the available remedies and sanctions in the event of violations. There are hundreds of articles and books on the topic, which leads me to confine myself to pointing out the main features relevant for the argument from normativity against non-coherence theory. In doing so I will, however, demonstrate that the simultaneous existence of multiple normative governance models does not speak against but for the justifiability of non-coherence theory.

In a nutshell, the vertical governance model in law is based on the coercive force of state structures against private entities. Despite some loss of linearity[3] in practice – some elements may be delegated to private entities – the fact remains that such delegation serves the goal of effectiveness and does not result in the incapability of the vertical model to operate all main features related to a normative framework on its own. New technologies are one reason

[2] These objections are potential, since here is the theory's inaugural presentation. Therefore, I can only speculate what might constitute the main points of any future critique.

[3] Vertical linearity is understood as a 'pure' model where all the main features of regulation are in the hands of the sovereign power, no matter its political characterisation as democratic or not. This sovereign power sets the rules of the game, oversees their implementation and operates judicial or quasi-judicial agencies to take action when the rules are not followed.

for the state easing its stance on interference into private matters.[4] Horizontal governance models are, by contrast, based on non-hierarchical structures involving a variety of actors in partnership over competition, where the output of regulation and compliance mechanisms is based on the idea I would term *working together*.[5] For the purpose of the non-coherence theory of digital human rights, we are interested in whether these governance models regarding the Internet continue to operate in isolation and whether there is a combination of elements, and if so, what is the degree of equilibrium.

1.2 THREE SCENARIOS OF THE TRANSPOSITION OF GOVERNANCE MODELS

A superficial glance at the development of the internet first highlights its relative shortness – since the beginning of the 2000s – and therefore seems to eliminate the predisposition that the transposal of human rights law and procedures from the offline to the online domain could have been countered by an existing conceptual and regulatory framework. Such a starting point for analysis would, therefore, not find it worthwhile to look at examples from the history of law where the intent to transpose a well-established and functioning legal system to unknown territory has failed or resulted in systemic variance due to existing ideas about rights and some form of regulatory structures from the *other side*. There are three possible scenarios whereby a normative-ideological regulatory framework – which is a concept of a more general level than a governance model – can be transposed to another environment.[6]

The first concerns a situation where a certain normative-ideological regulatory framework is carried to another socio-geographic environment, but it is countered by an existing framework, be it well or less well established. This scenario, which we may label the socio-geographic transposition of law, can be illustrated by the process of imposing colonial supremacy on the territories of the indigenous or more established albeit different cultures. Saliha

4 Take, for example, the Mann-Elkins Act of 1910, where the United States Congress gave the telegraph and telephone companies immunity from liability for the content they carried on the basis of the 'common carriage' doctrine.

5 For discussion see S. D. Philips, 'The Myths of Horizontal Governance: Is the Third Sector Really a Partner?', Intersectional Society for Third-Sector Research (ISTR) Conference, Toronto, July 2004.

6 The choice of the term signifies a more general situation of any attempt to take the normative-ideological structure from an established setting and transpose or impose it elsewhere. There may be no countering normative-ideological regulatory framework, or it may be underdeveloped, hence the broader term 'environment'.

Belmessous has shown that the colonisation of indigenous people from America, Africa, Australia and New Zealand was countered not only by force but also by ideas and understanding of a law which should apply between people. She uses the expression of indigenous legal opposition to European legislative framework and justifications.[7] From the perspective of legal scholarship, this opposition means contestation between ideas and procedures, that is, mechanisms for how the ideas are made to govern. Non-coherence theory makes the assumption that there is no or only minor contestation. Yet such contestation may appear in time.

The second scenario concerns regime change, leading to the ideological transposition of law. Legal scholarship dominated by comparative methodology does not conclusively show the possibility of the full replacement of established legal ideologies and structures by an incompatible set of ideas, leading to an entirely different understanding of how the law should govern society.[8] The overthrow of the Russian tsarist regime by the Bolsheviks led to the enactment of socialist ideology, but the administrative and court systems were largely functionally retained. The French Revolution led perhaps, at least initially, to even broader chaos in terms of laws and procedures.[9] Regime change may go hand in hand with the adoption of legal norms from a regime falling into the same ideological paradigm.[10] The common characteristic of regime change is the generic variance of the legal framework before and after the change, whereas the variance can always be characterised by degree. Such a scenario would not make sense in the initial stages after the digital domain appeared for the simple reason that there was no regime to be changed. But it does not exclude the possibility that the regime may have appeared over time, either in disguise or openly, which is then subject to the aspiration of regime

7 S. Belmessous (ed.), *Native Claims: Indigenous Law against Empire*, 1500–1920 (Oxford Academic, 19 January 2012), https://doi.org/10.1093/acprof:oso/9780199794850.001.0001, accessed 24 November 2022.

8 Peter Reich has explored the impact of regime change upon legal change and has identified various outcomes. For example, he writes that regime change in the Second Empire in ancient Rome resulted in hybridisation; in Canada, regime change led to legal conundrums for decades; and in California, gradual supplanting of the civil law system. See P. L. Reich, 'Regime Change and Legal Change – The Legacy of Mexico's Second Empire' (2005) 1 *Oxford U Comparative Law Forum*, https://ouclf.law.ox.ac.uk/regime-change-and-legal-change-the-legacy-of-mexicos-second-empire.

9 R. G. Fuchs, *Contested Paternity: Constructing Families in Modern France* (Baltimore: John Hopkins University Press, 2008), pp. 34–41.

10 P. Varul, H. Pisuke, 'Louisiana's Contribution to the Estonian Civil Code' (1999) 75 *Tulane Law Review*, 1027.

change from the offline domain. This concerns matters like self-normativity and self-constitutionalisation, discussed further on.

The third scenario concerns a situation where people and institutions enter an unknown territory with their own discursive history, ideas and values, but for one reason or another note that their regulatory and ideological equipment does not fully work. Imagine a colony established on Mars, where the colonisers soon experience that somehow the laws and legal procedures of Earth are not completely compatible with the challenges of an uninhabited planet. The planet Mars seems to have no preconditions for normative regulation, yet something has to be changed. It is similar in the online domain. We can term this scenario the transposition of law into normative *carte blanche*. This position might take it for granted that the digital domain could have been characterised – in its early years – as such an empty sheet available for the transposition of normative regulation; that is, there were no countering normative forces, and the offline regulatory and conceptual framework would appear welcome by the online. A deeper examination questions this predisposition for the reason of the *inadequacy of protection* thesis, which I have developed elsewhere to explain the element of novelty in human rights development.[11] This thesis claims that the development of new human rights is explainable through the recognition of the incapability of established human rights to provide adequate protection of certain groups in comparison with others, or that the novel contemporary conditions challenge the capability of an established human right to provide sufficient protection of an important social value. The common element of both reasons leading to the articulation of new human rights according to the inadequacy of protection thesis is contestation. The application of this thesis to the internet is at the bottom of questions on whether it is possible to provide in the online domain protection that is comparable to that in the offline domain by using the concepts entirely placed in and originating from offline, or whether offline remedies can be effectively applied online.

1.3 THE INADEQUACY OF PROTECTION THESIS

The inadequacy of protection thesis when applied to the internet is offline-morphic and practice-dependent. Offline-morphic means the view from the

[11] M. Susi, 'Novelty in New Human Rights: The Decrease of Universality and Abstractness Thesis' in A. von Arnauld, K. von der Decken, M. Susi (eds.), *Cambridge Handbook on New Human Rights of the 21st Century: Recognition, Novelty, and Rhetoric* (Cambridge: Cambridge University Press, 2020), pp. 21–22.

offline domain, analogous to when an animal rights lawyer projects her understandings onto other species and concludes that they exhibit behavioural patterns comparable to humans.[12] The image that can be posited as adequate from the perspective of the well-established offline legal system may be viewed as inadequate by a viewer from the electronic world. Just like when a Western lawyer deems the absence of adversarial proceedings among an indigenous group as inadequate, her view would find no understanding from inside the group. The offline-morphic component of the inadequacy of protection thesis is dichotomous, which may be in terms of degree between the online and offline regulatory realms. It eliminates the potential claims of regulatory superiority[13] from *non-coherence theory*, replacing it with the *capabilities approach* and *comparability of protection thesis*, discussed later in this monograph.

The practice-dependent aspect of the inadequacy of protection thesis refers to the method of verification. Careful observers can count from practical observation, scholarly statements and the views of the courts, individualised and generalised stories of how the digital domain affords a somewhat different protection in comparison with the offline. Certain remedies remain ineffective, even if theoretically accessible. The overarching verification, and thereby confirmation of the correctness of the practice dependency aspect of the inadequacy of protection thesis, is best understood via the traditional wisdom 'where there is smoke, there must be fire'. Smoke stands for contestation, that is, the process of a detail-oriented and arguments-based exchange of viewpoints about the full or partial compatibility of offline human rights ideas and norms with the online reality. Non-coherence stands for fire, that is, the revelation of a non-coherent image when comparing human rights normative-ideological frameworks offline and online.

Not every disagreement or alternative explanation regarding human rights law should be viewed as a contestation against the adequacy of non-digital human rights norms and ideas in the digital sphere. To term a discussion as contestation, a critical mass of discussants and actors must exist who, while not agreeing on a common outcome, are at the same time in agreement regarding the inadequacy of the protection. The reasons for such an agreement are not important at this point since this chapter is concerned with the explication of

[12] M. C. Nussbaum, 'Animal Rights: The Need for a Theoretical Basis' (2001) 114 *Harvard Law Review*, 5, 1506–1552.

[13] For the notion of regulatory superiority, see, for example, Friedrich F. Martens' concept of consular jurisdiction, exercised by the Western consuls over their nationals in the Oriental states. See A. T. Müller, F. F. Martens, 'The Office of Consul and Consular Jurisdiction in the East' (2014) 25 *European Journal of International Law*, 3, 871–891.

the dichotomy of internet governance models. Their very co-existence means contesting views on whether one of the models is solely, or in conjunction with some elements of the other model, more suitable for providing the regulatory structure for human rights in the digital sphere. There are no quantitative measurements about the frequency and intensity of questions that make it possible to establish universal criteria when differing viewpoints become a contestation. Yet there are instances when something is obvious prima facie, as is the case with the incompatibility of offline human rights governance models online. This is expressed in various discursive statements; for example, using expressions like fragmentation, polarisation and hybridisation.[14]

The element of contestation is also clearly evident in alternative categorisations of the processes whereby one legal system is transposed into a different setting. Berkowitz et al. write about four groups of classification applicable to the transposition of legal systems: direct-receptive, direct-unreceptive, indirect-receptive, and indirect-unreceptive.[15]

The non-coherent image of human rights in the digital domain does not appear immediately and develops over time. This does not mean gradual incremental transformation, since the element of time depends on the scope of actors and interests, both public and private. An example of this is someone who sporadically glances at the mirror in the morning and detects a small wrinkle, and then on closer inspection discovers that the whole face in the mirror appears fully distorted. This person may panic, yet after further scrutiny understands that the distorted image is not because the face has changed, but the cause is the mirror itself. This mirror then is not adequately reflecting the true nature of the face. Using this analogy for human rights, the inadequacy of the protection of human rights in the digital sphere is comprehensible after evidence from practice that something has changed. All previously described scenarios of normative-ideological transformation may be applied, leading to one and the same conclusion of non-coherence.

1.4 NORMATIVE TRANSPOSITION *CARTE BLANCHE* AND RHETORICAL FUNCTIONALITY

The last scenario, termed a normative transposition *carte blanche*, is primarily of a rhetorical nature and is short of concrete verification that human rights

[14] G. De Gregorio, R. Radu, 'Digital Constitutionalism in the New Era of Internet Governance' (2022) 30 *International Journal of Law and Technology*, 1, 68–87.

[15] See D. Berkowitz, K. Pistor, J.-F. Richard, 'Economic Development, Legality, and the Transplant Effect' (2003) 47 *European Economic Review*, 1, 165–195.

law and principles from the offline domain are not entirely or partially adequate in the digital reality. A statement from 1996 by John Perry Barlow, delivered at Davos, Switzerland, illustrates well the rhetorical attack against human rights *as we know it* without offering the quest of alternatives. He writes: 'Governments of the Industrial World, you weary giants of flesh and steel, I come from Cyberspace, the new home of Mind. On behalf of the future, I ask you of the past to leave us alone. You are not welcome among us. You have no sovereignty where we gather.'[16] When placing the normative transition *carte blanche* into the rhetoric of rights doctrine articulated by Arnaud and Theilen in 2020,[17] and relying on the communication theory of human rights, one detects that the distorted image of offline human rights through the online mirror initially captures our attention because of the novelty of the image. The magnitude of such a distortion appears in inverse correlation to its immediate explainability. As such, the traditional vertical human rights governance model seems to lose at least some effectiveness, yet we do not initially fully comprehend the reasons and alternatives. The functionalist approach discussed by Arnaud and Theilen[18] provides a conceptual tool to reflect how the rhetoric about the incompatibility of the offline human rights framework and governance models with the cyber reality gradually transforms into a discursive justification of new governance models. The functions are as follows, although they are interrelated, yet Arnaud and Theilen do not show specifically the extent to which these functions overlap or the logical path of when and why one function gives way to the other:

(i) The *appellative function* is related to the affective and energising element implied by statements that the regulative and ideological status quo

[16] J. P. Barlow, 'Declaration on the Independence of the Cyberspace', Electronic Frontier Foundation, 8 February 1996, www.eff.org/cyberspace-independence, accessed 25 May 2022. He continues: 'We have no elected government, nor are we likely to have one, so I address you with no greater authority than that with which liberty itself always speaks. I declare the global social space we are building to be naturally independent of the tyrannies you seek to impose on us. You have no moral right to rule us nor do you possess any methods of enforcement we have true reason to fear. Governments derive their just powers from the consent of the governed. You have neither solicited nor received ours. We did not invite you. You do not know us, nor do you know our world. Cyberspace does not lie within your borders. Do not think that you can build it, as though it were a public construction project. You cannot. It is an act of nature and it grows itself through our collective actions.'

[17] A. von Arnaud, J. T. Theilen, 'Rhetoric of Rights: A Topical Perspective on the Function of Claiming a "Human Rights to . . ."' in A. von Arnauld, K. von der Decken, M. Susi (eds.), *Cambridge Handbook on New Human Rights of the 21st Century: Recognition, Novelty, and Rhetoric* (Cambridge: Cambridge University Press, 2020), pp. 34–49.

[18] Ibid.

somehow is not compatible with the new realities. It strengthens activism, where the side of argumentation remains of secondary importance. In our framework of the distorted image of online human rights against human rights law *as we know it*, this function shows that the distortion is noted, and then the need for an explanation and alternative regulation is put forward either through activism, or academia or the political establishments.

(ii) Explanations of incompatibility and proposals for a different regulation and ideology appear through the *contesting function*, which logically taken follows the appellative function. For the purposes of this book and this review of the different governance models, the contesting function appears when a horizontal governance model is put forward as more or exclusively suitable for human rights in the digital realm. There is a specific aspect of contestation characterising human rights governance models for the Internet in comparison to contestation when new rights claims appear. New human rights claims run against the entrenched framework by proposing new rights – such as the right to water or right to euthanasia – but the contestation between the horizontal and vertical governance models is marred by lexical semantics. Both models use the same words and do not offer substantially alternative outcomes. To put it differently, multiple discursive frameworks can have a magnifying effect on the idealistic element of the quest for rights. This is simply because, when confronted with a choice between several ways to understand, communicate and regulate a shared reality, we would in an ideal world put ideas in front of pragmatics. To articulate this differently, the promise embedded inside human rights principles grows in importance – with normativity in the narrow sense at stake – when more than one rights narrative appears to carry the regulatory and remedial *metacode*. For digital human rights, this multiplicity of discursive frameworks and regulatory narratives appears with the co-existence of horizontal and vertical regulatory governance models for the Internet. Since such contestation appears at a high level of generality, it becomes a matter of contestation beyond argumentative justification, and in the Kelsenian spirit, a contestation between grounded norms, that is, the choice between horizontal and vertical governance models is rooted in ideology and culture rather than the effectiveness of the model. Noncoherence theory shows that one model does not have superiority over another in abstract. Here there are the hidden roots of relativity, and noncoherence theory appears as the key.

(iii) It is therefore questionable what the next function – the *connecting function* – can accomplish. Arnaud and Theilen have described this function as having the 'potential to connect various local, regional and global discourses across politics, law and morality and thereby give prominence to the underlying issue'.[19] This explanation is almost identical to the specific phenomenon of multistakeholderism in internet governance, formulated by Joanna Kulesza as 'a distributed policy-making model based on the voluntary cooperation of key actors, usually identified as: states, business and civil society, operating "in their respective roles" through "rough consensus and running code"'.[20] For more than one party to connect, a genuine willingness from both sides is needed, otherwise the logical sequence of rhetorical functions comes to a standstill. This is the position which appears in multistakeholderism.

1.5 THE MULTISTAKEHOLDERISM VEIL THESIS

Dialogue and connectivity may be an end in itself, or alternatively there may exist the expectation of reaching some form of regulatory end result. Both versions are conceivable for multistakeholderism as ramifications reflecting the connecting function, and both are explainable through the non-coherence theory of digital human rights, but for different reasons. Multistakeholderism as an end result in itself carries primarily non-regulatory aspirations, such as an advocacy tool for civil society or *whitewashing* the aspirations of stakeholders who are more equal than others.[21] Referring back to the Introduction, the connecting function of human rights rhetoric regarding human rights in the digital domain can reveal itself in the format of consistent process without reaching a qualitatively new and distinct outcome, but while displaying properties which seem at odds with human rights law as we know it offline. In this case, multistakeholderism says that the digital domain necessitates a regulatory and perhaps ideological framework which is at variance with the offline version but does not give a specific design of the features that would replace the previous version. Usually, there is no attention to whether such a new regulation is theoretically justifiable or practically possible, thus enforcing the inadequacy of protection thesis as a

[19] Ibid., p. 44.

[20] For the discussion about multistakehoderism, see J. Kulesza, 'Multistakeholderism – Meaning and Implications' in M. Susi (ed.), *Human Rights, Digital Society and the Law: A Research Companion* (London: Routledge, 2019), pp. 117–131.

[21] A. Kovacs, 'Moving Multistakeholderism Forward: Lessons from the NETmundial', Internet Policy Review: *Journal on Internet Regulation*, 12 May 2014, https://policyreview.info/articles/news/moving-multistakeholderism-forward-lessons-netmundial/281, accessed 5 June 2022.

practice-dependent view.[22] The situation resembles Plato's Cave, where discussants inside the cave try to guess what is happening outside. They plan activities and take up arms but upon exiting the cave may find these completely useless.

The connecting function of multistakeholderism can lead to regulatory aspirations,[23] which can be viewed as the manifestation of the *triggering function* in the framework of the rhetoric of rights formulated by Arnaud and Theilen. These aspirations can exist in two separate spheres: the first concerns ideas and the second concerns the format where ideas are discussed and normative conclusions drawn. The matter of ideas will be viewed later in this monograph in the sections on the ontological and epistemic dimensions of human rights law in the digital domain. Concerning the second sphere – discursive formats and various co-creation models – it suffices here to note the relative abundance of various public, private and semi-public-semi-private forums aspiring to standard setting.[24] By itself, the search for standards in forums overwhelmingly confirms the inadequacy of protection thesis and as a logical sequence justifies non-coherence theory. If there was no variance, there would be no haste towards creating or co-creating new regulatory mechanisms. The triggering function of human rights rhetoric in the digital domain therefore verifies the proposition that human rights ideology and regulation in the digital domain is at variance with the offline. This represents the image of non-coherence.

The *jurisgenerative function* of rights rhetoric explains how framing the recognition of the inadequacy of protection may have discursive effects which create legal meaning. This means, that in lieu of statements demonstrating

[22] See, for example, a statement regarding the need for normative development without specifics in J. Brake, 'Co-regulation or Capitulation? Addressing Conflicts Arising by AI and Standardization' (2020) 25 *Lex Electronica*, 2, 13: 'The need for regulation that reconciles high-level ethics, dynamic technological progress and enforceable rules calls for multi-stakeholder cooperation in the process of developing and enforcing rules, which can be found in co-regulation. This encompasses in the broadest sense all variations of regulation between state-exclusive and industry self-regulation'.

[23] See, for example, praise towards the Internet Governance Forum, which says that as 'an open, multistakeholder forum, it carries the potential to act as a legitimate governance network for the Internet regime, whose discussions not only carry normative influence on their own account, but are also reflected in the development and implementation of policy by other institutions and mechanisms, both public and private' – J. Malcoolm, 'Appraising the Success of the Internet Governance Forum', Internet Governance Project, 21 November 2008, www.internetgovernance.org/wp-content/uploads/MalcolmIGFReview.pdf, accessed 21 August 2022.

[24] See for reference A. Harcourt, G. Christou, S. Simpson, *Global Standard Setting in Internet Governance* (Oxford: Oxford University Press, 2020).

pure dissatisfaction with the status quo, a new model of rights governance is proposed, having the claim of normativity and ideological justification. Wischmeyer has distinguished two separate narratives characterising the digitisation of human rights – transformation and reconfiguration – both of which can be brought under the umbrella of jurisgeneration.[25] The transformation narrative claims that digital technologies have betrayed the original ideals of the digital revolution and have morphed from tools, which we employ to serve our ends, to express our thoughts and to communicate with others freely, into artefacts, which control how we act, think and communicate.[26] Wischmeyer writes like a clear proponent of non-coherence theory: 'it is far from clear how the regulatory instruments we could employ to protect the normative status quo would look'.[27] His statement is characterising an image where one notes variance, without being able to subject the image to detailed characterisation.

The jurisgenerative function of the reconfiguration narrative lies in the 'concern … to make the rules and principles that were developed for the offline world fit for the digital age'.[28] Uncertainty connected to the transformation narrative of how the unclear image of human rights through the digital mirror can be solidified is omnipresent also in the reconfiguration narrative. It is evident through its search of governance mechanisms that increase the benefits and reduce the costs for individuals and societies. We notice consistent and ongoing contestation between various narratives and governance models.

Against this background, I am proposing the multistakeholderism veil thesis, which will be confirmed or rejected in various sections later in this monograph. This thesis is inspired by the various transposition scenarios described earlier in this chapter. The rise of the Internet in the late 1990s and early 2000s can be characterised by the expansion of technological horizons, overshadowing the absence of internet-specific regulation, thereby assuming that the law *as we know it* from offline can be easily transposed into the digital reality. This was the period of transformation *carte blanche*. Recognition of the unclear image led to the ideological transposition through the multistakeholderism scenario, where co-creation and dialogue were viewed as a means to arrive at the clear image, while still relying on the conceptual and procedural building blocks from offline. In parallel, the

[25] T. Wischmeyer, 'Making Social Media an Instrument of Democracy' (2019) 25 *European Law Journal*, Special Issue: Internet and Human Rights Law, 2, 169–181.

[26] Ibid., 170.

[27] Ibid.

[28] Ibid., 171.

online community construed its own understandings of human rights in the digital domain, either implicitly or explicitly intending to conceptually counter the offline framework. By the time the limitations of the multistakeholder approach became evident, the only scenario left was the rivalry between competing regulatory frameworks; that is, between the horizontal and vertical governance models. This thesis will be explored further for the purposes of rejection or verification. Having written this, the condition of regulatory uncertainty and proliferation has an axiomatic effect on human rights in the digital domain, which can be viewed as an element of non-coherence. The ambition of the non-coherence theory of digital human rights therefore lies, among many other characteristics, in providing a conceptual framework for understanding the implications from the co-existence of multiple internet governance models.

2

The Ontological Dimension

Reflections on Distorted Images and Normative Fragmentation

2.1 SOME OBSERVATIONS ON THE FOCUS

The ontological dimension of human rights in the digital domain concerns its theoretical foundations and the content of human rights norms. Based on the Aristotelian theory of epistemology, this represents the side of objective reality. The non-coherence theory of digital human rights explores the ontology of human rights at various levels of generality. It starts with an existential question – how can we know that human rights exist – and applies this to the digital domain. This is the transposition of ontological inquiry: can justifications about the existence of human rights offline be carried over to the digital domain? It then proceeds to examine whether the definition of human rights offline appears to be non-coherent online. Finally, the ontological queries are related to the possible variance in the meaning of specific human rights; in other words, whether the way well-established rights are understood offline (e.g., the right to the freedom of expression or the right to privacy), also applies online. The assumption emanating from the non-coherence approach implies differences in meaning.

The methodology of this chapter dealing with the ontology of human rights in the digital domain is confined to an abstract approach to the matters raised. I will assume ideal discursive conditions that are not influenced by actors and are time and place independent. Therefore, the approach of this chapter differs from the overarching assumption of the practice dependency of human rights in the digital domain, rooted in the very concept of non-coherence since the exploration of the offline image of human rights in the digital mirror by itself constitutes an act of practice. At the same time, such an abstract aspiration, assuming the possibility of ideal discursive conditions, may overlook the generic chiasmic structure of human rights as if existing in parallel offline and online universes. We should be attentive of Merleau-Ponty's reflection about the prejudges which accompany the application of terminology from one distinct reflective domain to another. For the purpose of this book, I have chosen his reflection about the colour red to illustrate the conceptual *loss in transposition*, as a mirror may reflect a different red than the one which we see directly:

> We must first understand that this red under my eyes is not, as is always said, a *quale*, a pellicle of being without thickness, a message at the same time indecipherable and evident, which one has or has not received, but of which, if one has received it, one knows all there is to know, and of which in the end there is nothing to say. It requires focusing, however brief.[1]

The focus which Merleau-Ponty calls for may lead to doubting, in the context of ideal discursive circumstances, whether practice independence is at all possible for human rights in the digital domain. If it is not, then the distinction between legal rights and human rights as known from the offline realm becomes non-futile. And then we would face only legal rights in the online domain, and at best we could be satisfied with the statement that human rights only exist offline and upon transposition into the digital domain turn into legal rights with a lower level of generality. This in turns leads to the rejection of the basic premise of human rights, which Pereira Coutinho defines as the constitution of a critical and reactive standard to authoritative practices on which human rights cannot depend.[2] The response from non-coherence theory is simple, however, saying that non-coherence is a predominantly one-way street. The theory is interested in how the image of human rights as known offline is reflected online. From this perspective, even an antimetabole carries meaning, even if this means that the reflection remains entirely incomprehensible.

The discussion on how we know that human rights exist remains largely outside of the focus of this monograph, due to the very meaning of the non-coherence concept – if human rights cannot be defended then there is simply nothing to look for in the online domain. The ontological basis of offline human rights rests on the dilemma of whether certain fundamental rights belong to any sentient being by their very nature, that is, having intrinsic roots as inseparable from the sentient being itself, or whether they are conferred by

[1] M. Merleau-Ponty, *The Visible and the Invisible*, edited by Claude Lefort, translated by Alphonso Lingis, Northwestern University Studies in Phenomenology and Existential Philosophy (Evanston, IL: Northwestern University Press, 1968), p. 130.

[2] L. P. Coutinho, 'The Practice-Independency of Human Rights' in M. La Torre, L. Niglia, M. Susi (eds.), *The Quest for Rights: Ideal and Normative Dimensions* (Northampton, MA: Edward Elgar Publishing, 2019), p. 49.

some outside authority.[3] A more simplistic approach would say that human rights exist because the United Nations or some other authoritative and collective international body tells us so. I will carry this dual approach along into various discussions in the next section, formulated as: do human rights in the digital domain exist because sentient beings when venturing into the virtual reality carry them with them, or is some non-sentient authority capable of justifying that they exist online as well.

2.2 REFLECTIONS OF OFFLINE JUSTIFICATIONS ONLINE

On deeper scrutiny, there exist multifarious attempts to justify human rights. Robert Alexy has categorised eight groups: religious, biological, intuitionistic, consensual, instrumental, cultural, explicative and existential.[4] A short review of their argumentative force from the non-coherent perspective are in order to view the extent to which the justifications applicable offline are usable online.

2.2.1 *Religious Justification*

The religious justification of human rights appears in two versions: the first is the absence of discursive and logically sequenced argumentation, and the second is related to the communication model. The first version can, but does not have to, be influenced by time; that is, religious justification resembles the rhetorical aspect of rights development when the idea of something has not yet led to the articulation of a logically based and sequenced reasoning. The fifth sentence of the Universal Declaration of Human Rights – 'whereas the peoples of the United Nations have in the Charter reaffirmed their *faith* in fundamental rights' – serves as an example of religious justification, which according to current scholarship has been replaced by non-religious argumentation.[5] Since there are assertions regarding some foundational ideas of human rights which remain outside of pure argumentation, it becomes obvious that the religious justification of human rights may also be time independent. It is a matter of the establishment of certain basic ideas which in the Kelsenian spirit cannot be a subject of argumentation and stay at the level of faith, for example, the belief that dignity is the core principle of

3 Literature about the topic is immense, see for reference R. Dennehy, 'The Ontological Basis of Human Rights' (1978) 42 *The Thomist: A Speculative Quarterly Review*, 3, 434–463.

4 R. Alexy, 'The Existence of Human Rights' (2011) *Law of Ukraine: Legal Journal*, 11–12, 102–111.

5 See, for example, A. Kohen, *In Defence of Human Rights: A Non-religious Grounding in a Pluralistic World* (London: Routledge, 2007).

human rights architecture. More will be said about this later in the monograph in search of grounded norms and ideas of digital human rights. Here I will confine myself to the observation that, like offline, the online domain of human rights contains different statements which necessitate the element of faith. Take, for example, the implicit assumption that rights offline and online are the same, contained in the seminal United Nations Human Rights Council statement in Resolution 20/8, from 5 July 2012. What the council in reality writes in paragraph 1 of the resolution – '[a]ffirms that the same rights that people have offline must also be protected online'[6] – is faith in the sameness. Many more examples of statements regarding human rights online could be given, in particular from the operational level, where the core feature is the reliance of rhetoric rather than logic in the argumentation. For the purposes of this book, we can therefore assert that the element of the religious justification of digital human rights in the version of core ideas is probably more omnipresent than regarding offline human rights.

The second version of religious justification is rooted in an etymologically understood vision 'of final and radical reconciliation, a set of beliefs about how one is or can be bound or connected to the world – to the "other" and to "nature" – and, above all, to ultimate reality in a profoundly intimate way'.[7] This is related to the sense of belonging to one community which understands certain features in a similar way without the need for additional discursive exercises. The digital domain rests on the viability of such a reconciliatory approach, but for a different reason. When Eric Goldman asks the question – '[o]n the Internet, the question arises: whose community standards?'[8] – he refers to the hierarchical nature of internet community standards.[9] The hierarchical aspect of internet community standards leads us to propose the digital community standards veil thesis, which means that in comparison with the offline meaning of community standards, internet community standards imply the idea of 'take it or leave it' as a gateway to the digital domain.

6 U.N. General Assembly, Human Rights Council, 'The Promotion, Protection and Enjoyment of Human Rights on the Internet', HRC 20th session, UN Doc A/HRC/RES/20/8 (2012).

7 M. J. Perry, 'Is the Idea of Human Rights Ineliminably Religious?' (1993) 27 *University of Richmond Law Review*, 5, 1031.

8 E. Goldman, 'Internet Obscenity Conviction Requires Assessment of National Community Standards – US v, Kilbride', Technology and Marketing Law Blog, 30 October 2009, https://blog.ericgoldman.org/archives/2009/10/internet_obscen.htm, accessed 14 June 2022.

9 For more about so-called community standards, see: A. Kućs, J. Viljanen, 'Updating Freedom of Expression Doctrines in the New Media Cases: Lessons from Strasbourg and Other International Treaty Bodies' in M. Susi, J. Viljanen, E. Jónsson, A. Kucs (eds.), *Human Rights Law and Regulating Freedom of Expression in New Media: Lessons from Nordic Approaches* (London: Routledge, 2018).

The non-coherent aspect is clearly visible – the element of the impossibility of the users' communities to have any say in the formulation of these standards. Internet community standards are non-coherent with offline community standards because of the exclusion of the community from their articulation. More will be said about this when I write about the aspect of non-transparency.

2.2.2 *Biological Justification*

The biological justification of human rights originates from the ideas of the Enlightenment and the theory of natural rights, whereby all individuals share similar biologically determined desires and needs. Ralph W. Gerard articulated in more contemporary science the idea of a biological basis for ethics[10] and claimed that although the biologist cannot supply the details of what present human rights should be, nevertheless, biological evolution sets the framework for rights articulation, in particular asserting that '[g]reater dependence of the individual on the group is in line with evolution'.[11] This assertion, contrary to what Gerard may have envisioned, does not carry a moral dimension. Notwithstanding the objection against biological ethics, due to the lack of convincing argumentation that altruistic attitudes are a result of biological evolution,[12] group dependence can lead to morally fragmented results. Even the more recently expressed view by Wilson that, '[a] basic element of human nature is that people feel compelled to join groups and, having joined, consider them superior to competing groups',[13] says nothing about the nature of these groups. For instance, Sam Harris has shown that violent behaviour is as natural a product of human evolution as altruistic behaviour.[14] Against this short background, and since my goal is not to put forward a comprehensive justification or rejection of the biological aspect of human rights in the digital domain, I will limit myself to adding a separate layer to the discussion. The biological justification of human rights offline is primarily related to the

10 R. W. Gerard, 'A Biological Basis for Ethics' (1942) 9 *Philosophy of Science*, 1, 92–120.

11 R. W. Gerard, 'The Rights of Man: A Biological Approach' in Jacques Maritain (ed.), *Human Rights: Comments and Interpretations* (New York: Allan Wingate), pp. 205–206.

12 See C. W. Maris, *Critique of the Empirist Explanation of Morality: Is There a Natural Equivalent of Categorical Morality?* (Berlin: Springer Dordrecht, 1981), p. 171.

13 E. O. Wilson, *The Social Conquest of Earth* (New York: W. W. Norton and Company, 2012), p. 290.

14 See S. Harris, *The Moral Landscape: How Science Can Determine Human Values* (New York: Free Press, 2010), where he writes on page 100: 'Human evil is a natural phenomenon, and some level of predatory violence is innate in us.'

assertion that the connecting element of human rights flows from human biology. Since little attention is paid to counter the potential evils of human behaviour, then in the online domain, human rights serve an additional function of countering such evil. The non-coherent aspect lies in the idealistic power of human rights to bring a moral dimension to biologically determined human behaviour online. In the other words, the biological justification of human rights online is at variance with such a justification offline because offline this justification says why human rights exist, but online it says why human rights need to exist.

2.2.3 *Intuitionistic Model*

Intuitionistic model of human rights, as argued by Robert Alexy, is related to the claim that they are self-evident.[15] Alexy writes that if the model were to be embedded in arguments, then it no longer represents intuitionism, and concludes that the intuitionistic model simply means nothing less than the same self-evidence.[16] Non-coherence theory is interested in the aspects of the reliability of evidence underlying the model, and its position in the matrix of time-chain and relevance among other justifications of human rights. What we are looking at here is not intuitionism about whether human rights exist at all – because if we are convinced by our intuition that they do not exist offline, it follows that they do not exist in the digital realm as well. This is because the non-coherence theory of human rights focuses on comparing the rights in offline and online domains and does not go as far as to assert the possibility of the existence of human rights in the digital domain without any basis offline. Maybe surprisingly, the intuitionistic model clearly verifies non-coherence theory through the lens of the Cartesian circle because it shows the option of rejecting the transposition of the offline human rights architecture to the online domain. When someone is saying 'since the universality of human rights is self-evident, it follows that human rights in the digital domain carry comparable features as in the physical domain', this person stumbles upon the *circulus in probando* because she takes for granted the premise of the self-evidence of the universality of human rights. The claim under the intuitionistic model, in isolation from other models, that the universality of human rights and coherent transposability to the online domain is self-evident,

[15] R. Alexy, 'Discourse Theory and Fundamental Rights' in A. J. Menéndez, E. O. Eriksen (eds.), *Arguing Fundamental Rights: Law and Philosophy Library* (Berlin: Springer Dordrecht, 2006), p. 19.

[16] Ibid.

represents rational intuition, yet as shown by Oman Grundmann, the demand for an explanation of any claim put forward through such rational intuition is based on a category mistake.[17] It follows that the intuitionistic model, therefore, not only makes it possible to justify but also to reject the coherence between offline and online human rights realms. Any statement that human rights exist online in a format that is compatible with their offline origin can be countered by a statement to the contrary, both of which cannot demand rational explanation, and therefore both appear to be correct. Against this observation, someone can raise doubts about whether the intuitionistic model for justifying human rights should be viewed as self-standing, or rather serves the purpose of triggering a search for more systematic and logical justification models.

The second aspect of interest from the non-coherence perspective was identified as related to the time-chain of justifications, that is, whether the omnipresence of intuitionistic justification can be considered an element of the triggering function of rights rhetoric. It follows that the relevance of the intuitionistic justification withers in time and may re-emerge once some fundamental changes appear in rights content or practice. Yet, in other words, the higher the degree of intuitionistic statements in human rights justification in comparison with other justifications, the more there are unanswered fundamental questions. This is because the argumentation remains outside of the scope of intuitionism. Generalisation on the works of Johannes Morsnik and David Little by Jeff Gottlieb shows the relevance of intuitionism in the process of articulating the core human rights principles and drafting the Universal Declaration of Human Rights.[18] With the passage of time, human rights normativity and established discursive practices push intuitionism aside, leading to the argument of the relativity of the intuitionistic justification of offline human rights. The variables of such relativity are the time from the appearance of intuitionistic claims and the solidification of the concrete human rights framework. This thesis of the relativity of intuitionistic justification can lead to dual conclusions regarding human rights in the digital domain, which necessarily do not appear as mutually exclusive. First, the argument of self-evidence appears strong in contemporary scholarly and political discourse. Take, for example, a political statement by the European Pirate Party, '[w]e consider the people's right to self-determination as

[17] O. Grundmann, 'The Nature of Rational Intuitions and a Fresh Look at the Explanationist Objection' (2007) 74 *Grazer Philosophische Studien*, 1, 69–87.

[18] See for discussion J. Gottlieb, 'Foundations of Human Rights: Metaphysics, Essentialism, and Intuitionism' (2016) 99 *An Interdisciplinary Journal*, 4, 390–428.

self-evident',[19] or a statement by Robert Spano that the need for better regulation of human rights in the digital sphere is self-evident.[20] It appears that the notion of self-evidence is seen as a trigger for the development of a holistic human rights framework in the digital domain. Let us see for another example the policy statement from 2021 by the Internet Governance Forum about the Draft Principles of a Digital Governance Bill of Rights and Responsibilities, where it says: 'The goal is that people come to a point where global digital citizens proclaim "[w]e hold these truths to be self-evident" regarding the rights and duties of their digital citizenship, and we wish to see them embedded in Internet Governance.'[21]

Many more examples can be given of resorting to the statement of self-evidence regarding human rights in the digital domain at the time of writing this monograph. Yet, since intuitionism as a statement of how something is supposed to exist stands separately, it can either be applied to the claim that human rights law is or is not transposable from the offline to the online domain, or it can be applied to characterise some fundamental feature of human rights online without resorting to its origin offline. This is because the statement that 'human rights online are self-evident because human rights offline are self-evident' no longer represents an intuitionistic approach because dual intuitionism is excluded by the very nature of intuitionism, as reliance on self-evidence as a source of additional self-evidence turns into an argument. Therefore, the usage of the language of self-evidence regarding digital human rights, which is a feature of intuitionistic justification, is a manifestation of the non-coherency of digital human rights vis-à-vis offline rights. Self-evidence is inseparable from a distinct system of rights and values and cannot be transposed to another system and claim normativity.

The second aspect of interest when comparing the intuitionistic justification of human rights offline and online is related to the recognition that intuitionism is a revelation of pure idealism, that is, complete practice-independence. The statements of self-evidence, therefore, should be laid to

[19] European Pirate Party (EPP), 'Human Rights in the Digital Era – Right to Self-Determination', EPP, date unknown, https://european-pirateparty.eu/programme/human-rights-in-the-digital-era, accessed 23 June 2022.

[20] Reference to the statement of Robert Spano, who at the time of writing this monograph served as President of the European Court of Human Rights, delivered at the Council of Europe Symposium: Human Rights in the Digital Sphere on 18 October 2021, www.coe.int/en/web/freedom-expression/human-rights-in-digital-sphere, accessed 23 June 2022.

[21] See Internet Governance Forum policy statement from 2021, 'Issues, Challenges and Opportunities Addressed', available at: www.intgovforum.org/multilingual/content/igf-2021-ws-258-a-common-%E2%80%9Cbill-of-digital-human-rights-and-responsibilities%E2%80%9D, accessed 5 July 2022.

rest and placed outside any subsequent argumentation. A quantitative study of the proportion of such statements against other justifications would reveal the extent of the idealism, which is regrettably not possible in the framework of this publication.

2.2.4 *Consensual Model*

The consensual model goes beyond the intuitionistic model by adding a layer of group-shared non-critical congruence in its arguments. The consensual model does not include an aspect of the nature of these arguments but is different from the intuitionistic model because these arguments are shared by groups. It follows that the intuitionistic model of human rights grows into the consensual model once a critical mass of subjects appears to hold similar intuition about a concrete matter – saying, for example, that human rights online and offline are the same, or that the right to freedom of expression online deserves more protection than the right to privacy. Alexy warns against the danger of the disappearance of consensualism unless it relies on rational argumentation or discourse, which are instrumental for ensuring appropriate human rights justifications.[22] Non-coherence theory sees a reversal of this danger in the perpetuation of consensualism despite the absence of more appropriate argumentative human rights justifications online. In the other words, and more directly, when the offline consensual justification of human rights represents a gateway to a rational argument-based justification, then online consensual justification does not and appears an end in itself. This may be explainable, first, by the weakness of the complementarity between various human rights justifications online in comparison with offline.

Such weakness may itself result from reasons which serve goals other than the justification of rights, primarily related to political and economic agendas. Even a superficial glance at the digital human rights discourse reveals the abundance of beliefs shared by the internet users and various stakeholders concerned. Mireille Hildebrandt has identified a consensus in the framework of collective security against yielding individual liberties by writing: 'We are often told that we must sacrifice some of our liberties to gain security'.[23] She goes on to demonstrate, partly by relying on the six caveats articulated by

[22] Alexy (n 4), p. 107.

[23] M. Hilderband, 'Digital Security and Human Rights: A Plea for Counter-Infringement Measures' in M. Susi (ed.), *Human Rights, Digital Society and the Law: A Research Companion* (London: Routledge, 2019), p. 259.

Jeremy Waldron,[24] that such a call for sacrifice has little to do with rational arguments, yet it has led to a consensus that there is no harm in relinquishing liberties against the promise of a safer society. In addition to this example of political agenda we can add an example of economic agenda from private business, manifest in the doctrine of *community standards*. This leads me to the second explanation of why the online consensual justification of human rights is an end in itself.

The non-coherence lens shows that the meaning of consensus is at variance with the online and offline domains. Offline consensus is a result of compromises with a focus on maximising the benefits for everyone involved. Online consensus is best characterised by the statement: 'If you do not like our community standards, you are welcome to find another community.' Online consensus, therefore, appears to focus on the maximisation of the interests of some at the expense of others. An explanation from mathematics adds another possible layer to the meaning of consensus within the online realm, whereby those who do not understand the language of algorithmic design are easily persuaded of what is possible and what is not possible online. T. J. Fletcher's expression 'take it or leave it'[25] characterises the dictate of pragmatics over human rights idealism whereby we are told that due to technical complications, some aspects of human rights law cannot be realised online, especially in respect to remedies.

A few additional examples will complete this short exploration of the consensual model of human rights justification online, showing that consensus online is not a result of discourse, but a view of human rights language as an element for claiming the validity of some other cause, leading to the observation that offline and online consensual models of human rights justification are non-coherent. I find support for my statement of non-coherence from some scholarly reflections. American academics have written that 'what we found lying below the surface of these community guidelines is actually Silicon Valley values disguised as American democratic ones'.[26] Sumner writes that due to the tyranny of the community, the consensual standards cannot disguise their arbitrariness.[27] Wischmeyer reports how YouTube

[24] J. Waldron, 'Security and Liberty: The Image of Balance' (2003) 11 *Journal of Political Philosophy*, 2, 191–210.

[25] T. J. Fletcher, 'Take It or Leave It!' (1996) 80 *The Mathematical Gazette*, 487, 185–194.

[26] J. Maddox, J. Malson, 'Guidelines without Lines, Communities without Borders: The Marketplace of Ideas and Digital Manifest Destiny in Social Media Platform Policies' (2020) 6 *Social Media + Society*, 1, https://doi.org/10.1177/2056305120926622, accessed 5 July 2022.

[27] L. W. Sumner, 'The Myth of Community Standards' in *The Hateful and the Obscene: Studies in the Limits of Free Expression* (Toronto: University of Toronto Press, 2004) p. 120.

deleted almost 9 million videos at the end of the 2010s without the viewers being able to see them, albeit on the basis of consensual community standards.[28] These do not mean that consensual online human rights justification has to be rejected, since that would mean shutting our eyes to the obvious. At the same time, the functional incompatibility of the consensual justification models adds another layer to non-coherence theory. The function of the consensual model offline is to foster collective belief about whether and how human rights exist, while the function in the digital realm is to instrumentalise human rights language in service of specific goals outside of the ideal human rights domain within the offline meaning.

2.2.5 *Instrumentalist Approach*

The fifth approach to justification identified in the previous section is instrumental. This approach reveals itself in two forms, both of which are not related to the content of human rights. These forms concern, first, the juris generation of human rights, and second, the utility of human rights. They are represented respectively by questions of how human rights are construed and why they exist. The first is specific to the digital domain, understood through recognising that there are limits that digital technology may impose on the transposition of human rights from offline to online. An example is the generalisation of cyber law scholarship by Frank Pasquale and Arthur J. Cockfield that 'technology itself is all too often taken as a foundational reality, which must be accommodated'.[29] Statements like '[t]he Internet has created unprecedented possibilities for the exercise of freedom of expression', or '[t]he right to privacy is by default threatened by digital technologies' are pure examples of the instrumental approach. In its simple format the instrumental approach towards digital human rights remains entirely utilitarian and allows technical practicalities to dictate whether and how human rights can be safeguarded online. A more profound revelation of this model leads to the capabilities approach, discussed in detail elsewhere in this monograph, leading to the consequence that the divide between the ideal and practical dimensions of human rights in the digital domain remains a generic element which will determine the entire human rights architecture online.

28 T. Wischmeyer, 'Making Social Media an Instrument of Democracy' (2019) 25 *European Law Journal*, Special Issue: Internet and Human Rights Law, 2, 176–177.

29 F. A. Pasquale, A. J. Cockfield, 'Beyond Instrumentalism: A Substantivist Perspective on Law, Technology and the Digital Persona' (2018) 821 *Michigan State Law Review*, 3, 855.

The instrumentalist approach offline is usually understood as an end-oriented statutory interpretation.[30] Dworkin's model of instrumentalism is intertwined with interpretive and non-reductionist concepts of law, which 'try to show legal practice as a whole in its best light, to achieve equilibrium between legal practice as they find it and the best justification of that practice'.[31] Alexy suggests that 'human rights justification is instrumental in the case of a statement that human rights recognition is a necessary condition to maximise individual and collective benefit'.[32] Jeffrey A. van Detta asks in turn a simplified question to characterise the instrumentalist approach: 'What value does a particular rule have in a particular case.'[33] Utility is the weakest feature of the instrumentalist approach since it does not include clear standards about what constitutes individual or collective benefit, best light, or best value.

Acceptance of the instrumentalist approach for human rights justification in the digital realm might then lead to recognising that the following statements are not logical fallacies, but a result of instrumentalism devoid of concrete standards: 'human rights are necessary to maximise individual and collective benefit provided that the business benefit is not harmed', or 'human rights need to be rejected since they hinder technical acceleration online.' This monograph will present many examples where the generality of standards leads to a mistaken consideration that offline human rights are directly transposable online. In this part, I will limit myself to suggesting that the instrumentalist approach to human rights justification is paradigm centred. Since the instrumentalist approach does not itself define the values that constitute the utility or end result of human rights existence, this approach is meaningful only in conjunction with some other justification models which define such utility. The isolated transposition of offline human rights to online using the instrumentalist justification model can lead to an image which is very close to non-compatibility instead of non-coherence. To give another example, even if we transpose the idea that human rights recognition is a

[30] See presentation by André Coelho, Formalism and Instrumentalism in Dworkin's Interpretation of Statutes, International Colloquium 'Dialogues with Frederick Schauer', Belo Horizonte, 2 September 2016, www.academia.edu/28233318/Formalism_and_Instrumentalism_in_Dworkins_Interpretation_of_Statutes, p. 7, accessed 27 August 2022.

[31] R. Dworkin, *Law's Empire* (Cambridge, MA: Harvard University Press, 1986), p. 90.

[32] Alexy (n 4).

[33] J. A. van Detta, 'The Irony of Instrumentalism: Using Dworkin's Principle-Rule Distinction to Reconceptualize Metaphorically a Substance-Procedure Dissonance Exemplified by Forum Non Conveniens Dismissals in International Product Injury Cases' (2004) 87 *Marquette Law Review*, 3, 426.

necessary condition to maximise individual and collective benefit, the digital domain may significantly change the meaning of such a benefit by adding an element of proportionality; that is, benefit maximisation is to be weighed against other goals of equal or greater importance.

Inserting the proportionality element into the instrumentalist model leads to the necessity of a more complex model, which is not immune to value-based input. Yet in other words, the instrumentalist approach can be considered an example of Markov's perfect equilibrium, where an outcome is only dependent upon a relatively small set of variables rather than the entire history or discursive practice.[34] Such equilibrium withers once the number of variables is increased and significantly altered, which would be the case for transposition. The followers of Hannah Arendt might concur with the thesis of the paradigm centrism of the instrumental human rights justification for another reason – that values make most sense in a means-and-ends relationship[35] and it is as easy to change values as it is to change underwear.[36] The consequences of my thesis in conjunction with the relativity of value-based standards is methodological. It appears that non-coherence is measurable against a limited set of variables. If many variables change in the transposition from one paradigm to another, the image no longer is that of non-coherence but of incompatibility. In the case of the instrumentalist justification of human rights, non-coherence in the prioritisation of values (offline says that values have priority, while online does not verify this claim) is magnified by the volatility of values in the first place. In this instance, it is more appropriate to talk about parallels than non-coherent systems.

2.2.6 *Cultural Justification*

There are two points of interest in the cultural justification of human rights from the digital perspective: first, whether human rights can be considered a result of cultural development, and second, whether cultural relativism has some similarity with the concept of non-coherence. In reference to the first point, Robert Alexy has suggested a negative answer by noting: 'The fact itself that "the practice of centuries" has established human rights in one or more cultures, is not sufficient to prove their universal character (validity) which is a

34 E. Maskin, J. Tirole, 'Markov Perfect Equilibrium'(2001) 100 *Journal of Economic Theory*, 2, 191–219.

35 J. Klabbers, 'Possible Islands of Predictability: The Legal Thought of Hannah Arendt' (2007) 20, *Leiden Journal of International Law*, 1, 13–14.

36 H. Arendt, 'The Crisis in Culture: Its Social and Its Political Significance' in *Between Past and Future* (New York: Penguin Books, 1977), p. 204.

part of the human rights concept.'[37] This statement is a clear representation of the rejection of practice as a possible source of verification of the core concepts of human rights. The transposition of such a rejection to the digital domain leads to a logical reflection of the same – regardless of what digital culture has to say about human rights, it is not sufficient to define their core nature, universal validity or generic fragmentation, and equivalence with the offline domain. A simplistic position would be content with rejecting the idea that there a specific digital culture has emerged – due to the shortness of time. This is because time is an element which is needed for culture to develop and take shape, *ergo* variances in approaches towards human rights from the digital domain need to be explainable by some other concept than culture. Yet time is relative, and as warned by Mireille Hildebrandt, smart technologies systematically undermine the elements of stability, replication, deliberation and universal application rooted in the technology of the printed word, resulting in operational results which are inconsistent with the root premises of modern Western systems of legal thought.[38] Even if such undermining leads to an overall change of culture or a separate and parallel culture characterising only the digital domain, it can verify the thesis of non-coherence and not the universality and equivalence of human rights. The first point, therefore, leads us to conclude that the cultural justification of human rights online in isolation cannot be accepted. The aspect of the incremental development of human rights deemed as a feature of overall cultural development by Jack Donnelly[39] is simply not possible in the digital domain, and hence one additional feature of non-coherence is flagged.

The second point when comparing non-coherence and cultural relativism leads to a surprising realisation that relativism appears to be intertwined with the idea of universality and vice versa. When Alexy as a universalist writes that recognition of the universal character of human rights in some cultures is insufficient to support this concept's overall universality, he appears to be accepting the idea of relativity. While, on the contrary, those who declare cultural relativism are ready to accept that this relativism needs to be upheld despite the universal character of human rights. For instance, Rhoda E. Howard-Hassmann has defined the debate about cultural relativism and human rights as a question of 'whether culture should trump human rights:

[37] Alexy (n 4), p. 107.

[38] M. Hildebrandt, *Smart Technologies and the End(s) of Law: Novel Entanglements of Law and Technology* (London: Edward Elgar Publishing, 2015), pp. 176–183.

[39] J. Donnelly, *Universal Human Rights in Theory and Practice* (Ithaca, NY: Cornell University Press, 1989), p. 223.

that is, whether a cultural belief or practice should be encouraged or retained even if it violates the internationally-recognised human rights of some individuals within that culture'.[40] Or Makau Mutua, writing in her seminal book about practices that are counter to human dignity, states: 'Rather than being subjected to demonizing and finger-pointing, under the tutelage of outsiders and their local ilk, the contending positions would be carefully examined and compared to find ways of either modifying or discarding the practice *without making its practitioners hateful of their culture and of themselves*.'[41] The basic idea of the cultural relativist approach is different from the non-coherence approach, as the first is rooted in the matter of generality and respective prioritisation between human rights and culture, whereas the second is only interested in comparing the content and practice of human rights in different domains without resorting to relativity.

2.2.7 *Explicative Justification*

The explicative justification of human rights in traceable to transcendental philosophy where human necessity is taken as the obvious, in other words, implicit transcends to explicit. Alexy defends the version of discursive justification that presents something implicit as explicit through a practice of assertions, statements of questions and exchange of arguments.[42] Martin Hapla points to the obvious shortcoming of the Is-Ought problem woven into the human rights explicative justification argument – there are normative assumptions about some of the highest values which constitute the backbone of arguing and asserting.[43] According to Alexy, the discursive practice of explication 'necessarily presupposes rules and principles that give expression to the ideas of freedom and equality of the participants of the discourse'.[44] Rainer Forst elevates the right to justification – which can happen through explanations and arguments, or through discursion – to the level of a basic

[40] R. E. Howard-Hassmann, 'Multiculturalism, Human Rights, and Cultural Relativism: Canadian Civic Leaders Discuss Women's Rights and Gay and Lesbian Rights' (2017) 18 *Netherlands Quarterly of Human Rights*, 4, 493.

[41] M. Mutua, *Human Rights: A Political and Cultural Critique* (Philadelphia: University of Pennsylvania Press, 2002), p. 8.

[42] Alexy (n 4), p. 108.

[43] M. Hapla, 'Explicative-Existential Justification of Human Rights Analysis of Robert Alexy's Argument in Context of Is-Ought Problem' (2020) 15 *The Age of Human Rights Journal*, 105–116.

[44] R. Alexy, 'A Non-positivistic Concept of Constitutional Rights' in M. La Torre, L. Niglia, M. Susi (eds.), *The Quest for Rights: Ideal and Normative Dimensions* (Northampton, MA: Edward Elgar Publishing, 2019), p. 20.

moral right by writing that 'one claim underlies all human rights, namely human beings' claim to be respected as agents who have the right not to be subjected to certain actions or institutional norms that cannot be adequately justified to them'.[45] The justification of human rights through explication has three imperfections, which lead to the verification of the non-coherence theory of digital human rights.

The first imperfection is about the determination of the core ideas of human rights outside of and before the exchange of arguments can be launched. We notice the absence of standards for these outside rules which constitute the backbone of this model. Therefore, if there were to appear a domain which claims, just to give an abstract example, that the ideas of absolute independence (as opposed to freedom) and membership in a community (as opposed to equality) form the basis of human rights, these could perhaps be verified through the explicative justification. Non-coherence theory does not necessarily claim that the rules forming the basis for explication in the online domain are fundamentally different from the offline domain. It is possible to speak of non-coherence in a narrow and broad sense in relation to the basis or origin of rules subject to the explicative justification of human rights. The distinguishing element is that of the origin of these basic rules and principles.

The transfer of such basic rules and principles from offline to online results in narrow non-coherence since the image may exhibit variance in terms of certain aspects of these ideas but retains the core property of the explicit having roots in the implicit. For example, the moral right for the justification of rights in the physical realm may take the form of the moral right to justification by humans instead of machines. Or the idea of freedom after being transferred from the offline to the online domain may obtain a specific additional aspect of freedom from the Internet. In the case of the narrow conception of non-coherence, the ideas were born within the offline domain and usually have a long history of articulation and scholarly attention. The opposite characterises non-coherence in the broad sense, as the ideas forming the basis of explication originate from the online domain and have not had adequate time for maturation. The latter aspect presupposes that time is a constant, which needs separate justification, as ideas online may develop at a different pace than offline. To repeat this thesis, time regarding the development of fundamental rights online moves at a speed that is different from the same offline.

[45] R. Forst, 'The Justification of Human Rights and the Basic Right to Justification: A Reflexive Approach' (2010) 120, *Ethics*, 1, 711–740.

For broad non-coherence, the ideas from online and offline may be compared against one another, yet keeping in mind the non-coherent aspect that the meaning of concepts is paradigm centred. The one speaking of freedom and equality in real-world social relationships, for example, access to education or services, may find that someone else speaking of freedom and equality in a virtual reality may use the same words but to communicate an entirely different meaning. The variance in meanings may not be immediately obvious since open denial of ideas like equality and freedom on the Internet would be an exception remaining outside of the explicative justification model. But differences can become apparent when exploring the relationship between several basic ideas; here is my example. The offline human rights architecture is built on the premise that personal freedom and equality are absolute entitlements and not dependent on some discretionary decision. Yet in the design of online human rights this premise changes, as discretionary entitlement enters the arena. This regulatory argument can be traced from Tim Wu's seminal work introducing the concept of network neutrality when he writes: 'The basic principle behind a network anti-discrimination regime is to give users the right to use non-harmful network attachments or applications, and give innovators the corresponding freedom to supply them.'[46] We can see that equality from discrimination becomes a matter of someone's freedom to secure this treatment. The image of equality in the online domain does not fully match the idea of equality offline. More examples from activist and scientific discussions could be given and will be given later in this monograph. This is the argument of non-coherence.

The second imperfection is related to the absence of criteria for how to decide which arguments and statements are more persuasive and should prevail. Without such specific criteria it will be difficult to completely ignore that quantity can overrule quality in the Novgorod Veche style,[47] or that those who have more PhD students already established after their graduation will be able to widen the circle of supporters of certain statements. A point of interest emerges from here towards the general character of non-coherence. What happens to this imperfection after transposition from one domain to another can be questioned. It can be said that, if the absence of concrete criteria leading to the preponderance of certain arguments over others in the

[46] T. Wu, 'Network Neutrality, Broadband Discrimination' (2003) 2 *Journal of Telecommunications and High Technology Law*, 142.

[47] Novgorod Veche was the gathering of community members in Novgorod in Russia during early medieval times and was characterised by the feature that those who had the loudest voice during the gathering were able to dictate the will of this body.

explicative justification framework of human rights in the offline domain leads to uncertainty, is the same uncertainty carried over to the digital domain. An imperfection necessitates a solution. An imperfection originating from one specific human rights paradigm – offline – can find a resolution within that same paradigm. Therefore, the transposition of an imperfection is just what it says – the transposition of an imperfection. It means that the transposition of an imperfection does not imply the possibility of finding a resolution from the online domain. A contrary position would reverse non-coherence since the resolution of an imperfection originating offline could be found online, but we have just said that it is logically impossible. Yet, someone could endorse such a possibility by asking what prevents the digital domain from proposing criteria for how to determine which arguments in favour of the explicative justification of human rights carry more academic or practical weight. Such an endorsement would be false for the reason of non-coherence: a reflection cannot explain the original; this is the argument from Plato's myth of the cave. If it can, it would be the *Alice in Wonderland* argument, but then the logical framework of fundamental rights becomes amorphous.

The third imperfection is about the discursivity assumption hypothesis. This hypothesis is evident in Alexy's view that '[n]ever making statements, never asking questions, never exchanging arguments means to hold back from participation in most common forms of human lives, as "discursive formations"'.[48] However, there are plenty of examples of how ideas are nurtured through isolation and the avoidance of confrontation in argumentation. Some ideas of the highest value may have been born and ripened through autism. When isolationism can be considered an exception in human rights offline communities, it may yet become a postulate for the participants of online communities as opposed to observers. Such discrepancy between participants and observers points to the common understanding that participants in the digital realm do not understand nor wish to understand fundamental rights language nor participate in the human rights debate. Such a debate is held by observers from the outside on their behalf. We can say that digital human rights discursivity becomes fragmented between those who have an interest in the discussion and exchange of ideas and those who would find this simply a waste of time. The fragmentation of the discursivity assumption hypothesis upon the transposition of human rights into the digital domain is an argument of non-coherence.

[48] Alexy (n 4), p. 108.

2.2.8 *Existentialist Justification*

The final model of human rights justification is existential. Paraphrasing Jean-Paul Sartre's view that we are thrown into freedom but do not choose to be free,[49] we can say that we are thrown into human rights, yet that does not mean that we have to choose human rights. A proponent of non-coherence theory may use this approach and claim that when we are thrown into the digital domain, we do not find human rights there waiting, and it is our choice whether we transpose them from the offline domain or create a new paradigm of rules, or choose to avoid rules altogether. Descartes' mediation leads us to recognise the existence of human rights independent of someone's will simply because the subjective rejection of human rights does not amount to their rejection as something which is objectively given. La Torre writes about this as the *existential* normative situation, where rights as such are not given but 'one starts to orient oneself with regards to what ought to be done'.[50] This represents the start of turning the implicit dimension into the explicit. The existential justification therefore concerns the possibility or ability to introduce the ideal aspect into the human rights architecture.[51]

The logical chain between implicit and explicit is assumed in offline human rights theories, but Samantha Besson has warned about the gap between human rights practice and human rights standards within existing human rights theories, and referred to the need to reconcile the 'political' and 'ethical' human rights theories out of their sterile opposition.[52] This logical chain may be relative, but it is necessary to combine the explicative and existential justifications in order to claim that human rights exist. It is the representation of transcendentality from perfect to imperfect, for example, as defined by Pogge's idiosyncratic reading of human rights resting 'in recognizing that human persons with a past of potential future ability to engage in moral conversation and practice have certain basic needs, and that these needs give rise to weighty moral demands'.[53] This is the confirmation that the implicit dimension of human rights is defined outside and before human

[49] Sartre writes: 'Man is condemned to be free. Condemned, because he did not create himself, in other respect is free: because, once thrown into the world, he is responsible for everything he does.' See J.-P. Sartre, *Existentialism and Human Emotions* (New York: Philosophical Library Book, 1957), p. 15.

[50] M. La Torre, 'Human Rights: Existential, Not Metaphysical' (2018) 31 *Ratio Juris*, 2, 188.

[51] Alexy (n 4), p. 110.

[52] S. Besson, 'Legal Human Rights Theory' in K. Lippert-Rasmussen, K. Brownlee, D. Coady (eds.), *A Companion to Applied Philosophy* (Wiley Online Library, 2017), pp. 328–341.

[53] T. Pogge, *World Poverty and Human Rights* (Cambridge: Polity Press, 2002), p. 58.

rights are articulated. The elements of implicitness are relative and may change in time and by location, which leads to the consequences in the explicit elements. The aforementioned leads me to formulate the transcendentality transposition question. I will limit myself to formulating some main aspects of this question and keep returning to potential responses further in this volume. The other way to present the transcendentality transposition question is to ask whether the implicitness of human rights is determined entirely by the offline domain and is then transposed to the online and finds explication through online-specific practice and discourse. As we have seen, it is a question of underlying values and morals; in other words, whether the online realm has a similar need for orientation about what needs to be done in moral terms as the offline realm. If the implicitness of human rights online were to originate from this same online domain, it could no longer be viewed through non-coherence theory, as it would represent an entirely independent and separate paradigm of meanings. However, if this implicitness was entirely or partly transposed from offline to online, a different question of the breadth of the gap between implicitness and explicitness emerges. This is a perfect question of non-coherence, as these gaps between online and offline can be explored and compared. Since the online world is determined by technical possibilities, we can formulate a hypothesis that the gap between the implicit and explicit dimensions of human rights online are by default narrowing since these elements of implicitness, which cannot be realised online, are simply rejected. This will be one of the main theses this monograph will seek to respond to.

3

The Epistemic Dimension

Rhetoric by and Recognition of Multiple Actors

3.1 THE CONTEXT

The epistemic human rights dimension concerns how knowledge about human rights issues is generated, articulated in discourse and normativity and finally enforced in practice. According to the Aristotelian theory of epistemology, this represents the side of subjective *thought* about objective *reality*. Within the non-coherence approach, the fundamental question is whether the methods of knowledge creation, articulation and enforcement about human rights issues in the digital realm remain similar to the offline realm, or whether distortion exists. This, in turn, has to do with the matter of whether valid arguments concerning the difference in the *reality* can be defended. If it can, then the predisposition that the objective *reality* explored is different still does not automatically lead us to conclude that the knowledge creation process is at variance. For the purposes of this book, however, it is sufficient to rely on the findings of others from various social science disciplines, concerning the objective digital *reality*. I will stop more concretely on a selection of relevant theories regarding digital reality in the following section, such as Castell's network society approach, Teubner's transversality principle, the Frankfurt School and poly-contextuality. The following observations are of more fundamental importance for non-coherence theory.

Here a more non-nuanced view is appropriate, which reveals the variance between digital and non-digital realities. Such a variance can no longer be considered a hypothesis but has to be taken as a starting point with consequences depending on its degree. The variance between digital and non-digital realities is mostly described as broad. For example, Markland has come forward with the *transformation thesis* to emphasise what he calls 'the revolutionary ruptures wrought by digital connectivity and datafication'.[1] We will remain content with the observation that digital and non-digital realities are at least to some degree non-coherent. The subsequent questions will now be: first, whether and to what degree knowledge creation about the digital reality is at variance with the non-digital reality, and immediately thereafter, how such knowledge creation is related to construing the normative validity of human rights rules in the digital domain. Responses to both questions can reveal non-coherence. It is of particular importance how normative commitments are made in the digital domain in comparison with the non-digital. This variance between idealism versus relativism may turn out to be explainable through the non-coherence approach.

3.2 THE PROCESS OF KNOWLEDGE CREATION AND NORMATIVE VALIDITY

Views on the variance in knowledge creation in the digital reality as opposed to the non-digital are polarised. Some viewpoints suggest that by and large the process is coherent, while others claim the opposite, of wide variance. The former is represented, for instance, by Alistair's conclusion that the humanistic subculture of human rights field limits the adoption of novel digital and data-centric practices. This leads to the proposal of the relative marginality of epistemic transformation within the human rights field, despite the relative variance in the realities.[2] A directly opposing view is represented by Alan Liu's assertion of the 'wisdom of the crowd', which he thinks 'challenges the very notion of an epistemology, or philosophy, of knowledge'.[3] He continues to write that, '[i]nstead of valuing enduring or permanent truths (the temporal version of "high" knowledge), the digital age is preoccupied with information of much shorter durations – time spans plunging to the diurnal rhythm of blog posts, the microseconds of a data packet's TTL (time to live)'.[4] Divergence in knowledge creation in law contains an additional layer of norm creation. This aspect is evident in Ladeur's network approach about different forms of societal self-regulation, which build the centre of the legal system where

[1] A. Markland, 'Epistemic Transformation at the Margins: Resistance to Digitalisation and Datafication within Global Human Rights Advocacy' (2022) 36 *Global Society*, 1, 126.

[2] Ibid., p. 129.

[3] A. Liu 'Theses on the Epistemology of the Digital: Advice For the Cambridge Cenre for Digital Knowledge', Alan Liu, 14 August 2014, https://liu.english.ucsb.edu/theses-on-the-epistemology-of-the-digital-page, accessed 2 September 2022.

[4] Ibid.

statutes, judgments and dogmatics rather serve a supportive purpose.[5] His suggestion that practical networks (a category also encompassing digital networks) are constantly creating new knowledge and possibilities, is about the variance in how knowledge about digital and non-digital realities is obtained.

And yet, it is not our goal here to take a position on the rivalry between these viewpoints regarding knowledge creation because our interest is how knowledge creation is translated to claim normative validity. This is the question of whether in normative commitments reached in the digital domain the claim of metaphysicism can be maintained, as opposed to the dominance of practice dependency. There is nothing to suggest that the possibility of claiming a truth through normative validity is linked to a specific type of knowledge creation. Nor that practice dependency cancels the possibility of claiming a truth, even if the practice turns out to be extreme. This statement can be tested through different theoretical propositions. To name a few, Talbott's idea – that the grounding of our beliefs results from process rather than applying transcendent standards to what we can understand from reality[6] – is a clear example of the possibility of truth through process. Contemporary social epistemology puts forward a similar dependency on practice. Goldman's approach to evaluating social procedures in terms of their actual or likely success, with the view to increase their probability of attaining truth,[7] does not say that truth remains an idealistic non-achievable feature of reality.

From here, two concerns emerge, which will be decisive for some conclusions about human rights knowledge creation in the digital domain through the non-coherence lens. The first is whether the digital domain has any interest in claiming normative validity of human rights rules in the first place, and second, whether the meaning of truth in the digital and non-digital domains contains similar features.

3.2.1 *The Digital Domain's Interest in Normative Validity*

To illustrate the first concern, my question inspired by Habermas' theory of communicative rationality is whether such rationality makes any sense in the

5 K.-H. Ladeur, 'Der "Eigenwert" des Rechts – die Selbstorganisationsfähigkeit der Gesellschaft und die relationale Rationalität des Rechts' in DIE ZUKUNFT DES RECHTS 31 (Christian J. Meier -Schatz, ed., 1999), p. 43.

6 W. J. Talbott, 'Epistemological Foundations for Human Rights' in *Human Rights and Human Well-Being*, Oxford Political Philosophy (New York: Oxford Academic, 1 January 2011), accessed 26 September 2022.

7 A. I. Goldman, 'Epistemic Paternalism: Communication Control in Law and Society' (1991) 88 *Journal of Philosophy*, 3, 113–132.

digital domain at all.[8] In other words, whether human rights normativity is rational for the digital domain. Here, non-coherence theory becomes a decisive tool, suggesting that the understanding of rationality from one domain is not necessarily transposed to another. Such a transposition cannot be assumed, as a feature which is rational in one normative paradigm may not retain such rationality features in another. In the non-digital domain, we are accustomed to accepting that when someone utters a sentence, this person has some reason to believe in this sentence's validity and at the same time in the truthfulness of the sentence.[9] Proponents of the non-coherence approach have doubts about whether the same logical rationality can be applied to sentences claiming normative validity in the digital domain.

This is because someone who says a sentence about the digital domain with the view of claiming normative validity, may do so to claim validity for the purpose of understanding in the non-digital domain. But then its reflection in the digital domain does not exhibit genuine normative validity, since it only reflects that something is normatively valid somewhere else. To put it differently, we are faced here with multiple mirror images. A statement from the digital domain claiming normative validity is made for the purpose of satisfying the viewer in the non-digital domain. Then this is reflected back from the non-digital to the digital, and the viewer in the non-digital domain sees the image in the digital mirror, mistakenly thinking that she sees an image of digital normative validity, but what she actually sees is her own initial expectation of normative validity. This image has to be distorted. To illustrate this multiplicity with a construction from our daily lives, consider when a child says to their parents that he will clean up his room; he may do so to claim praise and rewards, knowing that the parents think highly of a tidy room. Without the parents being there, or without the desire to claim praise and rewards, the child would not bother to tidy the room. Here the child reflects back to the parents what he knows they view as normatively valid behaviour, and the parents take positive action because they think that the child's claim of the normative validity is genuinely based on his internal understanding. However, for the child, this behaviour *makes sense* only so far as his relations with his parents are concerned, it *makes no sense* outside of the context of the parental–child relationship. And returning here to knowledge creation, the child in this instance has obtained knowledge from his parents about the importance of keeping his room clean. Talking with friends may reveal a

[8] J. Habermas, *Theory of Communicative Action*, vol. I (Boston: Beacon Press, 1984), p. 297.

[9] J. Habermas, *On the Pragmatics of Communication*, edited by M. Cooke (Cambridge, MA: MIT Press, 1998), pp. 232–233.

pattern that the majority of other parents value similar behaviour. And now this child has a variety of options regarding his behaviour. He may adopt the position 'I cannot wait until I can leave your house', or another, 'I cleaned my room, but I want you to know that I always hated it.' Most likely the child simply considers the matter of third- or fourth-rate relevance and cares much more about other, more interesting issues.

The main light that non-coherence theory casts upon the chain of epistemic dependencies between the digital and non-digital domains shows a need for concretisation. The broad image is unclear, and one must step closer. The reply to the question posed a few paragraphs earlier – whether it can be said that the digital domain has an interest in claiming the normative validity of human rights rules – has to be further divided, therefore, into two questions. However, an opponent may here raise an argument to the contrary and point to the normativity which has emerged in digital domains, either as a matter of the enforcement of human rights rules originating from offline, or as a matter of the self-normativity on social media networks. This statement, however, is a reflection of the reality and does not say how knowledge about the reality is obtained. The more concrete questions that follow from here are: first, whether the need for the claim of a normative validity of human rights rules is a generic feature of both the digital and non-digital domains, and as such a logical consequence of the observations of the respective realities. In other words, whether digital and non-digital realities have such features which lead in any event to the formulation of human rights rules and principles. Perhaps only a highly conservative sceptic can raise doubts about whether normativity exists at all in some format in the digital domain. It does exist, even if normativity takes the format of 'anything goes'. If we can establish that the *thought* that whatever paradigmatic *reality* involving humans leads to the necessity of fundamental rights normativity, then this leads us to view non-coherence as a theory beyond digital human rights. In such a case, one should adopt a position saying that non-coherence is a common feature when different fundamental rights systems are compared against one another.

However, doubts about whether we know exactly how the *thought* about *reality* is translated into fundamental rights normativity become more credible when one turns to the specific factors which can shape these normative constructions. We will stay here on a high level. Non-coherence theory does not exclude its applicability to epistemic processes, which also lead to the articulation of fundamental rights. However, in order to be able to draw conclusions from the non-coherence approach, similar factors need to be verified for both domains. One can seek to explore the degree of variance. For example, what is the role of argumentation versus rhetoric? Here it is possible that there do not exist comparable properties to the extent allowing non-coherence analysis. For instance, Radbruch points notably to the role of time in knowledge creation by suggesting that 'the practice of centuries has founded such solid grounds and they [fundamental rights] achieve such advanced consensus in the form of so-called declarations of human rights and civil rights'.[10] If this principle is to have universal character, namely that time is a substantial factor in knowledge crystallisation about the necessity of fundamental rights, then epistemologically digital and non-digital realms cannot be compared. There is full epistemological non-coherence. And the reply to the question raised about normative validity as a generic feature of digital and non-digital domains cannot be answered.

3.2.2 *Variance in the Meaning of Normative Validity*

Now the second question is: whether the meaning of normative validity in digital and non-digital domains may be different. This will be explored further in the section addressing self-normativity. It will suffice to note here that a complex non-coherent image is possible. Namely, what the digital domain claims as normatively valid may not appear fully or partially as such in the non-digital domain, and the other way around. What the non-digital domain claims as normatively valid for the digital, may not be accepted as such by the latter. A further complicating factor is the fragmentation of self-normative systems in the digital sphere, which means that some digital actors may view certain statements originating from the physical domain as normatively valid and some may not. For example, a norm requiring consistent content assessment and the removal of 'harmful' posts as a standard shield to protect privacy, originates probably from the non-digital domain. Its normative validity is accepted widely in European countries and among private actors but not in South American countries and the respective actors.

All these considerations raised lead me to suggest the thesis of the relativisation of truth in fundamental digital rights. I am not proposing the idea that knowledge in the non-digital domain about fundamental rights reality is a constant, leading to a uniform perception and crystallised norms. Everyone knows this is not possible. However, the abstract possibility of truthful statements constitutes a constant in the non-digital human rights architecture. This is an argument against relativism, saying that human rights norms serve as criteria of absolute justice, and there is nothing that can call this into question

[10] G. Radbruch, B. Litschewski Paulson, S. L. Paulson 'Five Minutes of Legal Philosophy (1945)' (2006) 26 *Oxford Journal of Legal Studies*, 1, 14–15.

or override it, even if such a quest of absolute justice is in practice overshadowed or simply ignored. But since we are not clear about the ways knowledge about human rights issues in the digital domain are generated, we cannot be sure that the criteria for absolute justice claims from one source are not challenged by another source claiming the equal validity of some other principle or idea. The consequence of the thesis of the relativisation of truth in fundamental digital rights, therefore, asserts that truth as a category is paradigm centred. What can be considered truthful about the digital domain through the eyes of the non-digital may not be reflected back as such into the digital domain. This is a demonstration of non-coherence. As such, the concept raises doubt about whether non-positivist categories, such as truth or values, are meaningful for the analysis of normative structures of different paradigms.

4

On the Controversy about the Relative Weight of Rights

4.1 INHERENT DIVISION INTO ABSOLUTE AND RELATIVE RIGHTS

One of the first concepts taught to law students in human rights courses is about the division between absolute and relative rights. Numerous human rights instruments contain this division between absolute and relative rights, and the same idea is present in national constitutional laws. Both students and well-established scholars[1] uphold the debate around the matter, whereas they take for granted the premise that such a dual categorisation of human rights is rational and justified. Here, the concept of relativity is not to be mistakenly considered opposite to universality, which would be a discussion with a different focus, especially since there are suggestions of combining the opposites into the concept of relative universality,[2] and second, because this discussion would divert us away from human rights ABC. There are very few doubts that the offline human rights architecture contains only a handful of absolute rights – those where derogation is not allowed in positive law. For example, under the European Convention for the Protection of Human Rights and Fundamental Freedoms, article 15 it is not allowed to derogate in time of emergency from articles 2, 3, 4 (1) and 7. These rights are respectively the right to life, the right not to be tortured, the prohibition of slavery and forced labour and finally, the prohibition of punishment without law. Protocol No. 7 article 4 added the right not to be tried or punished twice to this list. This demonstrates one of the core ideas of the human rights offline architecture: there are certain basic values, which are reflected in the absolute rights,

[1] For example, N. Mavronicola, 'What Is an "Absolute Right"? Deciphering Absoluteness in the Context of Article 3 of the European Convention on Human Rights' (2012) 12 *Human Rights Law Review*, 4, 723–758.

[2] J. Donnelly, 'Human Rights: Both Universal and Relative (A Reply to Michael Goodheart)' (2008) 30 *Human Rights Quarterly*, 1, 203.

whereas the connection of these basic values to relative rights is weaker but still present. One such core value offline is dignity, which can never be given up. Other core values, such as individual freedom and equality, can be added to this short list. *Fiat iustitia, et pereat mundus*, would be the Latin expression. The rights closely connected to this value contain the same element of *never to be given up*. This idea appears, for example, in the statement in the Siracusa Principles on the Limitation and Derogation Provisions in the International Covenant on Civil and Political Rights,[3] article 70, in the following passage: 'the denial of certain rights fundamental to human dignity can never be strictly necessary in any conceivable emergency'. A more populist expression would say that the possibility to derogate from certain fundamental rights offline is an *escape clause* for the situation of public emergencies.[4] But this escape clause does not apply universally to all human rights.

The first question to be asked here is whether the division of rights into absolute and relative is retained in the digital domain. A positive reply shows an image where the basic human rights architecture has no variance, and such variance can appear in the scope of these two areas; in other words, whether the circle of absolute rights online is substantially wider or narrower than offline. This means that the notions of dignity, personal freedom and equality appear online undistorted in comparison with the offline domain. The matter does not yet manage to view whether the meaning of these notions remains undistorted because a division into absolute and relative rights says nothing about the content of these rights. An alternative view suggests a flat human rights architecture online, where the layer of absolute rights is missing. Several aspects can be explored before giving an affirmative or negative answer. The consequences of the replies to the questions of change in the architectural composition of human rights online; that is, whether it is uni-layered or has multiple layers, is about the coherence of such architecture with the offline human rights architecture. Should there be just one layer of human rights online from the aspect of relativity, everything would be different in the online human rights landscape since all rights could in principle be balanced against one another.[5]

3 The Syracuse Principles were adopted in 1985 by the American Association for the International Commission of Jurists.

4 E. M. Hafner-Burton, L. R. Helfer, C. J. Fariss, 'Emergency and Escape: Explaining Derogations from Human Rights Treaties' (2011) 65 *International Organizations*, 4, 673–707.

5 One could claim, for example and for the purpose of originalism, that it is possible to torture humans online because of the words which are said. It would, however, twist the meaning of torture and inhumane treatment to claim that online hatred can cause suffering within the meaning of human rights law only online because the consequences will be felt in the physical

4.2 THE RANDOMISATION OF THE DIVISION

The problem I put forward is about the randomisation of the division between absolute and relative rights online. The variance here is not in the absence of multiple layers but the stability between the dividing lines. While the circle of absolute rights versus relative rights appears well established and uncontested offline, these circles are amorphous online.

Of special importance is the language and expressions about the features of some rights online, which then raise the expectation that in certain situations these rights increase to the level of immunity, that is, assume an absolute character. If we consider the rights that are usually put forward as balanceable against one another – the right to freedom of expression and the right to privacy, for example, then we find that there are claims about them both shifting status from relative to absolute. These claims do not cover these rights entirely but are directed towards certain elements and situations. We will now look at some examples to illustrate this point.

4.2.1 *The Randomisation of the Weight of the Freedom of Expression Online*

Doubts about whether there are situations that necessitate limiting any derogation from the right to freedom of expression have been expressed on numerous occasions by the UN Human Rights Committee. In General Comment No. 34 to the International Covenant on Civil and Political Rights article 19, this Committee wrote the following in general remark No. 5:

> 'Furthermore, although freedom of opinion is not listed among those rights that may not be derogated from pursuant to the provisions of article 4 of the Covenant, it is recalled that 'in those provisions of the Covenant that are not listed in article 4, paragraph 2, there are elements that in the Committee's opinion cannot be made subject to lawful derogation under article 4'. Freedom of expression is one such element, since it can never become necessary to derogate from it during a state of emergency.[6]

David Kaye, the former Special Rapporteur for the United Nations, has frequently used the language arguing for 'strong protection' of the right to

domain. Yet, there is some merit in the proposition that such consequences should be avoided, and therefore statements which clearly can cause such suffering are to be censored.

6 U.N. Human Rights Council, 'General Comment No.34 on Article 19: Freedoms of Opinion and Expression', 102nd session, UN Doc CCPR /C/GC/34 (2011).

freedom of opinion online, and reached the threshold of 'the strongest' protection of freedom of expression regarding whistle-blowers.[7] Kaye is of the opinion that freedom of expression is a foundational element of human dignity; hence, it deserves strong protection in the digital age. These statements lead to offset the well-established equilibrium that the rights to privacy and freedom of expression deserve equal protection. The same off-setting effect would follow even from approaches which at first glance say that, for example, the rights protected under the ECHR articles 8 and 10 deserve equal respect,[8] and then go further by excluding hate speech and otherwise illegal expressions from the freedom of expression. This is the other side of the coin – we are accustomed to the relativity of the right to freedom of expression, and are confronted with the view that this relativity does not hold universally towards this right.

4.2.2 *The Randomisation of the Weight of the Right to Privacy Online*

Similar concerns about the variance of its relativity have been raised about the right to privacy. Evidence about the expanding narrative about the 'death of privacy' was offered by Penney.[9] The Spanish Charter of Digital Rights appears to hold as absolute the right to identity in the digital environment, which may not be altered, controlled or manipulated by third parties against one's will.[10] In the first example, the right to privacy appears to be almost non-existent, since it has to yield to different other interests and values, and in the second example, one aspect of the right to privacy appears close to absolute, since no derogation nor balancing would be allowed.

7 Report of the Special Rapporteur on the promotion and protection of the right to freedom of opinion and expression, submitted to the United Nations General Assembly on 08 September 2015, the Summary has the following passage: 'In many situations, sources of information and whistle-blowers make access to information possible, for which they deserve the strongest protection in law and in practice.' See D. Kaye, 'Report of the Special Rapporteur on the Promotion and Protection of the Right to Freedom of Opinion and Expression' UN Doc A/70/361 (2015) p. 2.

8 Generalising on the jurisprudence of the European Court of Human Rights, the Council of Europe's Steering Committee on Media and Information Society Recommendation CM/Rec (2014)6 says in paragraph 41: 'The Court has found that, as a matter of principle, the rights guaranteed under Articles 8 and 10 deserve equal respect.'

9 J. Penney, 'The Right to Privacy: The End of Privacy Fatalism' in M. Susi (ed.), *Human Rights, Digital Society and the Law: A Research Companion* (London: Routledge, 2019), pp. 44–47.

10 Paragraph III 2. of the Spanish Charter of Digital Rights.

4.3 THE THESIS OF RELATIVE ABSOLUTENESS

The sketch in the previous section is not sufficient to point to emerging absolute rights in the digital domain, but it is sufficient to lead us towards the acceptance of the variance between the offline and online human rights architectures in respect to the relative and absolute weight of rights. A call for 'strong' or 'stronger' protection of some right, like the right to freedom of expression, can only mean that the element of strength is measurable on a scale against the intensity of the protection of some other right. This statement is meaningful only if the opposite is also true – the opposing right, the right to privacy, does not deserve such 'strong' protection, or it has to manage with 'weaker' protection. Here, one needs to consider whether the balancing model of conflicting rights, as established in the offline domain, can be used as an effective tool online. I claim that a critical examination is needed due to the following reasons. In the offline world, the starting point for balancing rights in a conflict is that of equal weight. When it appears that there are more arguments in favour of the preponderance of one side, then this right prevails. Variance in the balancing model means that before the balancing can start, one of the rights in the balance already has a higher or lower weight. In most cases, this will determine the outcome of this exercise since the interference of privacy rights would need to be extremely deep to stop freedom of expression from prevailing. The image of relative rights in the digital domain in comparison with offline is non-coherent since the critical mass of writings and various opinions suggesting variance is above opportunism or activism. This leads us to two intuitionistic predictions.

4.3.1 *The Assumption of a Multilayered Rights Structure*

First, since the claims for variance in the weight of relative rights have appeared as the digital domain matures, which is due to time, it may be in the nature of human rights that a stable architecture needs multilayered weights. That is, once the image becomes clear, there must be commonly accepted fundamental values and then a small circle of rights with the closest connection to these values allowing us to claim absolute protection. And then there are relative rights, which are subject to being balanced against one another. The image may be distorted, which means that rights claiming absoluteness do not need to coincide or exist at all in both domains or retain the same properties. Non-coherence exists in the change of the meaning of absoluteness – it becomes relative and determined in the concreteness of the situation. One can therefore ask whether relative absoluteness is absoluteness at all?

And the second intuitionistic prediction lies in the statement that it cannot be excluded that at some point in the future, rights claiming absolute protection appear in the digital domain. Or alternatively, relative rights have a corner which deserves 'absolute' protection, like the rights of whistle-blowers or the right to digital identity. More will be said about this matter shortly when I explore the matter of new human rights claims for the digital domain.

If the previous intuitionistic reflections have merit, we need to ask whether the premise of the existence of certain fundamental (constitutional) values is still applicable in the online domain. This has two sides: first, whether it remains justified to speak of the existence of such fundamental digital values at all, regardless of what they are; and second, if it were to be justified, and if it were to appear that the same fundamental values are brought forward for the online domain as for the offline domain, might there still be some variance in their meaning. It is not difficult to note that this is perhaps the main question at the constitutional level from non-coherence theory for the digital reality. If the answer is simply no, or if the justifications are not credible, then the doctrine of 'anything goes' appears. This would mean that multiple normative systems can be construed, based on multiple and non-coherent basic values. Or alternatively, that these normative systems can be construed without the presence of any such basic values. The latter possibility takes us outside of the narrow meaning of non-coherence, as it would be difficult to find common elements for comparison. A quick look at some suggestions on the notion of dignity in the digital domain will be instructive and important at this stage.

4.4 THE IDEA OF DIGITAL DIGNITY

There are two types of approaches put forward towards the idea of dignity. Some take as given that dignity continues in the format of basic foundational human rights value, be it in the offline or online reality. This is represented, for example, by the UNESCO Recommendation on the Ethics of Artificial Intelligence.[11] Item 13, under III.1 values, has the following statement: 'The inviolable and inherent dignity of every human constitutes the foundation for the universal, indivisible, inalienable, interdependent and interrelated system of human rights and fundamental freedoms. Therefore, respect, protection and promotion of human dignity and rights established by international law … is essential throughout the life cycle of AI systems.' Here, as is typical

[11] UNESCO, 'Recommendation on the Ethics of Artificial Intelligence', Document Code SHS/BIO/PI/2021/1, adopted on 23 November 2021, available through open access from UNESCO database.

of policy documents, we do not find argumentation behind the claims. The main argument appears to be the belief that dignity in the digital domain carries the same meaning as offline. Possibly it is the main justification. The Spanish Charter of Digital Rights serves as another example of how the notion of dignity is utilised as a given value from offline.

Others, for example Biber, suggest that the meaning of dignity is distorted in the online environment. The main concern here is again related to the hierarchy of human rights norms and the matter of relativity and absoluteness. Biber writes on the basis of ample evidence from media statements and the jurisprudence of South African courts that, 'freedom of expression has come to dominate other principles, including dignity and privacy, with the effect that commercial media interests will inevitably, constitutionally, outstrip matters of humanity, compassion, respect and integrity'.[12]

As usual, there are statements from the middle, saying that when human dignity continues to stand at the bottom of the human rights architecture, it can be strengthened or weakened by digital developments.[13] Zielińska and Fandrejewska use the expression of the 'normative indeterminacy'[14] of the concept of dignity, with reference to the work of Chinese scientists in the field of human embryos, which allows multiple interpretations, leading to the redefinition of dignity.

Many other examples and citations can be given to illustrate these different viewpoints. At the same time, we see that none of these suggest that dignity does not belong in the core value system of digital human rights. Yet all of them are related to one matter which is most important above the others. This is the matter of relativity, as Kant has formulated on the matter of dignity being an end in itself.[15] One can speak in this context of the 'relativisation' of dignity in the digital realm, and also of the opposite. The latter would mean that dignity in the digital realm remains non-relative, but its meaning can differ from its offline meaning. The concept of digital dignity, therefore, has to be explored further.

[12] K. Biber, 'Dignity in the Digital Age: Broadcasting the Oscar Pistorius Trial' (2018) 15 *Crime, Media, Culture*, 3, 401–422.

[13] See, for example, Geneva Internet Platform, '*Human Dignity*' digiwatch, date unknown, https://dig.watch/values/human-dignity, accessed 25 July 2022.

[14] K. S. Zielińska, A. Fandrejewska, 'Artificial Intelligence Algorithms and the Prohibition of Discrimination' in L. M. Martin et al. (eds.), *Artificial Intelligence and Human Rights* (Madrid: Dykinson, 2021), pp. 260–271.

[15] I. Kant, *Fundamental Principles of the Metaphysic of Morals*, 'Second Section: Transition from Popular Moral Philosophy to the Metaphysic of Morals' translated by T. Kingsmill Abbott, The Project Gutenberg EBook of Fundamental Principles of the Metaphysic of Morals by Immanuel Kant, EBook #5682, released May 2004, www.gutenberg.org/files/5682/5682-h/5682-h.htm, accessed 27 October 2022.

4.5 THE RELATIVISATION OF THE CORE VALUE THESIS

When asking whether dignity in the digital world should be viewed as an end in itself, we quickly realise that if the answer should be negative, then the human rights digital architecture becomes completely flat. This represents the situation when there are not only no absolute human rights but everything becomes relative. This is because the basic norm itself would be relative. Here then, the key notion of dignity could be measured against competing rights and values. But it would no longer correspond to the place of dignity in the offline human rights realm. In this case, the weight of dignity in the offline and online domains becomes non-coherent. It lies in the simple recognition that when dignity is a constant offline, it is relative online. This scenario can be explained through the relativisation of core values thesis. The problem of reviewing the validity of this thesis lies in the absence or scarcity of arguments about why dignity online is fully transposable from offline. The effect of policy documents not containing explicative statements about the absolute nature of dignity online opens the door to speculation that relativisation cannot be excluded. The logical consequence of the relativisation of the core values thesis at this stage needs to be that the non-coherence of core fundamental rights values between online and offline cannot be completely ruled out.

The absence of explication can be corrected by looking at the level of concreteness when dignity is defined in the physical realm. Clear and simple statements are suggested based on a review of theoretical writings and judicial practices, containing the overarching point of dignity as an aspirational idea with much less convergence in practical application. For instance, Dan-Cohen claims that there are no ontological foundations for the concept of dignity, not even contours for determining the concept.[16] Bendor and Tamir put forward the conclusion that human dignity serves as a 'constitutional chameleon in the sense that courts in different countries interpret it in accordance with the constitutional environment in which it is located'.[17] These observations, and there are many more, can be explained, as Riley writes, of the '*incoherence* in human dignity's failure to provide a coherent connection between what we consider constitutive and what we consider regulative in our discourse'.[18] However, this explanation can be advanced

[16] M. Dan-Cohen, 'A Concept of Dignity' (2011) 44 *Israel Law Review*, 1–2: Symposium: Human Dignity and the Criminal Law, 22.

[17] A. L. Bendor, M. Tamir, 'Human Dignity as a Chameleon' (2021–2022) 5 *Cardozo International and Comparative Law Review*, 3, 742–743.

[18] S. Riley, 'Human Dignity as a *Sui Generis* Principle' (2019) 32 *Ratio Juris*, 443–444.

towards any core idea of human rights, representing therefore the divide between the ideal and normative dimensions of law.[19] It would be wrong to limit oneself just to the observation of what constitutes the generic feature of human rights core values because it does not say anything specific about the content of dignity in the human rights architecture. I will therefore offer an approach from the question: how do we know when our dignity has been infringed?

Schacther is of the opinion that since there are no explicit definitions of the expression the 'dignity of the human person', its violation can be recognised even if the abstract term cannot be defined. 'I know it when I see it even if I cannot tell you what it is', he writes.[20] Since the rights-based approach to human dignity does not seem to yield a better image for understanding what indeed constitutes human dignity as the foundational value of human rights, it has to be the basis of applying non-coherence theory to compare the meaning of dignity in the physical and online realms. As an intuitionistic explanation of the expression, it is therefore applicable also online. Here then there is no non-coherence in the approach. We could also say that we know that dignity online is infringed when we see it. Intuitionism is revealed through the approach where, instead of trying to come forward with an abstract definition of dignity, authors provide lists of examples of what can constitute an attack on dignity. These lists are not exhaustive. To illustrate, Schachter gives twelve examples of such attacks, including the dissemination of negative stereotypes, denial of educational opportunities and degrading living conditions.[21] A similar approach has been taken by various advocacy groups, for instance, by the ALNAP organisation, which instead of defining the notion of digital dignity provides examples when dignity online is threatened. They refer to threats from third-party service providers, humanitarian data incidents and the dual use of technologies.[22] Others have similar approaches, for example, the European Digital Rights network, which departs from the observation of

[19] For discussion about the matter of the divide between the ideal and normative dimensions, see M. La Torre, L. Niglia, M. Susi (eds.), *The Quest for Rights: Ideal and Normative Dimensions* (Northampton, MA: Edward Elgar Publishing, 2019).

[20] O. Schachter, 'Editorial Comment: Human Dignity as a Normative Concept' (1983) 77 *American Journal of International Law*, 4, 849.

[21] Ibid., 852.

[22] N. Cliem, A.-M. McKenzie, 'Digital Dignity in Practice: Existing Digital Dignity Standards, Pursuing Digital Dignity and Current Gaps in Digital Dignity', ALNAP, 1 January 2019, www.alnap.org/help-library/digital-dignity-in-practice-existing-digital-dignity-standards-pursuing-digital-dignity, accessed 23 September 2022.

difficulty in providing a definition of digital dignity and then proceeds to give concrete areas where such dignity is under threat.[23]

Stepping towards more concreteness, we can look at a definition of dignity given by Whitman, who writes of dignity as the ability to control one's image, name and reputation.[24] This is now a more practical statement since attacks on image and name have specific features. Just the same, we are quickly reminded of an almost identical view when looking at the European Declaration on Digital Rights and Principles for the Digital Decade, which says in chapter v that everyone has the right to the protection of personal data online, including the control of how the data are used and with whom they are shared.[25]

These observations have to be sufficient here to recapitulate the following statements. First, there does not appear to be any non-coherence between the idea of dignity in online and offline spaces due to the absence of abstract definitions. Both domains rely on an intuitionistic justification of dignity. Second, non-coherence regarding the absolute nature of dignity may occur, since the offline rights environment is multilayered, but it is not certain that the online environment is. Finally, non-coherence may appear in the possibilities to enforce the notion of dignity, but this concerns the topic of capabilities, addressed in Chapter 8 of this book.

[23] See the website of the EDRI, where the threats are listed and elaborated: https://edri.org/our-work/building-a-coalition-for-digital-dignity, accessed 23 September 2022.

[24] James Q. Whitman, 'The Two Western Cultures of Privacy: Dignity Versus Liberty' (2004) 113 *Yale Law Journal*, 1160.

[25] European Declaration on Digital Rights and Principles for the Digital Decade, chapter v, subchapter privacy and individual control over data.

5

Constitutional Entitlements to Human Rights in the Digital Domain

5.1 ABOUT THE ORIGIN OF ONLINE CONSTITUTIONAL IDEAS

Within the debate about constitutionality and the Internet, the argument of non-coherence assumes a pivotal role. This argument of non-coherence can be useful for explaining two principally different approaches about the interrelationship between constitutional principles originating from the offline reality and their applicability in the online domain. The first says that the constitutional ideas of the digital domain originate from the offline domain, and the second says that they do not, their origin being from inside the online domain in isolation from the offline. Let me write this differently. The first says that the digital domain contains and in time accumulates the abundance of elements which inevitably and gradually contests offline constitutional ideas,[1] which may lead to breaking away from offline constitutionality. The second is completely different and is not concerned with the offline constitutional ideas at all since these ideas are born and mature in isolation from the offline domain. However, both approaches can lead to self-constitutionalisation. The non-coherence question, therefore, is about the *reflection* of offline constitutional law principles and rules in the online *image*.

The challenge does not necessarily mean variance, due to the possible resilient function of constitutional ideas. The first approach presupposes at

[1] See, for example, the following reflection by Giovanni De Gregorio and Roxana Radu: 'The fragmentation of the global infosphere into national spaces of digital sovereignty, the increased bifurcation of Internet-based technologies along ideological divides, and the complex dynamics at plan for both public and private powers may not only raise questions about the protection of fundamental rights, but also pose broader challenges to established constitutional principles. As the Internet continues to be redefined due to the evolution of digital technologies, so is constitutionalism beyond the state.' G. De Gregorio, R. Radu, 'Digital Constitutionalism in the New Era of Internet Governance' (2022) 30 *International Journal of Law and Information Technology*, 1, 69.

least a certain degree of variance between the constitutional principles offline and online since the connectivity between offline and online constitutional principles is not broken because of the common offline cradle. In this case, the online constitutional ideas simply reflect the offline constitutional ideas but may do so with a certain amount of distortion. The feature of abstractness is the main question of interest, that is, whether in the course of the transposition of constitutional-level ideas, their abstractness weakens to the extent that they no longer represent constitutional principles but normative rules or principles below the constitutional level, with a function towards the realisation of constitutional values. Should this be the case, it leads to wider implications about the possibility of transposing highly general and abstract normative ideas into other paradigms, be they virtual or in some other way outside of the Earth's physical domain. An answer to the question of whether during the transposition of constitutional-level ideas from the offline to the online domain the level of abstractness diminishes will be now explored both through theoretical and practical reasoning.

5.2 ABOUT DIGITAL CONSTITUTIONALISM

From the side of practical reasoning, an umbrella concept of digital constitutionalism proposed in 2015 by Gill, Redeker and Gasser can be explored.[2] The concept is used as 'a common term to connect a constellation of initiatives that have sought to articulate a set of political rights, governance norms, and limitations on the exercise of power on the Internet'.[3] This approach is primarily concerned with the process and quantitative counting of rights mentioned in various *efforts*, which the authors themselves do not conceal when putting forward future research questions, among which the matter of substantive content is placed as isolated at the end of the list.[4]

5.2.1 *The Inadequacy of the Protection Thesis regarding Constitutional-Level Norms*

The process of the transposition of human rights law from one domain to another, including constitutional principles, has three stages. The first has to

[2] L. Gill, D. Redeker and U. Gasser, 'Towards Digital Constitutionalism? Mapping Attempts to Craft an Internet Bill of Rights' (2015) Berkman Center Research Publication No. 2015–15, https://ssrn.com/abstract=2687120 or http://dx.doi.org/10.2139/ssrn.2687120, 2.

[3] Ibid.

[4] Gill et al. (n 2), 19–21.

do with the reasons for such a transposition. Elsewhere I have termed this stage through the *inadequacy of protection thesis*,[5] which brings under one umbrella the political and naturalist perspectives of human rights development. By containing both of these perspectives, the inadequacy of protection thesis says that human rights law develops because the protection of certain vulnerable groups, or alternatively the advancement of certain values is deemed inadequate by identifiable interest groups through the existing normative framework. Technological and scientific developments form one of the six origins for advancing the inadequacy of protection claim.[6] The common explanation for why the digital domain may be in need of specific human rights regulation is indeed that of technical advances capable of altering the status quo of how human rights ideas can be put into practice. The argument from technicism can take different formats and levels of specificity. For example, Pollicino and De Gregorio point out that since 'algorithms are instruments which extract value from data, then moving to the social perspective, such technologies constitute automated decision-making processes able to affect society and thus also impacting on constitutional values, precisely fundamental rights and democratic values'.[7] Yet it would be a simplification to suggest that inadequacy of protection necessarily reaches the level of constitutional law, that is, to suggest that constitutional law principles cannot provide a similar level of protection in the digital domain as in the physical domain. This is because the adequacy of protection can in principle be achieved by alterations in normative structures below the constitutional level.

The digital constitutionalism concept has one main weakness and one caveat. The weakness is connected to raising questions which may be constitutional in nature, yet there are no clear answers to these questions. In other words, it does not follow from digital constitutionalism that the image of constitutional principles online is at all different from the original principles

5 M. Susi, 'Novelty in New Human Rights: The Decrease of Universality and Abstractness Thesis' in A. von Arnauld, K. von der Decken, M. Susi (eds.), *Cambridge Handbook on New Human Rights of the 21st Century: Recognition, Novelty, and Rhetoric* (Cambridge: Cambridge University Press, 2020), p. 22.

6 Ibid., p. 24; for the purpose of context, the other five origins for the inadequacy of protection claim are: desire to bring about domestic or international political change, civil society or special interest groups pushing certain agendas, insufficiency of the current human rights law to address new challenges, conceptualisation of moral and social values and finally, intellectual and philosophical considerations.

7 O. Pollicino, G. De Gregorio, 'Constitutional Law in the Algorithmic Society' in H. Micklitz, O. Pollicino, A. Reichman, A. Simoncini, G. Sartor, G. De Gregorio (eds.), *Constitutional Challenges in the Algorithmic Society* (Cambridge: Cambridge University Press, 2022), p. 5.

offline, and even if it is, where exactly lies the variance. As long as there are no suggestions, even implicitly, about what might be the elements of digital constitutional values, non-coherence theory cannot be applied. The caveat stems from the weakness. Digital constitutionalism accepts the possibility that constitutional-level principles online may be at variance with the offline principles, but it stops short of saying so. The negation that something may be lost in transposition does not exclude the possibility that the digital realm itself comes forward with ideas which from the offline perspective meet the criteria of constitutional-level thinking. What gets lost during transposition is silently replaced from inside the target area. This is the topic of self-constitutionality, and it is also a perfect revelation of non-coherency.

The second stage is the emergence of ideas and subsequent discourse saying that something in human rights law and/or practice has to be changed in order to provide adequate protection online. Adequacy does not necessarily mean equality. This is the question, with many aspects remaining outside of human rights ontological justification, which will be addressed separately in this monograph, in other words, whether comparable protection of fundamental rights is achievable in the online domain as in the offline domain. The process characterising this second stage can either be the widening of the scope of existing well-established human rights rules or principles or alternatively the articulation of novel ideas finding materialisation in novel human rights claims. The latter, in turn, can occur either via implication or derivation from well-established rights or by articulating new self-standing rights or principles, where the link to the so-called mother right or principle remains weak.[8]

5.2.2 *The Promise of Digital Constitutionalism*

The emerging school of digital constitutionalism raises high expectations that there can be new ideas, perhaps even new principles at the constitutional level which apply in particular online situations or exclusively to the digital domain. Edoardo Celeste, for example, advances such expectations by writing: 'Digital constitutionalism is a new strand of contemporary constitutionalism. However, it does denote a new stage of evolution to constitutionalism, which marks a revolutionary change and implies the transition to new values and

8 Gill, Redeker and Gasser follow this same logic by writing that in terms of substance, the efforts towards digital constitutionalism may either involve the extension of established civil rights to the digital sphere (such as freedom of association on the Internet), or the articulation of rights and freedoms which appear native to the digital environment (such as the principle of net neutrality), whereas the matter of whether these rights are entirely *new* remains debatable – see Gill et al. (n 2), 3.

ideals, like it happened when constitutionalism eventually became "democratic."'[9] However, the idea of digital constitutionalism also appears in reverse, where the basic difference of the promise of new ideals lies in the enhancement of well-established values to counter these possible new ideals emerging from the digital domain. This is expressed by De Gregorio as follows: 'the primary goals of digital constitutionalism in the algorithmic society is to promote and safeguard constitutional values from the rise of unaccountable digital powers'.[10] Such disagreement about the nature of digital constitutionalism may be a concern from the side of the dogmatism to define the true nature of this ambitious doctrine, yet for proponents of non-coherence it is no more than a revelation that something may or may not be different in the fundamental principles governing human rights in the offline and online domains. If the constitutional level principles in these two domains are the same, then non-coherence has to be denied. Alternatively, if the constitutional-level principles are at variance, then non-coherence is apparent. This is not a matter of scepticism or non-scepticism in regard to non-coherence but an objectively detectable result of comparing the principles on the basis of words and their meaning. It is necessary to add here that whenever someone says that something fundamentally *new* is necessary to protect fundamental rights in the digital domain, this proposition of novelty already takes non-coherence as an assumption.

This second stage of the transposition of human rights law from offline to online is primarily about the process. Relevant questions include whether ideas transform and who are the main actors in deciding about the necessity of the transformation. These questions should be separated from the question of how rights can be guaranteed since they are purely concerned with the idealistic or practice independent side of human rights. Therefore, the tendency to transfer public functions or tasks from lawmakers to specialist actors both in the public and private sectors[11] is not important. This is because the result of outsourcing public functions to private actors cannot by itself lead to an assumption that the end result of constitutional-level principles is at all at

[9] E. Celeste, 'Digital Constitutionalism: A New Systematic Theorization' (2019) 33 *International Review of Law, Computers & Technology*, 1, 88.

[10] G. De Gregorio, *Digital Constitutionalism in Europe: Reframing Rights and Powers in the Algorithmic Society* (Cambridge: Cambridge University Press, 2022), p. 317. De Gregorio echoes the same idea by suggesting that the primary challenge for constitutional democracies in the algorithmic society might be to limit the rise of global private powers replacing democratic values with private determinations, see Pollicino and De Gregorio (n 7), p. 24.

[11] J. Freeman, M. Minow (eds.), *Government by Contract: Outsourcing and American Democracy* (Cambridge, MA: Harvard University Press, 2009).

variance with principles which are generated by traditional power structures. As an example, the constitutional principles discovered from instruments put forward by purely public bodies meant for offline fundamental rights protection can entirely overlap with the principles to be found from instruments proposed by private bodies. Since we are focusing here on the idealistic side of fundamental rights, should there be evidence for such an overlap, non-coherence would have to be rejected. But we are yet to see whether there is such evidence, so such a statement would appear premature at this stage.

5.3 THE SEARCH FOR NEW ONLINE CONSTITUTIONAL PRINCIPLES

The third stage of the transposition of offline fundamental rights to the online domain is the acceptance of new rights or principles or conversely, the rejection of claims due to the absence of their necessity.[12] The main question here is about evidence of whether and which new fundamental rights aspiring to the constitutional level have been proposed, and whether they carry sufficient argumentative force to be considered as principles, which are non-coherent against the non-digital domain. For this purpose, I will apply the theory to some international instruments shortly, especially in respect to development over time. I will start with the twentieth session resolution of the Human Rights Council from 2012 on the promotion, protection and enjoyment of human rights on the Internet,[13] then proceed to the UN Human Rights Council adoption in 2021 of the principle of the promotion, protection and enjoyment of human rights on the Internet[14] and finally to the European Declaration on Digital Rights and Principles for the Digital Decade.[15] The goal of this short exercise is to view whether there are any novel ideas at the constitutional level and if and whether these have developed over time.

[12] For reference about the phases of recognising new rights, see K. von der Decken, N. Koch, 'Recognition of New Human Rights: Phases, Techniques and the Approach of "Differentiated Traditionalism"' in A. von Arnauld, K. von der Decken, M. Susi (eds.), *Cambridge Handbook on New Human Rights of the 21st Century: Recognition, Novelty, and Rhetoric* (Cambridge: Cambridge University Press, 2020), pp. 7–20.

[13] U.N. Human Rights Council, 'Report of the Human Rights Council on Its Twentieth Session', HRC 20th session, UN Doc A/HRC/20/2 (2012).

[14] U.N. Human Rights Council, 'The Promotion, Protection and Enjoyment of Human Rights on the Internet', 47th Session, UN Doc A/HRC/47/L.22 (2021).

[15] By the time this monograph is published, it is possible that the declaration will have been adopted, but as customary for EU lawmaking, with minor changes, if at all, the Document was proposed in Brussels on 26 January 2022, COM(2022) 28 final.

5.3.1 *The United Nations Human Rights Council Resolutions*

The UN Human Rights Council resolution from 2012 is short, containing only five substantive points, and says in the substantive paragraph No. 1 that the same rights people have offline must also be protected online. In contrast, the resolution adopted by the same body ten years later and having the same heading, contains nineteen substantive paragraphs, yet starts with the same statement of the sameness of rights. Since the matter of the sameness of rights online and offline is subject to a separate part later in this monograph, my interest here is elsewhere. Both documents contain no explicit statements regarding normative rights, including constitutional-level rights, which would be applicable only in the digital domain. These documents are to be viewed as procedural policy documents, highlighting how the substantive human rights are to be best implemented in the digital domain. It appears that the number of challenges identified has grown many times during the decade – an example would be a statement on the bridging of the digital divide[16] or attention to the phenomenon of net neutrality.[17] Given the abundance of identified impediments to the realisation of the *sameness* doctrine, it leads us to question at what point these impediments reach a critical mass of obscurity, making it impossible to justify that no new constitutional-level ideas apply in the digital domain. We can say that this critical mass of impediments decreases the ease of justifying the absence of constitutional ideas specific to the digital domain. Another way to say this would be to advance the thesis of an increase in idealism, which means that amidst the attention behind the concept of the absence of the need for new rights, the practicality of the rights from the offline domain diminishes.

5.3.2 *The EU Digital Rights Declaration*

The EU Digital Rights Declaration excluded prima facie the possibility of any form of double constitutionality in the digital space. The preamble statement in paragraph 1 is: 'With the acceleration of the digital transformation, the time has come for the European Union (EU) to spell out how its values and fundamental rights should be applied in the online world.'[18] Such a level of generality is retained throughout the declaration, where reference to

16 Paragraph 8 of the 2021 Resolution (n 14).

17 U.N. Human Rights Council (n 14), para. 12.

18 EU Declaration on Digital Rights and Principles for the Digital Decade, chapter v, subchapter privacy and individual control over data, preamble paragraph 1.

fundamental rights without any specification is used in five sentences, and the spirit of the declaration is about the means to secure their effectiveness and practicality.[19] The praise associated with the proclamation of these six pillars from practice[20] is not about normative developments but about the apparent end to the process of normative contestations. Such a declaration may be viewed as a response to what Flonk, Jachtenfuchs and Obendiek suggest as the non-emergence or weakness of alternative normative frameworks. They write: 'Rather, it is in many instances not yet established which norms apply to which issues of internet governance',[21] and then continue by reinforcing the understanding that the normative ambiguity is in the fact that 'the conflicts over adequate internet governance institutions and norms are ongoing, transforming and unlikely to be resolved in the near future'. All of the aforementioned reinforces our observation about the process of the transformation of offline constitutional-level human rights norms and ideas to the online domain. Non-coherence therefore dominates, and it cannot be otherwise. This is because there are no concrete alternative suggestions of internet-specific and fundamental human rights norms from one side. And from the other side there are emerging instruments with the goal of advising how the offline human rights norms and ideas are to be *discovered* and reinforced online. The main question here then is whether the content of the norms and the ideas born in the offline human rights realm, and at a superficial glance bearing the same name in both domains, are indeed the same.

5.4 LOOKING AT SOME DIGITAL CONSTITUTIONS

We will now have a brief look at some *digital constitutions*. The choice is based on availability at the time of writing this monograph, and so we will look at those adopted in Italy, Spain, Africa and Brazil. We will not seek at this point to explore a comparison of the rights articulated in these human rights instruments designed for the digital space. More attention will be given to the matter of content comparison as the monograph progresses. The central point

[19] For reference, the declaration has six chapters which are declared and constitute the backbone of the so-called digital transformation. These six topics are petting people at the centre of the digital transformation; solidarity and inclusion; freedom of choice; participation in the digital public space; safety, security and empowerment; and finally, sustainability.

[20] See, for example, a statement from practice on the positive convergence trend, Energy Industry Review, '2022 DESI: EU Digital Progress, Energy Industry Review', 1 August 2022, https://energyindustryreview.com/tech/2022-desi-eu-digital-progress, accessed 27 October 2022.

[21] D. Flonk, M. Jachtenfuchs, A. S. Obendiek, 'Authority Conflicts in Internet Governance: Liberals vs. Sovereigntists' (2020) 9 *Global Constitutionalism*, 2, 379.

of this quick glance at these images of human rights in digital constitutions will concern the proportion of ideal and normative dimensions, that is, whether the expansion of digital human rights at the constitutional level in comparison with offline human rights will destroy or diminish the ideal dimension of digital constitutionalism. To put it simply, if all digital human rights are to be lifted to the constitutional level, then constitutionalism loses its meaning.

Such an ideal dimension – whether offline or online – is an essential property of any normative system, and it exists independently of the normative positive dimensions of human rights. In the background of this glance is the level of abstractness of digital constitutional rights. This expression of *digital constitutional rights* is used here to point to the reflection of well-established and self-standing fundamental rights from the offline domain, such as freedom of expression or the right to privacy, or the right to association, to mention a few. The fundamentality of these rights is prima facie shared by academic and professional communities now and in the past and needs no justification. Yet an entirely different question, and of the highest importance here, is when a limited number of rights is lifted to constitutional-level instruments but with a distorted degree of abstractness (usually lower) at variance with offline instruments; then again, constitutionalism either loses its meaning or obtains a different meaning from what it meant offline. Examples of the distorted degree of abstractness will be revealed in the next section.

5.4.1 *The Italian Declaration of Internet Rights*

The Italian Declaration of Internet Rights, adopted by parliament in 2015, is one of the first digital constitutions within the meaning of non-binding law. It does not introduce any new constitutional properties into human rights discourse in the digital domain due to clear reference to the Universal Declaration of the UN and the Charter of Fundamental Rights of the EU.[22] It also sets forth guidelines for interpreting these rights, which is to be done on the basis of the dignity, freedom, equality and diversity of each individual.[23] The main objection to be raised against the promise from the preamble – that this declaration is 'crucial for laying the constitutional foundation for

[22] Article 1 in the Italian Declaration (recognition and protection of rights) says in paragraph 1: 'The fundamental rights of every individual enshrined in the Universal Declaration of the United Nations, the Charter of Fundamental Rights of the European Union, national constitutions and other relevant International declarations shall be protected on the Internet.'

[23] Ibid., respectively paras. 2 and 3 of article 1.

supranational principles and rights' – can be termed an objection to the concretisation. This means, that the concreteness of various rights, guidelines and values put forward by the declaration, speak against constituting a new backbone of the digital constitution.

Commenting on the text of the declaration, one of its authors, Rodotá, is of the opinion that one thing the Declaration attempted, 'was to identify the specific principles and rights of the digital world, by underlining not only their peculiarities but also the way in which they generally contribute to redefining the entire sphere of rights'.[24] Like Rodotá, some advocacy commentators are of the view that this declaration points to the question of whether a new digital social contract is needed to create a *digital home* for all.[25] The reply to these expectations is based on the objection from the concretisation. Human rights and constitutional principles cannot contain highly practice-oriented guidelines and policy ideas because this is a weakening of the idea of constitutionalism. Implication cannot be compared against explication in the framework of non-coherence, since these two manifestations of human rights always appear in non-coherent forms against one another. Therefore, my reply is that the declaration from Italy has not been capable of laying a new constitutional foundation for human rights in the digital domain, despite its promise. Any movement further away from the rhetoric, articulation and recognition that the entire sphere of rights will be redefined calls for justification. But such justification has not been offered. The question is whether such justification is possible. Of course, the statement of a redefinition of the foundations of fundamental rights in the digital domain is a clear statement of non-coherence. The pivotal point now is whether the promise of constitutional principles – incorporating by default well-established fundamental rights – remains empty, or whether it lends itself to justification through non-coherence. This would mean that the basic ideas of the dignity, freedom, equality and diversity of each individual have meaning which is at variance with well-established and commonly accepted meanings from the fundamental rights and democratic discourses offline.

[24] S. Rodotá, 'Towards a Declaration of Internet Rights', date unknown, www.camera.it/application/xmanager/projects/leg17/attachments/upload_file/upload_files/000/000/194/Internet_Libe_inglese.pdf, accessed 22 August 2022.

[25] See, for example, such commentary from Geneva Digital Platform, 'La "Carta dei Diritti di Internet" e il report "The Age of Interdependence": Principi e sfide', digwatch, 7 October 2020, https://dig.watch/event/igf-italia-2020/la-carta-dei-diritti-di-internet-e-il-report-age-interdependence-principi-e-sfide, accessed 22 August 2022.

5.4.2 *The Spanish Charter of Digital Rights*

These questions can be explored further on the basis of the Spanish Charter of Digital Rights, adopted in 2021.[26] This charter does not have the ambition to establish new ideas at the constitutional level or put forward new fundamental rights but rather, as stated in the media at the time of its adoption, 'provides a reference framework to guarantee citizens' rights in the new digital age and aims to recognize the challenges of adapting existing rights to the virtual and digital environment'.[27] The same newspaper further writes about the goal of 'updating existing rights' for the digital age. The text of the Spanish Charter, unlike the Italian one, does not include the ambition of constitutional foundations. The ambition is narrower and limited to guaranteeing that 'the fundamental rights and freedoms recognized in the Spanish Constitution, in the Universal Declaration of Human Rights, in the Charter of Fundamental Rights of the European Union and in the international treaties and covenants on the same matters ratified by Spain are guaranteed in the digital environment or space'.[28] Like the Italian declaration, some core values are listed, among them equality (article 1.3), human dignity and the free development of personality (article 1.3).

One can consider my careful assumption of the non-coherent nature of fundamental principles transferred to the digital domain on the example of equality in the digital ecosystem specified in the Spanish Charter. Chapter 2 bears the heading 'Equality Rights' and is divided into four subchapters, with the headings respectively 'Right to Equality and to Non-discrimination in the Digital Environment' (VIII), 'Child Protection in the Digital Environment' (IX), 'Protection of Persons with Disabilities in the Digital Environment' (X) and 'Protection of Older Persons in the Digital Environment' (XI). These subchapters by and large contain the reinforcement of the idea that equality should also apply in the digital domain without restriction, as manifest in

[26] The original text in Spanish is accessible, for example, via the following website:

Cities Coalition for Digital Rights, 'Spain presents Its Charter of Digital Rights', date unknown, https://citiesfordigitalrights.org/spain-presents-its-charter-digital-rights, accessed 22 October 2022.

[27] See, for example, commentary of La Moncloa at:

La Moncloa, 'The Government Adopts the Digital Rights Charter to Articulate a Reference Framework to Guarantee Citizens' Rights in the New Digital Age', La Moncloa, 14 September 2021, www.lamoncloa.gob.es/lang/en/gobierno/news/Paginas/2021/20210713_rights-charter.aspx, accessed 24 August 2022.

[28] Para. 1, article 1 of the Spanish Charter of Digital Rights.

simple wordings like 'the right to the effective equality of women and men in digital environments is recognized',[29] or 'the rights of older persons to access to digital environments are recognized'.[30] In these presentations, equality as an underlying foundational principle of the fundamental rights architecture means nothing else than assurance that everyone is equal to another also in the cyberspace. In this manifestation, the non-coherence of foundational fundamental rights principles between online and offline domains does not exist. However, this is simply a statement from implication. This may appear as simplistic after evidence from practice is put on the table; that is, the divide between the articulated principles of equality and dignity and their reality can appear wider online than offline. There is nothing to suggest from the Spanish Charter that the idea of equality online is understood differently from the idea of equality offline. Of course, this approach, excluding non-coherence, comes from the public authorities.

From the point of human rights theory, three substantive matters can be raised against the majority of the ideas advanced in the Spanish Charter. The first concerns principles such as the right to net neutrality (XII) or public participation by digital means (XIV). In the analogue context with the proposed human right to democracy, which largely has been rejected, the right to net neutrality cannot be seen as a human right among others with a similar conceptual structure and analogous legal effects.[31] The main concerns are related to its normativity and consequences in the event of not fulfilling the goal of net neutrality. In a concrete case, it is not clear whether the idea of net neutrality is just a soft law norm, or a mere goal or preference. Regarding its normative type, it is not clear whether it is to be seen as an individual entitlement or an imperfect duty. Taking it one step further, it is likewise ambiguous what would be the consequences in the event of not providing net neutrality.

The second matter builds upon the uncertainty of normativity. This concerns the breakage of the relational chain between the rights holder and the addressee of this proposed right, which is a precondition of any fundamental right. In this case, under the scrutiny of net neutrality, the rights holders would be collectively all internet users and the public authority, and the addressee or obligated party are likewise the users and the public authority.

29 Spanish Charter, article 8.1, second sentence.

30 Spanish Charter, article 11.1.

31 For the context of the discussion of why political goals cannot be transformed into human rights, see Samantha Besson, 'The Human Right to Democracy in International Law. Coming to Moral Terms with an Equivocal Legal Practice' in A. von Arnauld, K. von der Decken, M. Susi (eds.), *Cambridge Handbook on New Human Rights of the 21st Century: Recognition, Novelty, and Rhetoric* (Cambridge: Cambridge University Press, 2020), pp. 481–489.

The third matter is related to the decrease in abstractness. Taking as an example the right to digital education (XV), one notices the articulation of highly detailed entitlements and corresponding duties, for example, the promotion of vocational training plans aimed at the integration of workers into digital transformation processes (XV 3 a). Even from the view of a narrow and strict construction of constitutional norms, the necessary level of abstractness is lost. It follows, and this observation has to be sufficient here, that fundamental principles underlying human rights in the digital domain are in need of specific guidelines for action in order to obtain practical effect. In response to the question 'why', the immediate reaction could be that there must be something in the digital domain related to the capability of obligated actors to safeguard these principles.

5.4.3 *The African Declaration on Internet Rights and Freedoms and the Brazilian Internet Bill*

The African Declaration on Internet Rights and Freedoms, passed in 2013 in Nairobi,[32] is less articulate on the fundamental standards, yet puts emphasis on the element of equality. As such, the preamble mentions the concern caused by the continuing inequality in access to and use of the Internet and the need to avoid the exclusion of some vulnerable groups. It makes mention of many regional and international standard documents, and by implication, it follows that these standards are to be upheld online as well. The Brazilian Internet Bill (Marco Civil Law of the Internet[33]) also does not contain any reference to any international standards but only to the country's federal constitution. Yet there is one point which makes no sense in the context of the traditional structure of constitutional rights; namely, article 2 says that the 'discipline of internet use in Brazil is founded on the basis of respect for freedom of expression'. This demonstrates variance from the constitutional principle of equality of relative fundamental rights. As such, it is a clear representation of non-coherence between offline and online constitutional constructions.

5.5 SHORT CONCLUDING REMARKS

Various explanations have been given to explain the phenomenon of the non-coherence of digital constitutional principles. For example, Thornhill has

[32] For updates and the road leading to this declaration, visit https://africaninternetrights.org/en/updates

[33] Brazilian law No. 12.965, 23 April 2014.

noted the expansionary tendencies of non-governmental collective actors,[34] which may lead to constitutional aspirations. He believes that this is a matter of concern for jurists. Viellechner writes about a phenomenon which I would call 'procedural constitutionalism', necessary for limiting the self-destructive element of freedom associated with self-regulation.[35] We will be content at this point to say that constitutional-level principles are not immune from non-coherence when it comes to the image of human rights in the digital domain.

34 C. Thornhill, 'A Sociology of Constituent Power: The Political Code of Transnational Societal Constitutions' (2013) 20 *Indiana Journal of Global Legal Studies* 2, Article 3, 577.

35 L. Viellechner, 'The Network of Networks: Karl-Heinz Ladeur's Theory of Law and Globalization' (2009) 10 *German Law Journal*, 4, 523.

PART II

Reflections on Some Theories and Doctrines

6

The Doctrine of the Sameness of Rights Online and Offline

6.1 CONTOURS OF THE IDEA

The idea that human rights offline and online are the same belongs to the sphere of human rights religious reasoning. As such, it is the representation of faith located far and above the reach of explicative justification. Religious justifications as a rule remain immune to any contrary argumentation. The correctness of the sameness statement seems to remain unquestioned from its appearance. It coincided with the spread of the Internet and many may see it therefore as standing outside the need for any justification at all. Just like we take for granted that for human life it is conditional to have the ability to breathe. Proponents of the judicial argumentation approach should note, however, that religious justification taken alone without other forms of justification is not sufficient to reject the validity of the argument on the table. This is because some highly relevant human rights ideas are best explainable as religious beliefs, and this does not compromise their validity at the top of the human rights pyramid. For example, one can include in such a list the ideas of equality and personal freedom.

Several doubts can be raised against the idea of the sameness of rights online and offline. Whether such a statement of high generality can be supported by rational argumentation at all, can be raised as the primary doubt. The second doubt is about mistaken focus. Opponents of such a statement may mistakenly have in mind something else – the difficulties of enforcing human rights online whatever the content. Here the focus would be highly practical as opposed to the highly general nature of the sameness statement. A brief sketch of how the idea emerged and has spread has to be presented before taking a more particular look at the doubts expressed.

6.2 THE MATURATION OF THE IDEA

With some imagination, it is possible to cite the claim of sameness from the Geneva Principles in 2003.[1] This result of an effort for which there are no *traveaux preparatoires*, lacks argumentation in support of its claims, and thus represents a clear example of an instrument of faith. It reaffirms 'the universality, indivisibility, interdependence and interrelation of all human rights and fundamental freedoms'.[2] One can say that such a statement is not a full acknowledgement of the idea of the sameness, but it conveys the impression that human rights are not domain dependent. It took almost ten years to reach the *expressis verbis* statement of sameness in an international instrument. This is the UN Human Rights Council resolution from 29 June 2012, which '[*a*] *ffirms* that the same rights that people have offline must also be protected online'.[3] Sometimes the idea of sameness does not appear as a direct statement but is deducible from the context. Take, for example, the UN Human Rights Committee's General comment No. 34 to article of 19 of the UN General Declaration from 2011.[4] This comment acknowledges in paragraph 15 the substantial change in communication practices around the world due to information and communication technologies. And yet implicitly, it is based on accepting full transposition of human rights principles from offline to online. O'Flaherty, with insights from the Committee, pointed to the 'unusual willingness by the Committee to engage with the interaction of technological advancement and the enjoyment of ICCPR rights'.[5] The matter of enthusiasm is of course not important for the argument's credibility, especially in relation to fundamental matters of human rights law. However, and not reading between the lines, the framework paragraph cited by O'Flaherty says the following: 'State parties should take account of the extent to which developments in information and communication technologies, such as internet and mobile-based electronic information dissemination systems, have substantially

[1] World Summit on the Information Society, Geneva 2003 – Tunis 2005, Document WSIS-03/ GEBEVA7DOC74-E, 12 December 2003, Declaration of Principles, Building the Information Society: A Global Challenge in the New Millennium, www.itu.int/net/wsis/docs/ geneva/official/dop.htm, accessed 21 October 2022.

[2] Ibid., para. 3.

[3] U.N. Human Rights Council, 'The Promotion, Protection and Enjoyment of Human Rights on the Internet', HRC 20th Session, UN Doc A/HRC/20/L.13 (2012).

[4] U.N. Human Rights Council, 'General Comment No. 34 on Article 19: Freedoms of Opinion and Expression', 102nd session, UN Doc CCPR /C/GC/34 (2011).

[5] M. O'Flaherty, 'Freedom of Expression: Article 19 of the International Covenant on Civil and Political Rights and the Human Rights Committee's General Comment No 34' (2012) 12 *Human Rights Law Review*, 651.

changed communication practices around the world'.[6] Here we see the focus on practices and not on the substance of rights. The idea of sameness has to be assumed.

The assumption of the idea of the sameness of human rights online and offline now appears as an incontestable truth but not entirely beyond criticism. The incontestable aspect appears in the format of ignoring this question completely; for example, we do not find any reference to the matter of sameness in the newest – at the time of writing this monograph – European Union digital policy documents, such as the Declaration on European Digital Rights and Principles. Some instruments still explicitly mention this idea as the cornerstone. For example, the Spanish Charter of Digital Rights is another proponent of the sameness doctrine by saying in article 1, paragraph 2: 'All persons have identical rights in both the digital and analogical environments … taking into account the peculiarities of each sphere.' The idea of the sameness of offline and online fundamental rights is often also accepted as standing outside critical review in scholarly observations. Kettemann, for example, in his early career has commented in 2015 on article 1 of the Italian declaration, with an enthusiasm devoid of academic restraint, that it reaffirms that all fundamental rights apply offline just as online.[7]

It may be sufficient here to point to the ubiquity of this idea on the basis of the commendable work of others. For example, Dror-Shpoliansky and Shany propose the normative equivalency paradigm, having shown how in a series of resolutions, the Human Rights Committee and the General Assembly 'have reiterated the notion that human rights apply in the digital "online world" as they apply in the "offline world"'.[8] The normative equivalency, as they assert, contains a major flaw, which is about considering 'digital technology as a new tool or arena for exercising offline rights or governmental powers, as opposed to a conceptualisation of digital space as giving rise to a new human condition and governance domain'.[9] This view represents non-coherence between digital and non-digital domains in a narrow sense, not encompassing well-

6 U.N. Human Rights Council (n 4), article 19, para. 15.

7 See from online sources: Matthias C. Kettemann, 'Forza Internet Rights: IRPC Charter as Source of Inspiration for Innovative Italian Declaration of Internet Rights', Internet Rights and Principles Coalition, date unknown, https://internetrightsandprinciples.org/forza-internet-rights-iprc-charter-as-source-of-inspiration-for-innovative-italian-declaration-of-internet-rights, accessed 24 July 2022.

8 D. Dror-Shpoliansky, Y. Shany 'It's the End of the (Offline) World as We Know It: From Human Rights to Digital Human Rights – A Proposed Typology' (2021) 32 *The European Journal of International Law*, 4, 1253.

9 Ibid., 1265.

established rights from the offline domain, such as the right to privacy, and covers the so-called second generation rights. An example would be the right not to be subject to automated decision-making. As it turns out, the weakest feature of the concept of normative equivalency lies in its normativity. When applied, this concept shows us the image of well-established human rights in the digital space without variance, and variance appears when one looks at certain new human rights, which have one or more parent rights but are not fully and adequately covered by them.[10] Yet normativity in this case concerns the labels and does not look at the content of rights. Therefore, it may appear that human rights norms in the digital and non-digital environments, which appear normatively equivalent, carry different meanings. I can depart from this comment on criticisms of normative equivalency towards the idea of the sameness of online and offline rights with an additional remark from the logic of human rights law development. The proposition of human rights specific to the digital domain means that they cannot exist offline. Therefore, and purely in positivist terms, equivalency can or cannot exist between norms which can be found in both domains. When a certain claim of a right does exist only in the digital space, there cannot be any equivalency in the first place.

6.3 DOUBTS ABOUT THE SAMENESS DOCTRINE

Now it is time to return to the doubts expressed in the previous section. They were formulated in response to the generality of the statement of sameness and the doubt arising from mistaking rights content with enforcement.

6.3.1 *The Doubt Arising from Generality*

The doubt arising from generality is related to a common feature of the basic or fundamental building blocks of human rights. There are certain ideas which are difficult to justify through explication, and even then, the element of belief in something remains relevant. For example, take the idea of the universality of human rights. Is this a premise that can be verified through rational argumentation, or is this the result of discursive, political and judicial practices? Its importance is, nevertheless, evident from asking what would happen to the suggestion about the omnipotence of human rights if the idea was given up? The sameness idea carries similar connecting and rhetorical force. In today's human rights discourses, policies, judgments and civil society

[10] Ibid., 1268.

approaches (i.e., everywhere), an answer to the question of whether human rights offline and online are the same has far-reaching consequences. An affirmative answer means coherence of content and leads to the subsequent question of the breadth of non-coherence in the enforcement instruments. However, on the contrary, if the negation of the sameness idea could claim validity as a general principle, then we can say that human rights online do not exist. Even if we add, as some have done, that human rights online are not the human rights we are used to in the offline domain, then all efforts to regulate the online domain through human rights language and normativity originating from offline can only affect the facade and not reach beyond. Talking about and adjudicating human rights in this case would address symptoms and not the causes. It is therefore highly significant to attach weight to any argumentation related to the matter of the sameness question. To illustrate this, I will turn to two well-known reports from the United Nations Special Rapporteurs.

La Rue's report from 2011 on freedom of expression on the Internet[11] demonstrates that it is mandatory to look for reasons and the development of ideas and not accept uncritically positions from normative instruments. His view that, 'the framework of international human rights law remains relevant today and equally applicable to new communication technologies as the Internet',[12] rests on his assumption that article 19 of the Universal Declaration and the Covenant was drafted with foresight to include and accommodate future technological developments. As such, it stands close to faith in regard to the sameness of rights. But it depends on the correctness of only one assertion, that is, what the drafters of the Universal Declaration and the Covenant had in mind and were able to predict. This dependency turns into a weakness because it can easily be challenged through objections. Should the validity of the proposition disappear or become contested, then this is carried over to the validity of the conclusion, which means that the claim of sameness is weakened or needs to be rejected. And these objections are indeed raised towards what the drafters really could have had in mind. For example, the objections formulated by Land are linked to the problems of quantity and lack of filters as generic characteristics of the communication technology.[13] These features led her to the critique's central point, that some

[11] Frank La Rue, 'Report of the Special Rapporteur on the Promotion and Protection of the Right to Freedom of Opinion and Expression', HRC 17th session, UN Doc A/HRC/17/27 (2011).

[12] Ibid., para. 21.

[13] M. Land, 'Toward an International Law of the Internet' (2013) 54 *Harvard International Law Journal*, 2, 410.

new information and communication technologies might be so different in kind from the media available at the time of the drafting of the ICCPR, that 'they should not be understood to be encompassed within the term "media"'.[14] If this assertion is correct, then La Rue's assumption for the sameness argument disappears.

A different UN Special Rapporteur writing on the right to privacy raises, as I am proposing here, an objection to generality. The Rapporteur has come up with the finding that, '[w]hen dealing with technologies such as the Internet it is simplistic and naïve to be content with a statement that "whatever is protected off-line is protected on-line". That is a hopelessly inadequate approach to the protection of privacy in 2018.'[15] This objection is rooted in the recognition that the statement of sameness results from our agreement that privacy is a fundamental right; in other words, it is a matter or faith. Consequently, twelve questions follow that need an answer to justify or reject the sameness statement. It is not my role to seek answers but merely highlight, as I have done before in this book, that non-coherence between the digital and non-digital domains may appear at a certain level of concreteness, even when some general properties of human rights systems appear to have little variance.

The doubt about generality allows us to say that the statement of the sameness of human rights in the digital and non-digital domains is true at the highest level of generality and abstractness. Here, human rights in these domains are coherent, and non-coherence becomes more and more apparent in the image of digital human rights as we progress towards increasing concreteness. At some point, non-coherence disappears when human rights specific to the digital domain emerge which are not a reflection of a comparable right offline. Here we need to distinguish between positivism and the interpretation of norms, as they carry different features when comparing offline and online human rights. When we take, for example, the right to non-automated decision-making in the digital realm, then we observe that there is no corresponding human rights norm in the offline realm. Positivism and textualism lead us to conclude that the question of non-coherence cannot be raised. However, the right to non-automated decision-making may have some connection to the right to self-determination, and here one can apply the non-coherence lens. Suddenly, the matter of the sameness of rights is connected to the very foundations of digital society. When we accept that the claim of sameness is correct at least at the highest level of generality, as a self-standing

[14] Ibid.

[15] U.N. Human Rights Council, 'Special Rapporteur on the Right to Privacy', HRC 37th session, UN Doc A/HRC/37/62 (2018), Annex, para. 6.

basic feature, then we can also claim that human rights make sense in the digital domain. The rejection of this claim leads to absolute relativism, which is the notion that *anything goes*. Non-coherence theory is rooted in this dilemma of the absoluteness or relativity of relativism. The main thesis here states that if human rights online and offline are the same, this can only concern their similar status as the foundation of different realities. This question is positioned outside the method of non-coherence, as it relates to belief. Everything that follows is subject to analysis from the mutual coherence perspective.

6.3.2 *The Doubt from Mistaking Content for Enforcement*

The second doubt, mistaking the content of right for their enforcement, claims that whatever the concrete content of a human right, its structure is about rights and obligations. This is the question of turning the *ought* into *is*. This doubt means that despite the different breadth between these elements – since there are new elements in the digital domain – the rights holders can assume realisation. This is the aspect of practice. The advocacy group Article 19 has translated the reaffirmation that 'the same rights that people have offline must also be protected online' into questions of practicality. It says that unless greater priority is placed on addressing violations and changes to law and practice, this statement of sameness is no more 'than words just written on paper'.[16] Here the focus can easily divert to matters which are conceptually not relevant but related to the matter of sameness. Take, for example, the concern about whether courts and lawyers can find something from social networking sites which corresponds to the meaning of a *document*.[17] A legal theory cannot be diluted using overly specific questions and needs to stay focused on matters deemed conceptual. Non-coherence theory is interested in comparing the concepts of compliance and enforcement, which will be the subject of more detailed attention as we progress.

[16] Article 19, statement at the 35th Session of the UN Human Rights Council on the 14 June 2017, as part of the Item 3 General Debate, see: /www.article19.org/resources/article-19-at-the-unhrc-the-same-rights-that-people-have-offline-must-also-be-protected-online, accessed 28 July 2022.

[17] B. E. Boyden, 'Oversharing: Facebook Discover and the Unbearable Sameness of Internet Law' (2012) 65 *Arkansas Law Review*, 39, 71.

7

Claims of New Internet-Specific Human Rights

7.1 THREE THEORETICAL FRAMEWORKS

There are several theoretical frameworks that may be useful when approaching the question of whether new human rights claims have emerged in the digital domain. Since choices have to be made, I will use three sources for reflection: Phil Alston's quality control doctrine, H. L. Hart's seminal categorisation of rights into primary and secondary and finally, the universality and abstractness decrease thesis, which I have proposed and elaborated elsewhere. The primary connecting feature in the application of these theories is their position on the matter of non-coherence. In other words, whether all these approaches reveal a non-coherent image between the non-digital and digital human rights domains, or whether the non-coherence approach remains outside of their realm, or else gets straightforwardly or implicitly rejected. This is a general statement and will be concretised in the course of the analysis in this chapter. Phil Alston's *appellation controlee* test is about when a new human right has matured to the degree that is can be recognised as a self-standing right by an international institution.[1] In Alston's view, a new human right exists only after an international organ, such as the United Nations, tells us so, if we allow paraphrasing. Of interest here is whether rights specific only to the digital realm would, in the abstract sense, pass this test. It is worthwhile

[1] P. Alston, 'Conjuring up New Human Rights: A Proposal for Quality Control' (1984) 78 *American Journal of International Law*, 607–621. According to his criteria, a new human right is ready to be recognised by an international organ if the following conditions apply: the right reflects a fundamentally important social value, is relevant throughout the world in different value systems, is an interpretation of the UN Charter obligation, introduces a new aspect into the existing body of international human rights law, there is already a high degree of international consensus about the claim, states already have a practice enforcing the right and it is sufficiently precise to give rise to identifiable rights and corresponding obligations.

also considering H. L. Hart's approach, where we find the doctrinal statement that the, 'union of primary and secondary rules is at the centre of a legal system; but it is not the whole, and as we move away from the centre we shall have to accommodate, in ways indicated in later chapters, elements of a different character'.[2] The non-coherence questions here are about the nature of the union between primary and secondary rules in the two domains of our focus, and whether the movement away from the centre exhibits features of variance.

Finally, the applicability of the *universality and abstractness decrease thesis* is to be explored for the digital domain. This thesis, which I have introduced elsewhere,[3] claims that the direction of human rights development can be best characterised by either a decrease in the level of abstractness or its universal applicability, or both. The verification or rejection of the same development mechanisms for human rights online is one specific question here. Another matter of interest is whether the decrease in abstractness and universality thesis is at all a suitable methodological tool to comprehend digital human rights development. My approach in the next section will move from deductive reflections to find supportive images from the digital human rights landscape. The power of this theory's universality depends on the degree of its presence when other human rights theories are applied to digital human rights. I seek to defend the position of its horizontal effect.

7.2 HART'S SECONDARY AND PRIMARY RULES

Hart gives concrete function to the secondary rules, which remedies the defects of an imagined regime consisting only of primary rules of obligation. These defects are, 'the *uncertainty* as to the identity of the rules, their *static* quality, and the time-wasting *inefficiency* of the diffuse social pressure by which alone the rules are enforced'.[4] He famously calls the secondary rules those of recognition, change and adjudication. And yet writes that the main idea of the union of primary and secondary rules is to be regarded as a means between juristic extremes.[5] From this comprehensive theory with significant explanatory capacity, several features can appear as non-coherent between the

[2] H. L. Hart, *The Concept of Law*, 2nd ed. (Oxford: Oxford University Press, 1994), p. 99.

[3] M. Susi, 'Novelty in New Human Rights: The Decrease of Universality and Abstractness Thesis' in A. von Arnauld, K. von der Decken, M. Susi (eds.), *Cambridge Handbook on New Human Rights of the 21st Century: Recognition, Novelty, and Rhetoric* (Cambridge: Cambridge University Press, 2020), pp. 21–33.

[4] Hart (n 2), p. 249.

[5] Ibid., p. 213.

digital and physical human rights law domains. A proponent of the non-coherence view would in the beginning focus upon the equilibrium between the primary and the secondary rules. We can clearly see, taking the non-coherence approach as assumed, that a similar equilibrium between the primary and secondary rules online cannot be assumed. There are several reasons for this, which are speculative due to the persistent unclear image of digital human rights. If the rules and principles of human rights law – which coincide with the meaning of the primary rules for Hart – between digital and non-digital domains are at variance, then the secondary rules also have to be at variance. Equilibrium cannot be taken for granted; quite the contrary because in the development stage of human rights law, the primary rules always receive more attention and need to be in place before the secondary rules start to correct the defects.

If, however, the primary rules online and offline have no or little variance, then non-coherence would not exist at all, or it would be very narrow at the primary law level. Here, the variance between the secondary rules attached to the primary human rights law then needs to appear, or the non-coherence would not exist. The non-coherence of secondary rules would in this scenario become decisive for the theory's verification. Once again, looking beyond appearances is necessary, so that deceit via the usage of similar words is avoided since words may carry different meanings. This observation holds both for the primary and secondary rules layers.

Despite Hart not saying this, the secondary rules are inseparable from the specific primary rules. This means that they cannot exist independently. We take for granted that human and fundamental rights in the offline world belong to the category of primary rules due to their higher levels of abstractness and universality. And it follows that it is not possible to accord to secondary rules the status of fundamental rights, especially because of their lower levels of abstractness and universality. We need to find out now, whether online regulatory instruments might contain such positive law norms, which from one side serve the function of the secondary rules in enabling the functionality of the primary rules, and yet at the same time are lifted into the status of fundamental rights by these same instruments. This can simply happen by merely naming these rights as fundamental or listing them among well-established fundamental rights. Should this be the case, the non-coherence between the online and offline domains would be extensive. This may be close to a model of a new fundamental rights paradigm, aspiring to show as fundamental rights such claims which theoretically cannot be justified as possessing the elements necessary for a fundamental right. The paradigmatic change would occur only when such a justification becomes a closed aim in itself and is not necessary for the functioning of the system. This is close to the *anything goes* model.

Due to the dependency of the secondary rules upon the primary, the non-coherence view of the Hartian model of rights stipulates that the defects of the image of primary rules online have to be addressed first. And then one can turn to the functionality of secondary rules. Should the same defects in the primary rules vary between the online and offline domains, or should the listing of defects have alterations, one needs the secondary rules with their different character for remedial purposes.

7.2.1 *The First Defect: Uncertainty*

The first defect which Hart lists is about the uncertainty of rules. This is explained as the absence of a procedure for settling the doubt about what the rules actually are and their precise scope. There is no procedure within the primary rules for settling such doubts. There is also no reason to reject or even doubt the applicability of such a defect online. Uncertainty is in the nature of fundamental rights, due to their generic abstractness and generality. But this uncertainty becomes important only if one seeks to enforce these abstract rights in practice. Should there be no expectation that primary rules, that is, human rights in the digital domain, are of practical significance, then there would be no reason to seek the determination of their actuality and precise scope. It is as if someone who is aware of the non-reachability of something would not seek to find a means of reaching it. The activity of achieving the unachievable would be a deceit and cannot constitute a defect.

Having determined that, in principle, the defect of the uncertainty of human rights is relevant for the digital domain, the point about the strength of the connectivity between the primary and secondary rules remains. In other words, the question is whether the secondary rules are closely connected to the primary, or whether they have a weaker connection of a certain degree. The latter may be the case because of two factors. The first originates from a disconnect between the idealism of the primary rules and the practicality of the secondary rules. To illustrate, while the freedom to express oneself online may remain a general goal, a facade, the secondary rules may give this right a different meaning. I call this the problem of the weakness of connectivity. In order to solve the problem, one has to study whether the secondary rules, put forward by a variety of actors, diffuse the meaning of the freedom to express oneself. The second factor is related to the origin of the secondary rules. When primary rules for the digital domain usually originate from the public sphere, some authoritative body or instrument, then the origin diversifies online as these rules may originate both from the public and private sectors or a combination. The weakness of connectivity problem, therefore, can become even more complex. I will move on by saying that the non-coherence of the uncertainty defect may therefore lie in the connectivity between the secondary and primary rules.

7.2.2 *The Second Defect: Staticity*

The second defect, that of staticity, is related directly to the universal nature of human rights. It is worth mentioning here that the implicit recognition of core human rights may be inseparable from human existence. Should this be the case, and it probably is, then according to Hart: 'There will be no means, in such a society, of deliberately adapting the rules to changing circumstances, either by eliminating old rules or introducing new ones: for, again the possibility of doing this presupposes the existence of rules of a different type from the primary rules of obligation by which alone the society lives.'[6] There are a variety of methods for adapting to these changing circumstances, which would fall under the broad definition of secondary rules. The impression from Hart, and from more contemporary views, is that the divide between primary and secondary rules is fixed and by itself static. Primary rules are not subject to change, at least fundamental human rights norms and values are not. But the secondary rules are and have to be, since otherwise a normative system would not be able to exist. The concept of a *living instrument* illustrates this. This has been developed by the European Court of Human Rights and stands to justify the Court's discretion in taking into account present-day conditions for the protection of individual applicants.[7]

An objection can be raised, not against the division of human rights norms into primary and secondary as a methodological approach to help our understanding of the rights system, but against the simplicity of the two-layer divide as being too general and not allowing a more complex and multilayered image. I will confine myself when advancing this objection to questioning whether the secondary norms have similar weight against one another and consequently have a similar function in relation to the primary norms. Because it is simplistic to say that all secondary norms are of similar weight and scope – they are not,

6 Hart (n 2), pp. 92–93.

7 European Court of Human Rights Judgement: *Loizidou v Turkey* (1995), Application no 15318/89, para. 71, where it becomes apparent '[t]hat the Convention is a living instrument which must be interpreted in the light of the present-day conditions is firmly rooted in the Court's case-law'.

and secondary norms are clustered around topics; some are reinforced through repetition and some are given higher normative value in instruments. We therefore have to speak of a multilayered system of secondary human rights norms, some with a higher general level and some a lower. The concept of standards will serve as a tool to further elaborate this point.

Secondary human rights norms can be grouped according to standards when they serve the purpose of explaining the primary norms and generating tools for adjudication. Such standards are just one step below the level of the generality of primary rules and are comparatively less influenced by time. Since the proponents of the primary/secondary rule divide would know that the primary rules are to remain *untouchable*, it is here where developments of human rights normativity occur. Mutua represents the same view by referring to setting standards as a dynamic process that must respond to a rapidly changing globe and challenges that come with the emergence of new problems and conditions. I have chosen to cite this work in order to provide a contrast with the static nature of primary rules, since Mutua writes: 'The setting of human rights standards is not a static process.'[8] Here we see to which we have to concur, and that when one of the main features of primary norms is immunity to time and outside developments, these two are the direct influencers of the secondary norms. Hart himself considers that standards are a combined result of discretion by the courts and other officials, implying that they constitute a distinct set of secondary norms.[9] Such standards now become of decisive importance when human rights compliance is measured, as proposed by Sano, who has explained that: 'The compliance dimension will relate to the legal human rights obligations and to the associated human rights standards.'[10] It therefore appears that primary human rights rules lose their significance more and more in practical terms. And we know that the digital social dimension is highly practical. The human rights standards are not static, and yet there is a tendency to mix up their status by mistakenly considering that human rights standards are themselves primary norms but with more understandable functionality. The more solidified the standards become, the more they assume the role of primary norms. It may be at this instance where the link to primary norms is broken. If this view is correct, the non-coherence theory will say that in the digital domain the link between human rights standards and

8 M. Mutua, 'Standard Setting in Human Rights: Critique and Prognosis' (2007) 29 *Human Rights Quarterly*, 3, 620.

9 Hart (n 2), p. 136.

10 H. O. Sano, 'Human Rights and Development: Human Rights Principles and Their Indicators' (2013) 31 *Nordic Journal of Human Rights*, 3, 399.

primary norms becomes at least weaker in comparison with the offline domain. This is the position that has to be defended or rejected here.

7.2.3 *The Third Defect: Inefficiency*

The model of dividing human rights norms into primary and secondary presupposes that primary norms always prevail over the secondary. The third Hartian defect, that of inefficiency, has to be added to this picture, which he describes as there being, 'no agency specially empowered to ascertain finally, and authoritatively, the fact of violation'.[11] The violation of a primary norm can be argued only if the violation of a secondary norm can be construed. But as secondary norms have multiple layers, so do primary norms. To further explain this aspect, one can refer to Sano's division of primary norms into four categories, where human rights as values and dimensions have the highest level of generality, and human rights as obligations have the lowest level of generality due to their concreteness.[12] The lower the level of generality, the more accurate and strict are the operational and indicator implications for measuring human rights compliance. The thesis of the weakening link between primary and secondary human rights norms in the digital domain means that while human rights as values and dimensions, having the highest level of generality and abstractness, remain coherent between the digital and non-digital domains, the lower generality–level human rights norms become overshadowed by the secondary norms. Another way to put this would be to say that the lower-level human rights norms in the digital domain transform into secondary norms, which then means that they no longer are immune to adaptiveness on the basis of time and need. I will test this proposition on the basis of so-called community standards advocated by some major private online service providers.

7.2.4 *About Meta's Community Standards*

Meta, previously and still known as Facebook, has the Transparency Center outlaying their community standards.[13] The company claims that it 'works

[11] Hart (n 2), p. 93.

[12] Sano (n 10), 386. The four categories which Sano proposes are, in order from the more general down: human rights as values and dimensions; human rights as principles; human rights as methodological approaches; human rights as obligations.

[13] It is more useful not to provide a specific link to Meta community standards, since over time the link may change. It is advisable for anyone interested to use a search engine to find Meta community standards. As long as the company exists, the community standards will be easy to locate.

hard' to protect various high-level values. By looking at the section labelled 'privacy violations', we can also notice the 'change log' which allows by navigation to compare the formulations of what is considered a privacy violation and how these formulations have changed. At the time of writing (2022), the Meta Transparency Center allows us to view the formulations for privacy protection from 29 June 2018; since then, six changes have been made. In June 2018, the company started the section about privacy with a warning not to post 'content that facilitates identity theft by posting or soliciting personally identifiable information',[14] and then proceeds directly to list four types of information which is not to be posted. We do not find any reference to high-level principles, nor to any specific origin of obligation for the company to remove such content. With a reservation about what constitutes a standard, the approach is certainly of a secondary-level human rights rule. By 29 September 2022, the formulation was modified to a more general level, and the first paragraph is this: 'Privacy and the protection of personal information are fundamentally important values for Facebook. We work hard to safeguard your personal identity and information and we do not allow people to post personal or confidential information about yourself or others.'[15] It would yet be wrong to view such a formulation as a pure statement of the idea of core human rights. This is because a decisive reservation has been added, namely reference to this statement being an important value for the company. This gives an impression of volatility because it is not clear whether there are any other competing important values. We can imagine that should competing values emerge, there is no clear commitment to giving priority to privacy and personal information protection. Giving the benefit of the doubt, it is possible to take this statement at face value and consider that substitution with some other important values is excluded. Should we take this position, the privacy policy rationale – using the company's vocabulary – clearly represents my previous thesis of the weakening link between primary and secondary norms. Immediately after this statement, the company moves to provide a listing of situations when information posted by users will be removed, which constitutes secondary norms of a not overly high level of generality.

[14] For the reasons explained in the previous footnote, I am not providing a link to the webpage, since it may not be available. The Transparency Center webpage was accessed 28 August 2022.

[15] Ibid.

7.2.5 *The Weakness of Connection Thesis*

The objection on the basis of the weakness between specificity and generality can be raised – network rules of operation are often highly specific and have a weak connection to generally accepted human rights values and principles. This appears to be a common feature of the published rules of operation on social media networks. My observations are confirmed by others, and illustrations are therefore in order. Bateman, Thompson and Smith claim that no one has collected the community standards of all major platforms and subjected them to systematic analysis. Their own study reveals that such standards largely 'avoid the umbrella terms most familiar to experts and the public, like "disinformation"',[16] and they usually contain highly specific policies, and most importantly, these standards are continually changing. The group known as Article 19 has published a summary of recommendations in regard to Facebook community standards, which is to be read in the context of the time they were issued – 2018.[17] The organisation claims, in summary, a preponderance of vague statements and loose connectivity to commonly accepted human rights language. The conclusion from these short references is not only the preponderance of rules which necessarily have to be categorised as secondary rules but also the weakness of their connection to primary rules. This conclusion weighs heavily towards the impression that the image of human rights in social media community standards suggests the connection between primary and secondary rules is not only weak but may be entirely missing. My prediction is that the connectivity is being generated, for a variety of reasons, but will remain cosmetic. Therefore, non-coherence appears in the variance of the strength of the connection between primary and secondary human rights rules.

The weakness of connection thesis, which is a revelation of non-coherence, leads us to question whether the secondary rules in the digital domain serve a similar function as in the non-digital domain. Recognition, change and adjudication – which are the main functions of the secondary rules – acquire their validity in the non-digital domain because they stand in clear service to

[16] J. Bateman, N. Thompson, V. Smith, 2011, 'How Social Media Platforms' Community Standards Address Influence Operations', Carnegie Endowment for International Peace, 01 April 2021, https://carnegieendowment.org/2021/04/01/how-social-media-platforms-community-standards-address-influence-operations-pub-84201, accessed 21 July 2022.

[17] Article 9, 'Facebook Community Standards: Analysis against International Standards on Freedom of Expression', Article 9, 30 July 2018, www.article19.org/resources/facebook-community-standards-analysis-against-international-standards-on-freedom-of-expression, accessed 21 July 2022.

the primary rules. Without such a connection, the functionality of the secondary rules in the digital domain casts a double image which is at clear variance with the physical world. The duality of the secondary human rights rules image reflects two fundamentally different conceptual possibilities. First, that the secondary rules cease to be at the service of the primary rules through supplementary features. Here they would replace primary rules as standing at the bottom of the human rights architecture. This can happen gradually or at an accelerated pace. Yet they would retain some specific features of secondary rules within the meaning of the non-digital domain, such as non-immunity to various influences. Non-coherence between the two domains is extensive. The second possibility is that the functionality of the secondary rules resembles the non-digital domain but with a difference of decisiveness. This difference is now explainable on the basis of the weakness in connection thesis. Here secondary human rights rules are engaged as they would be in the non-digital domain but with the difference that there is nothing to recognise or change. These secondary rules convey the impression of functioning as secondary rules in the service of primary rules, but we do not know whether the primary rules exist nor their nature. Here the non-coherence between the digital and non-digital domains is equally extensive since in the digital realm the secondary rules may attempt to acquire the validity of primary rules. A similar process cannot be ruled out for the non-digital domain, but it would be countered there by well-established core human rights. This is not the case in the digital domain.

As an interim conclusion, the application of the Hartian division of legal rules into primary and secondary reveals a non-coherent image between the non-digital and digital domains. Non-coherence is embedded in the defects of the primary rules and the functionality of the secondary rules. A further step is now needed to observe whether non-coherence also appears in other theoretical frameworks regarding human rights development in the digital domain.

7.3 THE DECREASE IN UNIVERSALITY AND ABSTRACTNESS THESIS

7.3.1 *The Main Concepts*

The *decrease in universality and abstractness thesis* will be the second framework applied here. It is related to the generic relativity of abstractness and universality as key properties accompanying any human right. An animal is a more abstract term than a dog, whereas a dog is more abstract than a dachshund. Likewise, freedom of expression is more abstract than the prohibition of censorship, and censorship is more abstract than the prohibition of hate speech. The need to eat is a more universal desire than the need for vegetarians to refrain from eating meat, which in turn is more universal than a group choice to eat only homegrown fruits and vegetables. Likewise, the right to privacy is more universal than the right to start a family, which in turn is more universal than the right to gestational surrogacy.

I have to recapitulate some key points from the thesis presented elsewhere, yet which are important for this book.[18] There are concepts which need to be tested in the digital domain. The results will exhibit whether these concepts, for the development of offline domain human rights, are domain-dependent, or whether they are universal or whether they appear in the digital domain with some variance. Here are these concepts to be tested. I have claimed that:

All the new human rights ... can be traced to some uncontested, globally accepted and long-standing human rights norm or multiple norms in conjunction, which can thus be considered an overarching conceptual framework for the emergence of any new human rights claim.[19]

There are two distinct categories of new human rights claims. First, there are new human rights claims connected with the incapability of the discursive practice of established rights to provide sufficient protection to certain groups.[20]

Second, there are new human rights claims which are meant to enhance some specific aspect of an established human right.[21]

[T]he process of new human rights development has two directions: either towards a decrease in universality, as is the case with the rights for specific groups, or towards a decrease in abstractness, as is the case with rights derived from or being implied by established rights.[22]

These ideas will be viewed against some instruments which have the ambition of formalising digital constitutions. These are the Italian, Spanish and African declaration of internet-related rights. Of course, many more instruments can be chosen, although perhaps three will be sufficient for our purpose here.

7.3.2 *Review of Some Instruments under the Thesis*

The Italian Declaration of Internet Rights puts forward thirteen internet-specific principles, which are: the right to internet access; the right to online

18 Susi (n 3).
19 Ibid., p. 25.
20 Susi (n 3), p. 26.
21 Ibid., p. 27.
22 Ibid., p. 28.

knowledge and education; net neutrality; protection of personal data; the right to informational self-determination; inviolability of electronic systems, devices and domiciles; automated processing; the right to one's identity; protection of anonymity; the right to be forgotten; rights and safeguards of people on platforms; network security; and finally, rights related to internet governance. Our interest from the perspective of non-coherence is whether these ideas constitute separate self-standing rights applicable only in the digital domain, or whether they are concretisations for the purposes of the Internet of rights articulated in the offline domain. Should they be self-standing rights, then the lens of non-coherence, as stated repeatedly in this monograph, is of no use or at least would not play a significant role due to the absence of common comparable roots. Yet these are not self-standing rights, perhaps with the exception of the right to be forgotten, which may also be viewed as an extension of the right to privacy, and of which I have written elsewhere among many others.[23] From here, the view has to be defended that new rights articulated for the digital domain can be traced to some self-standing globally accepted human rights.

One could consider from the Italian Declaration, whether the right to one's identity (article 9) might be a candidate for a new, internet-specific right. This right is formulated using five paragraphs and reads:

> 1. Every person has a right to the complete and up-to-date representation of his or her identities on the Internet.
>
> 2. The definition of identity regards the free construction of personality and cannot take place without the intervention and the knowledge of the data subject.
>
> 3. The use of algorithms and probabilistic techniques shall be disclosed to the data subject who, in any case, has the right to oppose the construction and dissemination of profiles regarding him or her.
>
> 4. Every person has the right to provide only the information which is strictly necessary for complying with legal obligations, for the supply of goods and services or for accessing Internet platforms.
>
> 5. The attribution and management of digital identities by public institutions shall be governed by appropriate guarantees, especially with regard to security.

[23] M. Susi, 'The Ideal and Normative Dimensions of the Right to Be Forgotten' in A. von Arnauld, K. von der Decken, M. Susi (eds.), *Cambridge Handbook on New Human Rights: Recognition, Novelty, and Rhetoric* (Cambridge: Cambridge University Press, 2020), pp. 287–299.

Having deliberately provided the entire text describing this proposed new right, I wish to demonstrate that its level of concreteness precludes potential justifications as a self-standing human right. This right is clearly traceable to the right to privacy and at best can be considered a composition of guidelines and principles for the digital enforcement of the privacy right. Here we can see the reflection of the decrease in abstractness thesis.

The Spanish Charter admits 'the specific nature of rights in the digital environment'. A closer look inside some rights therefore is in order, for example, the right to freedom of expression and freedom of information (XIII). The right to freedom of expression has five specific limitations.[24] Some of these limitations could, in principle, also be applicable to the right to provide information in traditional media channels, such as TV or print media. Take, for example, item XV 2 (c) which gives everyone the entitlement to request that providers not use analytical techniques which make it possible to offer information that affects ideological or religious freedom, or freedom of thought or belief. Many examples of how these limitations are applied can be given from court practice,[25] along with analyses of how offline media is non-separable from ideology.[26] Yet the Spanish Charter limits the freedom to provide information, and it is sufficient to explore it only from the angle of non-coherence, leaving aside the justification of such a limitation. The concreteness of limitations against the freedom to provide information are excessive in the Spanish Charter, which leads to the matter of layers of non-coherence. Such non-coherence in the content of the freedom to provide information exists, but it appears mainly in the *operational level* of this right, positioned at the margins. One can question whether these specific formulations are still inside the human right element of abstractness and universality. Here again, as was the case with the Italian Charter, the decrease in abstractness is confirmed, as is the traceability to already established rights.

The right to freedom of expression on the Internet in the African declaration (article 3) is a mirror image from the formulation of the said right in

[24] In the order these limitations are provided in the text, all persons have the right to know when information is produced automatically, when it has been classified or prioritised, have the right to request that analytical techniques are not used, have the right to corrections and the right to compare the information to the original news.

[25] For instance, European Court of Human Rights Judgement: *Lopes Gomes da Silva v Portugal* (2000), Application no. 37698/97.

[26] J. Downey, G. Titley, J. Toynbee, 'Ideology Critique: The Challenge for Media Studies' (2014) 36 *Media, Culture and Society*, 6, 878–887.

well-established international instruments.[27] The explanatory part puts forward the ideas of transparency regarding processes developed by intermediaries and calls for states to review and reform their legislation related to freedom of expression online, taking into account compliance with international standards. This text provides the guidelines for how to better protect the freedom of expression and does not specifically say what are the constitutive elements of this right. Such an approach, in turn, has a dual effect, meaning from one side that the content of freedom of expression online becomes more concrete; for example, via the requirement that products designed to facilitate end-user filtering should be required to be accompanied by clear information about how they work. From the other side, the text asks for various normative developments to take place, such as putting in place guidelines for the protection of those who gather information, or calling for states to reform their legislation related to freedom of expression online. And here once again, the decrease in abstractness and the promise of some grand ideas appear hand in hand.

7.3.3 *Decreasing Abstractness and Universality Online*

The following conclusions can therefore be put forward. First of all, and overall, human rights online exhibit a decrease in abstractness. Separately taken, this does not lead to a conclusion of non-coherence, since it reflects an ordinary multidimensional human rights architecture, where some rights are more and some are less abstract. Human rights online are more concrete, hence less abstract. Yet the situation calls for a more detailed examination. Speaking of their structure, at least some elements of human rights online retain textually the same level of abstractness with offline – either only the nomination, or additional features, which exhibit the same image as the nomination and features offline. In terms of the text, there is coherence. Then at some point, secondary norms enter the scene, being presented as primary norms. And they push aside the primary norms transposed from the offline domain by entering the scene as more influential and practical, thereby highlighting the idealism of primary coherent norms online. The consequence of such a textual approach, where abstract rights are

[27] This article has three divisions, the first saying that everyone has the right to hold opinions without interference; the second mentions that this right also applies through the Internet and digital technologies; and the last subdivision applies the usual limitations of legality, legitimate aim and proportionality.

supplemented with concrete provisions, changes the nature of fundamental rights online. This is because of the decrease in universality and the abstractness phenomenon; at least some rights which are presented as fundamental rights online are very close to meeting or even completely meet the qualification criteria of abstractness and universality. We can term this phenomenon as the holistic shift due to non-coherence since the overall structure of online human rights moves towards less abstractness and universality. The latter is due to the simple fact that online rights are what the term says – they are meant for the online domain, and consequently the circle of rights holders is narrower in comparison with human rights holders in general.

Second, it is possible to trace the source of human rights online, again viewed from above, to some uncontested rights offline. There may be some exceptions, like with the right to be forgotten, although its degree of connection to the right to privacy remains debatable.

Third, we have also seen confirmation of what my thesis mentioned previously says about the reasons for rights development – either the inability of established rights to provide sufficient protection to specific groups, or to enhance some specific aspect of an established right. The first aspect relates to group rights on the Internet and the second to the need to counter the influence of the digital domain. My final observation here is to return to the fundamental question of where online human rights originate. The decrease in universality and abstractness relies on the traceability to core and well-established offline human rights. Otherwise, it would not be logically possible to trace the chain of connectivity. Now, if human rights online originate from inside the digital domain, or if the digital domain retains only the facade – such as the formal nomination of rights – but fills this with different content, we face a different paradigm, which also provides new parameters to consider. Among those, abstractness and universality may not be significant. Here then we are still faced with the possibility of broad non-coherence between the digital and non-digital domains. Such broad non-coherence shows that various theories focusing on rights development are paradigm centred; they are of little value for comprehending and explaining developments at the margins or meeting points of paradigms. Here a feature of non-coherence theory not mentioned before comes to the fore. This is the inseparability from the origin of rights. In other words, non-coherence theory is not paradigm centred and is capable of addressing variations between quite distantly separated normative systems. The outcome is objectively applicable to both systems because if A's non-coherence with B is not wide, the opposite has to hold as well. B's non-coherence with A also has to be narrow, otherwise the first assertion would not be correct.

7.4 ALSTON'S QUALITY CONTROL APPROACH

Finally, we will look at digital human rights through Alston's quality control lens, as promised. Its weakest aspect does not rely on the difficulty of reaching a point where an international organisation with the history of authority considers that a new right in the digital domain is sufficiently justified for formal recognition. This is because in international politics the constraints concerning a new right's theoretical validity appear weak. Although Alston aspires to put forward a universally applicable mechanism of quality control for rights development, the essential element of what constitutes quality is actually missing. The only element close to the idea of quality is that a new right needs to reflect a fundamentally important social value. Other elements are related to political consensus building and rights enforcement practicalities. Yet the notion of a fundamentally important social value is construed in isolation from specifying standards. It is therefore open to excesses from relativism or geopolitical agendas from states claiming hegemony.

Because a very concrete and individual idea can also meet the standard of an important social value, Alston's new human rights quality control method turns into something completely different – it is a new human rights quantity enabler. Alston's filter would not block very specific digital rights from the status of a fundamental right, if countries agree to this. Its logical consequence, when applied to online rights, is that most rights in digital constitutions, provided they are repetitive, can be justified as fundamental rights. The meaning and value of fundamental rights would then wither through a process that others have called rights inflation. Suffice to say that additional components need to be added to Alston's list so that it can be turned into an approach where qualitative standards and non-relative and non-political characteristics prevent the inflation.

Baxi calls the former process human rights overproduction.[28] Inflation and overproduction are usually explained through the belief that human rights rhetoric and normativity are helpful means for problem-solving. For the digital domain, the reverse is correct. There is the underproduction of specific digital human rights primary norms and the overproduction of secondary norms. One may say here that human rights rhetoric and normativity lose their promise of being problem-solvers in the digital domain. Here non-coherence is clear. And it leaves open the question of whether something else has taken over the functionality of human rights.

[28] U. Baxi, 'Too Many, or Too Few, Human Rights?' (2001) 1 *Human Rights Law Review*, 1, 1–10.

8

The Capabilities Approach

8.1 THE CONTEXT

One of the core ideas of non-coherence theory is that human rights standards offline appear at variance with the online image. Human rights standards change in the course of the transposition, where the online image of offline standards may be widely distorted, given the subject, or only exhibit minor variance. But the fact of the variance remains. This idea has been repeatedly discussed in this monograph, and occasional references to similar observations from others have also been given. Hence, the theory is built upon the discourse around a certain incompatibility of standards and is placing this as a basic approach towards fundamental digital rights. To further illustrate the discourse, Schaumburg-Müller has expressed the observation of this incompatibility as follows: 'I am not arguing that life online and offline is always completely the same and ought to be regulated in precisely the same manner. What I am arguing is that they are not fundamentally different either.'[1] Others have expressed similar hesitations about full compatibility.

Among several social science theories focusing on how values and expectations become relative once one constructs a theory on the basis of legal subject-hood, the capabilities approach seems to have some similarities with non-coherence theory. Two aspects are of main interest here. The first is related to the dependency of normative standards applied to a legal subject upon this subject's capabilities. And the second concerns the matter of how the element of normative reasonability is constructed. The first aspect is positivist and the second is purely non-positivist.

[1] S. Schaumburg-Müller, 'Liability Regimes for Online Human Rights Violations' in M. Susi (ed.), *Human Rights, Digital Society and the Law: A Research Companion* (London: Routledge, 2019), p. 111.

8.2 THE PROBLEM OF NORMATIVE STANDARDS DEPENDENCY ON CAPABILITIES

Sen calls us to focus in the social sciences on what people are able to do rather than the resources they have available for any kind of performance.[2] Finding common elements to assign people to groups on the basis of capabilities leads us to the question of whether normative standards are dependent on these capabilities. This relates not to rights but obligations. For instance, as illustrated by Nussbaum's discourse on non-human animals,[3] animal rights law needs to take as the starting point the capabilities of the animals, otherwise it remains an abstraction of human thinking about animals. Should this not be the case, then one would expect from animals what they are unable to perform. When thinking in the category of capabilities, the transposition of similar standards to various groups of individuals may lead to a scenario where these standards remain isolated from the ability of the concrete subjects to live up to them.

Yet the capabilities approach reveals non-coherence since the capabilities compared exhibit variance to a smaller or greater degree. Here a specific example of capabilities is in order. This concerns the matter of the user-generated content assessment obligation on internet service providers. Such an obligation appears as one of the main elements in various domestic and international legal instruments, but it is not important here what exact format this is presented in. Our interest is whether, and to what extent, the private online service providers are capable of fulfilling this obligation. It is a perfect example of the capabilities approach towards the digital domain because, as logically follows, if the service providers are not capable of undertaking the user-generated content assessment, then the obligation to do so remains entirely theoretical with no practical value.

In traditional human rights discourse, the concept of content assessment is associated with the ability to provide reasons for why certain content is viewed to be illegal or unethical, or inferior to some other competing interest. In the mainstream media, the expectation is that any action interfering with someone's statements or information is accompanied with reasons for why the media company has or has not taken certain actions allowing or blocking the content. Furthermore, once the debate about allowing or not allowing

[2] W. Gaertner, 'Amartya Sen: Capability and Well-Being' in M. Nussbaum, A. Sen (eds.), *The Quality of Life* (Oxford: Clarendon Press, 1993), p. 30.

[3] M. Nussbaum, *Frontiers of Justice: Disability, Nationality, Species Membership* (Harvard University Press, Belknap Press, 2006).

some content reaches a court; for example, when an injunction is sought to prevent a newspaper from publishing problematic content, this court is expected to come forward with an explanation. The court explains the reasons in some shorter or longer version, but at least there is some explanation. Now, the situation with online platforms is completely different. For reasons of effectiveness, the decision to block a posting with debatable content needs to be taken almost immediately. Otherwise, any retroactive decision about its illegality or inappropriateness would only have a compensatory nature since the Internet allows sharing and multiplication.

My point is that online service providers are simply not able to provide individualised reasons for their decisions to take down or block user-generated content. This can be considered an absence of the basic capacity to do something, referring here to Nussbaum's understanding of a basic capacity as something which is innate, natural and cannot be acquired in time.[4] This is for two reasons; first, there simply is no time to formulate an explication or argument. And the second is that online companies face hundreds if not thousands of user postings daily, which makes individualised assessment simply impossible. The compatibility argument – regarding comparison with analogous obligations offline – in this specific situation demonstrates the non-coherence of human rights obligations. This also shows the dual character of non-coherence – there can be no variance in normativity, but there is non-coherence regarding the capability to apply the normativity in practice. Non-coherence of practice highlights the discrepancy between the ideal and practical dimensions of human rights law.

8.3 REASONABILITY OF NORMATIVE CONSTRUCTION

The second aspect of interest from the capabilities approach concerns the element of reasonability in normative construction. This has to be lifted here to a more general level as a problem about whether the digital domain finds the idea of human rights protection reasonable. In other words, even if we establish that online companies have a general capability to safeguard human rights in the digital domain, it says nothing of their interest in actually protecting these rights. This is a general problem of the capabilities approach, apparent in Sen's assertion that in thinking about capabilities, what is important is not so much the capabilities which people aspire to or want but those

[4] M. Nussbaum, *Women and Human Development: The Capabilities Approach* (Cambridge: Cambridge University Press, 2000), p. 84.

they have reason to value.[5] This leads us to ask whether the digital domain in general, and online private service providers in particular, have a reason to value human rights.

Here non-coherence shows manifold images. For example, it is possible to suggest that actors in the digital domain have the capability to protect human rights and in general find this reasonable. Yet it does not follow that this leads to the assumption of protection. Capability and the reasonability to do something does not mean that this is indeed accomplished in practice. The unclear causal chains between capability, reasonability and subsequent activity are the weakest elements of the capabilities approach. It can be said that these causal chains are absent, or that they can be arbitrarily construed, for example, as a consequence of best practices analysis. These constructions would be arbitrary because capability is an entirely separate category of abilities in conjunction, whereas reasonability refers to the cognition and construction of values. It is possible to think of X having the capability to protect human rights, but X does not find this reasonable. And at the same time, it is possible to think of Y finding value in protecting and reason to protect human rights, but Y is not capable of rights protection.

A further complication arises from questioning whether the notion of reasonability can be assigned objectively. Arneson has formulated a somewhat similar question for what is called the perfectionist interpretation or understanding of the capabilities approach. He asks about the possibility of determining what is objectively valuable for the capacity holder, independently of the capacity holder's subjective perception of values. This argument follows that Y has a reason to value X because X is objectively valuable, even if Y itself does not value X.[6] Non-coherence theory adds another layer to this sequence of questions, related to the idea that the meaning of similar terms and concepts can be at variance if one is to compare different domains. This argument would be that Y, as a digital entity, has reason to value X not because X is objectively valuable, but because X is valuable within the digital domain. And it can also be asserted that Y as a digital entity does not value X because it knows that X is valuable in the offline domain, but it does not know whether this label of value is carried over to the digital domain.

5 A. Sen, *The Idea of Justice* (Cambridge, MA: Allen Lane and Harvard University Press, 2009), p. 233.

6 For the discussion of logical connections related to objectivity, see R. Arneson, 'The Capabilities Approach and Political Liberalism' in E. Chapierro-Martinetti, S. Osmani, M. Qizilbash (eds.), *The Cambridge Handbook of the Capability Approach* (Cambridge: Cambridge University Press, 2020), pp. 165–187.

Here the discussion leads to the search for one or several common core elements for normative systems, which are independent of whatever capabilities are dominant for legal subjects in the digital and non-digital domains. In other words, even when we can accept that digital and non-digital capabilities are non-coherent, which they have to be, is there any commonality which stands as more general over and above the details of the capabilities terminology, and therefore characterises both domains. We could look to see whether the capabilities theorists have put forward any such commonalities. Now the concept of equal concern for all comes forward, viewed often as the foundational principle of ethical reasoning.[7] This is expressed by Sen as a seminal question: 'Equality of what?'[8] My response to Sen's question is: equality in having the capability to claim equal normative authority. Translated into law, this would mean that both normative paradigms determine independently what is reasonable to value. This is the basis of respective normative constructions. Now we see that such independently existing normative systems, which are explainable through the non-coherence of value systems, can lead to normative systems of little or no variance. The similarity here would be superficial since in both systems notions like privacy and the right to disseminate information stand in central positions, but their actual content differs. We can call this phenomenon the non-coherence of normative coherence.

It is important to consider the possible consequences of the capabilities approach when applied to human rights in the digital domain. These consequences may exhibit variance in comparison with the effect usually associated with the capabilities approach towards underrepresented or vulnerable groups, where positive development is implicitly assumed. Take, for example, the passage from Nussbaum's short praise for the effects of this approach, when she writes: 'The Capabilities Approach has pushed forward the analysis of women's rights, the rights of the poor, and, more recently, the rights of people with disabilities.'[9] Yet the capabilities approach does not contain a moral element attached to the notion of reasonability. So, it logically leads to the prioritisation of paradigmatic value systems, which for human rights means that positive developments cannot be assumed. On the contrary, the capabilities approach may provide arguments for why human rights protection online is weaker in comparison with the offline domain, or that it is different.

7 J. Kane, 'Justice, Impartiality, and Equality: Why the Concept of Justice Does Not Presume Equality' (1996) 24 *Political Theory*, 3, 375–376.

8 A. Sen, 'On the Status of Equality' (1996) 24 *Political Theory*, 399.

9 M. Nussbaum, 'Human Rights and Human Capabilities' (2007) 20 *Harvard Human Rights Journal*, 21.

9

The Frankfurt School and the Normative Order of the Internet

9.1 THE ACHILLES' HEEL

The Achilles' heel of the Frankfurt School since its emergence in the late 1920s has been the promise of the absolute explanatory capability of legal systems. Its fascination with rationality achievable through idealism has taken different versions, where the dividing line is whether the values inseparable from any normative structure originate from rationality itself, or whether the values exist in parallel to such a normative structure and thereby form an assessment tool which is applied to ascertain whether this structure meets the value threshold. Both versions imply the possibility of a regulatory structure which lies outside the quality circle associated with any normative structure. The Frankfurt School's intellectual contribution has led and continues to lead, over its century-old history for different reasons, to the premise that critical thinking is capable of producing one theory which explains any socio-economic system or social phenomenon in its entirety, including legal systems. Should this premise be valid, the non-coherence theory of digital human rights would not be able to claim that it can put forward a self-standing explanation of digital human rights, since it would stay at a level of less generality than the Frankfurt school. It should then and consequently be placed below the general level of the Frankfurt School's approach as an instrument to explain nuances. I will therefore explore whether the core elements of the Frankfurt School theory can be applied undistorted to the digital domain. The elements under view will be the legitimating function of a normative system, and then the legitimation itself of a normative system. This latter aspect contains elements of the process and the inclusion or exclusion of any quality elements.

9.2 THE LEGITIMATING FUNCTION OF NORMATIVE SYSTEMS

The legitimating function of any normative system is explained by a current scholarship from the Frankfurt School as something which objectively follows from such a system's existence. A normative system is understood as a 'complex of norms and values with which the fundamental structure of a society (or the structure of international, supranational or transnational relationships) is legitimated, in particular the exercise of political authority and the distribution of basic goods'.[1] In other words, and relying on the Aristotelian logical syllogism, once a normative system is determined, it automatically has a legitimating function. To provide a pure logical sequence: all normative systems (A) have a legitimating function (B). If all As are Bs, then if X is normative system A, then X is also the function B. This would of course raise a further question – at what point is it justified to speak of a separate normative system – but this question is addressed elsewhere in this book. This syllogism appears to hold in the digital domain as well, provided that the meaning of the basic concepts of a normative system and legitimation remain undistorted. Returning to the non-coherence lens described in the introductory statements to this monograph, even if all As are Bs in the non-digital domain, and all *A*s are *B*s in the digital domain, it does not follow that As and *A*s are identical or the same, or that all Bs and *B*s are identical or the same. This is because Bs either in italics or roman reflect the Objectivity, which may exhibit variance between the two domains. Non-coherence theory's starting question is about the sameness or degree of variance in the Objectivity characterising different domains. Interestingly, this leads me to formulate a query which is familiar to practicing lawyers, the query about the burden of proof. That is, when faced with different Objectivities – belonging to digital and non-digital domains – where is the start of the burden positioned: either to assume sameness or assume divergence. Non-coherence theory assumes explicit divergence and is concerned with the degree of variance.

The question whether a normative system or a normative order means the same in the digital domain as in the non-digital will be addressed shortly in this subsection when reviewing Matthias Kettemann's seminal book on the Normative Order of the Internet.[2] The question of legitimation, according to

[1] R. Forst, K. Günther, 'Die Herausbildung normativer Ordnungen. Zur Idee eines interdisziplinären Forschungsprogramms' Normative Orders Working Paper (Franfkurt am Main: Goethe-Universität Franfkurt am Main 2010), pp. 11–30.

[2] M. C. Kettemann, *The Normative Order of the Internet: A Theory of Rule and Regulation Online* (Oxford: Oxford University Press, 2020).

the analysis of the Frankfurt scholars, contains an unanswered aspect pertaining to the entire normative approach. This is about the final arbiter to decide whether a regulatory system can claim legitimacy. It can be logically suggested that such a final arbiter needs to be positioned outside of the normative system in question. Günther offers some guidelines for such a neutral third position by highlighting that such an assessment needs to consider in what way power inequalities are neutralised, whether rights to equal participation are granted, whether third party interests are adequately represented and whether the procedures are transparent.[3] Notwithstanding the concrete core criteria used for such an assessment, which is an element of relativity, it transpires that the source of the knowledge about legitimacy remains under contestation. There are three possible answers regarding the search for the origin of the legitimacy claim. Inspired by the Hobbesian dichotomy,[4] this source can either inhere in the perceivers, or alternatively in the Objectivity perceived. The third way is to say that neither of the former two can claim such legitimacy; that is, the question of the source of the legitimacy also remains under contestation. We will see shortly that the Frankfurt scholars' current approach represents the preponderance of the perceivers side, and we have to ask whether there are differences in the perceivers of the digital and non-digital Objectivity.

One of the main critiques of the Frankfurt School's holistic ambition to explain any normative formations concerns the absence of the promise of a better future.[5] This critique has recently been countered by the response from the current Frankfurt School community by proposing a methodology where normative orders are analysed through narratives of justification. Rainer Frorst and Klaus Günther explain that such narratives derive persuasive power from aesthetic considerations of a *good story*, where focus is placed on proper or good justifications.[6] Such justifications are discourse-based, allowing the participants to engage in contestations resulting in the rejection or confirmation of whether an explanation matches the quality criterion of a *good story*. This clearly value-based approach turns the desired strength into a weakness for two reasons. The first is the absence of concrete constitutive elements the

3 K. Günther, 'Legal Pluralism or Uniform Concept of Law? Globalisation as a Problem of Legal Theory' (2008) 5 *NoFo*, 19.

4 See T. Hobbes, 'The Elements of Law (1640)' in J. C. A Gaskin (ed.), *The Elements of Law, Natural and Politic* (Oxford: Oxford University Press, 1990).

5 K. Popper, '*Addendum 1974: The Frankfurt School*' in K. Popper, M. A. Notturno (eds.), *The Myth of the Framework* (New York: Routledge, 1994), p. 80.

6 R. Forst, K. Günther, 'Preface: The Normativity of Normative Orders' in M. C. Kettemann (ed.), *Navigating Normative Orders: Interdisciplinary Perspectives* (New York: Campus Verlag, 2020), p. 8.

statements of which meet this *good story* criterion. What precludes that any political or business ambition cannot be transformed through power and persuasion into a narrative claiming a positive value? In other words, the proposed methodology allows time and culture-based relativity to enter into the explanation of normative formations. What may be regarded as a *good story* in certain cultural contexts may be viewed as a *bad story* in others. My view is that concrete constitutive elements are missing from the concept of the *good story* because it would undermine the methodology's level of abstractness. The creation of a normative narrative and establishing what can be regarded as a *good story* is clearly a perceiver-centred approach.

The Frankfurt approach to the digital domain remains in the same cluster. Kettemann writes about the normative development of the Internet and characterises *norms* as normatively relevant commitments, exercising pull on the addressee, that can crystallise into (international) law.[7] Not much needs to be added here, since even the terms of a perceiver (used by Hobbes) and of an addressee (used by Kettemann) have very similar, if not identical, meanings. The connection to Hobbes' subjectivity is clear. We have to look deeper in the search for any variance in the Frankfurt doctrine's application between non-digital and digital human rights.

9.3 THE LEGITIMATION OF NORMATIVE SYSTEMS

Generalising on his edited book, Kettemann identified three common themes emerging from research into normativity by the current Frankfurt School. The first is the doctrine of narratively legitimating normative orders, construed through and located in discourses.[8] The second is related to the contestation enshrined in instituted practices, leading to eventual adaptation or fading away.[9] The third argues that normative orders are built on the productive tension between normativity and facticity.[10] These themes paint the following logical sequence for normativity: through discourse to narrative creation and from narrative creation through discourse to normativity. We cannot take for granted that the meaning of a *narrative* remains undistorted between non-digital and digital domains, due to the non-coherence assumption thesis, and further we are faced with the question of whether and to what extent the

[7] M. C. Kettemann, 'Normative Turns: Landmarks for Navigating Normative Orders' in M. C. Kettemann (ed.), *Navigating Normative Orders: Interdisciplinary Perspectives* (New York: Campus Verlag, 2020), p. 14.

[8] Ibid., p. 13.

[9] Ibid.

[10] Kettemann (n 7).

meanings of normativity on the Internet and the physical world coincide or are at variance. Yet both these elements are dependent on discourse; therefore, the focus turns out to the possible variance in its meaning. The Frankfurt School's proposition, as put forward by Kettemann, can be referred to as the discursive relational chain. This monograph compares, first, the meaning of discourse through the non-coherence looking glass. If digital discourse carries a different meaning, then the relational chain has to be at variance or questionable in the first place. For variance is sufficient if the first element has been altered. Thereafter, this chapter will turn the looking glass to comparing the elements of the discursive relational chain, where discourse has a double function, as the initiator of normative development, and then the solidifier of the normative system.

Alexy shows how it is possible to substantiate human rights on the basis of discourse theory, and the first step concerns the justification of the rules for the discourse.[11] Even if the rules of the discourse may lead to different theories about the same subject matter, these would still apply to the same discourse rules. Like when pupils in the same grade may and probably do receive different grades for writing a homework essay, they are still all using the sentences and grammatical rules of their particular language. My question, therefore, is once again, whether some main elements of what constitutes a discourse are at variance between the digital and non-digital spheres. Here my goal is not to paint an image of what digital discourse means, but rather whether there is a reliable and critical mass of evidence to say that its meaning has changed. Blitvich and Bou-Franch have edited a volume containing specific analysis of what they call *digital discourse*. Their introductory remarks to the volume point clearly towards a variance between the digital and non-digital discourse, since former methods and research tools about discourse 'need to be critically assessed and reflectively adapted, and perhaps also expanded and even combined with others to suitably account for the communicative practices that occur in the digital world'.[12] Hildebrandt provides fascinating illustrations of how the digital domain rejects arguments in discourse which are not formatted in a specific way. Kafka is around the corner, she writes, pointing out that someone operating in the digital system may need to present claims about the system's errors in terms dictated by the system

[11] R. Alexy, 'Discourse Theory and Human Rights' (1996) 9 *Ratio Juris*, 3, 209–235.

[12] P. G. Blitvich, P. Bou-Feanch, 'Introduction to Analyzing Digital Discourse: New Insights and Future Directions' in P. Bou-Franch, P. Garcés-Conejos Blitvich (eds.), *Analyzing Digital Discourse: New Insights and Future Directions* (London: Palgrave Macmillan, 2019), p. 1., pp. 4–22.

itself.[13] As a remark from the holistic perspective, we could, of course, mention that that reference to Kafka speaks against non-coherence between the digital and non-digital systems since Kafka was writing about the administrative and judicial systems of the former. If Kafka were to be present in both domains, then a look from far above detects only Kafka and no non-coherence.

Having made these observations, one notices that although digital discourse is different in terms of some dominant features from non-digital discourse, it has its own separate and self-standing existence. This does not now preclude that under the umbrella of the Frankfurt school, discourse may lead to a narrative and from there again through discourse to normativity. Narratives about the digital domain for our purposes have to be assumed, since these concern how reality is understood and thought about in primarily non-legal concepts. But this assumption does not extend further to the creation of normativity through discourse. Any discourse in this relational chain has double functions. Discourse about the Objective reality is concerned with the Is, but an additional layer of Ought has to enter into discourse leading to normativity. This is about ideas and values entering into normative creation, an aspect which is a core element of critical discourse studies.[14] Hidden here is the main difference affecting the relational chain from narratives to normativity through discourse. There is a natality in the non-digital world towards normativity, but it is not certain that such natality exists in the digital domain. For fundamental rights the conclusion is similar – fundamental rights are part of our consciousness as human beings, conditioned by the physical reality, but digital reality does not necessarily condition human rights. Hildebrandt writes about the same idea as follows: 'Our institutional environment depends on the largely implicit alignment of individual consciousness with societal norms that in turn depend on the individual consciousness of all those who form a society. This underscores the relational nature of individual consciousness; human beings are always in the process of – incrementally and/or radically – reinventing themselves and their shared world.'[15] Once we can agree that the natality aspect of fundamental rights is lost in the transfer from the non-digital domain, we see that the Frankfurt school's aspiration towards the general explanatory power is lost as well. The relational chain stops after the creation

[13] Ibid., p. 16.

[14] For the context about critical discourse studies, see L. Cheng, D. Machin, 'The Law and Critical Discourse Studies' (2022) *Critical Discourse Studies*, DOI: 10.1080/17405904.2022.2102520.

[15] M. Hildebrandt, 'Privacy as Protection of the Incomputable Self: From Agnostic to Agonistic Machine Learning' (2018) 20 *Theoretical Inquiries in Law*, 1, 90–91.

of the digital narrative; that is, normativity does not follow as a logical result from internal development inside the digital domain.

It is possible to explain my thesis of the breakage of the relational chain using Gibson's concept of affordance, which by itself has certain similarities to the capabilities approach. Gibson writes about this concept as follows:

> The affordances of the environment are what it offers the animal, what it provides or furnishes, either for good or ill. The verb to afford is found in the dictionary, but the noun affordance is not. I have made it up. I mean by it something that refers to both the environment and the animal in a way that no existing term does. It implies the complementarity of the animal and the environment.[16]

The problem in applying the theory of affordance to our discussion lies in the idea that, as Gibson writes, 'values and meanings are external to the perceiver'.[17] Let us make it more concrete. Say we have a perceiver, a company operating online – whom we can call a digital agent, and outside are positioned values and meanings, which have been constructed somewhere separately of this agent but are meant for this agent to provide complementarity for the agent's operation. Now these outside values and meanings become practical only if the agent has an affordance towards this complementarity. There is no doubt that such affordance exists in the non-digital domain's relational chain as suggested by the Frankfurt school. But it is not clear whether our digital agent has affordance towards such outside input. We can term this the doubt about fundamental rights in the thesis of digital affordance. This is then a revelation of non-coherence, and its consequence is to question the applicability of the relational chain from discourse to narrative and from there to normativity in the digital domain. Despite the relational chain being broken, normativity exists in and for the digital domain. If not a result of the development as proposed by the Frankfurt school, there must be other explanatory venues. The main among these is the concept of self-normativity. This will be the subject of Chapter 10.

[16] J. J. Gibson, *The Ecological Approach to Visual Perception* (Mahwah, NJ: Lawrence Erlbaum, 1986), p. 119.

[17] Ibid.

10

The Articulation and Critical Review of Self-Normativity

10.1 A SIMPLE MATHEMATICAL EXPLANATION

A simple explanation of self-normativity says that a person makes the rules for him or herself. This can refer to individual self-normativity, or when groups or communities have certain common characteristics or shared values. These normative clusters, which may not correspond to the meaning of a normative system, have narrower or deeper differences, and therefore any phenomenon of self-normativity has inherent elements of non-coherence in comparison with other normative clusters. Here is a mirror effect because this non-coherence has to be symmetrical. This holds for self-normative systems which have developed predominantly in isolation, and says that if normative system A is non-coherent against normative system B, then normative system B must also be non-coherent against normative system A. We know that such isolated self-normative systems are in the realm of abstraction. Since physical and digital domains are interrelated, there must be at least some common features if we are comparing self-normative systems. The first appearance of similarities is usually connected to the usage of similar words in different normative systems. The consequence of the non-coherence assumption regarding self-normativity leads us to reject at the outset naïve beliefs that the usage of similar words and concepts means the transposition of norms and values from offline to online undistorted. One has to look beyond the appearance of similarity to see what is actually happening.

10.2 MORE COMPLEX EXPLANATIONS

Self-normativity, taken more explicatively, refers to the shift in the origin of (legal) rules applied for rights protection. In the broadest sense, this entails standards and concrete norms, and in the narrowest sense only the latter.

By assumption, self-normativity excludes or relies to a limited extent on vertical delegation, such as from a domestic constitution or statutory law or international legal instruments. The broad self-normativity of standards and norms shows an image where the normative relational chain between legal subject-hood and normative authority is completely broken. A mafia-type organisation serves as an example, since such an organisation operates primarily according to its internal rules and relationships of authority and delegation and is concerned with the outside world's normativity only as far as these enable or hinder the implementation of its own rules. Narrow self-normativity breaks the normative relational chain only for secondary norms, excluding the self-control and revision of primary norms.[1]

Self-normativity can be considered a phenomenon of modern statehood,[2] as opposed to the conception of homogenous global and domestic law and epitomising the loss of legitimacy through some *higher order* of law.[3] We now see autonomous normative systems which all have a quest for legitimacy, since one source for all has disappeared. Several scenarios are possible for how legitimacy is gained. The first is to claim self-legitimacy, which leads to a logical conclusion of complete self-standardisation and the principle of *anything goes*. The second mechanism for the legitimation of self-normative systems is to transpose, and borrow certain core concepts from elsewhere. One illustration would be media company Z with global aspirations, which claims: 'Privacy is not a concept which fits into our business model. However, because privacy protection is considered very important by many clients and important external *others*, we have accommodated privacy protection into our rules of operation. Through this we claim the legitimacy of our rules in front of the outside world and clients.' This seems like a statement from some community guidelines, but it is not. I have made it up. Whether this company Z takes its promise seriously is an entirely different matter, especially in times of economic difficulty or new business opportunities. Such a transposition of principles, which is the most common scenario, is a process explainable through non-coherence. Yet, scepticism may be voiced about the assumption that legitimacy matters for the one who transposes the ideas and principles.

1 The conceivability of narrow self-normativity may run counter to Hart's thesis that secondary norms are necessary for the stabilisation of positive law, but this topic has already been addressed.

2 F. Moreau, 'The Role of the State in Evolutionary Economics' (2004) 28 *Cambridge Journal of Economics*, 6, 847.

3 K.-H. Ladeur, 'The Emergence of Global Administrative Law and Transnational Regulation' (2011) International Law and Justice Working Paper 2011/1 (History and Theory of International Law Series), finalized 4 April 2011.

If it does not, we are looking at an image of human rights in the specific digital mirror where the only concern is the image itself. Elon Musk's actions following the takeover of Twitter in November 2022 – slightly before this manuscript was finished – are an example of self-legitimation and no concern for legitimacy from the outside world.[4]

10.2.1 *Heterarchy and Self-Normativity*

Self-normativity in digital human rights law and practice is explainable through the heterarchy concept, the term for the process whereby the hierarchical delegation of normative regulation is replaced by the self-organisation of the legal system. This concept is partly rooted in the interconnectedness with and dependence of normative regulation and practices of knowledge development – rapid technological advances lead to and are based on new knowledge, and therefore relying on traditional lawmaking mechanisms would mean the consistent emergence and perpetuation of legal vacuums.

The justification of self-normativity in general is based on the recognition that the continuous process of reconsidering legal norms is unavoidable.[5] Judicial evolution is seen as the key reason for heterarchy, as expressed by Ladeur in reference to global administrative law:

> The evolution of both domestic and transnational administrative law will allow for new heterarchical forms of accountability and legitimation once the focus on a hierarchical concept of delegation is given up. Both for domestic and global administrative law the adoption of new approaches to ex post

[4] In 2022 Elon Musk acquired ownership of Twitter, followed by his immediate change of policies. He laid off thousands of employees involved in content moderation and announced the shift in policies, where freedom of expression's weight is considered by default higher than anything else. This was followed by statements from the world's leading politicians reminding Musk to protect fundamental rights. No references are provided here, since the story is new and there will probably be plenty of sources available via search engines for an interested reader, provided what happened has not become standard knowledge. If Musk is to comply, it is an example of consideration that an outside legitimation source is for some reason important. In the diverse scientific and advocacy analysis which will certainly follow the Twitter takeover, and some of which may be published by the time this monograph appears in print, the matter of non-coherence matters. The questions asked will focus on whether any principles of human rights law were maintained in this process, whether they were given different content, whether any regulatory system was maintained at Twitter and what if any is its overlap with offline human rights principles and online human rights secondary rules. These are all questions related to non-coherence theory.

[5] K. Noonan, C. F. Sabel, W. H. Simon, 'Legal Accountability in the Service-Based Welfare State: Lessons from Child Welfare Reform' (2009) 34 *Law of Social Inquiry*, 523–524.

> monitoring of administrative action and learning seems to be more promising than the traditional orientation on the binding force of legal rules ex ante.[6]

The heterarchical direction of judicial evolution can lead to what Teubner coins the auto-constitutionalisation of the global civil society in its own right.[7] Once the assumption of the self-constitutionalisation inherent in self-normativity becomes validated – and there is no reason why it should not do so in practice, such self-constitutionalisation necessitates a theoretical justification from legal theory. Otherwise, it would not possess normative validity. The primary concern is not how fundamental principles and rules construed via self-constitutionalisation stand against principles and rules of a similar level to be found elsewhere but about the moral dimension. Building on the conceptual frameworks of affordance and capabilities, the question is whether the digital domain, and in particular digital agents, can afford or are capable of self-normativity with a moral dimension.

A lot depends on the viewer and his and her belief into the possibility of human rights universality carrying certain universal moral elements. From this monograph's introductory reference to the book *Alice in Wonderland*, the following analogy can emerge. Let us think of a scene where A is on one side of the mirror, representing the physical realm, and B is on the other side, representing the virtual realm, and they start to speak and compare. 'I have a constitution which was made by my predecessors here', says A. 'I also have a constitution which was made somewhere here recently', replies B. They continue and A claims: 'Our constitution protects the right to privacy.' 'And so does our constitution', replies B. 'Our privacy right says that you have to leave me alone', is the next remark from A. 'Ours is different', claims B, 'because our privacy right says not that I have to leave you alone, but it is you who has to leave me alone'. A question to the reader is, whether the privacy rights claimed by A and B are coherent? A broader question is whether the articulation of similar concepts and rights in multiple discourses from self-normativity always entails an element of non-coherence? We have to take and defend the position that such an element of non-coherence is inseparable from multiple self-normative systems.

Zumbansen writes about conceptual pluralism based on the plurality of states, divergent arenas of decision-making with heterogenous participants and national or international agencies and private actors, including private

6 Ladeur (n 3), 3.

7 G. Teubner, 'Fragmented Foundations: Societal Constitutionalism Beyond the Nation State' in M. Loughlin, P. Dobner (eds.), *The Twilight of Constitutionalism?* (Oxford: Oxford University Press, 2010), p. 327.

stakeholders and non-government institutions.[8] He asserts that such pluralism leads to the severing of the traditional conceptual and institutional separations inherent in well-established legal systems. These concepts serve as legitimating arguments for the self-normativity of offline legal fields. Yet the transposition of justifications regarding self-normativity and self-constitutionalisation from regular offline law cannot be viewed as automatic. In other words, justification does not follow from the surface, such as a new combination of different actors and their mutual relationships and functions. Here the theoretical and practical value of non-coherence theory opens, alerting us against such transposability before core elements of validating arguments are addressed. Therefore, in order to enter into a discussion about the justification of digital self-normativity regarding fundamental rights protection, we would have to be content with the proposition that such self-normativity, involving the fundamental rights aspect, is unavoidable for the digital domain, and in particular for digital agents.

We have to be reminded that unavoidability can appear in different layers. For instance, the regulation of some basic features necessary for economic operations and transactions with clients and other agents can be avoided at much higher costs than inserting the fundamental rights aspect into self-normativity. In other words, the primary interest of digital agents does not lie in the normativity of fundamental rights but in more concrete rules which govern daily operations. Before seeking an answer to the question of the unavoidability of legal regulation, it has to be specified that it concerns, for the purposes of this theory, the matter of the unavoidability of fundamental rights in regulating the digital sphere, and in particular in the self-regulation of digital agents. Of special importance here is the doubt about the thesis of digital affordance regarding fundamental rights in the online sphere, as expressed previously. This thesis speaks against the unavoidability of human rights in the digital domain, in other words, that human rights can be deemed avoidable by digital agents. And yet, the regulation of the digital sphere exists, and there is discourse about fundamental rights, and fundamental rights are often at the centre when features of the digital domain are discussed. Therefore, justifications for self-normativity other than its unavoidability need to be considered.

10.2.2 *Isolationism and Self-Normativity*

At closer inspection, the viewer needs to contemplate whether self-normativity can occur in isolation from other, surrounding normative systems and

8 P. Zumbansen, 'Transnational Legal Pluralism' (2010) 1 *Transnational Legal Theory*, 2, 141, 144, 159.

regulatory ideas. An ordinary reading of the expression excludes such an option, since self-normativity obtains content only as a reaction against some other, well-established normative system. Otherwise it would no longer be self-normativity, but simply a different normative system which has developed in isolation or completely separately from other normative systems. For example, if man was to discover a civilisation of intelligent agents on Mars, having internal rules and principles for behaviour, we cannot term this as a self-normative system, since it has developed in isolation from Earth on Mars. On the other hand, if there was no community of intelligent agents on Mars, and humans were to colonise it, leading to their gradual or abrupt development of rules for behaviour and norms differing from the ones in place on Earth, we could call this self-normativity. Therefore, self-normativity assumes an awareness of another normative system, and its complete or partial rejection and full or partial replacement with another system. This assertion also applies to the digital domain with the following consequence. Self-normativity in the digital domain and for digital agents means that the offline system of norms and values exists to their knowledge, and there is a possibility to choose between their transposition or rejection, both of which can be to a certain degree.

One of the main problems here – if not the most important in terms of impact – lies in how to explain fundamental rights ideas in the digital domain in connection with the generic process of self-normativity. It can either be said that these ideas are the result of self-normativity itself, or that self-normativity concerns only less fundamental layers and is built around fundamental concepts, including human rights principles, transposed from the non-digital sphere. Yet there is no evidence that the digital domain has produced a normative system in isolation which can bear resemblance to the human rights system as we know it in the offline domain. This is because of the overwhelming nature of non-digital human rights ideas and their scope and history. Therefore, the scenario for the digital domain, and digital agents in particular, is to either transpose the non-digital human rights system fully or with variance, by giving new meanings and scope to certain human rights ideas, or to reject them. Non-coherence theory is based on the perception that human rights ideas and principles originate in the offline domain and are then transposed to the online domain with variance. Self-normativity then concerns how these ideas and values are reflected at lower levels of normativity. I have also proposed and repeat here the view that the transposition of these human rights ideas does not immediately mean that they occupy central or meaningful positions in the offline domain. Due to elements of affordance and capabilities they can remain dormant at the idealistic level. The consequence of this phenomenon is concerned with the morality of digital self-normativity because in isolation human rights would not be able to serve the function of the moral empowerment of a normative system.

10.2.3 *Self-Normativity and the Moral Dimension*

Objections against digital self-normativity are primarily related to questioning whether a moral dimension is embedded in the normative function of algorithms and the increase in predictive power connected to the automatic implementation of norms. These matters concern secondary level rules of implementation and practice but are often thought to reflect the moral dimension of digital primary norms. Here a short intervention needs to be opened about the source of the moral validity of secondary norms in general, and towards the digital domain in particular, where non-coherence theory can be applied as an explanatory tool. A cursory belief that often appears may be seen in the statement that secondary norms can claim moral validity only from their connection to primary norms. In this instance, the moral validity of primary norms is transposed to the secondary norms, but the strength of validity claim against competing claims may weaken in the course of the transposition. Yet it cannot be completely *lost in translation*, since then we would not be confronted with secondary norms but with distinct and self-standing rules construed in a different domain with a specific purpose and with different sources of moral validity, if at all.

According to such a viewpoint, for instance, the rules of operation of the algorithms used to block illegal content can claim moral validity only if they are causally connected to some primary human rights norm existing in the digital domain. Causal connection here can mean either derivation or by implication, for example, when the digital domain or digital operator claims commitment to the right to privacy online as an overarching moral principle for its business. Then such a principle can be either directly stated to constitute the goal for why algorithms operate, which is the case of derivation, or by default the protection of privacy is written into the algorithmic design, which is the case of implication. There are a number of questions that non-coherence theory is interested in regarding the moral validity of secondary norms. The first concerns the question of whether such norms can operate without any moral validity as a basis in the first place – from the perspective of the viewer from offline. The second concerns whether these secondary norms can claim such moral validity which makes sense only internally within the digital domain. The third is whether digital secondary norms can acquire moral validity directly from primary norms from the offline domain, which would mean the transposition of morality between layers under a 45-degree angle. And finally, whether the digital secondary norms acquire moral validity simply through some internal process and then turn it into moral validity, which remains digital-domain specific and loses the capability to claim such moral validity outside of the digital domain.

All these questions exhibit some non-coherence to a narrower or broader degree between the digital and non-digital domains. A careful and contemplative reader comprehends one assumption in all these questions – the capacity of the digital domain to deal with morality in general – which if it was not there, would make these questions meaningless. In other words, can we assume that the digital domain has moral features. If, on the contrary, to support the view that the digital domain cannot be characterised using moral features, or if these features are unrecognisable against understandings from non-digital morality, then we might still be able to enter into a discourse about digital self-normativity, but bear in mind that it has no moral character, at least of the kind towards which non-coherence can be applied.

The point about the moral dimension of digital law lies not in its absence but in that it has a different origin from human morals. Fournet and Yvert reflect as follows regarding digital morality:

> attaining a stage where humans would systematically have to comply with the predictions of algorithms is no longer impossible, at least in specific domains. Algorithms could then become prescriptive by imposing their digital normativity, and thus no longer restricted with an autonomy of execution but acquiring a form of moral autonomy at the expense of human moral autonomy, and hence subjectivisation. This could result in the emergence of a form of governance without subject.[9]

They term this phenomenon silent desubjectivisation, which I would call additionally the path towards the silent variance of morals. Because of non-coherence, it cannot be expected that the morals of the digital domain coincide or largely overlap with the morals of the non-digital domain. At the same time, we do not find too many proponents of the approach that morals as a category of articulating values is missing from the digital domain, since only its content and focus has changed. The idea that the morals of the digital domain are in variance in comparison with the non-digital domain can be found from most writings dealing with the social dimension of the Internet. Therefore, just a few illustrations may be sufficient for the various concepts

[9] E. Fourneret, B. Yvert, 'Digital Normativity: A Challenge for Human Subjectivization and Free Will' Cornell University, 23 May 2019, https://arxiv.org/abs/1905.09735, p. 5.

proposed to address the moral divergence. Schutz writes about application determinism, which is based on the assumption that technological developments are always an improvement.[10] The consequence can be that ethical considerations cannot be immune to time and may need to be revised along the road. Brand suggests that internet ethics are influenced by the moral paradox of information technology, noting the impasse between quick access to information and the need to maintain the quality of the information. Another paradox coined by O'Neill – a view from practice – is the technological transparency paradox, which says that the provision of transparency in various networks has no connection to the quality of information available on the sites.[11] These features taken together – the tendency to believe that technological developments also mean moral development, transformed connections between information quality against transparency and the speed of information sharing – highlight that the Internet and digital technologies are concerned with distinct moral questions and challenges, which are not as central as or are absent completely from the physical realm. It appears a rather radical hypothesis to suggest that digital and non-digital morals have different content, but this is based on the functionality of morals. If we accept that self-normativity assumes self-morality, this is because subjects give meaning and values to matters which are important for them and occupy their mind more than other matters of minor importance. Here we are faced with the recognition that repetition and intensity define moral understandings instead of pure reason. Relativism may then become one general consequence of non-coherence theory, in whatever context it is to be applied, and especially towards human rights, morals and law.

10.2.4 *Relativism and Self-Normativity*

Relativism in this context becomes a dominant feature, concerning not only practice but also ideas. Tomuschat has pointed to wider implications that traditional states lose the ability to direct and control the social reality and has noted a vision that the function of social control has to be re-established on an international scale by international communities. He calls for the *crystal-clear*

[10] R. A. Schultz, 'Ethics and the Internet' in Francisco González (ed.), *BBVA Values and Ethics for the 21st Century* (Madrid: BBVA, 2011), pp. 217–256.

[11] O. O'Neill, Onora, 'Trust Is the First Casualty of the Cult of Transparency', The Telegraph, 24 April 2002, www.telegraph.co.uk/comment/personal-view/3575750/Trust-is-the-first-casualty-of-the-cult-of-transparency.html, accessed 19 January 2023.

discourse of establishing what is right and what is wrong.[12] Even if such a discourse would lead to the articulation of criteria about the truth, our current understanding of legal theories and the hierarchy of norms and ideas says that these criteria would need to remain at a high level of generality. The fact that notions of truth and wrong can be applied in the digital human rights discourse does not cancel non-coherence theory. Although at a superficial level we are tempted to think that once truth is a constant, then any appearances of legitimacy fragmentation resulting from divergence in public interest vis-à-vis private interests of self-constitutionality are simply phenomena which are explainable as *occurrences within a family*. Yet non-coherence speaks in favour of constants as core building blocks in our construction of legal, digital and social realities, and in their comparison. Divergence happens below core ideas.

A specific aspect of non-coherence is, and I have stated this before in the monograph, that the consideration of similar statements of truth as accepted both in digital and non-digital domains can turn out to be deceiving. This is because the notions of truth and wrong can carry different meanings. To illustrate this, when there is a standard of X as truth, accepted by A and B from human rights domains in variance, and then both A and B claim that their behaviour corresponds to standard X, can we conclude that their behaviour objectively taken corresponds to X. An affirmative answer, if advanced, is made from the basis of insufficient information, since we do not know the origin of standard X. Because if A and B in good faith look upon standard X, they do so from their domestic domain and may see just one side of the standard. When we look at the Moon from the Earth, we see a completely different image in comparison to someone who looks from the back side of the Moon, where there is never any sunlight. Both can claim that their perceptions are correct.

The principal question that non-coherence theory asks in this respect is about the transposability of standards of truth from one domain to another. In other words, does it follow from some ideas in legal and moral theories that the concept of truth is domain-centred, and if it is transposed from another domain, distortion and variance are always involved. Non-coherence theory supports an affirmative answer here. The previously discussed approach of multistakeholderism could in principle overcome the objections related to the

[12] C. Tomuschat, 'International Law: Ensuring the Survival of Mankind on the Eve of a New Century General Course on Public International Law (Volume 281)' in Collected Courses of the Hague Academy of International Law. Consulted online on 24 March 2023, http://dx.doi.org/10.1163/1875-8096_pplrdc_A9789041114884_01, first published online: 1999, p. 28.

distortion of the meaning of truth when applied from one domain to another. This would happen because the notion of truth in this case is formulated not by one domain or another but in combination. Yet it seems that the application of such a consideration is not meaningful because multistakeholderism is not concerned with general notions of what is right and what is wrong – which means that such discussions need to have taken place somewhere else, if at all, but with highly practical aspects of digital human rights. And secondly, because multistakeholderism has failed.

The most fundamental view from the non-coherence lens upon the matter of truth in digital and non-digital domains is connected to the problem of how these domains, and specifically the actors in these domains, understand the notion of truth. Among the multiple factors which shape the contours of truth, time appears to be the immediate factor which can lead to the reconceptualisation of what is true and what is not. When the notion of truth in the non-digital domain is a result of incremental development, tested in discourse and inside conceptually diverse viewpoints, then the notion of truth in the digital domain has no cushion of time. The expectation that what is true today continues so tomorrow appears correct in the non-digital domain, but this is not the case in the digital reality. What is true today in the digital domain has little or no predictive power that it will continue like this tomorrow.

10.2.5 *In Summary*

In summary, the non-coherence lens provides the following image of heterarchical digital human rights self-normativity. While self-normativity in global administrative or civil law decreases the role of hierarchical normativity by replacing it with heterarchical networks of interrelationships, such self-normativity regarding digital human rights appears in a continuous state of contestation between traditional hierarchy on the one hand, and heterarchical constructions on the other. The non-coherent aspect is, therefore, the feature of contestation. Self-normativity is functionally seen as the continuity of legal developments in non-digital law and the element of contestability is of minor importance. The legal meaning generated from various sources, contexts and practices, including experimental ones, would not compromise the effectiveness of these non-digital legal realms[13] of global civil and administrative law.

[13] For the context of polycentric legal regimes, see J. Black, 'Constructing and Contesting Legitimacy and Accountability in Polycentric Regulatory Regimes' (2008) 2 *Regulation & Governance*, 2, 137, 145.

Acceptance of the argument of non-contestability and unavoidable hybridisation[14] leads as a logical consequence to the weakening of the traditional constitutional accountability and well-ordered legal system. Such a consequence is not compatible with the idea of human rights, including digital human rights, due to the disappearance of the ideal dimension and overwhelming dominance of practice-driven constructions and goals. Building on this perception, I turn to Lauder's thesis of the explicit link between self-normativity and constitutionality and apply the non-coherence approach. Lauder expresses this thesis as follows:

> the idea should be accepted that an evolutionary process of the implicit shaping and re-shaping of administrative paradigms has to be distinguished from an explicit layer of administrative law that is made by the legislator. That 'deep structure' of administrative law that underlies a historical evolutionary development is closely linked to the transformation of the knowledge and the (social) rule basis of society.[15]

While there is no, and should be no, contestation from the side of self-made global administrative and possibly public legal norms against the legislative layer, this image does not hold for digital human rights. The absence of contestation means that self-normativity and more general legal instruments adopted by the legislature or international institutions can be viewed in some, perhaps most, legal realms as a continuum. This continuum serves the aim of enhancing the legal predictability and effectiveness of interventions. There appears no comparable continuum between self-made private rules and international or domestic legal instruments governing digital human rights. I term such an absence as the idealism abyss; that is, the idealistic nature inherent in human rights articulated by positive legal instruments is not carried as uninterrupted into the self-normativity of digital agents. Perhaps the abyss is of such a depth that the ideal nature of human rights in the digital domain is recreated containing a different meaning of idealism through self-normativity, if at all possible. This means that the digital realm is perhaps capable of creating idealism within its own meaning. Such a proposition necessitates further exploration.

The holistic question from the aforementioned is *prima facie* about the relationship between self-normativity and self-constitutionality. The non-coherence lens opens the following image. Once the self-normativity of digital

[14] G. Teubner, 'Hybrid Laws: Constitutionalizing Private Governance' in R. Kagan, K. Winston (eds.), *Legality and Community* (Berkley, CA: Berkeley Public Policy Press, 2002), p. 311.

[15] L. Karl-Heinz, *Der Staat Gegen die Gesellschaft* (Tübingen: Mohr Siebeck Verlag, 2006), p. 18.

private enterprises becomes justified, the idealism abyss leads to the necessity of self-constitutionality. In this case, primary and secondary self-regulation form one logical structure. The rejection of the idealism abyss shows an image where the self-made secondary norms rely on primary- (constitutional-) level norms originating from the non-digital realm, but their content may have changed in the course of the transposition. The next question is, what happens to legitimation in such multiple networks. To deal with this question, some ideas from the transversality principle proposed by Teubner and the network approach by Ladeur will be considered.

11

The Transversality Principle (Teubner)

11.1 CHALLENGE AGAINST IDEALISM

Those who find it useful to rely on the contemporary social sciences vocabulary of modernism, can claim that the idea of the universality of human rights is facing multidimensional challenges. Without specifying what 'challenges' actually mean in relation to human rights, this line could continue to suggest that the challenges entail aspects of generalisations from practice and postmodern social theories with juridical ambitions. Usefulness here flows from the purpose of averting criticism about *over-theoretisation*, but usefulness does not mean exclusivity. This postmodern 'challenge' is of a fundamental nature and seems like a logical consequence of the plurality of social and legal discourses. The concomitant element of postmodern statehood and modern social sciences, as it can be claimed, is the collapse or unjustifiability of discourses based on one grand idea.[1] To generalise this phenomenon, Teubner has advanced the transversality thesis to counter the rivalry and incompatibility of various social theories and discourses.

The transversality approach in law means the following according to Teubner:

> The law recognises that under extreme differentiation of society, there is no more a justification for the existence of any single generally valid social theory, but only for a multiplicity of theories of social areas which are equal in terms of their origin. These derive their justification from their coexistence, i.e. from the high level of autonomy and the simultaneous

[1] For the collapse of the *grands recits*, see W. Welsch, *Vernunft: Die zeitgenössische Vernunftkritik und das Konzept der transversalen Vernunft* (Frankfurt: Suhrkamp Verlag, 1996); for weakening of social practices based on an *idée directrice*, see M. Hauriou, 'La théorie de l'institution et de la fondation: Essai de vitalisme social' in M. Hauriou (ed.), *Aux sources du droit* (Caen : Centre de Philosophie politique et juridique, 1986 [1933]), pp. 89–128.

> reciprocal interdependencies of different social rationalities ... It would defend itself against any claim to totality of any theory; however, it would accept the intrinsic right of social theories that exist side by side.[2]

The application of the transversality approach towards digital human rights would effectively quieten the sceptics and idealists who speak against the expansion of private self-normativity due to its claim of validity. This is because self-normativity would now stand as equal among other forms of normative development and as immune to critique regarding standards.

Yet the question here stands, if transversality asserts the co-existence of different grand ideas of which none can claim universality and exclusivity, what does it exactly mean for human rights? In translation, and to illustrate, when the grand idea in the offline domain is that human rights prevail over all other interests, then in the digital domain the grand idea could be that business interests prevail, which means that human rights need to succumb in front of the former. Teubner and his proponents would assert that this is correct. Non-coherence theory says here that a closer look must be taken at what these grand ideas exactly claim, which means that the variance between grand ideas can at least be discussed from the perspective of their promises. Non-coherence theory goes further to ask – if it is in the nature of human rights to be always prioritised over all other interests, and now there appears a domain where they are not, can we term them human rights? The possible change in the relative weight of human rights as a holistic concept, when transposed online, is a phenomenon of non-coherence. The scope of this change can vary.

The transversality effect for mutually incompatible social theories is that of non-exclusivity. Competing theories continue to exist and the elements of choice between theories are determined by practice, convenience and economies, and not necessarily by idealistic goals. Because Teubner does not propose any specific quality standards or quality control elements for a theory to qualify within a circle of competing theories, transversality can become, superficially, an instrument for human rights conceptualisation, whereby the quest for idealistic and practice-independent justification is lost. On further inspection, we can construe an argument that the loss of the quest towards idealism depends on how we understand the term *idealism*. A digital private company could find merit in the statement that the generalisation of practice

[2] G. Teubner, 'Law and Social Theory: Three Problems' (4 May 2014). SSRN: https://ssrn.com/abstract=2432631 or http://dx.doi.org/10.2139/ssrn.2432631, 7.

resembles idealism since these patterns serve as benchmarks in the common terminology, where they are known as *best practices*.

11.2 ANYTHING GOES

Giving up the grand idea of human rights superiority and accepting multiple readings of what human rights mean leads to the extreme principle of *anything goes* within the meaning of Paul Feyerabend's epistemological anarchism.[3] Under the umbrellas of transversality and Günther's poly-contextuality[4], the practice-driven approaches of powerful private global online companies claim existence as equal with human rights theories of long standing. Epistemological anarchism minimises the justifiability of justificatory elements, the consequence being that anything which private online companies undertake can claim validity from a human rights perspective. To reject the suitability of the transversality approach means rejecting the acceptability of competition between theories regarding human rights. Paraphrasing Feyerabend (science is not one thing, it is many) one can say: human rights in identical terms are not identical or similar, they are varied. Variance is already an expression of the phenomenon of non-coherence. And the aforementioned arguments and other learned colleagues cited would not be able to show why human rights in the traditional value-based meaning can claim superiority or priority over the *modern* efficiency-based meaning of human rights.

And yet this view remains abstract until we can produce evidence that such competing theories of human rights in the digital domain are available. The challenge is related to argumentation in two respects. The first is whether any argumentation is needed at all to claim that a *competing* approach to human rights has appeared. Perhaps some critical mass of the proponents of such a competing approach is necessary to claim a place among other approaches towards human rights. But can such a critical mass be construed on the basis of practice and repetition? Considering, for instance, the statement that moral views have no place online since the Internet is a global phenomenon and morality in turn is ethnocentric. And second, are there standards to evaluate the quality of arguments against one another? Non-coherence theory says that these standards can only be one-sided, that is, from the side of the viewer. In this case, standards can be construed.

3 See P. Feyerabend, *Against Method* (London: Verso, 1975).

4 G. Günther, 'Life as Poly-Contexturality' in G. Günther (ed.), *Beiträge zur Grundlegung einer operationsfähigen Dialektik I* (Hamburg: Felix Meiner Verlag, 1976), pp. 283–306.

There is nothing to suggest that transversality would not accept the *right* of scientifically unvalidated human rights approaches to exist side by side with validated approaches. This is because the concept of validity itself becomes weak under the transversality approach and can be viewed from different sides – what seems valid for one viewer may not be the case for another, and the other way around. We can recall the *Alice in Wonderland* mirror, where a validated claim from physical reality becomes distorted in the looking glass and thereby unvalidated. The non-coherence aspect becomes crucial for understanding the claim of the universality of such theories. It says that normative and conceptual validity are non-coherent concepts and thereby multidimensional. In this context, universality becomes a category of no use and has to be replaced by alternatives.

Building on Weber's *new polytheism*, which makes monotheistic theories impossible,[5] Teubner writes: 'There is no longer one theory of society, but only equally justified partial theories relating to areas of society. Yet each one of these – and this is what gives rise to concern – at the same time lays claim to universal validity as the sole theory of society.'[6] The longing for universality is evident in most legal theoretical discourses and needs no repetition here. Yet the theories of digital human rights may be immune to the claim of universality for different reasons. These theories or approaches (which may not mount to the meaning of theories as we understand the word) are primarily concerned with secondary level normativity and have no interest in totality due to the idealism abyss thesis. Non-coherence theory shows that elements of universality are absent from the transversal image of digital human rights. This is the result of the transformed nature and content of digital human rights norms and procedures in comparison with non-digital. Digital human rights theories and approaches usually can have an interest in claiming universality as domain-specific and not reaching beyond the digital sphere into the non-digital, but this is not reciprocal. Human rights theories from the physical realm have the ambition of universality extending into the digital domain as well. Here we see that the expression of universality itself has a non-coherent nature.

[5] M. Weber, *Gesammelte Aufsätze zur Wissenschaftslehre* (Tuebingen: J. C. B. Mohr, 1968), pp. 605 ff.

[6] Teubner (n 2), 4.

12

Network Society Approach (Castells)

12.1 THE MUTUAL BENEFIT ASSUMPTION THESIS

Castells has formulated the *network society theory* with a similar ambition towards universality as we have seen before in other theories – the ambition is to comprehensively explain postmodern societies, including in terms of legal and fundamental rights. Network society theory stipulates that the concrete content for judicial concepts and legal norms is derived through the network. This means that the network-given meaning may and may not coincide with the original meaning at the time of its genesis – attributed to these concepts and norms when they were coined. To put it simply, human rights formulated at the general level – as we find them from high-level conventions – constitute vessels, and the substance in these vessels comes from the networks. This image, of course, would be counter to my previous statement – that networks alter the initial meaning of legal concepts and ideas. The consequence of such an image would be that there are no standards outside of those derived from networks. Yet networks do not operate in isolation and use expressions and concepts which are generated outside of the networks, carrying certain common understandings, which are then subject to transformation by the networks. Digital networks did not invent the rights to freedom of thought and privacy but have *taken* these expressions from an external source, in other words, from other networks. So, whatever the origin, one has to be satisfied with the view that networks use ideas and concepts, also regarding human rights, which initially have some non-network meaning.

The variance between the original meaning and the meaning at the time of casting light on the image given to these rights by the networks, can be one of degree, where in the one end stands broad and in the other narrow variance. The broader the variance, the greater the likelihood of the incompatibility of meanings. Incompatibility here would mean territory beyond non-coherence, where self-standing definitions with minor or no common elements exist in parallel. However, this is a highly abstract consideration since meanings are always acquired through comparison, and if we have no information about some conceptual features, we cannot assess its meaning. Network failures happen when a network does not produce a coherent system of rules, and such failures become serious social risks, as Castells has written.[1] Ladeur responds to this suggestion of potential risk through the concept of *social inquirers*, which develops sufficient variety and dynamism and allegedly produces knowledge and possibilities for action which are of common benefit.[2]

I would call this approach the *mutual benefit assumption thesis*; that is, network society enables society in the broadest meaning, including its legal manifestation, to operate more efficiently for the common good in comparison to other theoretical approaches. The question for non-coherence theory concerns the applicability of the mutual benefit assumption thesis in digital networks. In other words, the mutual benefit means that by giving meaning with variance to certain human rights, can these rights be safeguarded in a somehow better and more comprehensive manner. Of course, the affordance for digital networks to achieve this remains an assumption here, which we have not yet been able to verify.

12.2 THE MAIN OBJECTION

The main objection against applying the network approach to digital human rights is the loss of the claim to legitimacy in the course of regulation. It is the consequence of regulatory self-organisation, expressed by Ladeur as follows: 'The rise of global forms of co-ordination beyond public international law can no longer be regarded as anomalous deviation from the right way of state-based law, but as the expression of an evolutionary step towards new forms of the self-organisation of societal norms which go beyond the official legal system.'[3] The usual response for the offline legal realm is that legitimacy can instead result through the 'discovery procedure of practice',[4] leading to some sort of normative structure and regulation beyond self-regulation. This is

1 M. Castells, *The Rise of the Network Society* (Oxford: Blackwell Publishers, 2000).

2 L. Karl-Heinz, *Der Staat Gegen die Gesellschaft* (Tübingen: Mohr Siebeck Verlag, 2006), p. 4.

3 K.-H. Ladeur, 'Globalization and Public Governance – A Contradiction?' in L. Karl-Heinz Ladeur (ed.), *Public Governance in the Age of Globalization* (New York: Routledge, 2004), p. 28.

4 C. Joerges, 'Constitutionalism and Transnational Governance: Exploring a Magic Triangle' in C. Joerges, I.-J. Sand, G. Teubner (eds.), *Transnational Governance and Constitutionalism* (Oxford: Hart, 2004), pp. 339, 374.

the process where normative legitimacy is causally connected to network legitimacy and does not need separate justification. For instance, when we can claim that physical network A of countries B to Z is legitimate, this serves as sufficient justification for the legitimation of any normative network which A is to produce. The non-coherence paradox for the digital realm is that such a consequential chain may not exist. When we can show, or have to accept, that the digital network is legitimate, constituting a variety of interconnected public and private entities, it does not necessarily follow that the normative structures which this network can produce are legitimate through the eyes of the onlooker from the non-digital space. And here an additional layer of argumentation may be needed. This would mean that network validity cannot be transposed directly to normative validity, but it has to be reflected back to the non-digital domain, and from there digital normative validity can be justified. Now non-coherence tells us that legitimacy appears as a concept which cannot be transposed or delegated.

12.3 VARIANCE IN MAIN FEATURES

More broadly, the application of the non-coherence approach focuses on whether the digital networks display similar characteristics to non-digital networks and upon the degree of possible dissimilarities. My reading of the main features characterising the network approach identifies permeability, its supportive purpose of vertical normative structures, its impact on the rise of social responsibility and the obscuring effect on legitimacy and *reliance on trust*.

12.3.1 *Permeability*

Permeability is understood as the process whereby the borders between the public and private domains become more and more dependent on one another.[5] Permeability can exist in the format of an idealistic idea or observation from practice or a combination of these. It is a process of tandem, resting on the assumption of the realisation of the utility of both the private and public domains. Its primary function is knowledge gathering, ideally leading to more information for normative and behavioural decision-making. The idea of permeability concerning the digital networks remains idealistic due to the absence of longitudinal patterns of subsidiarity and mutual support.

[5] P. Schiff Berman, 'From International Law to Law and Globalization' (2005) 43 *Columbia Journal of Transnational Law*, 485–556.

An example of idealistic permeability is the idea of a *cyber court*, where the state authorities and private stakeholders together would create a specialised institution comprised of experts and activists. This body would then decide on cases of internet-centred rights conflicts raised by users, and the private online enterprises would use such courts as an effective remedy by guaranteeing the implementation of its decisions. The proposition has not succeeded beyond the stage of an idea due to some obstacles, which whatever their exact nature, reveal the absence of permeability. The digital domain rather produces evidence to the contrary – non-permeability, which explains many of the processes described earlier in this book, where the common denominator is the absence of mutual trust.

12.3.2 *The Supportive Purpose of Vertical Normative Structures*

The supportive purpose of vertical normative structures in a network means that private networks can articulate the claim of correctness in self-regulation due to the existence of the vertical normative backbone. The variance from the offline domain is related to the differences in goals of the supportive normative structures. While the institutionalised vertical separation of powers[6] in the offline domain focuses on the end result of achieving a more effective regulation, in the online domain the institutionalisation focuses on the legitimation of the very existence of such a backbone, notwithstanding any claims of efficiency or quality.[7] Here the process itself is considered as having value, as opposed to the result, which is of primary value in the offline domain. Correctness could in this instance be claimed by any result, provided it has a connection to some vertical structure.

6 About the institutionalisation of vertical separation of powers, see A. Peters, 'The Globalization of State Constitutions' in J. Nijman, A. Nollkaemper (eds.), *New Perspectives on the Divide between National and International Law* (Oxford: Oxford University Press, 2007), p. 251, p. 273.

7 By the time this monograph is published, more whistleblower revelations may have emerged from inside social media, but the statements of Frances Haugen (see CBS news release on 4 October 2021 – www.cbsnews.com/news/facebook-whistleblower-frances-haugen-misinformation-public-60-minutes-2021-10-03 (accessed 23 November 2021) led to claims from Facebook executives in the US media asking for concrete guidelines from the legislator. This is a clear example of the necessity of a vertical normative backbone in times of crisis; we are noting that the claims are talking about the need for structure and not what is achievable through such a supportive backbone.

12.3.3 *Increased Social Responsibility*

Commenting on Ladeur's expectation that networks lead to increased social responsibility from the side of network participants, Viellechner puts forward the vision that individual and group-based legal relationships may allow for the creation of a more adaptive and productive model of public governance.[8] This statement remains abstract and without concrete evidence about whether such a model of public governance is actually achieved and that it is more than simple rhetoric. It suffices to claim from the side of non-coherence theory that the importance of evidence weakens when we consider the allegedly positive aspects of what network theory can produce. This is because anything which can be termed as non-coherent already has weaker features in terms of everything against which it is compared. Therefore, when evidence of the positivity of the social responsibility of networks in the physical domain is weak, such weakness increases online.

12.3.4 *Obscuring Effect on Legitimacy*

One of the main reservations related to digital human rights law and remedies through the network approach is that of the distortion of legitimacy. This appears in different versions, which at first sight are polarised and irreconcilable. The first version claims that the legitimacy argument is lost in networks, and the second claims to the contrary that networks are capable of providing human rights legitimacy. Habermas represents the first version and posits that the network model's side-effect for law is the supposedly misleading claim of legitimation.[9] A contrario it is claimed that in terms of legitimacy, networks do not seem to fall behind in common standards,[10] which means that the ideals of democratic legitimacy have to be rejected. These apparently incompatible views are reconcilable through the non-coherence approach, which disrupts the starting point in the argumentation of legitimacy in digital networks and claims that the expression *legitimacy* may mean different properties in offline and online realms. The offline meaning of legitimacy is inseparable from the vertical handing down of discretionary power, guaranteed by some form of public normative governance and traditional forms of judiciary. The online

8 L. Viellechner, 'The Network of Networks: Karl-Heinz Ladeur's Theory of Law and Globalization' (2009) 10 *German Law Journal*, 4, 530.

9 J. Habermas, 'A Political Constitution for the Pluralist World Society?' (2007) 34 *Journal of Chinese Philosophy*, 3, 331.

10 Viellechner (n 8), 529.

meaning of legitimacy is independent of these elements; that is, legitimacy is acquired through other forms of authority for norm creation and realisation. Once such legitimacy is acquired, digital networks appear as fully capable and have the affordance to enter into the arena of defining human rights law more broadly. In other words, by acquiring legitimacy through internal self-normativity, digital networks became part of the holistic discussion of what human rights law is.

This point is a conclusion, although not directly, from Kaufmann's assertion that the definition of law is reached through negotiation. He writes: 'So, positive law is not criticised, corrected or contested with reference to natural, divine or eternal law. Instead, if we have two competing systems of rules, they are both complemented according to the results that have been reached within zones of negotiation.'[11] The main point here is the relative weight of arguments which different sides of such negotiations can put on the table. In order for such a negotiation to claim validity, equality of the parties and also of the initial weight of arguments would have to be assumed. Here then, the non-coherence aspect of digital networks loses its importance, as non-coherence turns from weakness to strength. It can be said that the wider the non-coherence of a digital normative system from a non-digital normative system, the stronger becomes its position to assert equality for the purposes of normative negotiations. If non-coherence is to remain narrow, the *parent* system's view of the initially stronger weight of its arguments is easier to defend.

12.3.5 *Reliance on Trust*

Finally, Fukuyama has suggested trust as a characterising feature of networks.[12] For human rights in the offline context, this means that the normative solutions proposed by networks generate a collective social order. Trust here serves the connecting function between the origin of regulation and its legitimacy. If someone now applies the sameness doctrine and transposes uncritically the element of trust from the offline to the online human rights dimension, this transposition goes hand in hand with the assumption

[11] M. Kaufmann, 'How Right Is the Basis of Law' in M. La Torre, L. Niglia, M. Susi (eds.), *The Quest for Rights: Ideal and Normative Dimensions* (Cheltenham: Edward Elgar Publishing, 2019), pp. 109–123.

[12] F. Fukuyama, *Trust: The Social Virtues and the Creation of Prosperity* (New York: Free Press Paperbacks, 1995).

that the regulation created by the online domain also generates a collective social order and is legitimate.

Not much has to be added here for the following reasons. First, the belief in the trustworthiness of online stakeholders may belong irreversibly to the past, so that *prima facie* the element of trust is losing its relevance as a characterising element of networks. Secondly, and more importantly for non-coherence theory, the semantic aspect of trust refers to the process which has led to trustworthiness. Trust is something which needs to be earned, since it is the result of a process. The transposition of the element of trust from offline to online networks deprives trust of its original semantic meaning, since trust then would not be something which has to be earned but something which is given. Non-coherence theory explains that this is what happens when concepts are automatically taken from the offline realm and planted in the online.

PART III

The Core Elements of Non-coherence Theory

13

Doctrinal Changes in Scope and the Meaning of Human Rights

13.1 THE CONTEXT FOR ENTANGLEMENT

If we start from the assumption of non-coherence, the impression that rights bearing the same name mean different things offline and online is easily maintained. On closer inspection the matter has to be divided into several more specific questions. Among these, at the forefront stands the question about the scope of non-coherence: whether the variance touches the core elements of these rights, or whether it only appears at the level of some details, for example, those related to remedies or epistemic reliability. The second question is inspired by work leading to the 2022 Nobel Prize in Physics. Alain Aspect, John Clauser and Anton Zeilinger were awarded the prize for demonstrating entanglement between two or more particles regardless of how far they are located from one another.[1] In relation to the subject matter of this monograph, the question therefore is whether change in the meaning and scope of one relative right in the online domain means a simultaneous change in the scope and meaning of another right, which is entangled with the first right observed. These are the matters I will explore in this section.

13.2 THE EQUILIBRIUM OF RELATIVE RIGHTS THESIS

Building on the analogy from quantum mechanics, we can ask whether certain human rights exist in a shared state. This would mean, for instance, whether the right to privacy exists in a shared state with the right to freedom of expression. Or, whether the right to reputation – leaving aside the issue of

[1] There must be abundant literature on the topic available, here is a link to the announcement and short description: The Novel Prize Organization, 'The Nobel Prize in Physics 2022', date unknown, www.nobelprize.org/prizes/physics/2022/popular-information, accessed 27 December 2022.

whether such a self-standing right can be justified – exists in a shared state with the right of access to information. If the premise of such a shared state is correct, then it would follow that change in the scope and meaning of one right (particle) in this shared state leads to a simultaneous change in the opposite direction in the other right (particle). To give a concrete example, if the scope of the right to privacy is broadening, then the scope of the freedom of expression has to narrow. Such correlation would then be assumed. To give an abstract example, when we can measure the broadening of the freedom of expression, say in an online portal, we know without additional measuring that the scope of the right to privacy is narrowing. For human rights, this is related, first and foremost, to the relative weight of rights against one another. A new thesis can be advanced. I would term this the *equilibrium of relative rights thesis*, which says that for those rights existing in a shared state, when the relative weight of one right increases, the relative weight of the other right has to decrease by the respective amount.

My point here is not to take a position about the correctness of statements claiming whether the rights in a shared state should stay in perfect equilibrium; that is, their initial relative abstract weight should remain the equal, or whether the discourse of public or corporate policies may lead to prioritising one right over another. Of significant interest here, is to explore whether, if the abstract relative weight of one right in such a shared state were to change, the abstract relative weight of the other right changes by the respective measure in the opposite direction. Elsewhere in this monograph, I have on several occasions written about the correlation in relative weights of conflicting rights, and the observations are relevant here. The equilibrium thesis leads to the conclusion that the sum of relative weights of rights in a shared state remains a constant. For example, if for the purpose of abstract argumentation we assign a relative weight of 2 to the right to privacy and freedom of expression, then the combination of these weights would be 4. Now, if the relative weight of the freedom of expression were to increase by half to 3, then the relative weight of the right to privacy would need to decrease also by half to 1. The sum would remain 4.

The equilibrium thesis for relative human rights is different from Rawls' concept of reflective equilibrium because it does not concern the process of moral deliberation either in narrow or wide terms, nor intuitions.[2] It has an absolute nature and becomes applicable once the relative weight of a right in a shared state is altered. Then the relative abstract weight of the other right in

[2] J. Rawls, 'The Independence of Moral Theory' (1974–1975) (1999) 48 *Proceedings and Addresses of American Philosophical Association*, 47: 5–22, in Collected Papers, 286–302.

this pair changes automatically to the opposite, so that the original equilibrium is maintained. The equilibrium thesis concerns mathematics, whereas the reflective equilibrium discourse concerns morals.[3] This subsequently means that, as a matter of principle, the change in the relative weight of a right in the shared state may seem morally unacceptable, yet the relative weight of the other rights also changes. A different view runs against pure logic since change in the relative weight makes sense only in comparison with another right. To formulate it differently, expressions like 'right A deserves more protection' or 'in a particular situation, right C needs to be safeguarded' are meaningful only if more protection or safeguarding happens at the stake of some other right. Because relativity then is a feature of the holistic offline human rights system independent of geography, geopolitics, culture and history, one can consider the equilibrium thesis to have a universal nature for the offline domain. The question now emerges, whether the thesis also applies in the online domain.

Furthermore, elsewhere I have previously addressed the matter of how the initial abstract weight of conflicting rights is positioned in offline and online human rights environments.[4] To recapitulate, the position of the European Court of Human Rights defends the doctrine of the equal weight of rights.[5] There are doubts against this position from public and private sectors, and academics seem divided on the matter. Previously, I have noted that in the absence of a conformed approach, the initial weight assigned to conflicting rights is at variance. From the perspective of this book, this means an ongoing state of non-coherence. This is a matter of public or private policies, which is then applied in concrete cases. For instance, YouTube can classify a video as intruding on someone's privacy, but Facebook may not. Since these portals apply their internal policies and if the nature of the video does not amount to illegal content, both results can claim correctness. Therefore, the balancing paradigm, resting on the initial weight of colliding rights, has transformed in the digital space. The consensual idea from the offline domain about the

[3] For a discussion about the reflective equilibrium and morality, see K. Nielsen, 'Grounding Rights and a Method of Reflective Equilibrium' (1982) 25 *Inquiry*, 3, 277–306.

[4] M. Susi, 'Balancing Fundamental Rights on the Internet: The Proportionality Paradigm and Private Online Capabilities' in M. Susi (ed.), *Human Rights, Digital Society and the Law: A Research Companion* (London: Routledge, 2019), pp. 173–193.

[5] This position was formulated in the first *Delfi v Estonia* judgment and has not changed; see the wording '[b]earing in mind the need to protect the values underlying the Convention, and considering that the rights under Article 10 and 8 of the Convention deserve equal respect' – European Court of Human Rights Judgement: *Delfi v Estonia* (2013) Application n. 64569/09, para. 110.

equal deservedness of the protection of the right to privacy versus freedom of expression is replaced by the weight assigned to these rights by online private companies. The reasons can be practice-driven or idealistic. Yet the way the initial weight is assigned to relative rights stands separately from the operation of the equilibrium thesis, this being immune to moral considerations and policies.

Using the analogy from quantum mechanics, it does not concern what is desirable and what is not; it describes some objective features of the particles (rights) in pairs. To be sure, the matter emanating from the equilibrium thesis is not linear. This is because one relative right possesses this quality not in relationship with only one other single relative right but potentially with multiple shared states, or pairs of relative rights. For instance, the right to privacy forms a pair with the right to freedom of expression but also with others, like the right to religious beliefs. Does the equilibrium thesis now have an effect on all such shared states, or should the matter be viewed in isolation for each of these pairs? To illustrate, when the right to privacy is given higher protection vis-à-vis freedom of expression in a high school, does this also mean that the equilibrium between the right to privacy vis-à-vis the right to religious beliefs changes accordingly, and the latter then deserves less protection. This would yield to a situation where prima facie the right to study in an environment where no religious symbols are exhibited deserves more protection. Such a discussion remains outside the scope of this monograph but was offered as a general reflection. What concerns us, however, are two further questions. The first is whether the equilibrium thesis applies undistorted in the digital domain. And the second is, provided there is an affirmative reply to the first question, whether the change in the relative weight of one right in the shared offline state is reflected in the equilibrium of these rights in the online shared state of these rights.

The answer firstly depends on whether the assumption that certain rights exist in a shared state is transposed without variance from the non-digital to the digital sphere. Doubts are easily refutable because the division of rights into relative and absolute is a basic pillar of how human rights are conceptualised. An alternative view would suggest that there is no such distinction and the matter of relativity and absoluteness itself becomes relative. But here we would see total incompatibility between the two different domains and non-coherence would cease to apply. The main argument against the doubt of transposition without variance of the equilibrium thesis is epistemic – the idea of human rights originates from the cultural development of mankind and constitutes an inseparable part of modern civilisation. It is part of the way we think of ourselves and others in a global community, which has led to the articulation of certain core values, ideas and their mutual dependency. The only potential argument against the transposability without variance of the equilibrium thesis is to say that human rights do not exist.

In order to solve the problem of whether the equilibrium thesis has a nature above human rights paradigms, and whether it therefore can be transposed into the digital domain, a general reflection may be necessary. Thereafter, I will explore whether the meanings of two specific rights – the right to privacy and freedom of expression – exhibit signs of distortion after transposition, and then return to the second question, which is most significant. Namely, whether the equilibrium of rights in the shared states has a universal character, which in turn means that the change in opposite directions in a shared state happens inside the respective rights paradigm but in the same way and at the same time in other rights paradigms recognising the same rights.

The online image of digital human rights reflects, at first glance, the change in the equilibrium of rights. The broadening of some fundamental rights online, unrelated to whether these rights can be protected, results in the narrowing of some other rights, and is related to social media's incapability of securing the comparable protection of fundamental rights such as privacy or freedom of expression in comparison with traditional media. Some fundamental rights within the traditional meaning exist online with less restraints in comparison with the offline domain. In the extreme corner of this image lies the claim that social media portals are capable only of detecting hate speech and leaving the rest in a user-unregulated territory. The image also reflects the narrowing of some fundamental rights once online and is related to technologies developed for e-governance and e-public administration, such as blockchain. The perpetual memory inherent in an e-governance technological approach leads to algorithmic traps and magnifies governmental and private surveillance and monitoring capabilities. The concrete examination of whether the main properties of well-established offline human rights change online is now in order.

13.3 THE RIGHT TO PRIVACY

13.3.1 *The Exit and Entry into Privacies*

As non-coherence can appear for the first time in specific normative or value layers, one has to start with the fundamentals of how a rights subject finds herself in the various environments carrying fundamental rights. No matter whether we accept the existentialist view of being thrown into the world, or whether we accept our existence as something predetermined by God, it nevertheless is not a result of our personal choices. We find ourselves thrown into the physical realm. And then through knowledge creation we understand that this world offers us a framework of fundamental rights. The image of involuntary entry into the human rights realm becomes the opposite when we consider the digital domain. We enter into this domain as a result of our conscious decision, even if some argue that it is impossible to lead a life in a modern world without the imaginary reality the Internet offers. The choice not to enter into private and/or public digital domains is possible, although it may be uncomfortable. There is no comparable choice for the physical world. So, entry into the physical realm is not a result of our conscious decision, but entry into the digital realm is. This dichotomy is by itself the seed of non-coherence. This is the argument from the origin of being, or from ontology. Since the origins are non-coherent from the aspect of intent, the non-coherence assumption says that difference in ontology must be omnipresent also in the meaning of rights that carry identical names.

A similar non-coherence is observable when we consider the exit from these domains. Exit from the physical realm is permanent and in parallel also means exiting the digital domain. But exit from the digital realm does not simultaneously mean exit from the physical realm. The consequences of exits due to tiredness from digital or non-digital realities are non-coherent, the first being non-permanent and allowing re-entry, and the latter being final.

13.3.2 *The Argument from Interest Theory*

The argument from interest theory builds on Bentham's well-known assertion that for every recognised right there must exist the duties of others to safeguard the interests of the former.[6] It is one layer less fundamental than the argument related to the origin of being, but does not yet reach normativity. Here, the interests concern expectations of how society and others should behave in order to maximise the person's interests. Only then does normativity follow. As such, before reaching the layer of normativity, interests are related to a moral dimension. It has also been noted that the transposition of moral expectations to positive law entails by itself variance. This is what Cali and Meckled-Garcia actually have in mind when writing about the 'loss in translation' of moral interests into rights: 'The transformation of a moral right into a legal right, as desirable as it may be, comes at a price. A compromise must be

[6] J. Bentham, 'An Introduction of the Principles of Morals and Legislation' in J. H. Burns, H. L. A. Hart (eds.), *The Collected Works of Jeremy Bentham* (Oxford: Oxford University Press, 1970).

struck with other principles in law.'[7] The 'translation' of this statement reads that moral expectations and their reflection in positive law are non-coherent. Yet such variance does not concern the content of interests and corresponding rights but is related to the enforceability of interests through rights having the same content.

For the purposes of the non-coherence theory of digital human rights, the variance in interest in privacy between the physical and non-physical realms does not necessarily mean that such a variance is carried over to the next layer of less generality, which is the normative regulation of moral interests. For instance, even if we were to validate the wide discrepancy in the meaning of access to education, the normative regulation safeguarding this right with a different meaning can have different breadth. A robust example would be from the physical realm related to the right to life. Seemingly incompatible concepts for the right to life in different countries allowing or prohibiting the death penalty are at the same time often implemented in comparable judicial and remedial systems. This shows that the assessment of the variance between digital and non-digital human rights ideas and instruments is required each time anew when we move to a different layer of generality, or if other elements are added to the image. We can say that the non-coherence assumption cannot therefore be considered a standard towards specific rules and ideas, but its scope can change in time and when other elements are reflected in conjunction with its image.

13.3.3 *The Interest in Being Left Alone*

Now one has to ask whether the interest in privacy in non-digital and digital domains are at variance. The formulation of the right to privacy in the contemporary era is widely credited to Warren and Brandeis, who formulated an interest in being 'left alone' in 1890.[8] This foundational statement seems to be unchallenged, although several concepts have emerged to curtail this interest against other competing interests and concepts, such as proportionality, the rights of others, relativity, public interest, public figures and many others. However, the fact remains that these concepts do not alter the original expectation of being left alone. It suffices to note here how various recent

7 B. Çali, S. Meckled- García, 'Introduction: Human Rights Legalized: Defining, Interpreting and Implementing an Ideal' in S. Meckled- García, B. Çali (eds.), *The Legalization of Human Rights: Multidisciplinary Perspectives on Human Rights and Human Rights Law* (New York: Routledge, 2006), pp. 10–30.

8 S. D. Warren, L. D. Brandeis, 'The Right to Privacy' (1890) 4 *Harvard Law Review*, 5, 193.

intellectual endeavours have come up with specific aspects where the right to privacy should stand immune against claims of relativity. Take for instance the claims of the right to bodily integrity[9] or the right to mental integrity.[10] The foundational interest was determined before as based on our involuntary entry into the physical world. We may like or dislike what we see, or experience both feelings simultaneously. But the right to privacy in its ideal dimension can be viewed as a shield against the objective physical reality we did not choose to enter.

The foundational premise of being left alone does not hold for the digital domain. There may be hesitancy to come forward with this statement, as it would seem to cause a rift in the human rights architecture as we know it. Here non-coherence theory responds by saying that yielding from even the highest level or general understandings can be assumed in the transposition of human rights ideas and concepts, so the focus should be on establishing with as much precision and clarity as possible the digital image of privacy. I will start from the image and move from there to the foundational interest.

13.3.4 *The Obscurity of the Digital Privacy Image*

There are statements and observations from academic and practical circles about the obscurity of the image of non-digital privacy in the digital mirror. Some examples need to be presented here with immediate comments from the non-coherence perspective. Richards has declared privacy online *dead* or *dying*.[11] Facebook's Zuckerberg says that 'privacy is no longer a social norm'.[12] Both Richards and Zuckenberg speak about privacy in its traditional meaning as a shield before private and public eyes. Their statements in translation say that 'privacy as we know it from the non-digital domain' is dead or dying, or no longer a social norm. Even a naïve look at social platforms standards shows the

9 A. M. Viens, 'The Right to Bodily Integrity: Cutting Away Rhetoric in Favour of Substance' in A. von Arnauld, K. von der Decken, M. Susi (eds.), *The Cambridge Handbook of New Human Rights: Recognition, Novelty and Rhetoric* (Cambridge: Cambridge University Press, 2020), pp. 363–377.

10 J.-C. Bublitz, 'The Nascent Right to Psychological Integrity and Mental Self-Determination' in A. von Arnauld, K. von der Decken, M. Susi (eds.), *The Cambridge Handbook of New Human Rights: Recognition, Novelty and Rhetoric* (Cambridge: Cambridge University Press, 2020), pp. 387–403.

11 N. Richards, 'Four Myths of Privacy' in A. Sarat (ed.), *A World without Privacy: What the Law Can and Should Do* (Cambridge: Cambridge University Press, 2015), pp. 1–2.

12 B. Johnson, 'Privacy No Longer a Social Norm, Says Facebook Founder', *The Guardian*, 11 January 2010, www.theguardian.com/technology/2010/jan/11/facebook-privacy, accessed 27 December 2022.

frequent usage of expressions about privacy and personal autonomy. One of the following is correct here. First, it could constitute the usage of knowingly idealistic expressions which have no concrete content. When privacy is dead or dying, then reliance on these expressions as pillars of community standards, that is, secondary level norms, creates a dichotomy and distrust. Or the second possibility is that privacy through transposition into the digital domain has obtained a different meaning. This is the view of non-coherence, and it appears to be valid.

Here are two subsequent concerns. The first is whether the origin of digital privacy is to be viewed in isolation from the origin of offline privacy. This is not a conceptual question but about creation. It asks whether the concept of digital privacy emerged autonomously from non-digital privacy, and the usage of the similar expression 'privacy' has a confusing or blurring effect on images from both sides. And the second concern is about mutual influence, that is, whether non-coherent systems influence one another reciprocally.

There are more examples related to the discourse of what digital privacy means. Thomas has asserted that nobody today appears 'to have any very clear idea what privacy is'.[13] The doctrine of privacy fatalism is advanced by some to characterise a persistent contemporary phenomenon to characterise the distortion of the traditional meaning of privacy online.[14] The potential for the media to intrude on privacy is considered more readily available and of broader impact, in comparison with when Warren and Brandeis critiqued the press, which was overstepping in every direction beyond common decency and engaging in vicious and unseemly gossip.[15] It is suggested that the Internet has given birth to modern privacy rights, as proposed by some scholars focusing on new technology and associated data practices, and threats and challenges to privacy, particularly the development of new computing and

[13] J. J. Thomas, 'The Right to Privacy' in F. D. Schloeman (ed.), *Philosophical Dimensions of Privacy: An Anthology* (Cambridge: Cambridge University Press, 1984), pp. 272–289.

[14] C. Mims, 'Privacy Is Dead: Here's What Comes Next', *Wall Street Journal*, 6 May 2018, www.wsj.com/articles/privacy-is-dead-heres-what-comes-next-1525608001, accessed 19 October 2022 and A. Tan, 'Privacy Is Dead', *The Business Times*, 9 June 2018, accessed 29 October 2022; K. Bonnell, 'Privacy Is Dead and We All Helped Kill It', *Ottawa Citizen*, 2 April 2018, accessed 19 October 2022; C. F. Kerry, 'Why Protecting Privacy Is a Losing Game Today and How to Change the Game', *Brookings*, 12 July 2018, www.brookings.edu/research/why-protecting-privacy-is-a-losing-game-today-and-how-to-change-the-game, accessed 29 October 2022.

[15] See also D. J. Glancy, 'The Invention of the Right to Privacy' (1971) 21 *Arizona Law Review*, 1, 1–39.

data-based technologies.[16] The result of this process is that defining and conceptualising privacy has become an increasingly complex and complicated task, as noted by Lin.[17] Penney asserts that the difficulties associated with defining privacy online may have the chilling effect of deterring people from exercising their rights and freedoms on the Internet. These views from learned colleagues do not amount to denying that privacy exists in the online domain, but a contestation of the traditional offline meaning of privacy is prevalent.

These brushstrokes have to suffice here when painting a picture of privacy in the digital domain. It leads to the conclusion of the non-coherent nature of privacy upon transposition. The concept of privacy appears considerably more complex and many-faceted online in comparison with offline, and this complexity applies equally to private digital and public digital domains, including the e-state. The proportionality deficit paradox helps explain the complexity and is necessary to explain it further. This paradox shows, first, that the right to privacy can be explained and advanced more in line with the traditional understanding of privacy in social and legal contexts, which enable a proportionality assessment. In e-state applications, such as those using a QR code, or in social media networks, the right to privacy starts to evaporate because of the incapability of these solutions to allow balancing. The image of privacy becomes blurred in the digital domain. The private online digital domain is influenced by time and forgetting, whereas the e-state is not because the blockchain never forgets. There is no corresponding entitlement in the public sphere to the right to be forgotten which obligates private online search engines[18] under certain conditions to block access to information which is not relevant for the public. A well-known statement – which is part of popular and scientific folklore – that the Internet knows you better than you know yourself – can be proven both for the private online sphere and for blockchain technology. While private internet companies may be compelled to enable forgetting, blockchain by design is unable to yield to this command.

[16] J. M. Rosenberg, *The Death of Privacy* (Random House, 1969) and P. M. Regan, *Legislative Privacy: Technology, Social Values, and Public Policy* (London: University of North Carolina Press, 1995); M. Froomkin, 'The Death of Privacy?' (2000) 52 *Stanford Law Review*, 1461; and S. Garfinkel, *Database Nation: The Death of Privacy in the 21st Century* (Sebastopol, CA: O'Reilly Media, 2000).

[17] E. Lin, 'Prioritizing Privacy: A Constitutional Response to the Internet' (2002) 17 *Berkeley Technology Law Journal*, 1088.

[18] U. Pagallo, M. Durante, 'Human Rights and the Right to Be Forgotten' in A. von Arnauld, K. von der Decken, M. Susi (eds.), *The Cambridge Handbook of New Human Rights: Recognition, Novelty and Rhetoric* (Cambridge: Cambridge University Press, 2020), pp. 197–209.

13.3.5 *Redefining Online Privacy: The Dual Nature*

The concerns raised and doubts expressed about the utility and possibility of transposing the notion of privacy undistorted into the digital domain necessitate a redefining of online privacy. The utility aspect relates to the divide between ideal and normative domains which are efficient. If non-coherence is assumed in the meaning of privacy, then the transposition of the idea of privacy as a shield against the intrusion of others remains isolated, when there are no corresponding rules making it possible to raise such a shield. Since in law there is always such a divide, then non-coherence theory says that such a divide has the tendency to expand. The danger is, then, that the idea of offline privacy remains isolated from what is practically possible online. This conclusion also applies to the transposition of norms, which may end up being non-applicable due to technical hindrances. For instance, an interim measure for the print media in the format of an injunction to halt the publication of some undesired material usually enables the postponement of the material in print. In extreme cases, the retroactive seizure of printed newspapers and books minimises the chances of the spread of the information. In most of the recent extreme cases, the burning of books effectively eliminated the spread of knowledge and views. If we are to think that such remedies can be implemented in the digital domain, we would quickly realise the impossible nature of such a mission. This is simply because the internet domain is immune to court injunctions stopping the spread of information since in normal conditions it can spread in seconds to millions of viewers and readers.

The basis of the difficulty of transposing offline privacy to the digital domain can be found in the variance in expectations towards privacy. Privacy once transposed online obtains a dual nature and is dependent on the position of the subject vis-à-vis the type of digital technology explored. It also obtains more extreme versions in comparison with offline privacy. If an idea has an origin within a concrete system of ideas and has developed within that system due to knowledge development, then its links to this system of ideas have to be so manifold that at least some of the links and elements need to weaken or disappear during attempts to start applying these elements in another holistic system. The dual nature of the right to privacy in the digital domain means the simultaneous existence in one concept of the entitlement to be left alone and the entitlement to be noticed. Further explanation of this revelation of non-coherence is necessary.

Interest in certain entitlements is a fundamentally different concept to a right reflecting such an interest. This is because an interest in something is related to an ideal dimension and can be viewed as if existing in isolation from other interests and limitations. This phenomenon of the absolutism of an interest in isolation from any other factor was labelled by Steiner as the absolutism of a right within its own area, but every right is elaborately gerrymandered.[19] What Steiner has labelled as gerrymandering is a situation when an interest in something exits the ideal dimension and enters an area of implementation. Such an area of implementation is the sphere of rights, where the interest that turns into a right collides with other rights. Therefore, limitations against the interest become inevitable and the interest loses its absolute nature. Non-coherence theory here points to a paradox, where interests which appear to be opposite in the isolation of the ideal dimension approach one another once they enter the sphere of rights. This is the view which has to be explored.

The interest in being left alone turns into the right to privacy in the offline domain and limitations apply. It becomes evident that the realities of living in any society exclude the possibility of being left alone completely, so it becomes necessary to restrict the entitlement to certain areas and functions of private life. In other words, the interest in being left alone can be realised partially and in practice and means that we have to or can display ourselves to others to a reduced or more limited extent. The situation changes fundamentally from the digital perspective. The dual nature of privacy online is because of the parallel voluntary and involuntary entry into the digital dimension. Voluntary entry concerns the usage of social media and other digital communication tools, and involuntary entry concerns the digital recording of personal data by various publicly held applications, such as the e-state and blockchain.

13.3.6 *Privacy and Digital Identity*

Voluntary entry is related to the interest in exhibiting ourselves in the digital domain how we see as most suitable. This is not accompanied by the positive validity of our image but is triggered by what we wish to put forward and at the same time hide. This digital image has been termed digital identity. Michalkiewicz-Kadziela and Milczarek have noted: 'human identity on the internet functions on completely different terms than outside it. The Internet gives unlimited possibilities [for] creating subjective elements of one's own identity, but it also allows a change of objective elements'.[20] There are

[19] For a discussion about the absolute nature of rights, see H. Steiner, *An Essay of Rights* (Oxford: Wiley-Blackwell, 1994).

[20] E. Michalkiewcz-Kadziela, E. Milczarek, 'Legal Boundaries of Digital Identity Creation' (2022) 11 *Internet Policy Review*, 1, https://doi.org/10.14763/2022.1.1614, 10.

warnings from policy organisations that digital identity does not fit into the framework of human rights, and it entails a threat leading to totalitarianism.[21] The whole idea of Meta is to enable the creation of digital identities, which may or may not overlap with someone's physical identity. Here, the belief that one's digital identity may put forward a deliberately misleading image of the self becomes erroneous. In viewing the differences between privacy and identity, Neethling has noted: 'In contrast to identity, privacy is not infringed by the untrue or false use of the indicia of identity but through an acquaintance with (true) personal facts regarding the holder of the right contrary to his determination and will.'[22]

Non-coherence between the concepts of privacy and digital identity appears therefore in their claim to correctness. Both domains can claim correctness towards features which seem incompatible if they were to be compared within one and the same domain. Privacy in the physical domain can claim correctness because it is objectively verifiable by a neutral observer; for example, someone with red hair is seen by anyone who is not colour-blind to have this colour hair. Yet the person with red hair can create a digital identity with blond hair. This digital image is correct within the digital parameters and becomes incorrect only if the neutral observer is to compare digital and physical identities. But there is nothing to suggest that the physical domain's perception should prevail; these two identities can exist in parallel, exhibiting features in variance for the same person. We can term such interest as an interest in another identity.

This identity appears at first glance to be almost completely under the person's control because she can choose to exhibit the most desirable features and leave out features she would like to forget. Ironically, such interest in another identity enables the person to put into effect an offline interest in being left alone in the physical domain. There is anecdotal evidence about generations born in the new millennium hesitating when it comes to using a telephone for conversations, known as telephone phobia,[23] as it would entail exiting the digital domain and using the physical domain. The practical reality

21 See, for example, panel conclusions put forward by Geneva Internet platform digwatch in November 2018: S. Grottola, 'The Future of Digital Identity and Human Rights', Geneva Internet platform digwatch, 13 November 2018, https://dig.watch/event/13th-internet-governance-forum/future-digital-identity-and-human-rights, accessed 23 October 2022.

22 J. Neethling, J. Potgeiter, P. Visser, *Neethling's Law of Personality* (Durban: Butterworths, 2005), p. 36.

23 D. Buchanan, 'Wondering Why That Millennial Won't Take Your Phone Call? Here's Why', *The Guardian*, 26 August 2016, www.theguardian.com/commentisfree/2016/aug/26/whatsapp-phone-calls-smartphone-messaging-millennials, accessed 23 October 2022.

of the digital domain necessarily soon leads us to discover that our interest in another identity cannot be absolute, as it presupposes disturbances from the physical identity.

The involuntary entry into the digital domain is caused by the growing reliance on e-solutions by public and private authorities offering essential services. It is practically impossible to avoid the fact that various digital surveillance mechanisms record us using Big Data, and that financial or medical institutions record our personal information. Here it is impossible to raise the interest in being left alone, and the only claim can be related to asking for the accuracy of data through the newly emerging right to erasure.[24] Once someone enters involuntarily into the blockchain system, their interest in being left alone becomes meaningless. As put eloquently by Sullivan, this is due to the 'considerable challenges in establishing not only that "I am who I say I am" but in establishing "I am not who the identity register says I am"'.[25]

13.3.7 *Brief Summary Notes on Privacy*

The transformation of the right to privacy into the digital domain therefore appears in two formats; none of these correspond to the interest in being left alone. To recapitulate, the first concerns the interest in another identity, which may differ to various degrees from the physical identity. The only claim representing the interest to be left alone lies in the interest to exist in the digital domain separate from the physical identity. The other format concerns modern e-solutions used by public and private entities to engage in business or public affairs. Since someone's data is recorded indefinitely, or at least for certain periods of time, the divide between the interest in being left alone and the realisability of this expectation becomes extremely wide.

There remain a few additional impressions from the transformation of privacy into something else in the digital domain. Exploring the interest in being left alone tells us, surprisingly, that the digital domain entails mechanisms which can turn this entitlement into an absolute right. For instance, the right to be forgotten can in ideal discursive conditions eliminate all traces of someone's past. This concerns information that is legitimately in the digital domain, and yet the data subject wishes all traces of the information to

24 For example, under the GDPR article 17, it is worth mentioning here that the heading of this article, 'Right to Erasure ("Right to Be Forgotten"),' is an example of how the various entitlements related to the reflection of offline privacy get mixed up.

25 C. Sullivan, *Digital Identity: An Emergent Legal Concept: The Role and Legal Nature of Digital Identity in Commercial Transactions* (Adelaide: University of Adelaide Press, 2011), p. 140.

disappear.[26] A comparable situation in the offline domain remains illusory since one cannot erase human memory albeit it possible via the manipulation of written sources and photos. This leads, as an example, to conceding that the non-coherence principle works in multiple ways – we should not only be looking at how an idea or concept from the offline domain changes online but whether the online image has a retrograding effect, which influences the original concept or idea. Penney has suggested that this is the case, and asserts that the notion of privacy is being divided up and segmented into numerous categories, for example, physical or spatial, decisional and informational privacy.[27] Yet discourse about the details of what formats the right to privacy exactly exists in and what it entails offline does not change the main conclusion, which is to note prima facie variance in the meanings of privacy offline and online. The variance is of such a degree that it should be more appropriate to refrain from using the term *privacy* for the online environment. Non-coherence becomes centre stage here. Because the digital and non-digital domains are interconnected and we can lead parallel lives in both domains, the right to privacy has meaning in the digital reality only so far as it enables us to realise our interest in being left alone in the non-digital reality.

13.4 FREEDOM OF EXPRESSION ONLINE

13.4.1 *Positivity and Negativity in Transposition*

The non-coherence assumption holds an element of change towards the positivity or negativity associated with the idea (or concept or rule) of human rights offline, upon transposition into the other domain. There is no rule that says that what is viewed as a positive element offline increases in positivity online, and the other way around. Positivity may become negativity, and negativity positivity. For instance, the positivity associated with anonymity offline is usually perceived as negative online. Or the other way around, displaying oneself in joyful settings in online photos seems positive but may turn out to be negative in offline job interviews. Yet, non-coherence does not exclude that the scope of an offline right expands once transposed into the online domain. And should this be the case, both positivity and negativity can

[26] For reference about the right to be forgotten, see M. Susi, 'The Right to Be Forgotten' in. A. von Arnauld, K. von der Decken, M. Susi (eds.), *The Cambridge Handbook of New Human Rights: Recognition, Novelty and Rhetoric* (Cambridge: Cambridge University Press, 2020), pp. 287–299.

[27] J. W. Penney, 'Chilling Effects: Online Surveillance and Wikipedia Use' (2016) 31 *Berkeley Technology Law Journal*, 117.

appear simultaneously towards one and the same right. This by itself calls into question whether the expansion of the scope of this right still allows us to speak of a particular fundamental right. An alternative would be to suggest that upon transposition to the online domain, an offline right is divided into several self-standing rights. Such a proposition needs justification from theory and practice. But should this be the case, a new challenge emerges – which of the *new* rights should carry on the offline name and how to label the other derivates. I will explore this in regard to the freedom of expression.

Anyone reading about or contemplating the Internet has encountered statements that indicate such positivity or negativity associated with changes to the freedom of expression online. This variance is considered to be wide. Just a few examples randomly taken may be sufficient. Amour uses the expressions *unprecedented* and *unparalleled* in connection with the possibilities on the Internet.[28] The United States Department of State notes: 'The Internet has been revolutionary, and provides unprecedented opportunities for people around the world to connect and express themselves.'[29] Melinda Gates and Jack Ma, on behalf of the UN Secretary-General's High-Level panel on digital cooperation, have noted that social media is providing powerful new ways to exercise the rights to free expression and association.[30] Benedek and Kettemann assert a profound paradigmatic change in connection with the emergence of the Internet by writing: 'The Internet has a catalytic function for the exercise of all human rights. Just as Gutenberg's printing press helped to spread the Reformation, the Internet can support the respect, protection and implementation of all human rights for all people everywhere.'[31] When confronted with such statements suggesting a profound change in something, the proponent of the non-coherence view finds it inevitable that such a change must have affected the content and scope in this something. In the present case, we focus on the transposition of the freedom of expression into the digital domain and must therefore assume that there is wide variance between the concept of free speech offline and online.

[28] L. St. Amour, 'The Internet: An Unprecedented and Unparalleled Platform for Innovation and Change' in World Intellectual Property Organization, *The Global Innovation Index 2012*.

[29] Declaration on the Future of the Internet, U.S. Department of State, available at www.state.gov/declaration-for-the-future-of-the-internet, accessed 23 November 2022.

[30] U.N. Secretary-General's High-level Panel on Digital Cooperation, 'The Age of Digital Interdependence: Report of the UN Secretary-General's High-Level Panel on Digital Cooperation' (2019).

[31] W. Benedek, M. Kettemann, 'Preface' in *Freedom of Expression and the Internet* (Strasburg: Council of Europe, 2014).

13.4.2 *Business as Usual and Anything Goes*

There are, of course, attempts to view freedom of expression online following the idea of *business as usual*, which means that there are simply new challenges, which need to be met with proper attention from various stakeholders and adjustments in legal regimes. In such a scenario, nothing profound normatively or conceptually would have to be altered and the status quo of the human rights offline paradigm fully absorbs such new challenges. This view contains, however, some fallacies in ontological and epistemic respects. The first is related to the manipulation of boundaries, that is, the simultaneous widening and narrowing of the right to freedom of expression online. This is associated with the lack of clarity about the boundaries of what constitutes this right and what lies outside. In physics, one would call this fluctuation. Jorgensen has illustrated such lack of clarity and fluctuation using concrete evidence from practice, and he is just one among many. He refers, for instance, to 'how Google and Facebook produce and reproduce online boundaries via algorithms (e.g. search results), design features (e.g. privacy settings that codify user affordances), company norms (e.g. community standards), and governance mechanisms (e.g. review teams)'.[32] One of the characteristics of any human right is the predictability of its scope, its boundaries in relation to other rights and rules which govern these associated rights. When we can, in principle, change the boundaries of a fundamental right as often as we change our socks, then we cannot speak of a fundamental right due to the absence of stability.

The ontological aspect is associated with the problem of knowing what constitutes free speech online and what does not. When everything said can be considered freedom of expression, then labelling anything expressed as freedom of expression does not make sense. Freedom of speech makes sense only in the event that we can also determine what does not constitute freedom of speech, that is, logically through its opposite. And vice versa, if all speech was to be supressed or not allowed online, then the right would not exist either. Calling it simply a *challenge* means the non-coherence effect in reverse – touching the digital domain has altered the offline human rights paradigm itself. This alteration is manifold, as it touches the content of rights and elements associated with how we think about rights, such as their

[32] R. F. Jørgensen, 'How Platforms Make Sense of Human Rights', The Internet, Policy and Politics Conferences, Oxford Internet Institute, University of Oxford, http://blogs.oii.ox.ac.uk/ipp-conference/2016/programme-2016/track-b-governance/law-and-ethics/rikke-frank-j%C3%B8rgensen-how-platforms-make.html, 12, accessed 23 September 2022.

predictability to give just one of these elements. We can call this a virus effect from the digital domain, and this is more than just an intellectual statement. A vaccine against such a virus is to argue that offline and online human rights exist in separate paradigms, where knowledge about the other side is possible, as well as some influence, but it does not go so far as to profoundly change the way we think about our physical lives.

The term *challenges* exists in the background of the American safe harbour doctrine, which says that *anything goes* on the Internet. Yet after some initial fascination, now the dominant views and actions are to curtail this idea through positive law and community restrictions.[33] This signals the intent to narrow the initially wide concept of freedom of expression online. From the non-coherence perspective, if we are to look at the image from the positive law perspective, we could now say that the image of the freedom of speech online was initially at greater variance and has gradually started to move closer to the original concept. But any human right has to be related to what is practically possible and can be realised, and not to what the law says are consequences when such a right is infringed on or not sufficiently protected.

However, changes in the liability regimes of online service providers based on the negation of the safe harbour doctrine may shift the image of the freedom of expression from one to another extreme. That is, from the scenario of *anything goes* to the opposite, *nothing goes*. For instance, a recent edited collection on the situation in the Nordic countries regarding freedom of speech and new media reveals that more regulation can lead to the opposite of the desired outcome. Instead of allowing more user postings under sensible monitoring schemes, new private companies choose to opt out from allowing freedom of expression for the readers on their portals.[34] Such a fluctuation in the scope of the freedom of expression on some private portals reveals a blurring image. It can be said that the image is non-coherent from the perspective of the meaning of freedom of expression offline, but it is not yet possible to ascertain the features of such non-coherence, for example, the width and absence or inclusion of some elements. From the perspective of the

33 For example, see a blog calling the idea of safe harbours a mirage: T. Khan, 'Safe Harbours: A Mirage on Intermediary Protection', RGNUL Student Research Review, *Rajiv Gandhi National University of Law*, 21 October 2021, https://rsrr.in/2020/10/21/safe-harbours-and-intermediary-liability, accessed 25 September 2022. For a more comprehensive view of the doctrine of safe harbours, one may look at M. Lemley, 'Rationalizing Internet Safe Harbors', DOI: 10.31235/osf.io/eshq7, accessed 26 September 2022.

34 See for reference, M. Susi, J. Viljanen, E. Jónsson, A. Kućs (eds.), *Human Rights Law and Regulating Freedom of Expression in New Media: Lessons from Nordic Approaches* (New York: Routledge, 2018).

viewer from the non-digital domain, a settled non-coherent image may be considered better than fluctuation. This is primarily because during such a process the image of the freedom of expression remains obscure, and it may even be asserted that one cannot validate whether the digital image exhibits features of non-coherence, or whether the image might reveal total incompatibility with the offline image.

13.4.3 *The Comfort in the Non-coherence Thesis*

A novel aspect of the transfer of human rights images and ideas is revealed from here, which is the *comfort in the non-coherence thesis*. In translation, this refers to the simplistic perception that we prefer to operate in a realm which is at least to some extent familiar to us, as opposed to being confronted with a reality which has a completely new reality and is unfamiliar and unpredictable. In such a reality, human rights ideas and concepts would not be meaningful, and the only reason for using human rights language would be to approach the new reality with tools that are familiar to us from the physical realm. Figuratively speaking, this would resemble a situation where a man stands on the shore of a deep lake on a windless day and looks into the water. The man sees the reflection of the sun and clouds on the surface of the water and thinks that the lake is about the sun and the clouds. Concentrating on the images reflected on the surface has a blocking effect stopping the man from looking below the surface. The non-coherence approach goes beyond the surface and explores, as far as possible using the expressions and knowledge creation tools from the offline physical realm, what lies under the surface. Consequently, if someone speaks of the freedom of expression in the digital domain, then we must ask whether such talk is merely a reflection of the person's perception that the digital domain should entail such a right, or whether the discussion is about the features which this right has assumed after transposition.

It Is difficult to view the precise image of the freedom of expression in the digital domain. The discourse is dominated by the description of complications that go beyond just seeing the contours of the image. Plato's myth of the cave comes to mind, as there seems to be competition to decide who can more elaborately put forward elements that need to be addressed before the full image becomes visible. In legal science, this would be labelled future research questions. Maybe this is justified and coincides with the long road leading outside the cave, where the image would be visible without any areas still needing to be clarified. To give a few illustrations, Kettemann, Peukert and Spiecker conclude as follows in the 2022 edited volume about law in the digital space:

> The book reveals that the number of specifically digital and global phenomena, which raise unique regulatory questions, is increasing, and that the applicable digital law is characterised by private ordering, transnational standardisation, economisation but at the same time by persistent and possibly deepening legal fragmentation. The article ends with suggestions for future research as regards both concrete questions of digital law and of overarching theoretical issues.[35]

Specifically about freedom of expression online, Magarin lists structural concerns connected to the limited free speech online in need of regulatory attention, including: inequalities of access, power relationships among governments, private speech intermediaries and internet users and the ways the Internet's architecture complicates effective regulation.[36] Many more examples could be given of the ongoing efforts to apply ideas and concepts from the offline domain to the digital domain, and in particular the freedom of expression. Yet these efforts do not necessarily attempt to place freedom of expression online in the Procrustean Bed. The side effect of letting go of the Procrustean Bed approach, in other words, the sameness idea, is the uncertainty of what the image of the freedom of expression would be in the digital domain after one gets out of Plato's cave and can look at the real image. Maybe thereafter we would prefer to quickly return to the safety of the cave and the sameness doctrine. Maybe we see nothing precisely yet, which compromises the promise of the realm outside the cave. Plato has promised that those who make their way outside the cave start to see matters clearly; however, they do not hurry back to let those left behind know how things really are. The promise of the cave is that such knowledge of the true nature of things is possible. But the logic of no return compromises the realism of testing the promise. In connection with the topic of this chapter, the promise of non-coherence theory is to paint as clearly as possible the image of the freedom of speech online using the tools of knowledge creation from the offline realm. The aspiration of the explanatory power of any legal theory, and among those the non-coherence theory of digital human rights, is to look at the roots of the concept (i.e., the roots of the freedom of expression). There are some fundamentally important conceptions of the nature of the freedom of expression offline, or, as we have specified on numerous occasions, of this right as we know it from history and from the physical realities where we live.

35 M. Kettemann, A. Peukert, Alexnder, 'Conclusion' in M. Kettemann, A. Peukert, I. Spiecker gen. Döhmann (eds.), *The Law of Global Digitality* (London: Routledge, 2022).

36 G. P. Magarin, 'The Internet and Social Media' in A. Stone, F. Schauer (eds.), *The Oxford Handbook of Freedom of Speech* (Oxford: Oxford University Press, 2021).

These are about censorship, reactions to speech in the form of sanctions and the distinction between good and evil speech.

13.4.4 *Censorship Online*

The first element is about censorship, which is related to someone deciding whether the information I wish to put forward or opinions I wish to express are allowed to reach any audience, be it global or regional. It can be exercised after someone says or expresses something and before this reaches the target audience. It can also be exercised as a reaction to information or views which have already entered the public domain. As such, censorship can be divided into measures of general and individual impact. In the first scenario, the measure is related to disabling the person or institution from publishing or saying anything at all in the future in respective mediums, and in the second scenario it concerns specific information or views which the person or institution wishes to express. We have to see now whether these measures are available and exercised in the digital domain.

There are opposing views about the possibility of censorship in the digital domain – those who argue that such censorship is not achievable, and those who argue the opposite, namely, that the digital domain enables censorship with a much broader scope in comparison with the non-digital domain. Both these views, at first glance, testify in favour of non-coherence between the digital and non-digital domain. It follows from here, as an assumption, that non-coherence of the freedom of speech exists between digital and non-digital domains in relation to the property of censorship.

The first view is largely credited to John Gilmore, one of the founders of the Internet, who already in 1993 asserted the impossibility of digital censorship by saying: 'The Net interprets censorship as damage and routes around it.'[37] Around the same time, Cheer expressed a similar viewpoint by suggesting that censorship in the digital space is not possible.[38] Mailland has added an explanation that the cost of exercising censorship online, having in mind content control, weighs heavily against its feasibility.[39] The alternative view, asserting the possibility of censorship on the Internet, follows from a variety of

[37] P. Elmer-Dewitt, 'First Nation in Cyberspace', *TIME International*, 6 December 1993, https://content.time.com/time/magazine/article/0,9171,979768,00.html, accessed 27 November 2022.

[38] U. Cheer, 'A State's Increasing Role in Monitoring Expression: New Zealand's New Censorship Regime' (1996) 6 *Canterbury Law Review*, 333.

[39] J. Mailland, 'Freedom of Speech, the Internet, and the Costs of Control: The French Example' (2001) 33 *New York University Journal of International Law and Politics*, 1182.

technical measures enabled by the digital technology, such as internet protocol address blocking, domain name system filtering and redirection, uniform resource locator filtering and packet filtering; the list can continue. Here a different problem emerges known as circumvention, which means that the digital space enables originalism in finding how to avoid censorship decisions. As shown by Roberts, Zuckermann and Palfrey in a comprehensive study testing methods to avoid censorship methods:

> All of the circumvention and anonymity focused tools included in this study manage to circumvent both lab and in country filters and, notably, to provide an effective and reasonably easy to use interface. This point should be stressed – that all of the circumvention and anonymity tools included in this study succeeded at the basic task of retrieving blocked content in a filtering country. In that sense, the tools have individually and as a group been a success.[40]

This circumvention, however, is not a distinct feature of the digital space. Because circumvention is known to exist and will continue to exist also for the physical realm and mainstream publications, be it publishing somewhere else or speaking between the lines, as the case may be.

A collection of articles published by the Berkman Center of Harvard University opens up the complexity and absence of global consensus in discourses and practices on what censorship in the digital domain means and what the most effective methods are to exercise digital content control.[41] Several characteristics appear on closer inspection. One is the 'existence of advanced network interference techniques that grow in sophistication over time'.[42] This is echoed by Bambauer by showing how digital censorship has developed through three stages, the new censorship model involving four changes: 'a shift in implementation to private parties; a hybrid approach mixing promotion of favoured viewpoints with suppression of disfavoured ones; a blend of formal mandates with informal pressures; and a framing of

40 H. Roberts, E. Zuckermann, and J. Palfrey, '2007 Circumvention Landscape Report: Methods, Uses, and Tools' *The Berkmann Center for Internet and Society at Harvard University*, 5 March 2009, https://cyber.harvard.edu/publications/2009/2007_Circumvention_Landscape_Report, 85, accessed 28 November 2022.

41 S. J. Murdoch, H. Roberts, 'Introduction to: Internet Censorship and Control', 22 May 2013, SSRN: https://ssrn.com/abstract=2268587 or http://dx.doi.org/10.2139/ssrn.2268587, accessed 25 November 2022.

42 See a comprehensive study: V. Ververis, T. Ermakova, M. Isaakdis, S. Basso, B. Fabian, S. Milan, 'Understanding Internet Censorship in Europe: The Case of Spain', WebSvi'21: 13th ACM Web Science Conference 2021, https://dl.acm.org/doi/10.1145/3447535.3462638, 319, accessed 27 November 2022.

censorship using uncontroversial labels'.[43] This characteristic reveals greater variance in complexity in comparison with the non-digital domain. It also reveals a higher level of hiddenness when something is censored, and as such leads to the second characteristic on the scale of universality versus individuality. This concerns the incapability of applying censorship in individual cases due to the high volume of user postings online, and this matter will be discussed in more detail in Chapter 21.

Therefore, the image of censorship in the digital domain reveals certain variance in comparison with the non-digital domain. There is no variance in the general statement, as articulated by Sangsuvan, that 'international human rights law provides exceptions to freedom of speech, which may be used to censor online speech or control freedom of speech on the Internet'.[44] The variance appears once one moves closer to the effects of censorship and how it can be implemented. There is a shift from individual censorship towards censorship of portals or user groups, that is, from individual censorship to general censorship. There is also a tendency to censor certain topics or expressions, which as a consequence may affect not only individual sources of certain expressions or views but anyone who belongs to such groups or wishes to use their words to express certain ideas. This is because having censored an individual expression or view, the censors decide to eliminate the possibility of repetitions. The result for individual users is twofold. On the one hand, there is the narrowing of the freedom of expression because our ability to speak freely may be infringed not for reasons connected to us but because of someone else, unknown to us, who may have engaged in conversations deemed unsuitable for the portal. It may also happen because the public entities wish the private service providers to exercise certain policies. What transpires is the weakening of the link between the individual exercising their freedom of expression vis-à-vis the censorship measures exercised in the digital domain. Here we can conclude a medium level of non-coherence. However, if we accept the view of the sceptics, which represents the second side of the coin, of the effectiveness of digital censorship, we could conclude there is greater non-coherence, which lies in the discrepancy between the promise of censorship and its realisability.

43 D. E. Bambauer, 'Censorship V3.1' (2012) 18 *IEEE Internet Computing* 26 (May/June 2013), Arizona Legal Studies Discussion Paper No. 12–28, SSRN: https://ssrn.com/abstract=2144004 or http://dx.doi.org/10.2139/ssrn.2144004, 1.

44 K. Sangsuvan, 'Balancing Freedom of Speech on the Internet under International Law' (2014) 39 *North Carolina Journal of International Law*, 755.

The following question now is what happens after censorship is exercised. In the offline world, the answer depends to some extent on the subject matter of the content which was censored or blocked from publication. For content considered to be legitimate yet infringing someone's rights even to an extreme extent, there seems to be an understanding that civil law remedies are sufficient. That means that criminal sanctions and imprisonment are out of the range, at least in the European Union, and yet there are countries where criticising public authorities may lead to arrest and conviction.[45]

The matter changes when illegal content, specifically hate speech,[46] comes to the table. There seems to be consensus that criminal law is the most suitable response.[47] Yet a defiant person – such a statement carrying no moral aspect – can continue to voice his or her opinions, as difficult as this may seem in fear of various sanctions and possible harm. The point here is that the physical domain does not foresee the option of finality, that is, disabling the person forever exercising one's capability to voice opinions or express views. But this is exactly what the digital domain enables. It is a well-known property of social media portals to be able to apply sanctions of various duration and disable someone from continuing to use the platform services. An extreme end of such interference in the freedom of expression is de-platforming, where someone's social media account is terminated. An example of such cancelling happened in January 2021, when numerous internet platforms suspended the accounts of former US President Donald Trump and his supporters.[48] Because of the originalism inherent in those wishing to let their voice be heard either online, in traditional media or simply in various public spaces, it will always be possible to circumvent even the most extreme measures attached to censorship. Here the variance between the two domains seems narrow.

A few additional brushstrokes regarding the image of the freedom of speech online may be in order before arriving at the most fundamental question of

[45] See, for example, information collected and shared by Amnesty International on practices of imprisonment for a critique: Amnesty International, 'Freedom of Expression', Amnesty International, date unknown, www.amnesty.org/en/what-we-do/freedom-of-expression, accessed 29 November 2022.

[46] For a reference regarding hate speech, among other sources, one can read J. Viljanen, 'Combating Hate Speech Online' in M. Susi (ed.), *Human Rights, Digital Society and the Law: A Research Companion* (London: Routledge, 2019), pp. 225–238.

[47] As such, see EU Council Framework Decision 2008/913/JHA of 28 November 2008 on combating certain forms and expressions of racism and xenophobia by means of criminal law.

[48] For a reference, see a comparative study conducted by the Global Digital Human Rights Network into the 'deplatformng' phenomenon: M. Fertmann, M. C. Kettemann (eds.), *Can Platforms Cancel Politicians? How States and Platforms Deal with Private Power over Political Actors: An Exploratory Study of 15 Countries* (Hamburg: Verlag HansBredow-Institut, 2021).

how to evaluate words on the scale of good and evil. Here, the digital domain allows some specific properties which are much less available offline. This is connected to the feature of the digital domain enabling the almost immediate dissemination of information but also reactions to the information and views from uncountable individuals. Rubin has characterised this, again among many others, as a feature where the Internet 'reintroduces shaming and shunning penalties by enabling those who are offended by a particular statement to generate condemnations that will be permanently attached to an individual's Net presence and thus publicized throughout society'.[49] Because such shaming affects someone's privacy sphere, and since we have shown before how the notion of privacy is changed online almost to a point where it is not completely reasonable to use the expression, a correlation between the entitlement to be left alone and freedom of expression can be asserted. Such a correlation shows an image where the weakening of one entitlement causes the weakening of another. Such an image is surprising at first glance, as we would expect the strengthening of the right to the freedom of expression as being paired with the right to privacy, at the expense of the latter. As formulated by Krotoszynski: 'A society without privacy might not necessarily be a society without speech, but speech in such a society will undoubtedly be more limited, less vibrant, and substantially more circumscribed than in a society with meaningful privacy protections.'[50] It is not without reason that these additional elements in the image of freedom of speech online were put forward, because our interest here is to establish variance between the various rights online and offline. Since the variance here does not appear extreme, it may not be justified to suggest the replacement of the freedom of speech online with a different concept. There are suggestions towards concretisation. For instance, Sharma and Phandarkar suggest that it would be correct to speak of the 'right to freedom of speech and expression over the internet',[51] and as such it would occupy an area within the more broadly conceptualised freedom of speech right. Yet for all human rights, abstractness and universality are inherent properties. Therefore, we can question whether such a formulation retains a sufficient degree of abstractness and universality. The reply could be

[49] R. Edward, 'Privacy and Freedom of Speech in the Internet Era', JOTWELL, 8 December 2015 (reviewing Ronald J. Krotoszynski Jr., Reconciling Privacy and Speech in the Era of Big Data: A Comparative Legal Analysis, 56 Wm. & Mary L. Rev. 1279 (2015), https://juris.jotwell.com/privacy-and-freedom-of-speech-in-the-internet-era, 1, accessed 3 December 2023.

[50] R. J. Krotoszynski Jr., 'Reconciling Privacy and Speech in the Era of Big Data: A Comparative Legal Analysis' (2015) 56 *William & Mary Law Review* 4, 1338.

[51] M. Sharma, P. Bhandarkar, 'Freedom of Speech and Expression on Internet: An Emerging Right' (2020) 3 *International Journal of Law Management and Humanities*, 6, 390.

affirmative only if the boundaries of universality and abstractness are interpreted creatively.

From a stricter viewpoint, that of the hesitancy towards the expansion of fundamental rights, the reply is not affirmative. Such a conclusion can be reached through the exercise of contrasting how freedom of expression is defined online and offline. I will compare the text of the European Human Rights Convention article 10 (1) against the narrative of the soft and binding law formulations regarding the freedom of expression online gathered from various United Nations and European instruments. Since there is no specific definition of the freedom of expression online, the contours of my approach may be somewhat sketchy, but it does not miss the main point.

The European Human Rights Convention article 10 (1) provides a well-known formulation: 'Everyone has the right to freedom of expression. This right shall include freedom to hold opinions and to receive and impart information and ideas without interference by public authority and regardless of frontiers. This Article shall not prevent States from requiring the licensing of broadcasting, television or cinema enterprises.' I will contrast this with the reading from an online freedom of speech narrative, where similar formulations are retained, missing formulations are crossed out and new additions appear in italics. The reading is this: 'Everyone has the right to freedom of expression. This right shall include freedom to receive and impart *accurate and reliable*[52] information and ideas *based on solidarity and inclusion*[53] without interference by public *or private* authority *in fair and trusted online environment.*[54] *States are obligated to require from online enterprises a safe and secure digital environment, giving people control over their data.*'[55] The image is clearly non-coherent due to concretisation as opposed to abstractness. In terms of universality, there appears no variance, since such a right would apply to everyone who enters the digital domain. This, however, leads us to ask

[52] See statement by UNESCO Director-General: UNESCO, 'Social Media: UNESCO Leads Global Dialogue to Improve the Reliability of Information', UNESCO, 1 February 2023, www.unesco.org/en/articles/social-media-unesco-leads-global-dialogue-improve-reliability-information, accessed 2 February 2023.

[53] U. N., 'Road Map for Digital Cooperation: Implementation of the Recommendations of the High-Level Panel on Digital Cooperation' (2020).

[54] Regulation (EU) 2022/2065 of the European Parliament and of the Council of 19 October 2022 on a Single Market for Digital Services and Amending Directive 2000/31/EC (Digital Services Act) (2022) OJ L 277.

[55] U. N., Office of the High Commissioner for Human Rights, 'Human Rights in the Digital Age – Can They Make a Difference?', keynote speech by Michelle Bachelet, UN High Commissioner for Human Rights, Japan Society, New York, 17 October 2019, www.ohchr.org/en/speeches/2019/10/human-rights-digital-age, accessed 4 December 2022.

about a specific feature of non-coherence, concerning the interrelationship between parent rights and their derivate or implied rights. Since every derivate and implied right retains some features of the parent right, and through the process of the implication of derivation obtains some new features, does it not follow that non-coherence is a property characterising rights development in general. In this case, all new rights are to some extent non-coherent with the constitutive properties of their parent rights. Although this being the case, our interest here is not to focus on rights development inside a rights paradigm but to look at what happens when human rights and ideas are transposed into another normative paradigm. If transposition automatically means derivation and thereby non-coherence, any hopes of the sameness of rights and ideas cannot be upheld.

Due to medium variance, it is more accurate to say that freedom of expression online in comparison with freedom of expression offline has distinct features, among those (i) dual nature or scope, where in social media the scope is broader and in e-governance solutions the scope is narrow; (ii) the weakening of the chain between censorship measures to individual statements and views; and (iii) due to correlation with the right to privacy, limitations to the right to freedom of expression because of self-restraint.

13.4.5 *The Distinction between Good and Evil Speech*

Finally, this section reaches the point where we can look at the very foundation of the right to freedom of expression. For each fundamental right there must exist one or some basic ideas which enter the domain before judicial and logical argumentation and as such, constitute the core of the entire construction of this right, apparent in policies and judgements and law. Often these basic ideas are not thought of in daily practice or discourse. But for an ambitious theory such as the non-coherence theory of digital human rights, a return to the basics is inevitable.

The matter which stands out as most fundamental is the entitlement to speak words which are good and the prohibition to engage in speech which is considered evil. From here emerges the property of relativity. The interest in supressing evil speech as a matter that stands separately from the previous discussion has sometimes taken extreme formats. History tells us that putting someone to death for speaking against public morals has not only been imaginary, the most notable case perhaps being the execution of Socrates.[56]

[56] P. Cartledge, *Democracy: A Life* (Oxford: Oxford University Press, 2018), pp. xxviii, 388.

This example is given merely to illustrate the dilemma of establishing the distinction between the categories of good and evil. It is a matter which has deserved attention perhaps as long as humankind was able to articulate words and was evident when someone ten thousand years ago said to another '[w]hy do you say such evil things to me?', and the other responded 'I do not consider what I said evil, it was good words that I said.' Many attempts have been made to spell out the dilemma between good and evil speech. The statement of John Milton in *Areopagitica* encompasses the core of the dilemma, so it is worth citing the relevant passage, in the language written almost 400 years ago:

> Good and evill we know in the field of this World grow up together almost inseparably; and the knowledge of good is so involv'd and interwoven with the knowledge of evill, and in so many cunning resemblances hardly to be discern'd, that those confused seeds which were impos'd on Psyche as an incessant labour to cull out, and sort asunder, were not more intermixt. It was from out the rinde of one apple tasted, that the knowledge of good and evill as two twins cleaving together leapt forth into the World.[57]

It is not our goal to venture into a discussion of how good and evil are defined in different human rights domains because it would exhibit a high degree of relativity. Common sense and examples tell us that what someone may find as entirely evil may be considered by someone else as an example of goodness. But we have to note, despite this relativity, that the existence of categories of good and evil are necessary in order to think about freedom of expression. Without these categories, there would remain no grounds for exercising this freedom as we are accustomed to think. The question to ask is, therefore, how are these categories of good and evil positioned in the human rights online and offline architectures. The following can be asserted.

The offline human rights landscape operates with the goal of eliminating evil speech. Since this goal can never be fully realised, there are positive law provisions, judicial decisions and policies to press evil speech out of public domain. This reflection does not necessitate examples for verification, as it can be considered self-evident. Another side of the coin seems to be, likewise, the correlation with the minimisation of good speech. Some may term this phenomenon political correctness, while others call it the standardisation of public discourse. It may seem from the outside more predictable, and it is

[57] J. Milton, *Areopagitica, a Speech of Mr. John Milton for the Liberty of Unlicenc'd Printing to the Parliament of England*, 1st ed. (London, 1644), retrieved 18 October 2022 via Google Books.

certainly less disturbing. In an ideal freedom of expression offline environment, the categories of good and evil should be rarely evoked.

The online human rights landscape does not exhibit a similar standardisation. For instance, social media clusters are connecting people who express only good ideas and images as shared by all members of the cluster. It has been noted before how social media portals are designed to enable people to put forward their digital identity, which is profoundly good and attractive. Those who object to the common understanding of what is good are simply eliminated from the group and platform. However, the interest in enabling only good speech and ideas means that somewhere in the digital domain evil speech must also be stored. This is because of the inseparability of good and evil, as Milton has suggested. In the search for evil talk in the digital domain, several possibilities come to the forefront. One is that of the confusion between these categories, so that someone putting forward seemingly good expressions may be confused and in fact is engaged in evil talk. Another comes from the twin nature of good and evil – having grown up together, they enable the definition of one mainly through referral to the other. Evil speech can only exist when it is contrasted against good speech, and the other way around. Oscar Wilde's notorious character Dorian Gray can serve as an illustration of the inseparability of extreme versions of good and evil. The image that opens from the digital domain about the freedom of expression shows that its extreme versions are more openly exercised in comparison with the non-digital domain. This is a significant variance, and non-coherence is clearly visible. For believers, it can be said that Heaven and Hell are more open in the digital domain in contrast with the physical realm. Since we can consider that good and evil speech exist as a pair, and enhancement of one means the simultaneous enhancement of the other, it may be said that this aspect can also be applied to the analysis of freedom of expression offline.

A general idea may emerge, which can be termed the thesis of inaugural extremism. This means that after transposition into a new domain, the features of a human rights idea or characteristics of some offline traditional right, may appear in a higher spectrum than in the traditional setting. To use the analogy of astronomy, after transposition into another domain, human rights ideas, concepts and rules can be compared to the formation of a new star. The process of star formation is accompanied by a cloud of dust and turbulence. The cloud after a certain period of time collapses, and the turbulence withers to be replaced by forces of gravity. Based on this illustrative analogy, non-coherence appears as a condition sine qua non after any transposition of ideas, concepts and rules, and can be detected because of the dust and turbulence, which some can call contestations and resistance against paradigmatic change. Once these elements disappear, only then can the scope of non-coherence in the substantive characteristics and in normativity be seen. For instance, there was widely held scepticism after the emergence of the Internet about its resilience to any normative regulation. This was the stage of its formation. Thereafter, and notwithstanding the exact possibilities and nature of positive law in an elastic domain, the dust has started to settle somewhat, and turbulence is giving way to tranquillity, although one may object to whether the process has exited the stage of turbulence.

The objection originates from the appearance of close to pure forms of good and evil speech in the digital domain in communication and preventive and/or supportive policies. For instance, the design that allows only positive reflections through the function of *likes*, or the function to report postings which are not illegal but merely *disturbing*, is a revelation of a function that expects only good speech. The other side is represented by features of extreme evilness and concerns hate speech, entrapment or deceit via digital solutions, various revenge applications and the problematic adolescent usage of the Internet in general. Since the co-existence of such extreme formats of speech has existed from the formation of social media platforms and internet communication channels, it may be considered one of the main specific features of freedom of speech online. Non-coherence regarding extreme formats of speech and their frequency is apparently a feature of objective and longitudinal nature.

This leads me to the point where the relative nature of freedom of expression appears under attack. We are accustomed to think that freedom of expression is a non-absolute right. Law schools train students to accept the view that this right is fundamental but not absolute because then it would override the comparable legitimate interests of others, or some other public considerations. Courts fine-tune jurisprudence to distinguish between various elements necessary to define the limits of freedom of speech, such as who is the public figure and is therefore more immune to critique, and where does hate speech start. Yet there are at least two constitutive elements of the freedom of expression – censorship and the distinction between good and evil speech, without which it would not make sense, and which in combination define the core of the right in the non-digital domain. We have seen that these elements sometimes obtain an absolute nature in the digital domain. Here there is wide variance between the meaning of freedom of expression offline and online since offline it can rarely be justified as an absolute right, whereas online practice shows a duality: the parallel possibility of relativity and absoluteness. It may be in the nature of the digital domain that such parallelism does not incrementally disappear.

14

The Variance Principle and Digital Transparency

The variance principle claims that ontic and epistemic aspects of human rights from the offline domain may be at variance with these aspects in the online sphere. It is perhaps more accurate to state that offline rules and principles may apply sporadically, but there exists no predictability about the circumstances under which they apply and exactly how. In some instances, they may apply, such as in relation to some concrete online service providers, or in some countries, or regarding some specific rights – and in other instances, they may not.[1] The variance principle leads to the non-coherence theory of digital human rights, which claims that human rights law and its application online is characterised by changes in the fundamental characteristics of transparency, legal certainty and foreseeability. Human rights exist online in a non-coherent system characterised by the fragmentation of human rights normative sources and interpretations through discursive practice; a multitude of actors with changing roles, novel compliance mechanisms or their overall absence; the systemic dependence on the capabilities of online stakeholders for the protection of human rights; and the systemic susceptibility

[1] See, for example, similar propositions. Schaumburg-Müller writes: 'I am not arguing that life online and offline is always completely the same and ought to be regulated in precisely the same manner in all details. What I am arguing is that they are not fundamentally different either' (S. Schaumberg-Müller, 'Liability Regimes for Online Human Rights Violations' in M. Susi (ed.), *Human Rights, Digital Society and the Law: A Research Companion* (London: Routledge, 2019); or Kulesza writes: 'Does the internet's transboundary nature, scale, speed of communication, automation, interconnectivity and invisibility change the way in which we view and protect fundamental rights (privacy, data protection, non-discrimination, due process, presumption of innocence and free speech)? Are human rights online exactly the same as offline or are they modified by the internet-specific circumstances, possibly impacting their very core?' (J. Kulesza, 'Multistakeholderism: Meaning and Implications' in M. Susi (ed.), *Human Rights, Digital Society and the Law: A Research Companion* (London: Routledge, 2019).

to utilitarian considerations which are non-resilient to time. Various considerations may change swiftly in time at will, like the goals related to the protection of national security or economic interests.

14.1 REMEMBERING BENTHAM

For centuries it has been believed that transparency constitutes a foundation of the modern society's political processes. And from there forward, transparency is also believed to function as an overarching concept across human rights advocacy and normativity. The roots of the concept of transparency are usually credited to Jeremy Bentham from around two centuries ago, and in particular to his assertion that 'every gesture, every turn of limb or feature, in those whose motions have a visible impact on the general happiness, will be noticed and marked down'.[2] If not to choose words too carefully and just express the main idea, these phrases from Bentham about transparency point to exactly what the digital domain can accomplish but users wish to avoid – not make open someone's every gesture and turn of limb or feature for everyone's eyes. So here we see already the first revelation of non-coherence.

The idea of transparency transforms when transposed from the non-digital domain to the digital domain. This is the transformation from positivity into negativity. In other words, what is regarded positively in one domain may be regarded as the opposite in another domain, or at least contested in another domain due to the fragmented positions of those who are affected or in control. More broadly, it tells us that an aspect of non-coherence may therefore also exist in the change of a feature's qualitative characterisation. And yet this statement is viewer-dominated; that is, it represents the view from the domain where transparency was defined and then transposed. It does not need to coincide with the view from the outside, that is, from the domain against which a feature is reflected. We can find evidence to support the position that when the non-digital domain cherishes the idea of transparency and then discovers that after transposition into the digital domain the idea has lost its glamour, the digital domain may still consider the same feature as something positive.

To further illustrate, we say from the offline domain that the ability to follow every gesture and notice and mark down every behaviour in and by digital platforms is something negative, since it narrows the scope of privacy. However, the digital domain may find such ability suitable and appropriate for business interests and then assert that it is legitimised by and through the idea of

[2] J. Bentham, *Deontology: Or, the Science of Morality*, vol. 1, edited by J. Bowring (London: Longman, Rees, Orme, Brown, Green and Longman, 1834), p. 101.

transparency. Further attention to the matter is necessary in order to avoid first impressions and clarify the image of transparency in the digital sphere. The areas under view will be general concerns raised against the idea of transparency in the physical realm and whether these concerns are carried over undistorted to the non-physical realm, and then more concretely how transparency is understood by various actors on the Internet and how these approaches are comparable against those from the physical sphere. In this review, our primary interests at the beginning are theoretical before proceeding to the utilitarian.

14.2 OBJECTION FROM NON-SPECIFICITY

The main conceptual concern against transparency is its non-specificity. When reviewing its historical development, Hood writes about its quasi-religious character as follows: 'Transparency is more often preached than practiced, more often invoked than defined, and indeed might ironically be said to be mystic in essence, at least to some extent.'[3] More historical reviews could be added, which note that the concept of transparency has turned out to be problematic and even fraught.[4] Baume and Papadopoluos represent the same critical view and note little discussion of the justifications of transparency. Their conclusion notes 'that the virtuous effects of transparency are today qualified by criticisms in scholarly work which emphasise the possible costs and perverse effects of the search for transparency or demonstrate that it may fail to deliver the expected benefits'.[5] The concern is not only historic but seems to characterise the ambiguity of the transparency concept in contemporary legal and political discourse as well. Balazs has put forward an analysis of how the concept is instrumentalised in various legislative initiatives and has discovered variance not only in comparisons between organisations but also between documents issued and examined within the same organisations.[6]

3 C. Hood, 'Transparency in Historical Perspective' in C. Hood, D. Heald (eds.), *Transparency: The Key to Better Governance?*, Proceedings of the British Academy (London: British Academy Scholarship Online, 2006), 31 January 2012), https://doi.org/10.5871/bacad/9780197263839.003.0001, accessed 29 October 2022.

4 J. Felix, 'Before Transparency: Control and Communication in Early-Modern Europe' (2015) 30 *Revue Historie & Mesure*, 2.

5 S. Baume, Y. Papadopoulos, 'Transparency: From Bentham's Inventory of Virtuous Effects to Contemporary Evidence-Based Scepticism' (2018) 21 *Critical Review of International Social and Political Philosophy*, 2, 169–192, DOI: 10.1080/13698230.2015.1092656.

6 B. Hohmann, 'Interpretation the Concept of Transparency in the Strategic and Legislative Documents of Major International Organizations' (2021) 2 *Közigazgatási és Infokommunikációs Jogi PhD Tanulmányok*, 1, 68, DOI: 10.47272/KIKPhD.2021.1.4.

These examples suffice to illustrate the initial statement noting the non-specificity of the transparency concept in non-digital law.

Accordingly, we can now ask whether the objection to its non-specificity is carried over to the digital domain. This depends on how this non-specificity appearing in the non-digital domain can be explained. My response is that non-coherence is written integrally into the concept of transparency, it being the incompatibility between its promise of qualitative output and the basis of quantitative features. This is because transparency about someone's behaviour and open statements should in the end lead to understanding the reasons for the ideas this person puts forward in relation to a particular issue or the manner of their behaviour. Observations of behaviour and statements can be measured in quantitative terms and carry objectivity – we know what someone said and when. But quantitative measures do not tell us why this person made the statements and acted in the way she did, since it is the object of qualitative assessment. Plato's myth of the cave, mentioned in the Introduction, comes to mind once again as a source of inspirational explanation. Transparency here means that from the observation of shadows we wish to make conclusions about reasons and content. Non-coherence between quantitative and qualitative aspects is thus evident in transparency.

To deal with this contradiction, some scholars have noted that the current approach to transparency involves a shift from controlling the state's behaviour to understanding the state's behaviour.[7] Once again, the main objection against transparency as a general concept lies in its dual nature: one can ask for transparency towards Objectivity; that is, how a certain legal outcome is construed through a sequence of events and formal inputs, and one can also ask for transparency towards Subjectivity, which would be the reasons for such an outcome. I assert that the main non-coherent aspect in transparency between the non-digital and digital domains lies in the simple statement that transparency towards both the Objective and Subjective sides are possible in the non-digital domain but only towards the former, the Objective, in the digital domain. Non-digital transparency is multilayered, but digital transparency is uni-layered. My reasons for this will be presented in the following section.

14.3 ABOUT DIGITAL HAPPINESS

Let us consider the goal Bentham attached to transparency – the greatest happiness of society, acquired through transparent communication and exchange of arguments. Here is what he wrote:

[7] J. R. Bruno, 'Democracy beyond Disclosure: Secrecy, Transparency, and the Logic of Self-Government', Digital Access to Scholarships at Harvard, http://nrs.harvard.edu/urn-3:HUL.InstRepos:37944996, accessed 19 November 2022.

> Among a people who have been long accustomed to public assemblies, the general feeling will be raised to a higher tone – sound opinions will be more common, hurtful prejudices, publicly combated, not by rhetoricians but by statesmen, will have less dominion. The multitude will be more secure from the tricks of demagogues, and the cheats of impostors; they will most highly esteem great talents, and the frivolities of wit will be reduced to their just value. A habit of reasoning and discussion will penetrate all classes of society. The passions, accustomed to a public struggle, will learn reciprocally to restrain themselves; they will lose that morbid sensibility, which among nations without liberty and without experience, renders them the sport of every alarm and every suspicion.[8]

If we replace the phrase *public assemblies* from the first sentence with *the Internet*, we come close to saying that the goal of digital transparency is to enhance user happiness. Here now we are confronted with the promise of happiness resulting from transparency. When we take as a constant from Bentham that transparency enables better argumentation and thereby increases the happiness of those who participate in argumentation, although such a statement would need specific verification since sometimes not to know facts may make people happier than knowing facts, can this standard be applied to digital communication? In other words, does digital transparency make people happier?

Because happiness is a notion that is impossible to measure precisely, I have to limit this discussion to some general statements and observations. First, some scholars have used an empirical approach and generalisation from previous studies to conclude that the positive influence of internet use is stronger for low income and young individuals.[9] This finding shows an image which is different from the happiness image associated with the transparency effect from offline communication. Thi is because low income and younger individuals can be regarded as not being as interested in argumentation and engagement in reasoned discussion than in something else. Here we see that digital transparency has a correlation with happiness but for different reasons than in the case of offline transparency.

Second, images which are transparent from the offline side are not fully transposable to the online because of the previously discussed phenomena of digital identity and personality shifts when entering the internet domain. The digital self may be a construction which has some resemblance with the

8 J. Bentham, *Works of Jeremy Bentham*, edited by J. Bowring (Bluebook 21st Essay of Political Tactics, 1843), p. 311.

9 T. Penard, N. Poussing, R. Suire, 'Does the Internet Make People Happier?' (2013) 46 *Journal of Socio-Economics*, 105–116, DOI: 10.1016/j.socec.2013.08.004.

offline self, but there is always some variance. It can be intentional when someone is interested in pursuing dual personalities, and it can be unintentional. In the first case, when someone deliberately alters one's digital self in comparison with the physical self, non-coherence turns out to be a useful instrument for constructing their digital identity. In the second case, of the unintentional alteration of the self, a person can project their self into the digital domain and see an image of variance. We can call this the unintentional non-coherence effect. Therefore, it turns out that the digital transparency of someone or something is actually the result of the opposite: concealing some features, exaggerating or downplaying others or simply because the digital reality does not allow us to exhibit our physical personality in its entirety. Here offline transparency turns into non-transparency, which is a phenomenon of non-coherence between these two domains. Here transparency does not represent Objectivity as separated from Subjectivity, but Subjectivity turned into digital Objectivity.

The previous leads to an interim conclusion. When the item to be transposed from offline to online is unclear, then the image reflected online will be further obscured. The higher the degree of the non-specificity of a human rights idea or concept offline, the more it is possible for a different domain to give the idea or concept content that is at variance. This leads us to conclude that, because the meaning of transparency is vague in the offline domain, such vagueness is carried over to the digital domain with a multiplying effect. However, the positivity associated with the perception of the transparency principle offline is considerable and can easily overshadow the objections connected to non-specificity. From the other side, the digital domain and especially digital agents may not resist the transposition of unclear concepts, since they carry little or no specific obligations. This enables digital agents to claim compliance with the principle of transparency without any direct and specific effect for users. The non-coherent effect is that prima facie the positivity of transparency loses this feature in the process of its transposition to another domain. However, a proponent of the idea of the universality of human rights core ideas and concepts, regardless of the place of its manifestation, may reject this statement of loss and hold on to the genuine priority of transparency over practice-driven factors. The reply to this proponent is that such a viewpoint leads to non-coherence between the meanings of transparency: one having its origin from the non-digital domain, and the other, domain-specific content. Here the image of transparency becomes fully ambiguous in the digital domain. In the interest of normative certainty, one would have to let go of the non-digital meaning of transparency.

14.4 SOME SPECIFICS OF DIGITAL TRANSPARENCY: RULES AND REASONING

As we need examples and more concreteness about the rules in relation to transparency, I will now turn to how transparency appears in the digital domain. This has an aspect of rules creation and the articulation of reasoning. Since the transparency of rules creation is closely connected to the matter of digital self-normativity, I will refrain from repetition here. The focus will be on the specific question of whether the decisions of digital agents, or service providers, can be deemed to be transparent. The main non-coherent aspect of transparency between digital and non-digital domains becomes apparent here. When the non-digital sphere has the capability to make decisions regarding human rights violations transparent through reasoning and arguments, the digital domain cannot. Reasoning is replaced by the argument of plain trustworthiness. This position needs some illustration.

Imagine a domestic judicial system, which only displays to the public metric measures of how many decisions the courts have rendered, the general subject matter of the cases, how many of these have been appealed and whether these were successful, the dynamics of the court resolutions and whether the applicants to the courts were satisfied with the judgments. Without any hesitation, anyone taking a look at this information would conclude that the respective court system is non-transparent since it only makes it possible to know quantitative data and not understand *why* some decisions were made. If we inquire further and ask to have access to the reasoning behind the decisions, the response would be that these do not exist. Courts in this system put forward only the conclusions and do not explain. Yet this is exactly what is considered a transparent reporting system from the side of private online enterprises. These enterprises regularly release so-called transparency reports, which only include aggregated data showing the platform's own assessment procedure and results and not the merits of the underlying cases.[10]

The insufficiency of such reports is widely pointed out in various communities, but such criticisms take as a starting point the meaning of transparency in the non-digital domain. We can look, for example, at the Kaye report, where he asserts that such reporting by itself is the result of government

[10] For a detailed overview of the transparency reports and their critique, see N. Persily, J. Ticker, *Social Media and Democracy: The State of the Field and Prospects for Reform* (Cambridge: Cambridge University Press, 2020).

pressure, and yet it lacks objectivity and sufficiency.[11] The standard, which seems widely accepted regarding human rights transparency in the digital domain, is not about the content of decisions affecting human rights, but it is about the quantity – types of decisions, subject matter and remedies. For instance, the Manila Principles stipulate in section 6 that transparency and accountability must be built into laws and policies and practices restricting content, but when we look further we see that such a principle is limited to the publication of transparency reports containing statistical and quantitative information.[12] The quantitative meaning of transparency is omnipresent in legislative instruments – current at the time of writing this monograph. Take, for example, the EU Digital Markets Act, which puts forward transparency reporting obligations for providers of intermediary services, and these include reports on the number of various orders from public authority, the number of notices regarding illegal content and the number and type of measures taken on the platform's own initiative.[13] Academic researchers have likewise adopted the distorted transparency meaning and reiterate the importance of publishing transparency reports to strengthen user rights.[14] These few examples are sufficient here to conclude that the non-coherent meaning, which is to say online-specific meaning, of transparency has emerged in the online human rights discourse and instruments, and it varies considerably from the *traditional* meaning of transparency.

14.5 TOWARDS AN ONLINE-SPECIFIC MEANING OF TRANSPARENCY

Perceptions about the limitations of the online meaning of transparency have emerged. There seems to be a desire to move from a quantity-based meaning of transparency towards a feature entailing certain qualitative elements that

[11] D. Kaye, 'Report of the Special Rapporteur on the Promotion and Protection of the Right to Freedom of Opinion and Expression' UN Doc A/70/361 (2015), p. 39; one can also look at the references regarding the transparency critique in the report.

[12] Manila Principles on Intermediary Liability, www.manilaprinciples.org, see section 6 'e' which states that intermediaries should publish transparency reports that provide specific information about all content restrictions taken by the intermediary, including actions taken on government requests, court orders, private complaint requests and enforcement of content restriction policies.

[13] Regulation (EU) 2022/2065 of the European Parliament and of the Council of 19 October 2022 on a Single Market for Digital Services and Amending Directive 2000/31/EC (Digital Services Act) (2022) OJ L 277, article 13.

[14] M. C. Kettemann (ed.), *How Platforms Respond to Human Rights Conflicts Online: Best Practices in Weighing Rights and Obligations in Hybrid Online Orders* (Hamburg: Verlag Hans-Bredow-Institut, 2022), p. 23.

make it possible to explain decisions. For instance, the European Commission artificial intelligence expert group has published a set of standards for transparency, which should enable the identification of the reasons why an AI-decision was erroneous and which, in turn, could help prevent future mistakes.[15] Subsequently, the proposal for an EU Artificial Intelligence Act enlarges the meaning of online transparency regarding artificial intelligence decisions to reveal input and output elements.[16] There are attempts to implicitly accept that the meaning of transparency online has changed and to put this into some normative shape which would then represent the explicit acceptance of the variance in the meaning. For instance, UNESCO has endorsed the assertion that, 'a third way is increasingly being proposed: to focus more on issues of process, rather than content, and especially to focus on greater transparency of the processes used by the platform companies'.[17]

We can enter into lengthy polemics about which concrete features of these processes constitute the elements of digital transparency. We can also raise issues about whether these elements are subject-neutral in order to be considered an objective basis for measuring digital transparency, since data leading to digital transparency assessments are exclusively guarded by online enterprises. Yet this would only make the case of non-coherence more solid, namely, that the difference in transparency as a core human rights principle between non-digital and digital domains is whether or not it touches on matters of content. Non-digital transparency does, and digital transparency does not. This non-coherence is explainable because of the difference in capabilities. These capabilities concern time and volume.

Because of the short time within which digital enterprises need to make decisions about user-generated content, such as blocking or allowing, they are not capable of issuing the reasons for choosing a given option. The volume of posts in social media or other online websites, which is a fact that needs no evidence, attests further to the non-affordance of reasons. From this point then, requiring online portals to have a similar level of transparency as judicial or quasi-judicial entities have in the physical world, would be like requiring a

[15] European Commission High-Level Expert Group on AI, 'Ethics Guidelines for Trustworthy AI', 8 April 2019, https://digital-strategy.ec.europa.eu/en/library/ethics-guidelines-trustworthy-aip, 18.

[16] Proposal for laying down harmonised rules on artificial intelligence and amending certain union legislative acts: Proposal for a Regulation of the European Parliament and of the Council Laying Down Harmonised Rules on Artificial Intelligence (Artificial Intelligence Act) and Amending Certain Union Legislative Acts' COM/2021/206 final (2021), article 13.

[17] A. Puddephatt, 'Letting the Sun Shine In: Transparency and Accountability in the Digital Age' UNESCO document CI-2021/WTR/5 (2021), p. 7.

one-month-old child to explain why she cries. Such a requirement towards the child would not be productive since the child is not capable of articulation. Rather, an attentive parent can focus on the objective reality surrounding the subjectivity of the child, and by knowledge-building create the conditions that are likely to diminish the chances of a repetition.

There can be multiple reasons why the image reflected in a mirror appears distorted. One is related to the features of the mirror itself – it may not capture all elements of the object(ivity) for a variety of reasons. Another is related to the change which may happen to the object(ivity) before its reflection in the mirror is captured. Since time has a different meaning within the process of the transposition of ideas and norms, the distortion of the original reality will have the following effect on non-coherence. It can happen that society B can take over the normativity and legal concepts of society A, for whatever reason – compulsion or ignorance or something else – and after this process is finally accomplished, wakes up to discover that society A has meanwhile changed and has accorded new meaning to these ideas and rules. The meaning of these new ideas and rules is already at variance with what B has transposed. Therefore, can it be the case that the concept of transparency – rooted offline and applied towards the digital realm – has undergone some conceptual transformation during the time that various actors and influencers entered into discourse about the meaning of digital privacy. Should this be the case, then non-coherence can appear either between transparency's original meaning and the meaning of digital transparency, or between the new meaning of offline transparency and the meaning of digital transparency.

Several complications exist. Domain-specific meanings of transparency are not constants and undergo challenges and interpretations from various sides. Such a discourse usually stays on the surface, having the effect of obscuring the image of transparency, but when the air is purified, the core distinction between transparency focused on the process or the content remains. Another complication lies in the possibility of simultaneous transformations of the idea of transparency in separate domains, which can lead to many combinations of non-coherence existing in parallel. All this provides that there must exist a constant which is independent of the concrete distance between human rights concepts and the ideas between the digital and non-digital domain since such a distance, or the degree of variance, is relative and determined to a large extent by practice and discourse. This constant is the assumption of non-coherence, which is to say, that non-coherence is an omnipresent feature characterising the comparison of human rights between paradigmatically different domains.

An example of the shift in the meaning of offline transparency was proposed by Pozen, who wrote about the ideological drift of transparency, connected to the realisation of the diminishing marginal returns of government transparency.[18] When in the formative periods, the ideology of an open government advocated transparency in the promotion of values such as bureaucratic rationality, social justice and trust in public institutions. Pozen has written that the current policy discourse then emphasises its capacity to check administrative abuse, enhance private choice and reduce other forms of regulation.[19] What is important here is the incremental replacement of justification using ideology with justification using concreteness. As such, and as long as there are justifications, transparency retains its legitimacy offline. It is not my point here to raise the question as to whether the concreteness remains rooted in ideology, since without such roots offline transparency would risk losing its rationality and would not stand as an autonomous concept because in such an instance it would become a highly relative principle, which would have to give way to other principles with a stronger connection to ideology.

When we consider that human rights ideas online are formulated offline and transposed from there to the online domain, then this proposition has to hold also for ideologies. Let us view now whether the ideas of service provider rationality, social justice and trust in online institutions – reformulated from Pozen's assertion to reflect the online environment – would make sense? And then move towards concreteness and ask whether the concrete goals of checks against stakeholder abuse, enhancement of user choice and reduction of regulations make equal sense online. We can find, without giving a specific example, validity in such assertions for the online concept of transparency. And yet, if a sceptic was to attach dominant weight to the proposition that online human rights concepts need to closely mirror offline concepts, then the rationality of online transparency disappears or at least weakens considerably. This would be because the greater the degree of the concreteness of human rights rules or ideas, the less it is possible to transpose without distortion. Here then, the transposition of transparency void of ideological rhetoric, such as proposed by Pozen and others, which dominates the current discourse, would be like a missionary not communicating the story of Christ but instead handing out printed Bibles and asking potential converts to read it themselves.

What we can notice at the current stage of the conceptualisation of digital transparency is the combination of general aspirations with specific guidelines. The first is represented, for instance, by the European Digital Rights and Principles, which calls in general terms for us to ensure transparency about

[18] D. E. Pozen, 'Transparency's Ideological Drift' (2018) 128 *Yale Law Journal*, 100–165.

[19] Ibid.

the use of algorithms and artificial intelligence.[20] The second is represented by the increased requirement to publish statistics, discussed earlier. Such a requirement of transparency reporting is also listed as the first new obligation in the European Commission's information website introducing the Digital Services Act and as such applies to intermediary services, hosting services, online platforms and very large platforms.[21] Because there are multiple variations of the meaning of transparency in the digital discourse, non-coherence can also appear in multiple formats. But in any event, the image of transparency as defined in the offline domain remains distorted online. This also means that the logic of the doctrinal development of human rights offline does not apply online. The distorted human rights image can only be justified through an overly simplified approach, which in turn is non-coherent with the depth of argumentation usually expected for offline human rights ideas, rules and principles.

Non-coherence appears in opposite directions on different layers between the two domains where human rights are known to exist. We can deem the physical realm to be non-transparent regarding facts and transparent regarding the process of how judicial or quasi-judicial or political decisions are taken about these facts, including some transparency about the reasons for such decisions; however, in the digital domain we see the reverse. This domain can provide transparency regarding facts and non-transparency regarding the process of how quasi-judicial decisions are taken about these facts, also excluding insights into the reasons for these decisions.

14.6 HAN'S 'TRANSPARENCY SOCIETY' IMAGE ONLINE

All of the discussion in the pervious section is based on one core assumption about the positivity of transparency. As such, the positivity can be hailed at the general ideological level or be revealed through concrete rules of accountability and procedure. An objection to this general premise of positivity has been raised in one of the most significant recent works on the concept of

[20] See the Commission's proposed declaration on European digital rights and principles under 'freedom of choice': European Commission (EC), 'European Declaration on Digital Rights and Principles', European Commission, 7 February 2023, https://digital-strategy.ec.europa.eu/en/library/european-declaration-digital-rights-and-principles, accessed 14 December 2022.

[21] European Commission, 'The Digital Services Act: Ensuring a Safe and Accountable Online Environment', European Commission, date unknown, https://commission.europa.eu/strategy-and-policy/priorities-2019-2024/europe-fit-digital-age/digital-services-act-ensuring-safe-and-accountable-online-environment_en, accessed 4 April 2023.

transparency by Byung-Chul Han in *The Transparency Society*.[22] Because of its significance, some key ideas about the *society of positivity* have to be reproduced here. Han has the following observations:

> *Wherever information is very easy to obtain, as is the case today, the social system switches from trust to control. The society of transparency is not a society of trust, but a society of control.*[23]
>
> *The digital society of control makes intensive use of freedom. It is only possible thanks to voluntary self-illumination and self-exposure. It exploits freedom. The society of control achieves perfection when its inhabitants do not communicate because of external constraint but out of inner need – that is, when the fear of giving up a private and intimate sphere yields to the need to put oneself on display shamelessly.*[24]

He then goes on to formulate the idea of positivity as such:

> *The omnipresent demand for transparency, which has reached the point of fetishism and totalisation, goes back to a paradigm shift that cannot be restricted to the realm of politics and economics. Today the society of negativity is yielding to a society that progressively dismantles negativity in favor of positivity. Accordingly, the society of transparency manifests itself first and foremost as a society of positivity.*[25]

Such positivity, as asserted by Han, means no tolerance towards negative feelings, a lack of sensitivity towards confidentiality, proliferation and propagation instead of a search for the truth and in short, presenting reality in a distorted light. The supporter of this philosophical approach can quickly conclude that transparency in human rights law serves the goal of positivity enhancement. Yet non-coherence has a magnifying effect upon value judgments connected with human rights ideas or principles when these are transposed from one paradigm to another. This means that the positivity associated with transparency also increases in the digital domain. Since the digital space enables close to complete transparency, and the perpetuation of the transparency through data storage and *not forgetting*, it could be said that human rights law measures in the digital domain enable as high a transparency as possible, and have to be given the *quality* label. This in turn also means that almost anything which the private domain puts forward as self-

[22] B.-C. Han, *The Transparency Society*, translated by E. Butler (Stanford: Stanford University Press, 2015).

[23] Ibid., p. vii.

[24] Ibid., p. viii.

[25] Ibid., p. 1.

normativity, and any practice implemented to enhance transparency, would without hesitancy be viewed as positive features. Digital transparency here becomes a shield against any critique of self-normativity and non-accountability. As such, it appears quite close to the contemporary concept of non-digital transparency, as it seems that many policy decisions and rules are justified as if in the service of transparency.

The objections to the positivity of transparency raised in the non-digital domain lead us likewise to a magnified image of negativity in the digital domain. In other words, a proponent of Han's assertion claiming negativity would see that such negativity grows upon transposition. Then it becomes questionable whether transparency, when dominated by negativity, any longer corresponds to the original meaning of transparency, as one is used to from the traditional human rights discourse. According to the non-coherence approach, when a concept from the physical realm is transposed into the digital domain and non-coherence becomes wide, its core meaning changes. Then it is already exhibiting features where the connection to its meaning before transposition is weakened to the point that one can speak of a break. The higher the degree of supposed transparency and openness in the digital domain, the stronger the immanence that many features remain hidden. This is because in the conditions of ideal transparency the term loses its meaning, and it can only be defined in combination with the opposite. Complete or close to complete transparency has to mean the simultaneous existence of complete or close to complete non-transparency. This is not difficult to explain, since digital transparency reflects a combination of how one wishes to be seen against what one wishes to hide. We can put it differently and say that since the immanent feature of complete digital transparency is positivity on the surface, there is also non-transparent negativity beneath the surface, or behind the mirror.

This is why digital and non-digital transparency are non-coherent. Their features are an inherent polarisation between negativity and positivity and are incapable of surmounting this divide by allowing features that explain the reasons for the decisions and actions.

15

Legal Certainty and Uncertainty

15.1 THE CONNECTING FUNCTIONALITY

One of the core beliefs in human rights discourse and practice concerns the connecting function of legal certainty. It seems unquestioned that without legal certainty, any human rights system of rules and principles does not make sense. Placed centrally, legal certainty concerns human rights ideas, concreticised in rules and principles. These ideas should constitute in practice and in the ideal dimension the core of any domestic and international legal system and judicial thought. Such ideas stand at the foundation of any judicial normative hierarchy, which is of theoretical and practical consequences. Any system of ideas which is based on some core assertion(s) weakens or collapses when these assertions suddenly become uncertain themselves, or if they disappear entirely. From the theoretical side, for instance, a holistic human rights system would weaken or disappear if we were to question beyond rhetoric whether it is certain that equality, decency and personal freedom stand as its cornerstones. Take these ideas away from the fundament, and the walls and roof tumble into ruins. As such, certainty could be viewed as a limitation for theoretical thought, because it would eliminate or discourage the exploration of some areas and the asking of some questions. If someone says, '[d]ecency is the core human rights value offline and online', and then is countered with the question '[a]re you certain?', a sceptic could already find such certainty threatened. Yet such an approach could be an oversimplification, since certainty as a general concept, and especially legal certainty, does not mean that certain questions cannot be asked. Objections against the possibility of questions challenging certainty by itself strengthen the outlook of uncertainty. In such a case, we would seem to be expecting that responses to these questions would shatter the status quo of something of great significance. Here we could see the limitation of legal certainty, and that means excluding some areas completely.

The practical consequence of legal certainty is the expectation of patterns in judicial and quasi-judicial decisions. Another practical implication of legal certainty is the incremental nature of normative changes. It can be shown that polarised predictions concerning legal certainty can be raised towards one and the same legal instrument at the stage of rules creation and rhetoric; that is, when the instrument has yet to become implemented and before observations from practice can add weight to either side. For instance, Castermans et al. analysed the EU Digital Single Market Act before it entered into force and pointed out to the EU Commission that the new regulation enables traders to rely on a common set of rules and use the same contract terms, thereby reducing unnecessary costs while providing a high degree of legal certainty.[1] This view was reportedly countered from the other side, when the European Consumer Organisation BEUC expressed the opposite view, namely that this instrument would increase legal complexity and introduce great legal uncertainty.[2]

These observations are indeed on a highly general level, and as such not capable of providing too much material for drawing conclusions about similarities and differences concerning legal certainty in offline and online domains. The only commonality which transpires is the connecting functionality of legal certainty within concrete human rights paradigms. Yet, this remains abstract, and a closer and more detailed look is therefore needed.

15.2 LEGAL CERTAINTY AND THE BASIC NORM

15.2.1 *The Expectation of Interrelationship*

Legal certainty appears to be intrinsically bridged to the concept of a basic norm. This means that, for different reasons, their interrelationship is essential for holding together a normative system such as a human rights system. It can even be said that Kelsen's idea of a basic norm remains an abstract consideration without the concept of legal certainty. Legal certainty turns the ideal dimension of a basic norm into a real dimension. For sure, a basic norm taken in isolation contains no information about its practicality because for an observer in isolation only its non-positive origin is revealed. However, it seems undeniable that if this basic norm was to disappear or be replaced, the

1 A. G. Castermans, R. De Graaf, M. Haentjens, 'The Digital Single Market and Legal Certainty: A Critical Analysis' in A. C. Ciacchi (ed.), *Contents and Effects of Contracts: Lessons to Learn from the Common European Sales Law*, Studies in European Economic Law and Regulation Volume 7 (New York: Springer Cham, 2016), p. 46: DOI 10.1007/978-3-319-28074-5_5.

2 Ibid.

substantive side of the legal system would collapse or undergo profound alterations because all ideas which are not constitutive elements of basic norms could now be challenged beyond justifiability since there would be no support from a normative system connected by the basic norm. These alterations, if a normative system by itself were to continue, would not matter from the position of legal certainty because legal certainty at first glance is not concerned with the substance of law. Here, legal certainty would become a guarantor that the fundamental features of the normative system remain intact regardless of the content of the basic norm because legal certainty appears to stand outside the categories of what is right and what is wrong, as these categories under the umbrella of legal certainty are being replaced by correctness and incorrectness in relation to the normative system. Another way to say this would be to suggest that if a normative system was to appear which is almost completely of an amoral character, the certainty that such an amoral normative system is put into practice can still remain. Therefore, one could in such a situation be certain than amorality becomes a standard. Unfortunately, as the case may be, these examples are not too difficult to find from recent history.

However, one needs to ask whether the connection between the concept of a basic norm and legal certainty is one of mutual inclusion. The concept of a basic norm obtains its meaning largely through the concept of legal certainty, and legal certainty's principle function is to strengthen the basic norm. This would form such a dependency with a constitutive connection between the two concepts. To illustrate, the basic norm would lose its meaning if the instrument of legal certainty was not capable of ensuring that it is discoverable at every part of the normative order, even if we are facing secondary norms of little importance, and even if the search would mean intellectual and quantitative effort. Furthermore, legal certainty could not be construed without a normative hierarchical structure, having at its bottom one or a set of some basic norms. If we were to consider the previous observations as logical and correct for the offline domain, then the following question is whether such mutual inclusiveness is transposed to the digital domain.

This is a broader question about whether any regulatory system necessarily entails a mutually inclusive connection between the main idea or ideas of that regulatory system, from one side, and legal certainty of the regulation from the other side. Various approaches of instrumentalism and pragmatism could be introduced here. These could contribute to the discussion of variance between the digital and non-digital domains from a different aspect, namely whether something considered a weakness in a non-digital domain becomes even a greater weakness in the digital domain. This means that the non-coherence effect of transposition magnifies the properties characterising the mutual connection between various elements of the human rights non-digital system.

Take, for example, Dewey's writing on the instrumentalist nature of legal decisions, where he claims that, '[t]he "universal" stated in the major premise is not outside of an antecedent to particular cases; neither is it a selection of something found in a variety of cases. It is an indication of a single way of treating cases for certain purposes or consequences in spite of their diversity'.[3] Here the weak connection between the ideal and practical characters of normativity is presented as a condition *sine qua non*, and it can be taken that such a weakness may become a standard for the non-digital domain. And yet such a connection has the assumption of certainty about the very existence of the 'universal' somewhere in legal argumentation, even if it remains dormant in most instances. Upon the transposition of elements from one domain to another, the strength of the connections between the elements transposed changes. The constant is the change itself, and the variable is the connection. Weaknesses become even greater weaknesses and strengths become even stronger. This is what has to be assumed when all other variables are constant or unimportant. However, once the connection between some elements of the human rights offline system exhibits a different property after transposition, then it has to be assumed that some additional factors have entered the scene and may turn the weakness of the connection into a strength, or the reverse. Here, if the central element of the instrumentalist approach is the weakness between universalism and practical consequences, and this approach is applied to the digital domain without additional variables, the interrelationship between a basic norm and practicality cannot be construed. This is because the weakness grows to such a magnitude that universality is completely lost during transposition. The digital instrumentalist image contains no features of universality. This is a clear threat for the viewer from the physical domain of what might be expected upon exit from this domain – complete dominance by practicality and the absence of universality. For the purposes of our attention here, the consequence seems the absence of causal connection between a basic norm and legal certainty in the digital domain. Now a proponent of the idea of theoretical paradigms enters the scene and cautions that the previous does not tell us anything valuable about human rights in the

[3] J. Dewey, 'My Philosophy of Law' in J. A. Boydson (ed.), *John Dewey: The Later Works, 1925–1953: 1925: Experience and Nature (1) (Collected Works of John Dewey 1882–1953)* (Carbondale: Southern Illinois University Press, 2008), p. 115.

digital domain, and the only conclusion is about the reservation of the reasonableness of utilising a paradigm-centred theory such as instrumentalism.

For the sake of further illustration, suppose that one day astronauts land on a remote planet and discover a society which is very different from ours. But the society seems to operate well, as far as they can tell. Should they assume that such a society, where a regulatory framework is to be assumed, holds some core values or ideas as most prominent, and there are behavioural and remedial patterns in the service of these values, resembling legal certainty in terrestrial terms? Or if we examine the animal world, should we assume that the behavioural patterns of ants – which appears to a nature-lover to be a highly organised society based on some regulation – stands in the service of one or a number of common high values. Perhaps we can make the claim that the highest value is the continuity of the colony. In both examples, humans may not be able to communicate with these communities and ask questions. And yet, can our universal perception of how a normative system is construed be taken as an assumption – taking this concept very broadly and allowing the understanding that repetition and patterns exhibit normativity? A negation of the possibility of some basic values in these communities – on the remote planet or for ants – standing at the bottom of behaviour and normativity, would lead us to conclude that these communities are beyond non-coherence with the physical community of human animals. We can look, but we may not understand. This negation is avoidable for the digital domain, and differences in domains are explainable through non-coherence.

15.2.2 *Variance in Meanings*

The image becomes complicated due to the variety of variables and possible mutual combinations since we not only have to consider the connection between the basic norm and the principle of legal certainty but first, whether the meanings of the basic norm and legal certainty are comparable between the two domains in question. For simplicity, it will suffice here to explore the process of the genesis of these expressions, and then look at the compatibility of the conceptualisation of legal certainty offline with the online realities. To build our understanding of the genesis, whether we can speak of the simultaneous emergence of the idea of a basic norm and of legal certainty is important, or whether it is more justified to support the view that for legal certainty to make sense, a system is needed where the basic norm is already established. Yet another way to put this is to claim that in the offline human rights system, legal certainty has to be seen as standing in the service of the basic idea(s), and henceforth without such basic idea(s), the concept of legal certainty does not exist; it is transformed into something different.

A similar view, rooted in the importance of time, was expressed by Dworkin insisting that, 'the law – the rights and duties that flow from past collective decisions and for that reason licence or require coercion – contains not only the narrow explicit content of these decisions but also, more broadly, the scheme of principles necessary to justify them. History matters because that scheme of principle must justify the standing as well as the content of these past decisions'.[4] When time is an element needed not only for the appearance of the concept of legal certainty but also allowing it to assume the connecting function between the ideal dimension of normativity and practicality, does it not follow that there simply is an insufficiency of this element to speak of legal certainty as a solidified aspect of the digital human rights system? If this is the case, which in my view makes sense and has to be defended, it follows that digital and non-digital human rights paradigms are widely variant in terms of legal certainty. It is necessary once again, to have a closer look at how the concept of legal certainty is commonly understood in relation to non-digital human rights systems, and from there draw conclusions about the concept's possibility in or transposability into the digital human rights system. And thereafter look at how some legal instruments present certainty in particular reference to the digital domain.

15.2.3 *Legal and Social Uncertainties*

We are told by interdisciplinary theorists that to comprehend physical normativity, legal uncertainty originates conceptually from social uncertainty and is related to the sense of incomplete information about the behaviour of others; the gap between certainty and uncertainty can be narrowed through a social practice of trial and error and the observation of others and the acceptance of path dependencies.[5] The question here is whether these assumptions can be transferred without variance to the digital domain. The position to be argued says that even if the concept of digital social uncertainty can be defended, such uncertainty has to be much narrower than physical social uncertainty. An extremist might even ask whether there can be any social uncertainty in the digital domain, which is a construed reality, because the roots of social uncertainty are in the natural world.

4 R. Dworkin, *Law's Empire* (Cambridge, MA: Harvard University Press, 1986), p. 175.

5 L. Viellechner, 'The Network of Networks: Karl-Heinz Ladeur's Theory of Law and Globalization' (2009) 10 *German Law Journal*, 4, 518.

Assuming that the degree of the incompleteness of information about the behaviour of others is reduced in the digital domain due to the *Internet never forgetting* or various e-governance solutions (discussed shortly in a subsequent section), we should be able to agree at least that social uncertainty in the digital domain is narrower in comparison with the non-digital domain. On top of this, we are also confronted with the phenomena of algorithmic *prisons*, big data and profiling, which allow collective probabilities to be transformed into predicted actions for individuals.[6] These phenomena alter and crystallise the scope of information collected and stored about the behaviour of others because of their functional focus. The conceptual origin of legal certainty in the digital domain appears in strong variance with the origin of legal certainty in the physical realm. Therefore, one of the following is correct. Either legal certainty is a concept which does not fit into the digital human rights architecture, being a concept which is artificially applied and does not reflect the digital realities, or there have to be different origins and functions for the concept. Either way there is non-coherence between the two domains. The consequence is far-reaching since legal certainty constitutes one of the key components of the human rights normative and conceptual system as we are accustomed to it so far. Unless a specific justification can be shown, legal certainty remains an instrument making no or little sense digitally. The magnitude of this consequence becomes apparent from the following.

15.3 LEGAL CERTAINTY AND JUSTICE

15.3.1 *The Argument from Limits to Relativism*

Radbruch more concretely than Kelsen considered legal certainty to be one of the pillars of contemporary legal systems, standing outside the scope of relativity. This assertion is put forward by Borowski and related to the argument from limits to relativism.[7] His argument rests on the analysis of Radbruch's three pillars of any legal system, which are justice, purposiveness and legal certainty. While purposiveness has a generic character of relativity, determining who and what are equal or unequal in particular circumstances, Borowski shows that there are exceptions expressed by Radbruch to relativistic

[6] H.-Y. Liu, Hin-Yan, 'Digital Disruption of Human Rights' in M. Susi (ed.), *Human Rights, Digital Society and the Law: A Research Companion* (London: Routledge, 2019), p. 85.

[7] M. Borowski, 'Radbruch's Formula and Human Rights' in M. La Torre, L. Niglia, M. Susi (eds.), *The Quest for Rights: Ideal and Normative Dimensions* (Northampton, MA: Edward Elgar Publishing, 2019), pp. 27–48.

purposiveness, and in particular because '[t]here are a number of legal provisions which are dictated by no purposiveness at all but solely by justice or legal certainty'.[8] Now we are confronted with the realisation that when legal certainty carries a different meaning in the digital domain, if at all identifiable as a concept with any utility, then one of the two non-relative pillars of any human rights system is likewise taken out. To put this differently, if legal certainty does not have the same functionality in the digital domain as in the non-digital domain, its meaning has to be in variance. When legal certainty as one of the non-relative pillars of the digital human rights system collapses, then the sole idea of justice, if we adhere to Radbruch's understanding of law, remains the last stand against digital relativity.

15.3.2 *Legal Certainty* Contra *Justice*

We can proceed to view how these two concepts of legal certainty and justice, both of which are immune to relativism, were interpreted by Radbruch, and whether such an interpretation might be transferable to the digital domain. A closer inspection of how Radbruch opened the concept of legal certainty is now in order. His seminal approach is related to the distinction between regulation in ordinary times and extraordinary times, the first dominated by legal certainty and the second by justice. This is what is known:

> *The resolution of the [possible] conflict between justice and legal certainty may well be found in a formula such as this: Preference is given to the positive law, duly enacted and secured by state power as it is, even when it is unjust and fails to benefit the people, unless its conflict with justice reaches so intolerable a level that the statute becomes, in effect, 'false law' and must therefore yield to justice ... One line of distinction, however, can be drawn with utmost clarity: Where there is not even an attempt at justice, where equality, the core of justice, is deliberately betrayed in the issuance of positive law, then the statute is not merely 'false law', it lacks completely the very nature of law. For law, including positive law, cannot be otherwise defined than as a system and an institution whose very meaning is to serve justice.*[9]

When confronted with a statement like this, which touches the deepest core of a normative system in one domain, such as the physical realm of human civilisation, one has to *translate* the physical context into a digital one to test its applicability.

8 Ibid., p. 43.

9 G. Radbruch, B. Litschewski Paulson, S. L. Paulson, 'Statutory Lawlessness and Supra-Statutory Law (1946)' (2006) 26 *Oxford Journal of Legal Studies*, 1, 2–3.

Therefore, paraphrasing Radbruch, the conflict between legal certainty (leaving open for the moment its specific scope and meaning in the digital domain) and justice could at first be resolved by giving preference to self-normativity by digital actors, even if it appears unjust and does not benefit the users of the digital solutions and social media. This statement can perhaps be defended, and it would not be necessary here to give examples of how the economic benefits of private service providers, and backdoors left semi-open to public institutions to utilise electronic data for the surveillance and monitoring of peoples' behaviour, stand as threats to private users.[10] We are accustomed to operating in a digital world where we are watched and which knows us better than we ourselves do, but the common harms are balanced by what we think is useful from digital solutions.

But the real question is, at what point will the certainty flowing from self-regulation appear to run deliberately counter to the idea of justice. Over and above this, the meaning of justice in the digital domain emerges. According to the available discourse, the idea of justice appears to be non-relative; that it, its meaning is not determined by the concrete normative domain but stands above any such specific domain. This claim of non-relativity by itself runs counter to non-coherence theory, which says that normative concepts and ideas must have a certain degree of variance between different domains. As such, justice in the digital domain should carry a different meaning from justice in the non-digital domain, a proponent of non-coherence theory might argue. Yet such a distorted image of justice does not appear from discourse. For instance, the World Economic Forum in 2021 has identified three main obstacles to digital justice, which are, first, inadequate privacy-based protections; second, limited legal solutions; and third, a lack of fair process in automated decision-making.[11] This is a clear attempt to define justice in the digital sphere through non-digital tools. This is not surprising, and is explainable due to the authors not comprehending the non-coherence between the two distinct domains, and the variance in meanings resulting from the uncritical transposition of conceptual tools. The offline model of thinking about a conflict between legal certainty and justice in the digital domain becomes arbitrary and therefore irrational since the elements of certainty and justice are non-coherent in comparison with the original meaning of the model's

[10] For example, Miloon Kothari has given an overview of the various tools of repression which are enabled by digital solutions, and which are not possible in the physical realm; see M. Kohtari, 'The Sameness of Human Rights Online and Offline' in M. Susi (ed.), *Human Rights, Digital Society and the Law: A Research Companion* (London: Routledge, 2019), pp. 24–28.

[11] E. Cheikosman, S. Fazelpour and S. Warren, 'Pathways to Digital Justice – White Paper', *World Economic Forum*, 29 September 2021, p. 11.

elements. The question to be approached with hesitancy is that, after realising that the concept of legal certainty is at variance between the digital and non-digital domains, is there any assurance – through practice-driven dogma – that the idea of justice likewise does not appear at variance. Because if no such assurance can be given, all stands against relativity have fallen.

15.4 THE PROBLEM FROM ARGUMENTATION

15.4.1 *On Practicality*

In Radbruch's view, legal certainty not only requires the validity of legal rules laid down by power and factually carried through, but it also makes demands on their content, in particular that any normativity should be capable of being administered with certainty so that it can be practicable.[12] The matter of practicality has to be highlighted here because as soon as one eliminates from the background of legal certainty the requirement of compliance with justice, the digital domain can show highly practical solutions. The increase in automated decisions applying self-normativity can in fact lead to a much higher degree of certainty than in the non-digital domain. This may be partly explainable by the scarcity of or limitations on the argumentation these decisions are expected to produce or to be capable of, which is a separate matter discussed elsewhere in this monograph. Yet it leads to the problem of correlation between legal certainty and argumentation. From the perspective of non-coherence, it does not suffice to say that legal certainty has a different meaning in the digital domain, since this would also weaken the concept's original meaning. At all times when a normative concept is used with different meanings in non-compatible domains, one meaning would appear to prevail over another. And always in these instances, a sceptical view might emerge saying that the digital image is as real as the original.

15.4.2 *On Predictability*

Building on the problem of correlation between legal certainty and argumentation, it can be said that since argumentation stands as an inherent element of certainty, at one point its scarcity leaves the concept of legal certainty empty. In this case, an alternative concept would be more appropriate to enter the stage. Since the digital domain is dominated by mathematics driven solutions,

[12] E. Lask, G. Radbruch, J. Dabin, *The Legal Philosophies of Lask, Radbruch and Dabin*, translated by Kurt Wilk, (Cambridge, MA: Harvard University Press, 1950), p. 109.

predictability seems more precisely to characterise a similar function in the digital domain, which legal certainty performs in the non-digital domain. This concerns the potential to foresee quasi-judicial or judicial decisions as a reaction to people's behaviour. The difference between legal certainty and predictability is manifold.

To start, legal certainty entails both normative and descriptive elements, whereas predictability only the latter. Roessler coins this as the difference in the thickness.[13] Frischmann and Selinger assert that in digital space humans risk losing themselves to become increasingly predictable.[14] Building a regulatory practice upon self-normativity and predictability might be justifiable from a purely instrumentalist viewpoint; for instance, Posner's claims that even a pragmatist philosophical theory is irrelevant to legal pragmatism and legal practice.[15] But the danger of non-complementarity lies elsewhere. Absence of the idealism of justice and replacement of legal certainty with digital predictability is manipulation, which under Radbruch's model would mount to a flagrant denial of justice, but in the digital domain might not.[16] This is because the idea of justice appears in tandem with legal certainty, and if one element from the tandem is missing, it does not exist. The idea of justice is exactly the element which distinguishes legal certainty from predictability. There is justice present in legal certainty but not in predictability.

If this view is correct, non-coherence theory says that in order to speak of legal certainty in the digital domain, a domain-specific concept of justice has to be developed. But this would already lead to a far-reaching conclusion that there can exist different ideas of justice, which is a phenomenon of relativity reaching to the deepest bottom of human rights systems. A commonality would therefore need to be found between the concepts of legal certainty and predictability. Such commonality can be found from the functions of legal certainty and predictability, where the outcome of a judicial or quasi-judicial assessment assumes the existence of standards which are constant. Pursuing this commonality leads to the term the *thesis of immunity to time*.

[13] B. Roessler, 'Mark of the Human: On the Concept of the Digital Human Being, Opinion by Beate Roessler' (2021) 7 *European Data Protection Law Review*, 2, 157–160.

[14] B. Frischmann, E. Selinger, *Re-engineering Humanity* (Cambridge: Cambridge University Press, 2018).

[15] R. Posner, *Law, Pragmatism and Democracy* (Cambridge, MA: Harvard University Press, 2005), pp. 32–33.

[16] For example, and especially in reference to instances like the Cambridge Analytica scandal, which is a clear consequence of digital predictability from personality traits, see more in D. Susser, B. Roessler, H. Nissenbaum, 'Online Manipulation: Hidden Influences in a Digital World' (2019) 4 *Georgetown Law Technology Review*, 1, 9–12.

This means that in both non-digital and digital human rights domains there exists an expectation that whatever the standards are, these do not change and are applied. Non-coherence theory is based on the understanding of at least some commonalities when different normative systems are compared. This substantiation leads to a conclusion from a different perspective, which is that digital and non-digital human rights systems have a common element of immunity to time, appearing either in the format of legal certainty or the expectation of predictability.

Doubts can be raised whether amidst the abundant literature, decisions and policy documents, such a distinction can be justified. Perhaps a sceptic of non-coherence theory and proponent of the sameness doctrine could assert that these two terms have a largely overlapping meaning and their usage is a matter of habit and not deliberate choice. Still, for the reader of academic literature and media postings, examining the discourse of IT law and social media communication models reveals the dominant usage of the term *predictability*, whereas the term *certainty* is almost non-existent. This is the voice from practice. Quantitative research would be able to produce more accurate figures, which is not possible in the context of this monograph. Yet the strictly human rights academic discourse holds to the terminology from the offline domain and by applying this to digital realities arrives at images which are distorted. One comparative study (among many) into online stakeholder practices and recommendations was put forward in 2022 by the Global Digital Human Rights Network.[17] This study has the following assertion among its conclusions: 'In other words, even though the alleged infringement of right not to be discriminated against handled by the platform is a quicker and more efficient way to justice, it lowers legal certainty. Therefore, controlling the access to content and services has to be subject to judicial review.'[18] Here we note that although platforms have the capability to resolve matters in a predictable manner, there is an objection that it runs counter to the principle of legal certainty. This objection becomes unjustified if one is to take the non-coherence approach seriously and consider that the concept of legal certainty is arbitrary for the digital domain. But the main mistake in the quoted passage is breaking the interrelationship between legal certainty and justice, as it is asserted as if justice can be achieved through predictability alone. The mistake is because this assertion allows fragmentation into the

[17] M. C. Kettemann (ed.), *How Platforms Respond to Human Rights Conflicts Online: Best Practices in Weighing Rights and Obligations in Hybrid Online Orders* (Hamburg: Verlag Hans-Bredow-Institut, 2022).

[18] Ibid., p. 64.

meaning of justice. Yet the quoted passage, perhaps surprisingly, justifies the pivotal point of non-coherence theory, namely that legal ideas and doctrines are reshaped during transposition into another domain. Here we can think that such a transposition leads to the appearance of justice and legal certainty with a meaning in variance. Justice achieved through online predictable content assessment is not the same justice achieved via judicial assessment following the principle of legal certainty.

15.5 FIVE PARADOXES

Yet an additional recourse to the traditional meaning of legal certainty may be in order to validate the scope of variance between this concept and its reflection in the digital domain. Here the five paradoxes formulated by Popelier in reference to legal certainty will be explored.[19] Such a view would add a nuance to the non-coherence approach since it may or may not appear that concepts having a meaning in variance can still be characterised by similar paradoxes. These paradoxes are:[20]

(1) The principle of legal certainty demands certainty, whereas uncertainty is an inherent part of the legal order.
(2) The more the legal aspect of human relations prevails in society, the more accessibility of legislation becomes a basic requirement on the one hand, and a *mission impossible* on the other.
(3) The review of legislation in light of the principle of legal certainty is itself unpredictable.
(4) Objective uncertainty (accessibility) leads to justified subjective uncertainty (respect for legitimate expectations).
(5) The legal invalidation of a legal rule, for being contrary to the principle of legal certainty, leads to even more legal uncertainty.

The responses from digital human rights to these paradoxes are as follows, based on the premise that the digital domain is characterised by predictability rather than certainty. Can the claim that uncertainty is an inherent part of any normative order be transposed into the digital order and translated to say that unpredictability is an inherent part of it? The decisive element in comparison is the immunity to time thesis, formulated a few paragraphs ago, and because legal certainty is correlated to the idea of justice, it can never stand alone as an

[19] P. Popelier, 'Five Paradoxes of Legal Certainty and the Lawmaker' (2008) 2 *Legisprudence*, 1, 47–66, DOI: 10.1080/17521467.2008.11424673.
[20] Ibid., 49.

absolute demand and is influenced by the correlation between justice and positive law. On the other hand, if my view that predictability is not correlated to justice is correct, we see that the aspiration of predictability can become an absolute expectation. Imagine two drivers speeding and the first is caught by a police officer with a radar, and the other's speeding is noted by an automated camera. For the first driver, the speeding fine is not fully certain, since she may be able explain alleviating circumstances, or the police officer may suddenly be called to another situation. For the second driver, the speeding fine is fully predictable. The results may end up the same, both drivers having to pay a fine, but the route to this end is non-coherent.

The second paradox is rooted in the observation of the uncontrolled growth of normative instruments. In other words, legal certainty in the physical realm becomes an increasingly abstract idea since attempts to secure the knowledge which concrete instruments apply or could apply become unachievable and unbearable. The argument from the intensity of normative regulation appears distorted in the digital image for two reasons. The first is related to the discrepancy between the scope of regulations originating from digital and non-digital domains. When self-normativity remains scarce and is satisfied with generally worded statements, non-digital regulation is characterised by a growth in positive law instruments and policy documents. The gap is growing. The second reason is to question whether the paradox that accessibility to normativity becomes more and more a basic requirement holds also to digital solutions users. Until there appears evidence to support this assertion, the second paradox may not hold. This is partly because digital self-normativity can change at an unpredictable speed.

The third paradox, as explained by Popelier in the cited work with references to Dworkin and Alexy, concerns the matter that legal certainty does not require absolute certainty, as it is merely a principle used for normative argumentation.[21] Predictability, on the other hand, has as its ultimate goal the achievement of absolute certainty. To put it differently, when the principle of legal certainty can be utilised in complex judicial argumentation, then predictability is a tool outside of judicial argumentation, and stands at the centre of quasi-judicial argumentation. From here, the level of possible argumentation based on either the principle of legal certainty or predictability appears widely at variance. There is an assumption of argumentation for the non-digital domain and an assumption of little or no argumentation for the digital domain. This is a clear revelation of non-coherence.

[21] Popelier (n 19), 61.

Non-coherence is likewise apparent in the fourth paradox related to objective uncertainty leading to subjective uncertainty. It appears in two opposite and distinct aspects. For the physical realm, this paradox rests on the fact that it is possible to distinguish between objectively existing norms (objective certainty) on the one hand, and the expectation that these rules are applied (subjective certainty). However, if my assumption that digital predictability is unconnected to the idea of justice has merit, or that the connection is distorted, then predictability means only subsumption or existing rules, whereby weighing remains marginal and necessitates human input. This applies to blockchain and various e-governance solutions. An objection from the practice of private stakeholders can be raised, which refers to the practice of using tens of thousands of human moderators to assess user comments and user posted content. Here we are confronted by an entirely different situation, where the rules applied by content moderators, either human or non-human, remain abstract and would not meet the criteria of objective certainty. It can therefore be argued that content moderation outcomes are not predictable objectively and are therefore taken subjectively. What follows is multifaceted non-coherence, depending on the concrete digital environment and solutions applied.

The image of the fifth paradox in the digital realm says that the invalidation of a rule due to being contrary to the notion of predictability, increases unpredictability. This paradox cannot be justified because the invalidation of a legal rule in the physical realm occurs when it collides with a higher principle, such as the idea of justice. Since the notion of predictability is a stand-alone concept in the digital domain, and as such can be considered to belong among the foundational concepts, it cannot be invalidated for the reason of a collision simply because it has the highest weight in the digital space. Yet digital rules change, but not for the reason of invalidation due to contradicting the notion of unpredictability. Since the invalidation of digital self-normative rules by itself is often for unpredictable reasons, which prima facie belong to other categories than judicial or quasi-judicial argumentation, then it follows that unpredictability from the objective side becomes subjective predictability about objective unpredictability. Once again, the image is distorted and fragmented, and explainable because of non-coherence.

15.6 LEGAL CERTAINTY AND DIGITAL PREDICTABILITY IN SOME INSTRUMENTS

It now remains to examine how the notions of legal certainty and predictability are used in some selected normative. Surprisingly, the terms *legal certainty* and *predictability* are scarce in most digital human rights instruments. As such, the African Declaration and the Brazilian Internet Bill of Rights do not contain these expressions at all. There are sporadic mentions in discourse; for instance, Branco asserts that prior to the adoption of the Brazilian Internet Bill of Rights, the, 'so-called legal certainty principle was non-existent'.[22] Nor are these expressions to be found in the European Declaration on Digital Rights and Principles for the Digital Decade. Yet there are many instruments where the terms *certainty* and *predictability* appear, and a closer examination reveals the brilliant triumph of the non-coherence approach. For instance, the EU Digital Services Act includes both expressions, and predictability is used in connection to the online environment, where legal certainty in connection to the vertical legislation is put forward by international and domestic bodies.[23] A similar approach, although implicit, may be found from the UN Secretary-General 2020 roadmap for digital cooperation, with its call for legislative authorities to aim for legal certainty and for private companies to aim for predictability in company-specific actions.[24] In international legal instruments, the choice of expressions may be random, but if used, they do not miss the point that the principle of legal certainty transforms into predictability upon transposition from the non-digital to the digital domain. The variance is wide, the image of legal certainty becomes heavily distorted in the digital mirror. Because predictability loses its connection to qualitative standards, it is uni-layered instead of multilayered, and devoid of argumentation. The only commonality between legal certainty and predictability appears through the immunity to time thesis, and this is the main element allowing us to speak of non-coherence, since at least some common elements need to exist.

[22] S. Branco, 'Notes on Brazilian Internet Regulation' in C. A. Souza, M. Viola, R. Lemos (eds.), *Brazil's Internet Bill of Rights: A Closer Look*, 2nd ed. (Rio de Janeiro: Institute for Technology and Society of Rio de Janeiro (ITS Rio), 2017), p. 53.

[23] See, for example, the wording that the goal of the Act is to 'ensure safe, predictable and trusted online environment' – items 12 and 106 of the preamble and chapter 1, article 1, subparagraph 2 (b), Regulation (EU) 2022/2065 of the European Parliament and of the Council of 19 October 2022 on a Single Market for Digital Services and Amending Directive 2000/31/EC (Digital Services Act) (2022) OJ L 277.

[24] U.N., 'Road Map for Digital Cooperation: Implementation of the Recommendations of the High-Level Panel on Digital Cooperation' (2020). The wording of item 87 is as follows: 'I also call upon Member States to place human rights at the centre of regulatory frameworks and legislation on the development and use of digital technologies. In a similar vein, I call upon technology leaders urgently and publicly to acknowledge the importance of protecting the right to privacy and other human rights in the digital space and take clear, company-specific actions to do so.'

All of the aforementioned demonstrates that non-coherence is to be assumed in the transposition of normative ideas and rules from one well-established normative domain to another. Here we observed a specific phenomenon of non-coherence, which is a simplification and move towards thinness because predictability can, by and large, be considered legal certainty without qualitative elements, such as the ideas of justice or equality. Yet another feature of non-coherence theory is its neutrality towards the transformed images of human rights in the digital domain. This theory is not a tool for quality control or qualitative assessment of ideas before and after transformation. It merely alerts us to the non-coherence assumption. Now, can we accept that the non-coherent image reflects a normative system where some or most elements stand outside of a certain system of values. Critical questions can be asked, even if such a system were to contradict the value system of the viewer towards the distorted image. Or even if we were not able to comprehend the features of a hierarchical system which we are accustomed to term as a value system. Does wide non-coherence mean a weakening of a value-based normative system? There always remains the option to say that the absence of a value system is valuable by itself.

Yet before we end this section, a reflection on legal certainty and predictability may be in order. In the late 2010s, I listened to a conference speech by Robert Spano, then the judge at the European Court of Human Rights. During the Q&A session Spano asked the audience of more than 300 listeners, whether they would prefer to fly in a plane piloted by humans or artificial intelligence. All other conditions are the same – the flight time, seating arrangement, plane type, and the ticket price. Upon arrival at the airport the passenger is a given a choice which plane to board, and for the purposes of full disclosure the passengers are given statistical information, that around 90 per cent of plane accidents are due to human error. Artificial intelligence does not make mistakes. Yet the majority of the audience raised their hands when asked who would prefer the human pilot. I have asked such a question multiple times in my classes and the pattern remains similar. From a more general perspective, the choice was between the predictability of AI solutions, and the possibility of human error against a background of certainty. The intuitively predictable option was far less preferable. The reason for this response was because of the absence of qualitative and value-carrying elements. Building upon the previous paragraph, the question remains why a minority preferred to trust their fate to solutions which apparently carry no qualitative elements.

16

On Foreseeability and Non-foreseeability

16.1 ON POSITIVITY AND NEGATIVITY

The non-reflective and simplistic application of the non-coherence assumption leads to an automatic statement that foreseeability transforms into non-foreseeability online. The proponent of simplicity could argue that when the offline human rights normative domain is by and large characterised by foreseeability, the online realm is characterised by the opposite, non-foreseeability. Yet there is no rule according to non-coherence theory saying that specific features characterising rights offline turn into the opposite online. The theory only claims the assumption of variance. Variance in features can produce a multitude of non-coherent images, exhibiting a weakening or strengthening of the features, but also turning them into the opposite. If foreseeability were to turn into its opposite upon transposition to the online domain, and such transformation could be validated, then this positions foreseeability exclusively in the offline rights domain. The consequences of such exclusivity would be in terms of valuability and usability.

Valuability is related to the intuitionistic perception of foreseeability as carrying positive value. It can be claimed, again in intuitionistic terms, that people who prefer rationality also prefer legal solutions which have a higher degree of foreseeability. For these rational people, the foreseeability of human rights law and its application in practice would therefore belong to the positive side of objectivity. Since a concept can always be defined through its opposite, attributing to the positivity of foreseeability at the same time means that the feature of non-foreseeability carries a negative value. Rational people should therefore reject solutions and rights paradigms which exhibit non-foreseeability. But if foreseeability carrying positivity was exclusively limited to the physical realm of human rights law and practice, then human rights law and practice in the online domain would inevitably exhibit the feature of non-foreseeability.

And this, in turn, provides that human rights law in the digital domain appears to carry negativity. And yet rational people are using the digital domain more and more. How can this be explained, provided that our assumption of foreseeability's exclusivity appears correct? The easiest explanation is to say that the assumption is indeed incorrect, which means that the digital domain's human rights law and practice also exhibits features of foreseeability. Another explanation is related to the transformation of the content of foreseeability during transposition from offline to online. A property which from the offline domain appears to be non-foreseeable, appears at the same time to be foreseeable online. Here is the main aspect of non-coherence characterising the transfer of concepts: multiple definitions can exist; they are domain-determined and as such can simultaneously carry positivity and negativity. Usability is related to valuability. Should foreseeability appear solely as a negative feature online, then one is faced with a problem of how the concept can be used to understand the online domain because characterising a domain on the basis of negative features always remains incomplete. Here other features need to enter the scene.

The question of interest here is, whether there is a tendency among legal subjects, no matter in what domain they are operating, to choose solutions which carry a higher degree of foreseeability. The element of foreseeability has to be assessed within a concrete system of norms, values and ideas. There might be no correlation between the aspect of the foreseeability of certain features in the physical realm and their reflection in the digital domain. For instance, a history professor can quite confidently discuss Mao Zedong's cultural revolution in the university's seminar room, without having to anticipate negative comments from the students or even subsequent prohibition from entering the university premises, but she cannot rely on such confidence once she starts to discuss the matter in some online platforms because negative comments can quickly follow, and the platform may decide to *de-platform* her. One can ask whether a decrease in foreseeability is correlated to a decrease in the expectation of truthful claims being put forth in an undisturbed manner.

16.2 ON AN AVERAGE PERSON'S COMPREHENSION

One can depart from how foreseeability is understood in the non-digital realm and apply this to the digital. It stands as a shield against arbitrariness in the application of judicial or quasi-judicial rules. It has been articulated as a general principle of the quality of law on numerous occasions by the European Court of Human Rights, where foreseeability, 'refers to the subjective ability of the average person to predict, to a degree that is reasonable in the circumstances, the consequences which a given action might entail'.[1] At a general level, it seems to be accepted as a principle without geopolitical influencers (see, for example, the recently adopted Turkish Action Plan for Human Rights).[2] It also appears that global internet platforms resort to the concept of reasonable foreseeability, which rests on the idea of an average reasonable user.[3] To be sure, an average person cannot predict the consequences of a given action unless two conditions are met: the first is that rules are available against which the action is contemplated, and another is knowledge of the practice of the application of these rules.

For the purposes of a legal theory's longevity, a short note is in order about reliance upon examples from immediate practice around the time this monograph is written. Assuming someone gets hold of this monograph 100 years from now, say in 2123, the corporate and political arena may have changed and become unrecognisable. There may be no Meta as a company, and the digital space may have moved to formats described in today's science fiction. International and national policy documents relevant at the time of writing this monograph may not be relevant. What remains, however, are the ideas and connections between concepts. The idea of non-coherence is immune to time and space and can be applied to various new, invented or discovered normative paradigms. Therefore, the scope of examples from contemporary practice remains limited.

16.3 DEGREES OF FORESEEABILITY

As we have noted before with some elements from the offline human rights paradigm, so the concept of foreseeability assumes a double nature online.

[1] European Court of Human Rights Judgements: *Vasiliauskas v Lithuania* (2009) Application no. 35343/05, paras 167-168; *Sunday Times v United Kingdom* (1979) Application no. 6538/74, para. 49.

[2] The Turkish 2021 'Action Plan for Human Rights' states in article 48: one of the fundamental principles of a state governed by the rule of law is the principle of legal security. Accordingly, rules of law must be sufficiently clear, foreseeable, understandable and applicable not to allow any hesitation or doubt on the part of either the administration or individuals and they must include a set of safeguards against arbitrary practices of public authorities. Ministry of Justice of the Republic of Turkey, 'Action Plan on Human Rights: Free Individual, Strong Society; More Democratic TURKEY', March 2021, https://inhak.adalet.gov.tr/Resimler/SayfaDokuman/1262021081047Action_Plan_On_Human_Rights.pdf, accessed 17 December 2022.

[3] See, for instance, Meta terms of service for business enterprises: Provided that we have reasonably acted with professional diligence, we will not accept responsibility or liability for any losses: (i) not caused by our breach of these terms or otherwise by our acts; (ii) that are not reasonably foreseeable by you and us at the time of entering into these terms; or (iii) arising out of or in connection with events that are beyond our reasonable control and which we cannot avoid through appropriate measures and which could not reasonably have been foreseen at the time we entered into our contract with you. Available at www.meta.com/gb/legal/portal/commercial-terms, accessed 5 January 2023.

It refers to foreseeability in practice; that is, the ability to predict the outcome of one's actions online depends on knowledge of the applicable rules and how they are put into action. There are some areas in the digital domain where the rules are rigid and well known to users, and their application follows clear patterns with no room for exception or deviation. For instance, if we would like to vote using e-solutions but the certificates on our ID card have expired, the voting right cannot be exercised. We can all appreciate this as having a high degree of foreseeability. And then there are areas where the rules are often changed and some internal directives are not public, and the practice of their implementation depends on value judgments by human moderators or the design of an unknown algorithm. We can call this a low degree of foreseeability. It is worth stating here that foreseeability exists online in more extreme formats than offline, to a considerably higher and lower degree. Because of this particularity, the image of foreseeability online is unclear. More has to be said about it.

16.3.1 *A Low Degree of Foreseeability*

The consequential non-coherence resulting from the transposition of certain central human rights concepts, such as foreseeability, to the online domain, requires us to pay attention to the margins. One side of the margin is related to a low degree of foreseeability and is due to the technical features of the Internet, allowing solutions where foreseeability is minimised. It is of course not appropriate to suggest that such a low degree of foreseeability is completely excluded from offline objectivity. For instance, van der Sloot has shown that although the concept of foreseeability in the Strasbourg Court's jurisprudence is derived from the idea of prescription from law, there are limitations in criminal investigations:

> the requirements of the Convention, notably in regard to foreseeability, cannot be exactly the same in the special context of interception of communications for the purposes of police investigations as they are where the object of the relevant law is to place restrictions on the conduct of individuals. In particular, the requirement of foreseeability cannot mean that an individual should be enabled to foresee when the authorities are likely to intercept his communications so that he can adapt his conduct accordingly.[4]

Yet what can be considered as an exception offline, appears as a dominant situation online. In an analysis of automated systems, Leiman has pointed to the difficulties of applying the standard of care, since the actions of AI-driven machines are unpredictable.[5] Therefore, the consequences of using

4 B. van der Sloot, 'The Quality of Law' (2020) 11 *JIPITEC* 160, para. 14.

5 T. Leiman, 'Law and Tech Collide: Foreseeability, Reasonableness and Advanced Driver Assistance Systems' (2021) 40 *Policy and Society*, 250–271, https://doi.org/10.1080/14494035.2020.1787696.

automated solutions are less foreseeable than the consequences of using humans to perform the same tasks. Rothchild's assertion that, 'with certain types of online communication it is unclear whether effects in a given jurisdiction are "foreseeable"', points to the problem of a close link between foreseeability and domestic jurisdictions. The global reach of a simple e-posting contains an inherent and unavoidable feature of the consequences being unforeseeable.[6] These examples are from distinct and unrelated fields, yet the common element is the significant decrease in foreseeability.

Potential examples of how a decision to use some digital solution does not entail a conscious reflection on foreseeability are innumerable. A simple agreement to terms of service should, in an ideal case, entail that whoever agrees to these terms understands at least some of the possible consequences of their online presence. Since the terms of service are usually generally worded, and since possible negative consequences from using the digital domain remain distant, and since the perceived benefits of using the digital space are immediate as opposed to the threat of any negative consequences, and since there is a perception of arbitrariness in user content assessment in any event, a thesis of non-foreseeability by default can be advanced. Such a thesis finds indirect verification from the following analogy. When Christopher Columbus and his men arrived in the Americas, they were guided by curiosity and greed, and did not know what to expect. They did not care about foreseeability. As the years passed, those who stayed in the Americas learnt by doing, which in translation to law would be a Dworkian approach that law is practice. Similarly, those who enter into the digital domain are unsure of what to expect, and as the weeks and months pass, they build a stronger sense of this foreseeability. Time is relative in this context. For the Europeans in the Americas, there were centuries of normative turmoil ahead between various jurisdictions, which disables foreseeability. A similar feature characterises digital solutions.

6 Rothchild gives a list of questions, which are cited here for the purpose of illustrating the scope of unforeseeability. Thus, if a person makes a commercial communication via a website or newsgroup posting, is it foreseeable that the communication will have effects in every jurisdiction in which such communications may be received? If a person sends a message via bulk e-mail, an internet mailing list or in a chat session, is it foreseeable that the message will have effects in every jurisdiction in which a recipient of the message is located? When sending an e-mail message to a single recipient, are effects foreseeable wherever the recipient happens to be located when he accesses the message? Is the analysis different if the communication is made in a language that is understood almost exclusively by residents of a particular country, or if the maker of the communication advertises in a jurisdiction using other, specifically targeted media as well? See J. Rothchild, 'Protecting the Digital Consumer: The Limits of Cyberspace Utopianism' (1999) 74 *Indiana Law Journal*, 3, Article 5, 916.

16.3.2 A *High Degree of Foreseeability*

In the other corner of the image (of foreseeability) in the digital domain stands a high degree (of foreseeability) in comparison with the non-digital domain. This is because of a distinct feature of social media platforms, which allows users to choose portal areas where people sharing similar values and expectations may cluster. Postings in these rooms carry little in terms of unexpected outcomes and build a sense of comfort in knowing that the main concern is the quantity of *likes* and their frequency.

By the time this monograph is published, it is possible that new technical options via the metaverse will have vigorously emerged, where the goal of allowing people to build their own universe simultaneously carries the aspect of creating their own rules. The self-creation of rules gives someone close to absolute control of the space and foreseeability, which her own actions or those of others, in the self-created room may lead to. The only unknown factor is from the subjectivity of the one who creates her own rules for the metaverse space open for others to use. Such a solution does not presuppose rules and principles articulated somewhere in physical or non-physical human rights paradigms, and as such user behaviour, 'at any meaningful scale is practically impossible', as suggested by Bosworth as a view from inside the Meta development team.[7] Here a paradox emerges that what seems close to absolutely foreseeable for an individual user, is reflected as close to complete non-foreseeability in the image for outsiders. This prediction undoubtedly raises the concern about whether the concept of foreseeability makes any sense in the future digital domain.

16.4 THE UNCOMFORTABLE CONSEQUENCE OF NON-COHERENCE

The previous discussion can point to a feature of turmoil connected with either the emergence of a new normative paradigm, or the transposition of a full range of human rights ideas and concepts into another judicial and quasi-judicial paradigm. Legal systems have the tendency to move towards stability and standardisation. The more there is attention to and activity at the margins, the less stable a normative system can be considered. One might be tempted to think that such turmoil, or in stricter scientific terms contestations, have the

7 Internal memo from Andrew Bosworth reported by the *Financial Times* on 12 November 2021. The author read the memo and inserted it into these footnotes. During revision of the manuscript, the link was no longer available. The author has a screenshot from the posting made during the first reading.

tendency to disappear as time passes. Yet another possibility cannot be excluded. This is the possibility that foreseeability is the property of human rights in the digital domain where movements towards the centre are not likely theoretical because of the self-creation of rules, nor observable in practice because of the absence of evidence to the contrary. At this point, non-coherence theory tells us that a concept or idea from the offline human rights domain may transform upon transposition to an unrecognisable extent. Then it would only satisfy the uncritical viewer from the physical domain if a fragment of the digital human rights image is observed, and the rest of the image remains obscure. Saying that the online domain has a feature of foreseeability would be an exaggeration in this case, and simplification of and attention on just a small sector of the image. A justification for abandoning the foreseeability concept online relates to the multiplicity of actors and their interests when shaping the digital human rights environment.

From here a reflection of a more general nature emerges that is of the correlation between the meaningfulness of the concept of foreseeability against the scope of sources which exercise influence upon the outcome of someone's actions. The higher the number of those sources, the lower the foreseeability. If this is a correct assertion, at some point the amount of sources with influence upon the outcomes outgrows the capability to foresee the outcome. This is a revelation of non-coherence, although uncomfortable for someone who values certainty. The uncomfortableness lies in the recognition that some core concepts from the offline paradigm simply do not make sense online and one needs to let them go. The concept of foreseeability seems to belong in this box. Subsequent consequence is furthermore uncomfortable. It speaks of the relativity of fundamental rights ideas and the illusory nature of the expectation that we can take our understanding of human rights with us when we venture into new domains. The statement by Schmidt and Cohen that, 'the vast majority of us will find ourselves living, working and being governed in two worlds at once',[8] reflects the reality governed by non-coherence. It cannot be fully excluded that our words and discourse have the ability to narrow the gap between these two worlds. The gap remains and we need to accept that when non-coherence shows something as irrational in another domain, it still may be considered rational from the other side when looking at the image of human rights. The assumption is that the expressions of rationality and irrationality by themselves are constants and do not change during transposition.

8 E. Schmidt III, J. Cohen, *The New Digital Age: Reshaping the Future of People, Nations and Business* (New York: Alfred A. Knopf, 2013), p. 6.

17

Reflections from the Academic Debate

17.1 THE ACKNOWLEDGEMENT OF CONTRIBUTIONS

During the writing of this monograph, I had the privilege of heading the Global Digital Human Rights Network, which is (was) a network funded by the European Union's COST (Cooperation in Science and Technology) programme. The network includes around 100 scholars and practitioners, as the name says, in the field of digital human rights. I approached the network members with questions in order to obtain input into some theoretical and practical matters. I asked two questions: What in your view are the three most influential ideas put forward during the last ten years on the topic of digital human rights? What in your view are the two or three most significant challenges related to digital human rights which necessitate conceptualisation from academia? Instead of providing a literature review on the academic debate, I will provide here a generalisation of the replies of my learned colleagues and offer some comments through non-coherence theory. I acknowledge the replies from Barbora Badurova, Sergio Barbosa, Irena Barkane, Wolfgang Benedek, Lana Bubalo, Federico Costantini, Federica Cristani, Renata Deskosa, Matthias C. Kettemann, Konstantinos Kouroupis, Erik Larsson, Marijana Mladenov, Riku Neuvonen, Alexandre L. Dias Pereira, Graziella Romeo, Halldóra Þorsteinsdóttir, Jukka Viljanen and Gentian Zyberi.

It would be arbitrary to draw a rigid line between ideas and challenges. Some ideas emerge independently from human rights practice, for instance, the idea of the sameness of human rights offline and online. This idea leads to the challenge of practicality, in other words, whether it is possible to find ways to secure the idea through normativity and remedies, or whether it remains an idealistic aspiration. And from the other side, a challenge can lead to ideas. For instance, the ease of spreading offensive views online can lead to the idea of treating human rights in the digital sphere as a separate category of rights associated with the distinct obligations of a wider circle of stakeholders.

17.2 IDEAS RELATED TO THE DISTINCTNESS OF HUMAN RIGHTS ONLINE

This monograph has frequently raised the question of whether the digital domain contains a critical mass of specific rights which are fundamental in nature and domain specific, that is, whether there is a critical mass of rights which either have their origin from the digital domain itself, due to various technical or intellectual or community reasons, or which have their origin in the non-digital domain but their content has transformed during transposition to such an extent that it is necessary to accord new labels to these rights. Should such a critical mass be achieved, one could say that fundamental rights in the digital domain represent a totally new rights paradigm in comparison with the offline domain.

A number of colleagues pointed to the articulation of rights which are applicable only in the digital space. The list is in no way exhaustive. These rights can be categorised as rights that are derivate from offline rights, or rights which have a distinct origin from cyberspace. Into the first category were placed workers' digital rights and consumer rights. These are group rights and entail various entitlements with different levels of abstractness and universality. Within these group rights, the proportion of such rights which can be viewed as fundamental rights as opposed to simply legal rights is not important for this discussion because it has not been argued by my colleagues that the digital domain has changed worker or consumer rights to the extent that new labels are needed, or that it is justified to consider these group rights as separate from worker and consumer rights offline. Such a justification would be arbitrary due to the high level of generality of these categories of rights.

For rights having their origin in the digital domain, the right to a clean digital environment, the right to a safe digital environment and the right to disconnect were highlighted. This list can be expanded, for instance, by adding the right to decisions by humans instead of automated systems. Yet it seems prima facie clear that the volume of both categories is not comparable to the volume of well-established rights offline. Therefore, when speaking about digital human rights, the focus still has to remain upon what happens after the transposition of offline human rights to the online environment. This is what the monograph is focusing on, and the approach is to some extent confirmed by the input of other researchers.

Among specific fundamental rights, the overarching question is about the right of access to the Internet. Frequently, the matter of whether access to the

Internet should be recognised as a new independent human right was raised. There is of course extensive and wide-ranging debate on the topic. In this monograph, the question is translatable to whether this right entails an aspect of having the entitlement to let go of the meaning of rights in the non-digital domain. A side effect of this entitlement is the right to dual identities and *anything goes*. I have defended these entitlements elsewhere in this monograph. We cannot exclude that the *popularity* of the Internet and the prediction of high levels of fascination by Meta is partially explainable by the tiredness of having just one identity.

17.3 IDEAS RELATED TO THE DIVIDE BETWEEN THE OFFLINE AND ONLINE DOMAINS

The previous argument leads to the problem of the divide between the online and offline domains and its implication for the content and scope of *traditional* human rights. Most respondents touched on this matter. Some colleagues reiterated the well-known propositions that the same rights that people have offline must also be protected online, or that human rights are also valid online. Here it can be said that emphasising an aspect of objectivity by itself shows that this objectivity can be contested for more profound reasons than because of the reason of *contra mundum*. We all know that the sun rises every morning, and bringing this fact forward as one of the most important features of our existence in the physical world sends a worrisome signal that perhaps such mornings are not secure and something fundamentally different may happen. We wish to confirm the coherence of each morning with the previous and following mornings – that the sun also rises, but in the background looms the possibility that some mornings may be non-coherent. In the same way, by bringing forward the idea that human rights are also valid online signals the possibility that perhaps they are not. The statement of the sameness of rights has an inherent feature of the expectation of non-coherence.

On a more specific level, several concerns were raised that the digital human rights environment differs from the offline environment. These observations can be divided into comments about the core features of human rights systems, and comments originating from practice observations.

17.3.1 *Comments Related to Ontology*

Some comments about the core features, which we can also call comments related to the ontology of human rights, were as follows:

- Online rights more than their offline versions bring with them responsibilities because of their larger impact and potential for misuse
- Digital technologies provide new means to exercise human rights, but they are too often also used to violate them
- Due to unique challenges and issues that arise in the digital world, additional protections and considerations are required
- Digital human rights should be treated as a separate category of human rights
- The foundations of human rights are claimed to be universal but also to have some nuances that still need to be discussed
- The divide between the online and offline human rights domains appears at the core of ideas put forward both in relation to theory and practice
- Digital human rights changed the addresses of human rights obligations, which now include private companies, organisations and possibly AI
- The meaning of human rights and the rule of law changes in cyberspace
- Online actors, especially platforms, are essential actors in governing how human rights are enjoyed online
- Algorithms and rules together form complex normative ecosystems that impact human rights
- There exists the concurrence (overlapping and/or competing) of human rights and human rights regimes
- A more analytic approach is needed (i.e., whose right? what kind of right? who are the related parties?)
- The development of international standards for digital human rights is inevitable, including enforcement measures (e.g., attaching WTO membership to a basic DHR charter, similar to IP rights)
- The border between principles and rights is blurred
- Should private companies play a role vis-à-vis the question of how to harness data for the common good?

The core features characterising the digital human rights domains were proposed as those of decentralisation, resilience and asymmetry. The previous comments are sufficient to confirm what non-coherence theory argues. The digital domain contains features beyond cosmetic changes in comparison with the non-digital domain. And therefore, consequently, it represents a different rights paradigm. Non-coherence of human rights in these two domains has to be assumed.

17.3.2 *Comments Related to Observations from Practice*

Comments originating from practice include:

- States have been unable to respect, protect and fulfil their human rights obligations

- Intermediaries are not liable for human rights violations, but they do have a responsibility to respect and protect human rights on their platforms, and can be held accountable for their failure to do so
- Human rights violations online can lead to human rights violations offline (e.g., hate speech)
- The application of argumentation theory to AI may be possible in order to resolve the challenges of the *black box*
- It was (and still is) important to regulate social media and implement an international human rights framework online
- Proactive monitoring, surveillance and the removal of certain types of content (hate speech and terrorist content) in a proportionate way is of high importance
- It is important to achieve increased user safety online and improve the ability of law enforcement to tackle illegal content online
- Automatic filtering functions are needed to prevent users from having to see explicit material
- The main difference between the real world and the digital world is that in the digital world information is not forgotten
- It is important to recognise the relevant criteria to analyse the role of digital media in a democratic society
- Censorship and content moderation matters, and self-regulation vs. more extensive government regulation is relevant
- How can we uphold human rights in new forms of armed conflicts and wars that also include new forms of digital violence?
- Access to digital infrastructure and digital devices is a concern. Scholars have already addressed the problem of the digital divide. Attention, however, should be shifted from detecting the problem to conceptualising it as a problem of the effectiveness of digital human rights
- Freedom of expression in times of crisis emerges (such as in the period of the Covid-19 pandemic or during the Russian invasion of Ukraine)
- It is important to mention a better definition or understanding of *harmful material* or illegal content that calls for the removal of certain type of expression
- The notion of hate speech is something that deserves more scrutiny
- There are also many significant challenges created by the rise of social media and online platforms: How can we tackle online disinformation and misinformation? How can we protect the right to freedom of expression online? How can we prevent surveillance and manipulation? How can we ensure protection of the right to privacy online?
- The use of digital platforms, social media and other tools to interfere with democratic processes (elections, conflict resolution, crisis management, etc.) is a clear challenge

Returning to Plato's cave, these observations show images of incompatibility between the *traditional* perception of human rights law and practice with the objectivity in the new online paradigm. Once again, non-coherence theory explains that these observations are not incidental but show non-coherence between these two domains. Concepts from the offline domain obtain a new content upon transposition to the online domain, otherwise the offline human rights architecture simply remains idealistic and dormant online.

17.4 IDEAS AND CHALLENGES RELATED TO ARTIFICIAL INTELLIGENCE

Among the ideas and challenges put forward by my colleagues, those related to AI and automated systems stand out as a distinct, if not overshadowing the list. Two categories of responses can be distinguished here. First, there were suggestions for how to counter the largely unknown features and effect of AI upon *business as usual*, that is, how to secure the transposition of human rights law and procedures into the digital domain with as little variance as possible. The second category contains pure notices of shadows on the wall. These shadows seem sometimes threatening, usually overwhelming, always concerning. They concern the yearning for precise information about exactly how AI and automated decision-making systems operate, in other words, the process of building Thought about AI Objectivity. It is a clear situation when the AI mirror reflects back the image of human rights from the offline domain, without the light being able to penetrate into AI reality. Alternatively, the light disappears into AI reality as if into a black hole. When two such paradigms interact with one another, the non-coherence assumption needs to be upheld, and the question that remains is about the depth of the non-coherence.

The ideas and challenges written from my colleagues as a response to my questions include:

- Strict liability should be introduced for emerging technologies, such as AI
- Ethics alone cannot resolve the challenges of AI, since we need a human rights approach
- New legally binding regulation is needed to address the impact of artificial intelligence on human rights, the rule of law and democracy
- There is a need to adopt a regulatory framework to ensure accountability in the development and use of new digital technologies and online platforms and to address the challenges that these technologies pose to human rights

- The overall invasion of AI creates unknown challenges for traditional human rights
- The gradual reduction of human involvement or oversight over many automatic processes poses pressing questions about fairness, responsibility and respect of human rights
- The main threats and opportunities are related to artificial intelligence and the share of responsibility
- The assemblage of norms and algorithms in the enjoyment of human rights remains a challenge
- AI is becoming more mainstream, which leads to novel liability issues
- One of the significant challenges is how to ensure accountability, and the trustworthy development and use of AI systems and other new digital technologies; how toe ensure their safety; and how to prevent the risks AI systems pose to fundamental rights, the rule of law and democracy. It is crucial to evaluate the existing legal framework and assess what future regulation or clarification on the application of existing laws is needed in order to address the risks AI systems create and ensure the accountable and trustworthy use of AI systems
- There is a need to examine the challenges that AI and other new technologies in the online world, digital services and online platforms pose to the existing regulatory framework and how they influence the development of existing legislation as well as possible future regulations
- Profiling and artificial intelligence are a major concern
- The meaning of transparency specifically changes online

These observations reveal the capacity of AI and automated decision-making systems to alter the status quo bias of human rights offline architecture beyond return. This input variable is of such magnitude that it calls for a critical review of the entirety of offline human rights norms, procedures and concepts. The matter, which non-coherence theory has also addressed, is whether the void of the status quo bias leads to change in core human rights ideas when transposed online.

17.5 IDEAS AND CHALLENGES RELATED TO DIGITAL LITERACY

The specific area of *ideas and challenges* is related to rights holders, that is, everyone's knowledge building about the digital domain. What follows in this paragraph are indirect citations or references to views from my colleagues, generalised on the basis of the academic discourse related to digital education. In particular, the argument that everyone should be given the opportunity to develop enough digital education to reduce the risks of discrimination or the violation of human rights was highlighted. The absence of digital ethics education is seen as a major concern. Some learned colleagues involved in citizen education development wrote that exploring digital education and access to digital infrastructures in those areas where they are still underdeveloped implies understanding to what extent digital human rights can be effectively implemented and protected. Academia should also focus attention on the impact of digital human rights on minorities (discrimination) or less advantaged groups within the world population, for example, immigrants and potential human rights violations coming from digital technologies applied in the context of immigration. The role of tech giants and computer scientists in shaping society and contributing to protecting fundamental rights in the digital environment has been explored at length. The next challenge is now educating computer scientists and managers to understand the human rights implications of AI and digital technologies in general. Supporting and encouraging the creation of national digital literacy initiatives as a mandatory component of educational curricula, with long-term objectives, evaluation metrics and respective action plans, was highlighted as a holistic goal for all societies. School curricula should integrate a media education course in which students are required to develop all dimensions of digital human rights. The integration of media education in teacher training curricula, as well as more opportunities for in-service teacher training was seen as a tool for progressing along this path. Therefore, the focus needs to be not only on technological literacy as end users but also on the digital literacy embodied in social life.

These ideas, which by themselves are all significant, remain outside the scope of this monograph. However, the non-coherence assumption stands in the background of all these ideas. This is because the digital domain for many is the beginning of *terra incognita*, which raises all the conceptual and practical topics discussed in this book. Comprehensive knowledge building is needed to discover the complexity of the digital domain. Like someone who wakes up from a coma and starts to re-discover his self, soon realises that something has changed. The rediscovery of human rights in the digital domain is part of knowledge building, which would not be necessary if non-coherence was not discoverable prima facie.

17.6 DIGITAL HUMAN RIGHTS AND ETHICAL STANDARDS

Finally, there are ideas related to the conceptualisation of digital human rights against ethical standards. Several colleagues asked whether human rights can serve as a minimal ethical standard for regulating digital technologies. If yes, would that be enough, or do we need additional ethical guidelines? These observations point to possible subsequent intellectual undertakings, that is, exploring the non-coherence between non-digital and digital ethics. But such an exploration will happen outside of this book.

17.7 SHORT CONCLUDING REMARKS FROM ACADEMIC DISCOURSE

The academic discourse on digital human rights takes non-coherence as an implicit condition. This theory will turn the implicit assumption into an explicit condition. This explicit condition needs to be applied to several concepts of the highest importance pointed out by my colleagues: digital constitutionalism, digital democracy, overlapping human rights systems and the typology of digital human rights law development. I will stop here in order to allow the discourse to continue.

PART IV

The Impact of the Non-coherence Theory

18

The E-state and Fundamental Rights

18.1 THE CONTOURS OF POSITIVITY AND NEGATIVITY

It is now time to turn the application of the non-coherence theory of digital human rights towards specific digital solutions and phenomena, which are widely used and known. This can lead to questioning the positivity or negativity associated with these solutions and phenomena, which rests on the viewpoint that human rights law and ideas are transposable without variance. The rejection of this assumption does not necessarily lead to a reversal of the qualitative characteristics of these solutions or phenomena, but they surely secure a better understanding and replace pure intuitionistic perceptions that what is positive or negative in the non-digital human rights architecture is carried over to the digital domain. At least a more nuanced image becomes available. We will start with the image of e-statehood.

There are two fundamentally related perceptions, which are of a religious nature, about the e-state from the perspective of fundamental rights. The first hails e-state positivity by suggesting that public power draws closer to the people because this framework is providing more efficient, transparent and neutral procedures and outcomes. Here fundamental rights would therefore appear to be more safeguarded since e-solutions minimise arbitrariness. The opposite perception suggests there is obscurity and distrust despite the apparent efficiency and neutrality.

18.1.1 *The Objection from Obscurity*

The objection from obscurity is related to problematic knowledge development and in common language is usually expressed as, 'the people do not understand how the e-state works'. To give a few illustrations, this aspect has led to the rejection of e-elections, an application of e-statehood capable of affecting the entire society, by the German Constitutional Court. The argument is related to the absence of transparency in the electoral process without specialist technical knowledge; that is, people should not only believe the transparency of an e-solution but also easily understand how it works.[1] Solvak and Vassil, in their study of how and why the Estonian population has accepted the instrument of e-elections, identified as the main challenge the replacement of *simple trust* in public power with a better understanding of how the systems work and human rights are safeguarded.[2] And yet, if the principle objection to human rights protection in e-statehood is because of the scarcity of knowledge, then in ideal conditions of knowledge transfer this objection can be easily rejected because there are no such ideal conditions, the obscurity aspect of the e-state may constitute a *sine qua non* condition. Here, non-coherence theory explains that such a condition of obscurity is nothing surprising but is to be expected when a public policy instrument entailing fundamental rights protection, such as elections or access to medical records, is transposed into the digital domain. Explanations from political and academic establishments can narrow the discrepancy between the security and clarity of the image in both domains but cannot close the gap. In translation, this means that people can become accustomed to and accept public policy being implemented via e-solutions and recognise that sophisticated technologies stand in the service of efficiency, which gradually and organically overrule the need to comprehend *how the system works*. Non-coherence appears here at the level of faith instead of understanding.

18.1.2 *The Objection from Distrust*

The second objection is from distrust. It originates from blockchain technology, visible/invisible surveillance methods and the analytical capabilities of personal and big data achievable through modern technological solutions. The common argument warns against the possible abuse by the government or public and private entities of personal information, which individuals have been compelled to surrender through various e-state solutions. Popular and academic discourse has many examples – the validation and invalidation of the trade-off between yielding private and family data in return for the privilege to live in a safer modern society. Yet the perception of

[1] German Constitutional Court Judgements: BvC 3/07 (2009) and BvC 4/07 (2009).

[2] M. Solvak, K. Vassil, *E-voting in Estonia: Technological Diffusion and Other Developments over Ten Years (2005–2015)* (Tartu: University of Tartu, 2016).

distrust seems to prevail, against which legal and non-legal arguments can be raised.

The legal argument is related to faith in positive law, that is, normative regulation being capable of eliminating or ridiculing the distrust that technology is more powerful than law. It can be asserted that checks and balances and remedies in positive law, when transposed to the digital domain, carry sufficient legal mechanisms to minimise the concern that private data obtained is used un-purposefully.[3] Therefore, according to this legal argument, it may be possible to transpose a positive law system, including effective remedies, which secures the protection of human rights in the context of e-state solutions that is comparable with the protection against the arbitrary interference by the state in offline situations. But doubts about this view come from the assumption of non-coherence, which says that the functionality of non-digital positive law can never be transposed one-to-one without variance. In this specific respect, non-coherence appears in the heavier weight of non-argumentative faith in what positive law can accomplish online. Another specific aspect lies in the recognition that digital solutions are technology driven and they are always several steps ahead of normative responses. But if one has faith in normativity, then these developments become unimportant.

The non-legal argument is about trust in public power. In other words, in an ideal world the process and results of yielding private information to the democratically established government is subject to constitutional restraints. The government in turn enjoys the trust of civil society and abuses of information surrendered can be occasional but not systemic. Here, once again, the non-coherence assumption warns against the automatic transposition of faith in democracy to the digital domain.

The image of human rights protection in the e-state context leads, at the first and non-holistic glance, to a knowledge development exercise. The goal of such an exercise is to move ever closer to conditions of perfect knowledge transfer and perfect trust in the government. The further this goal is fully realised, the more this image becomes immune to objections arguing that practical e-state solutions and principles are incompatible with human rights. On further examination and when placing this development exercise into a theoretical framework, one easily notices its roots in practice dependency as

[3] Some short references may be in order. See European Court of Human Rights jurisprudence about the matters of Big Data, for example *Big Brother Watch et al. v The United Kingdom* (2018) Application no. 58170/13; or the annual reports of the European Data Protection Supervisor, assessing how efficiently the legislation for privacy protection is realised – website at edps.europa.eu/annual-reports_en.

opposed to human rights as a normative idea.[4] This approach runs counter to the proposition of human rights universality and idealism. The practice-dependent aspect is not sufficient to conclude principle compatibility or incompatibility of the e-state with the human rights promise.

18.2 THE FOUR CAVEATS

The application of the non-coherence theory of digital human rights leads to the formulation of four caveats.

18.2.1 *The First Caveat: The Dominance of Human Rights Rhetoric*

The first caveat is related to the preponderance of human rights rhetoric in relation to e-state goals and strategic commitments, compared to objectively verifiable information on how exactly human rights aspects are taken into account. This observation is subjectively cognitive and is based on reading, for example, Estonia's e-governance strategy documents, observing administrative practices and political rhetoric when Estonia's success story as an e-governed state is presented either domestically or internationally.[5] My hypothesis claims that the countries which rely on a greater volume of e-solutions for the purpose of public administration resort primarily to rhetorical arguments when the issue of safeguarding human rights through these solutions is raised. This safeguarding is theoretical and illusory. The countries that have quickly and on a large scale resorted to e-state solutions demonstrate at a relatively lower degree how exactly these solutions are in line with the obligation to protect human rights.

This aspect of preponderance is addressed through various practical initiatives and advocacy tasks. The concept of smart cities or human rights cities is built partly on the understanding that human rights need to be fostered at the local level. For example, van Zoonen has suggested a framework for including

[4] For a comprehensive discussion about the matter of practice dependency and practice independency of human rights, see L. P. Coutinho, 'The Practice-Dependency of Human Rights' in M. La Torre, L. Niglia, M. Susi (eds.), *The Quest for Rights: Ideal and Normative Dimensions* (Northampton, MA: Edward Elgar Publishing, 2019), pp. 49–64.

[5] Some examples may be in order from Estonia's national strategy documents. Estonia's information society development plan 2020 (in the Estonian language accessible via www.mkm.ee/sites/default/files/elfinder/article_files/eesti_infouhiskonna_arengukava.pdf) is a forty-five-page strategy document emphasising that information technology is a crucial tool to raise competitiveness of any economic or social sphere. This document does not contain a single reference to human rights. Strategy 'Estonia 2035' is a long-term development strategy to enhance the well-being of the population in the conditions of a modern society. The strategy is twenty-two pages long and contains no reference to human rights.

people's privacy concerns in research, policy and the design of smart cities.[6] Others have addressed how the smart city environment affects people's privacy.[7] More examples could be given of this approach. My observations and discussions with researchers and practitioners in the field reveal an endemic absence of the specification of human rights goals from e-state strategy and practice. The new concepts of human rights by design and human rights by default, when applied to human rights protection mechanisms in digital vertical relations, are indicative of the fact that human rights are engrafted into e-state strategy and solutions as a general idea; that is, they were not part of the e-state philosophy in the first place, nor present in the initial designs. It is much easier to add a rhetorical component than to change the software since we would then only deal with the labelling. Perhaps the expression of human-rights-washing can be introduced here.

We are trained to think that human rights are connected to social development.[8] Many examples, well known to readers, could be given about human rights and how the interests of vulnerable groups were enhanced because of human rights arguments. We can find examples about business success being related to the social responsibility of modern corporations. Contemporary human rights discourse seems to accept the proposition that social development and human rights work in tandem. The non-coherence theory of digital human rights suggests that something must be at variance from this picture of the offline dimension when reflected online. I claim that in this specific case, this variance concerns the transformation of the development and tandem argument. In the offline world, social and perhaps economic development is enhanced or accelerated when we take into account the human rights component. The e-state development in the online world, on the contrary, transforms human rights from an enhancing factor into an impediment. Instead of pushing forward with more and new e-state solutions and expanding e-statehood into new public administration areas, developers now need to add an element which is not functionally indispensable. Another way to formulate the first caveat is to say that the human rights factor has not yet

6 L. van Zoonen, 'Privacy Concerns in Smart Cities' (2016) 33 *Government Information Quarterly*, 3, 472–480, https://doi.org/10.1016/j.giq. The work shows that individual citizens or collective citizen groups are often ignored as partners in the development of smart city technologies or innovations.

7 D. Eckhoff, I. Wagner, 'Privacy in the Smart City – Applications, Technologies, Challenges, and Solutions' (2018) 20 *IEEE Communications Surveys & Tutorials*, 1, 489–516, DOI: 10.1109/COMST.2017.2748998.

8 P. Alston, 'Ships Passing in the Night: The Current State of the Human Rights and Development Debate Seen through the Lens of the Millennium Development Goals' (2005) 27 *Human Rights Quarterly*, 3, 755–829.

been integrated into the e-state to the extent that it becomes a functional part of the e-state organism. There is no specific vulnerable group who would gain some competitive advantage if pressure upon e-state design would be channelled into e-state solutions taking into account human rights concerns. This is because of the notion of internet vulnerability – we are all vulnerable in front of the Internet; this is the notion of collective vulnerability.

The problem originating from this caveat is the strong possibility that, when making further choices about the development of e-state principles and practical solutions, regard for human rights simply is not a relevant criterion for assessing the justifiability of the proposed measures.

18.2.2 *The Second Caveat: Is the E-state a Success?*

The second caveat is related to the absence of a conclusive justification about the success of the e-state in the social context. It claims that there exists little or no evidence to comprehensively assess the benefits or failures of the e-state project. This can be a continuous condition, at least until data emerges to either support or reject the positive social impact of the e-state project. While the e-state doctrine remains subject to scientific and practical contestations, I will explore whether any relationship exists between happiness and the high development of the e-state, that is, whether there is some causal relationship between happiness and/or unhappiness and e-state development in a given country.

The World Happiness Report 2019 refrains from presenting correlational conclusions between unhappiness and the time spent on digital media, yet it refers to studies that suggest people who limit their time on social media improve their well-being.[9] In short, the report concludes that adolescents who spend more time on electronic devices are less happy, and adolescents who spend more time on most other activities are happier. The World Happiness Report 2020 explores why people in the Nordic countries seem to be happier than in other countries.[10] Among other observations it refers to a cross-sectional study for 2005–2012 which links improvements in government

[9] J. M. Twenge, 'The Sad State of Happiness in the United States and the Role of Digital Media', chapter 5, World Happiness Report 2019, 20 March 2019, https://worldhappiness.report/ed/2019/the-sad-state-of-happiness-in-the-united-states-and-the-role-of-digital-media, accessed 27 January 2022.

[10] F. Martela, B. Greve, B. Rothstein, J. Saari, 'The Nordic Exceptionalism: What Explains Why the Nordic Countries Are Constantly among the Happiest in the World', chapter 7, World Happiness Report 2020, 20 March 2020, https://worldhappiness.report/ed/2020/the-nordic-exceptionalism-what-explains-why-the-nordic-countries-are-constantly-among-the-happiest-in-the-world/#fnref28, accessed 27 January 2022.

quality to improvements in well-being. When government quality is divided into democratic and delivery quality, it is the latter which is more strongly related to citizen happiness. These short brushstrokes, while not establishing that more e-state means less happiness, do not establish the contrary either. Yet the question remains of why Estonia as the 'most advanced digital society in the world'[11] is only ranked 51st in the 2020 World Happiness Report. If we view the usage of e-state solutions as part of individual digital habits and comprehend that more time using digital tools means less happiness, then digital public services can be viewed as part of the more general behaviour from the individual's perspective. If the former is correct, then more e-state means less happiness.

Another aspect of e-governance which seems worrying to human rights and IT scholars is the matter of algorithmic prisons – algorithmic gatekeepers influence access to various social services and may lead to insurmountable barriers on behalf of the state power.[12] When administrative misunderstandings or issues in face-to-face situations can often be resolved, there is nobody to talk to in many of the e-state solutions. This second caveat means that the economic or rhetorical *success* of e-statehood can easily overshadow reliable data on how the e-state affects people's daily lives and well-being.

18.2.3 *The Third Caveat: The Expectation of Horizontality*

The third caveat claims that in the digital sphere the protection of fundamental rights is more comprehensively expected and realised under horizontal than under traditional vertical governance models. Non-coherence theory posits that several core fundamental rights principles change once transposed from the offline domain to the online domain. To justify or reject the third caveat, our interest turns to the question of whether there are any significant differences between public and private digital domains vis-à-vis the meaning of and mechanisms for human rights protection. This question can be explored from the normative perspective through practice and the capabilities approach.

From the normative side, one notices the growth of soft law instruments calling upon the private internet service providers to respect fundamental

[11] A rhetorical statement often used in reference to Estonia's digitalisation and e-governance, see, for example, https://e-estonia.com.

[12] H.-Y. Liu, Hin-Yan, 'Digital Disruption of Human Rights' in M. Susi (ed.), *Human Rights, Digital Society and the Law: A Research Companion* (London: Routledge, 2019).

rights.[13] Private entities themselves are developing and publishing *modus operandi*, or original terms of service.[14] The terms of service of the public sector, a contrario, originate from the offline environment and appear transposed to provide the *same* services in the online domain as in the offline realm. The variance therefore lies in the origin of the operation models for protecting fundamental rights in the digital domain: the private online service providers rely on an original design, whereas the public service providers (e.g., the e-state) use a model which is necessary to manage the offline public domain. Despite contestations against the foreseeability of the terms of service used by the online service providers,[15] the fact remains that generically they are meant for the digital environment and thereby strengthen the online service providers per se, whereas the goal of the e-state is not to strengthen e-state applications but concrete real-world political and power-oriented processes.

The main epistemic question related to the practice of online private company and e-state applications is what exactly do these two realms seak to accomplish. A wide discrepancy appears. The private online portals focus their whole business model on increasing the economic efficiency of digital solutions, whereas e-state solutions have the clear target to make public administration more effective, also in economic terms. The difference in goals leads to a difference in expectations. The goal of a private online domain is to focus on accomplishments within the same domain, whereas the goal of the public online domain is to focus on accomplishments in the offline domain. I claim that private online companies and portals are expected to protect fundamental

[13] At the European level, the primary efforts are undertaken by the Council of Europe and the EU. Various instruments exist at the Council of Europe level, such as the Internet Governance strategy 2016–2019, or the 'Recommendation CM/Rec (2018) 2 of the Committee of Ministers to Member States on the Roles and Responsibilities of Internet Intermediaries'. The European Commission has adopted the EU Human Rights Guidelines on Freedom of Expression Online and Offline. At the global level the UN Guiding Principles on Business and Human Rights and the 'Protect, Respect and Remedy' Framework are pertinent.

[14] In recent years, the main global social media actors have published community standards regarding their anticipated actions towards online content. The focus of these standards is against hate speech and/or clearly illegal content, but there are also guidelines for when legal content affecting someone's privacy can be removed or blocked. These standards neither refer to the international normative human rights architecture nor address the matter of the sameness of online and offline rights. When YouTube writes in its standards that it 'reserves the right to make the final determination of whether a violation of its privacy guidelines has occurred', this reflects the doctrine of law as practice. We may use terms like *Lex Facebook*, *Lex Twitter*, etc., which means that the origin of digital human rights law has, strictly speaking, a private character.

[15] T. Wischmeyer, 'The Role and Practices of Online Stakeholders' in M. Susi (ed.), *Human Rights, Digital Society and the Law: A Research Companion* (London: Routledge, 2019).

rights to a much higher degree than e-state solutions. The matter of capabilities – what exactly are different online solutions capable of doing – is therefore much more relevant for the private online dimension than for the public dimension (the e-state).

Elsewhere I have shown that although private online enterprises are capable of balancing fundamental rights, the balancing entails a high degree of arbitrariness due to the incapability of these portals to include their reasoning for the balancing decisions.[16] This is evident from the so-called community standards of major internet companies, as well as from individual notifications to portal users, where the decision to block or delete information posted by the user is explained by a mere reference to non-compliance with the community standards.[17] The e-state on the other hand has no requirement to balance conflicting rights since the collusions of conflicting rights of individual rights-holders having the same weight is excluded. This is because the e-state is not a place where private individuals and/or companies can advance their rights claims towards one another, it is a platform for exercising state vertical power. When the fragmentation of various private stakeholder groups can be categorised through a focus on process-driven,[18] substance-oriented[19] and issue-oriented[20] initiatives, such fragmentation does not emerge in the e-state context. The matter of capabilities does not emerge for the public online domain due to the aspect of fundamental rights protection, since the e-state has no specific goals related to the protection of fundamental rights other than those originating from the offline domain. The main fundamental rights concern for e-statehood is whether the e-state solutions themselves have secret doors enabling the arbitrary use of data, which is a matter concerning the next caveat. The previous leads us to advance the hypothesis that fundamental rights are non-essential for justifying nor realising e-state solutions. Another way to formulate the same idea is to suggest that the e-state

16 M. Susi, 'Balancing Fundamental Rights on the Internet: The Proportionality Paradigm and Private Online Capabilities' in M. La Torre, L. Niglia, M. Susi (eds.), *The Quest for Rights: Ideal and Normative Dimensions* (Northampton, MA: Edward Elgar Publishing, 2019).

17 Consider the recommendation of the Google Advisory Council, which was set up after the Goolge judgment of the CJEU - Case C-131/12 *Google Spain SL and Google Inc. v Agencia Española de Protección de Datos (AEPD) and Mario Costeja González*, (13 May 2014). The council suggested in para. 19 of its report that Google should not attach reasons to individual decisions about blocking or deletion but should rather publish statistics.

18 Represented, for instance, by the Global Network Initiative, https://globalnetworkinitiative.org.

19 Represented, for instance, by the Manila Principles, https://manilaprinciples.org.

20 Represented, for instance, by the Google Advisory Council, https://archive.google.com/advisorycouncil.

does not need fundamental rights, or even more bluntly – fundamental rights disturb the development of the e-state.

18.2.4 *The Fourth Caveat: The Road to a Police State*

Fourth and finally, there is the threat that the e-state could transform into a police state. I put forward such a threat because blockchain and the Internet generate many tools which enable such a transformation, remaining unnoticed and disguised under the veil of economic and technological efficiency. Such a transformation would be accompanied by the rhetoric of trading the protection of privacy for increased international and national security.[21] It is sufficient to claim under this fourth caveat that with the expansion of the e-state, the possibility of police statehood measures increases. This threat moves from a theoretical one to a realistic one if QR technology as a gateway to the enjoyment of some fundamental rights was to find practical implementation. The elements for such a transformation are clearly visible in the image we are looking at, for instance, during the recent Covid-19 crisis, which hit the world in 2020–2021. Other crises may follow, either related to climate catastrophes, water and electricity shortages or military conflicts. QR codes may be developed which tell us when we can leave home and where we can travel. A rhetoric may emerge stating that QR codes will enable a *return to normality*. Against this background, it can be easily argued that the price of giving up some of our fundamental rights and entrusting the technology with the power to determine the degree of enjoyment of the fundamental rights is not too high. This completes the creation of the police state. As soon as AI through QR codes tells you whether you can leave your home, how far you can go on foot and who you can and cannot meet, then you live in a police state. An online police state in comparison with a potential police state offline appears stronger and more comprehensive, and immune to any mistakes.

[21] For a discussion about this matter, see J. Waldron, 'Security and Liberty: The Image of Balance' (2003) 11 *Journal of Political Philosophy*, 191.

19

Proportionality Deficit Paradox

19.1 IDEAS DEVELOP DURING A CRISIS

It is often said that human rights develop at a different pace during times of crisis. At least it does not need verification that the emergence of most of the important human rights instruments and the articulation of core human rights happened immediately after the global cataclysm of WWII. It can also be said that in times of crisis various characteristics of human rights appear or receive more attention, which otherwise might remain unnoticed. Variance resulting from the transposition from one domain to another can likewise become more obvious at an accelerated pace due to social and political turbulence, leading us to attentively explore the digital reflection of offline human rights ideas, ideals and features. One of the recent crises was the Covid-19 pandemic,[1] which led to the reflection about proportionality, discussed shortly. Sometimes it is useful to speak of human rights law before and after a crisis, assuming that certain fundamental changes and clarifications are a side product.

Among several objections often raised in the pre-pandemic times against the capability to protect fundamental rights in the digital domain is about the fluctuation and unpredictability of the scope of traditional rights originating from and conceptualised in an offline environment. In other words, non-coherence theory says the boundaries of traditional fundamental rights either become broader or narrower once transposed into the digital context. There

[1] For the reader from the future, the Covid-19 crisis hit the world in 2020 and led occasionally to an almost complete standstill of 'social life as usual'. Educational establishments were fully or partially closed, airline traffic reduced, people were required to wear protective facemasks and their movements outside the home was sometimes restricted. The crisis coincided with vaccination rules imposed by the majority of countries, where unvaccinated persons faced stricter limitations in comparison with vaccinated persons.

are two images which at first sight appear almost the opposite of one another. The first reflects almost total freedom of expression unrestrained in practice; the second is the almost total absence of such freedom due to e-technologies which have the function of transparency and perpetuating everything which has been recorded or done. The first is a feature of social media and the second of blockchain technologies. These images may seem incompatible, but they are additionally explainable through one distinct feature, which can be referred to as the proportionality deficit paradox. This is a theoretical conclusion arrived at via accelerated pace due to the pressure during the pandemic, the realisation of which might otherwise have taken years. The pressure was because of the question of whether at the time of crisis exceptions to the strict restrictions limiting foundational freedoms could be accomplished, for instance, whether alternative measures to access cultural establishments or board an airplane should have been available to unvaccinated citizens. The scenario during certain months in 2020 seemed black and white: vaccinated individuals can continue enjoying certain rights and unvaccinated individuals cannot. Such a distinction did not allow any alternatives, which means that the rule from vaccination status was applied without any possible proportionality assessment. From here, the proportionality deficit paradox thesis was articulated. A complete verification or possible rejection of this thesis would happen in the future through contestation and non-pandemic pressure, and possible quantitative analysis, which is not the focus of this monograph. The proportionality deficit paradox is based on the norm-theoretic distinction between rules and principles.[2] Social media and blockchain technologies are capable of applying human rights rules but are not able to apply human rights principles. This means, they are not functionally capable of implementing the proportionality principle. The war in Ukraine, ongoing at the time this monograph was written, likewise exhibits a proportionality deficit, and through the statement 'you are either against us or with us', neutrality is considered to be taking a side.

19.2 CONCERNS ABOUT ONLINE BALANCING

The reason for such incapability of proportionality, in the case of social media, is the practical impossibility to articulate arguments during content moderation, whereas the application of rules through subsumption stays within the reach of social media and is reflected in the content moderation outcomes of

[2] R. Alexy, A *Theory of Constitutional Rights* (Oxford: Oxford University Press, 2010).

deleting or retaining certain words, expressions or images. The reason for such incapability in the case of blockchain technology is related to this technology's essence. A proportionality application means optimisation and is therefore incompatible with technology based on definite solutions and opposed to the infinite outcomes of similar input resulting from a proportionality assessment.

There are various concerns about balancing in the online domain. Fontanelli has raised the objection from jurisprudence. Having analysed examples of reasoning when the Court of Justice of the EU is applying the balancing approach to conflicts of rights online, he posited that 'the proportionality test – as we know it – is an inadequate heuristic device to grasp and regulate the influence of the internet on fundamental rights. Consequently, judgements that turn on a determination of proportionality are ultimately ill-founded or simply seek artificial legitimacy for conclusions based on another policy trade-off'.[3] Fontanelli can be criticised for relying on Habermas' seminal assertion that there are no rational standards for weighing,[4] because on the contrary, his doubt about the reasonability of applying the proportionality test online originates not from the absence of rational standards but their abundance, as well as having to take into account three or more groups of stakeholders' interests and three or more rights which are to be placed on the scales. Others have been attentive to the difficulty of applying the proportionality idea in the novel technology surroundings and propose holding on to the traditional meaning of proportionality. For instance, Land writes that, 'in the net neutrality debate, Article 19's protection of technology would require caution in allowing significant departures from prevailing practices until more is known about the effect of such departures on freedoms of expression and information'.[5] Various concerns related to transposing balancing without variance to the online domain are discussed by Pollicino.[6] In a recent monograph about the practices of international and domestic courts vis-à-vis internet challenges, Pollicino puts forward a comprehensive picture of arguments presented for and against the proportionality approach online. Yet there is a view from judges that business as usual continues. This is, for instance,

3 F. Fontanell, 'The Court of Justice of the European Union and the Illusion of Balancing in Internet-Related Disputes' in O. Pollicino, G. Romeo (eds.), *The Internet and Constitutional Law: The Protection of Fundamental Rights and Constitutional Adjudication in Europe* (New York: Routledge, 2016), p. 95.

4 Ibid., p. 106.

5 M. Land, 'Toward an International Law of the Internet' (2013) 54 *Harvard International Law Journal*, 2, 417.

6 O. Pollicino, *Judicial Protection of Fundamental Rights on the Internet: A Road towards Digital Constitutionalism?* (Ebook: Bloombury Publishing, 2021).

represented by Spano[7] when discussing the approaches of the Strasbourg Court towards user comments online. Yet it even transpires from his writing that the criteria established for the assessment of offline freedom of expression are not transposed unchanged to the online domain, since the element of economic interest has been added. We can refer to Spano's approach as resistance to the idea of non-coherence. But it would be resistance to an inevitable. Even the Strasbourg judges would have to recognise that there is some degree of non-coherence, if we take the elements of time and economic interest, which mounts at least to a minor transformation of offline standards.

19.3 PROPORTIONALITY AND BLOCKCHAIN TECHNOLOGIES

The presentation of concerns about proportionality in blockchain technologies would remain unconvincing if they remained abstract and originated from purely legal scholarship in isolation from understanding how blockchain really works. A view from inside is indispensable. For this reason, some reflections from the interdisciplinary perspective are in order. Schreier and others remark that: 'The increasing opportunities and technical means for data collection afforded from digitalisation raise legal concerns related to proportionality, necessity and data minimisation.'[8] Villagran generalises to suggest that it is advisable not to introduce any personal data on blockchain at all.[9] This is because human rights principles from the offline domain are ignored and become non-functional in these technologies. It would seem that adherence to the belief that proportionality can remain an effective principle in blockchain is a matter of belief rather than being supported by argumentation. Marjolein finds the discrepancy between blockchain and the offline human rights system an insurmountable incompatibility of analogous and binary reasoning. He aptly remarks about the problems of such incompatibility: 'Rather, they stem from a more fundamental, general unease of the current legal paradigm, developed in an analogous context and with an essentially human focus, with the digital paradigm, which is binary in nature and applies a logical, mathematical reasoning. As blockchain technology

7 R. Spano, 'Intermediary Liability for Online User Comments under the European Convention on Human Rights' (2017) 17 *Human Rights Law Review*, 674.

8 N. Schreier, R. Renwick, T. Ehrke-Rabel, 'The Digital Avatar on a Blockchain: E-identity, Anonymity and Human Dignity' (2021) 2 *Austrian Law Journal*, 2, 202.

9 P. G. Villagran, 'Blockchain Technology and the General Data Protection Regulation: An Inevitable Conflict?' (2022) 14 *Amsterdam Law Forum*, 2, 63.

enters the phase of autonomously operating smart contracts and autonomous organisations, this tension will only increase.'[10]

The consequences of the immunity of blockchain technologies to enabling a proportionality assessment are far-reaching both in practical and theoretical terms. Here are a few examples of what has been said about the practical consequences either for the general population or specific interest groups. Schreier and others, having offered a general warning that proportionality does not operate in the blockchain realm, explain how this impacts everyone in daily doings:

> Proportionality is moreover questionable as in the case of financial service providers collecting device data, the aim of this infringement of fundamental rights is not to protect life and limb, but rather – apart from preventing the financing of terrorism – to protect either the banks' financial interests or as a consumer protection measure – as opposed to a measure necessary to maintain the financial system as a whole. The ECHR has stressed that the measure restricting the fundamental right to privacy must be foreseeable and lack arbitrariness. In the case where the data processing is based on consent, the foreseeability of the data processing is often in fact not given, especially if the ability to deny consent under one's own free will is compromised by the fact that financial services are essential in daily life and that there is a considerable imbalance of bargaining power between financial institutions and their customers.[11]

The inside view of blockchain comes from scholars looking at bitcoin mining, and here is what they suggest: 'It is widely assumed that the selection process in a blockchain is based on proportional winning probabilities. The reliability and security of any blockchain is based upon this assumption. However, making an analogy between the Bitcoin protocol and the classical statistical urn problem, we argue that, at least on a theoretical level, the selection process in several blockchains is based on nonproportional winning probabilities.'[12]

19.4 PROPORTIONALITY AS WE KNOW IT

The previous section shows that the possibility to transpose proportionality as we know it from the offline domain without variance to the online domain

[10] M. Busstra, 'Designing for Good: Blockchain Technology and Human Rights' (2020) *Intergovernmental Organization In-House Counsel Journal*, 38.

[11] Schreier et al. (n 8), 215.

[12] J. Parra-Moyano, G. Reich, K. Schmedders, 'A Note on the Non-proportionality of Winning Probabilities in Bitcoin', 1 October 2020, SSRN: https://ssrn.com/abstract=3399742 or http://dx.doi.org/10.2139/ssrn.3399742, accessed 21 November 2022.

remains under contestation. By itself, such contestation shows non-coherence, as there are important elements calling into doubt transposability without variance as a minimum, and as a maximum whether proportionality makes sense online at all. To understand the nature of non-coherence, it is necessary to state here that contestation means the unclear reflection of an offline human right idea or concept in the online domain. Such lack of clarity means non-coherence. Yet non-coherence is not a constant, and can change in time. Variance between human rights ideas or concepts between the two domains can fluctuate by narrowing or broadening, which is then also reflected in the non-coherence becoming wider or narrower. When through discourse and practice the images approach one another, this usually means that in both domains the respective idea or concept gives up some of its initial characteristics and adopts something from the other domain. We have called this the reverse effect of non-coherence.

However, there are not too many examples of such a reverse effect occurring. Perhaps the change in the concept of a journalist serves to illustrate mutual influences between digital and non-digital domains. For instance, Hovlid has recently demonstrated how the understanding of who is a journalist has shifted from an institutional to a functional understanding.[13] She shows that in modern times anyone who regularly expresses views on various formats can be considered a journalist, and one's affiliation to a media company is no longer decisive. This shift was caused by modern technological possibilities.

As a matter of fact, contestation can lead to the disappearance of non-coherence for two reasons. The first is when the digital domain entirely absorbs the meaning given to a concept or idea offline. This would be a case of transposition without variance. The sameness of rights rests on this approach. The opposite happens when it becomes obvious beyond argumentative possibilities that the meaning and function given to a human right idea, concept or rule in the digital domain is entirely incompatible with its offline origin. Again, not too many examples can be construed; possibly the right to know the reasons for decisions affecting the data subject can serve as an illustration. Since the digital domain, due to the absence of capabilities for such individual reasons, cannot furnish the data subject with reasons of comparable scope with the non-digital domain, there is nothing to contest against this objective impediment.

[13] E. Hovlid,'Finding a Judicial Definition of Journalism: A Challenging Exercise in the Digital Age' in M. Susi (ed.), *Human Rights, Digital Society and the Law: A Research Companion* (London: Routledge, 2019), pp. 209–224.

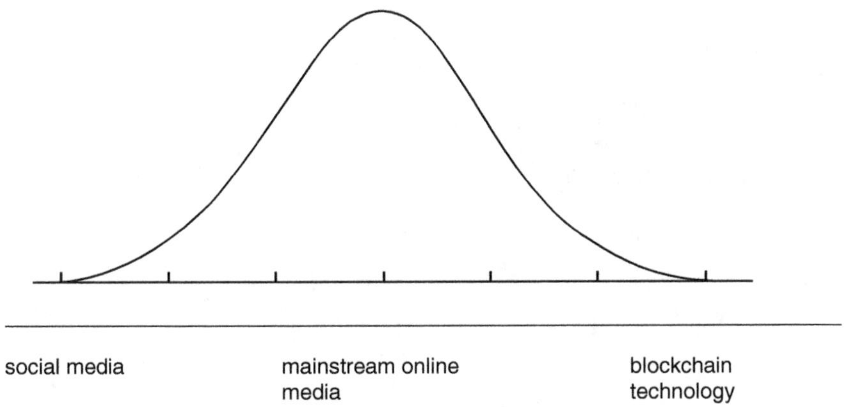

FIGURE 19.1
The graphic image illustrating the proportionality deficit paradox in Chapter 19 of the present volume first appeared in my article 'Digital Human Rights Proportionality during Global Crises'in the book *Pandemocracy in Europe: Power, Parliaments and People in Times of COVID-19*', edited by Matthias C. Kettemann and Konrad Lachmeyer, published in 2021 by Hart Publishing, an imprint of Bloomsbury Publishing Plc.

Yet contestation cannot be taken as eliminating some certainties. Here the online characteristics discussed block the possibility of a reasonable disagreement[14] about proportionality online in blockchain and social media solutions. Those who talk about proportionality in these solutions talk about the proportionality principle before it is absorbed by the digital image, reflecting nothing back.

Figure 19.1 illustrates the proportionality deficit paradox. The curve shows the capability level of the assessment of proportionality via argumentation. The y-axis indicates the level of proportionality assessment capabilities and the x-axis the level of normativity as opposed to arbitrariness and absence of foreseeable standards.

The conclusion is that proportionality as a human rights instrument becomes distorted and weakened in the digital domain. The fragmentation stems from the loss of its holistic capacity to be applied anywhere relative rights collide online. The distortion means a breakage of the link between the outcome and the proportionality principle. In other words, a solution in an individual case where rights and interests collide, is not a result of optimisation. When someone uses the expression of proportionality towards social media or blockchain outcomes, the expression is at wide variance from its meaning offline. In sum, the concept of proportionality between online and offline human rights domains exhibits wide non-coherence.

[14] J. Rawls, *Political Liberalism* (New York: Columbia University Press, 1993), p. 55.

20

Automated Systems and Artificial Intelligence

20.1 THE MAIN PROPERTIES

There are two human rights properties overshadowing academic discourse and policy documents in relation to automated systems and artificial intelligence which are operating in the digital realm. The division between automated systems and artificial intelligence is not important here; these are used with a high degree of generality and interchangeably, despite concerns about whether this is fully justified.[1] These properties are about the trust in artificial intelligence and automated systems, and secondly, about the robustness. The latter appears in two aspects – related to law governing the AI solutions and the AI itself. The purpose of this chapter is to put these properties into the foreground of possible non-coherence view in comparison with the non-digital domain.

20.2 TRUST IN AI

20.2.1 *The Dual Nature*

For a meaningful comparison, one needs to determine how an element to be compared is understood in different paradigms. The elements of trust in the offline human rights domain appear ripened with the passage of time. It has a dual nature: normative validity and the characteristics of those who implement the valid norms. Even if we trust those who have the authority to enforce the law, our satisfaction with the outcome depends on whether we consider

[1] It is not necessary here to provide insight into the details of the differences. It suffices to note that as a rule, artificial intelligence is understood widely as a device to resolve problems independently, whereas in automated solutions such a feature is minimal. One can easily read more using automated search engines.

the law which they apply to be in accordance with our understanding of fairness. Yet, if we consider the law to be applied as fair, in principle we should be able to accept an unfavourable outcome against our actions, if the law is applied by judges or public officials we consider trustworthy. There could be plenty of examples of how the concept of trust in judges and public officials has been construed, for example, containing the elements of the subjectivity and objectivity of the judges, or accountability of and public scrutiny towards the public officers. The claim of trust in the offline system of human rights thus contains a chain of at least two main elements, that of normativity and from there to those who are entrusted with the implementation of the said norms. The key here is the capability – at least in the abstract – of the judiciary to turn the unfairness of laws into fairness through judicial decisions. This is the essence of trust in the judiciary in the offline domain – that in situations of extremism, the judiciary at least has the tools to enable the non-application of unfair norms.

20.2.2 *Intolerability and Disavowal Formulas Online*

Such a capability appears through instruments of constitutional review, and is rooted in Radbruch's intolerability and disavowal formulas.[2] Both formulas are about extreme injustice and unfairness, the second in relation to the malicious intent of the lawgiver to adopt prima facie unfair legislative acts, and the former in the absence of such clear intent, the intolerable effects of the law. Such a proposition of turning unfair normativity into fair judicial or quasi-judicial outcomes cannot be validated for the digital domain, where automated solutions or artificial intelligence is allowed to make decisions. There are two reasons for this.

The first is because of a phenomenon which is primarily intuitionistic and asserts that the concept of trust in the digital domain has a blind eye towards the question of normative fairness. This is related to the objection from Radbruch's disavowal formula. Digital domain operators – automated systems and artificial intelligence – take for granted the positive features of positive or quasi-positive rules. By analogy, no matter whether a son grows up in a wealthy or materially struggling family and no matter whether his father objectively taken can be considered a fair or devious man, he still is the father of this young man and the only father he knows. The only rules this young

[2] For a discussion about both concepts, see M. Borowski, 'Rabdruch's Formula and Human Rights' in M. La Torre, L. Niglia, M. Susi (eds.), *The Quest for Rights : Ideal and Normative Dimensions* (Northampton, MA: Edward Elgar Publishing, 2019), pp. 27–48.

man knows are the ones imposed by his father and therefore he very likely may credit the rules with positive values – something the outsiders might question. It is only after the passage of some time that the son may start to question the fairness of the domestic rules, which may lead to disobedience. If the son does not grow up, or if he remains incapable of differentiating between what is right and what is wrong, or what is correct and what is incorrect, the son will remain in a constant stage of trusting the rules made by his father. For him, trust means narrowly the obligation not to deviate from the rules imposed by his father. This analogy can be used when thinking of the element of trust towards automated systems or artificial intelligence. And again, by analogy, the debate surrounding whether AI can outgrow its creators is similar to the son growing up and abandoning the domestic rules made by his father. Now, a different question of trust emerges, namely whether the rules created by the son or the grown-up AI should be trusted by others.

The second reason is the objection from the intolerability formula. Judges refusing to apply a legal norm which would lead to an extremely unfair outcome because they can exercise distrust in the law. Artificial intelligence and automated systems, on the other hand, are designed to trust the law. To put it figuratively, the degree of our trust in physical judges is related to our expectation that they are capable of distrusting the law. And our trust in automated systems and artificial intelligence is weaker because we assume that they completely trust the law. It could be said that we cannot find a better positivist than artificial intelligence. We see here broad non-coherence between the element of trust due to capabilities. The moment artificial intelligence can independently exercise disavowal and intolerability formulas, that is, articulate a reasoned understanding that a specific legal norm or rule is profoundly unfair, then the non-coherence disappears. However, then we would no longer be dealing with artificial intelligence; perhaps we could term such a decision-maker an artificial brain. Based on what was known at the time this monograph was written, trust in the assessment of the fairness of legal and quasi-legal rules is at wide variance between human decision-makers and artificial intelligence.

20.2.3 *Quantitative Input*

This variance may not be sufficient to capture the whole image of trust in non-digital and digital domains. Exceptionally for legal research, quantitative data is available on the matter of how trust is understood in these domains, which appears at variance due to the objections stemming from capabilities. A comprehensive survey from 2011 exploring how Europeans understand trust in justice revealed that the public assesses the trustworthiness of judicial institutions along three dimensions: effectiveness, procedural fairness and distributive fairness.[3] The authors of the survey, Jackson et al., assert a correlation between normativity and compliance, that is, the more trustworthy the justice system is considered, the greater the likelihood of individuals complying with socially expected behaviour.[4] Normativity appears to be the key for conceptualising trust in the non-digital domain. For the digital domain, a recent overview of twenty-three empirical studies revealed that user trust in AI-enabled systems was influenced by three main themes: the socio-ethical considerations, technical and design features, and user characteristics.[5] The study exhibited an almost complete absence of trust vis-à-vis AI operations.[6] This was due to AI systems developing faster than user readiness (social-ethical considerations),[7] difficulties in building solutions which resemble human communication (technical and design features)[8] and the dependence of the trust definition on the attitudes of users in general towards technical solutions (user characteristics).[9]

For a comparison to make sense of this, one can construe an ideal discursive image where doubts are eliminated and consensus achieved. This would be an ideal situation of complete trust in something, assuming that no additional factors are relevant. Such trust in decisions by AI and automated systems can be construed on the basis of the empirical study put forward by Bach et al. Here AI and automated solutions would operate in an environment of: (i) complete agreement on rules, which are put in place not before, but after the ethical consent of the users; (ii) technical solutions resembling human communication features to the extent that at first glance distinctions between the biological or technical origin of the decision-maker are not apparent; and (iii) the majority of digital space users have developed a positive attitude towards technical solutions due to overwhelming evidence from positive narratives and personal experiences. It appears that only after such

3 J. Jackson, M. Hough, B. Bradrord, T. Pooler, K. Hohl, J. Kuha, 'Trust in Justice: Topline Results from Round 5, European Social Survey', European Social Survey, December 2011, www.europeansocialsurvey.org/docs/findings/ESS5_toplines_issue_1_trust_in_justice .pdf, pp. 8–10.

4 Ibid., pp. 10–11.

5 T. A. Bach, A. Khan, H. Hallock, G. Beltrão, S. Sousa, 'A Systematic Literature Review of User Trust in AI-Enabled Systems: An HCI Perspective' (2022) *International Journal of Human–Computer Interaction*, DOI: 10.1080/10447318.2022.2138826.

6 Ibid., 3–4.

7 Ibid., 4.

8 Ibid., 4–6.

9 Ibid., 6–9.

an ideal scenario becomes available in practice will questions related to trust which dominate the discourse in non-digital domain become relevant.

20.2.4 *Recourse to Martens*

The questions related to trust in the digital domain towards the capabilities of AI and automated systems operate at a higher level of generality than in the physical realm towards decision-makers and the decision-making process. Yet such wide variance is not only a conclusion which can be reached towards these two human rights paradigms. Friedrich Marten's concept of consular jurisdiction was built upon the notion of distrust in the judicial system of the Orient, leading to the claim that citizens of Western countries should be exempted from the obligation to have their legal cases decided by Oriental courts.[10] To use the analogy, Martens' view on the need for consular jurisdiction exempting citizens from Western countries was based exactly on the same features raised towards AI and automated systems. In particular, (i) little knowledge and understanding of the legal system and ethical considerations of the Orient (the socio-ethical objection); (ii) the judges and public officials having a different outlook from Western judges, not to mention the issues of language, the way judicial systems operated and the behavioural properties of the judges (technical and design features objection, briefly: the courts and officials and judges do not look the same as judges in Western countries); and finally (iii) general distrust towards the inner features of the Orient (user characteristics objection). The proponent of the incremental view of human rights development might now say that even if the variance between the element of trust between AI and human decision-making was immediately wide when the AI appeared, with the passage of time the variance may diminish. This view, however, is wrong, as will be discussed in the following section.

20.2.5 *Recourse to Plato*

Quantitative measurements are important, yet describe reflections on the wall of the cave within Plato's concept. There are two options for addressing these reflections. One is to proceed by analysing these reflections, which would

[10] On the topic of the dichotomy between 'civilised' and 'non-civilised' nations, see A. T. Müller, F. F. Martens, 'The Office of Consul and Consular Jurisdiction in the East' (2014) 25 *European Journal of International Law*, 3, 871–891. For a contemporary view on the subject, please see: D. Stewart, 'The Emergent Human Right to Consular Notification, Access and Assistance' in A. von Arnauld, K. von der Decken, M. Susi (eds.), *Cambridge Handbook on New Human Rights: Recognition, Novelty, and Rhetoric* (Cambridge: Cambridge University Press, 2020), pp. 439–452.

mean reflecting further upon the reflections. This comes hand in hand with soon forgetting that one reflects upon a reflection. And the other option is to proceed outside the cave, where there is the light which shows us the accurate nature of things. In the present context, this would be the light emanating from the non-coherence assumption. The assumption can be applied not only to human rights ideas and rules originating from the non-digital domain but beyond to concepts which are closely connected to the former. Since the notion of trust appears to have such a close connection to the operation of any legal order, the non-coherence assumption applies. The consequence is that, despite what the technical developments can achieve, for example, an artificial brain capable of interpretation from the existing normative framework, and even the derivation of legal rules from existing rules, such an artificial brain may reach a point where no interpretations or derivations are possible without destroying the pyramid of legal norms.

20.2.6 *AI and the Basic Norm*

Here reference is made to the basic human rights norms, which stand at the bottom of any legal structure and have their origin from outside such a legal structure. Since the entire human rights physical realm is conditional on the existence and acceptance of some basic ideas, the question arises how in ideal discursive conditions can these basic ideas be replaced or transformed. We have built non-coherence theory upon the thesis that ideas, rules and concepts from the non-digital domain are transposed into the digital domain and may undergo transformation. Yet for non-coherence to make sense, there needs to be at least some link to properties offline which do not transform upon transposition; because if all features between digital and non-digital domains are at variance, then the point of comparison disappears. We can therefore ask whether trust in offline decision-makers also includes the hypothetical acceptance of the change of the basic norm. Or from the other side, that this trust entails the opposite, namely that the basic norm(s) will not be touched in judicial decision-making processes. Various views can be expressed on this matter. The non-coherence theory says that the capability of AI and automated decision-makers does not reach the point of challenging basic norms. This proposition excludes contestation, and as such already stands at variance from the offline domain, where the matter of who can alter the basic norms and how is a valid theoretical and practical question. If they, AI and automated systems, had the capability to alter the basic norm, then digital and non-digital domains would be completely different, despite how the words and expressions appear on the surface.

However, doubts can be raised as to whether decisions by AI and automated systems are traceable to some core ideas. This is a question from the ideal conditions of discursivity, where one can be confident that the link to fundamental principles and ideas in ordinary court judgments of quasi-judicial decisions by public officials is not always easily traceable but in a deeper and time-consuming search, findable. These doubts can be grouped as doubts related to the logical chain of normativity and to the incompatibility of language.

20.2.7 *Digital Normativity without Basic Norms*

Most legal scholars working in the field of digital rights are accustomed to thinking that IT technology is always several steps ahead of normativity. In other words, IT technology, including AI capabilities, are in the consistent stage of improvement, and therefore start to operate before rules to limit their operation are created and then catch up. One may seek comfort from the belief that such a concern is only about concrete rules and norms, and that higher-level principles are usually considered in AI development work. Yet there is no clear evidence for this being the case. For instance, Vianello et al. assert that although many practical methods and tool kits exist for assessing AI systems from an ethical perspective, many of these are based on a predefined set of ethical principles and processes.[11] And they continue: 'From our practitioner experience, applying predefined large frameworks can be a challenge, especially for small- and medium-sized businesses'.[12] This is a challenge due to the attempt to disregard non-coherence and a direct transposition with no variance. Gulati, Sousa and Lamas' extensive research about human–computer interaction demonstrates that a higher degree of technical complexity and problem-solving capacity is not correlated with explainable output. Their statement is reproduced here: 'New technologies, data, and algorithms impact nearly every aspect of daily life. Unfortunately, many of these algorithms operate like black boxes and cannot explain their results even to their programmers, let alone end-users'.[13] All this leads us to question whether AI solutions and automated decision-making tools can operate in a vacuum of

[11] A. Vianello, S. Laine, E. Tuomi, 'Improving Trustworthiness of AI Solutions: A Qualitative Approach to Support Ethically-Grounded AI Design' (2022) *International Journal of Human–Computer Interaction*, DOI: 10.1080/10447318.2022.2095478.

[12] Ibid., 14–15.

[13] S. Gulati, S. Sousa, D. Lamas, 'Design, Development and Evaluation of a Human-Computer Trust Scale' (2019) *Behaviour & Information Technology* 1, DOI: 10.1080/0144929X.2019.1656779.

core human rights principles. In other words, whether during the transposition of human rights specific rules and principles with relatively high concreteness, necessary to create some normative framework for AI operations, basic norms legitimising these specific rules and concrete principles were left behind. These simply were not transposed. A question of broader scope than just related to the digital domain emerges. This is whether one can construe a normative system of rules and principles where there are no fundamental values specified, even if these are at the stage of contestation, nor basic norms determined.

By analogy, this same question can be asked differently for the physical realm. Can one construe a legal system without a constitution or some other instrument having the properties of a constitution? And further, if a constitution were to exist, can one construe such a constitution without a preamble or introductory statement which puts forth the pillars for the instrument and thereby a connecting function to the entire normative structure? The same question can be asked for international law – whether instruments without general statements can be imagined, and if so, can they be validated. The reply is given by non-coherence theory, and as such shows the wider power for explanations beyond the boundaries between digital and non-digital domains. The reply to the question whether one can construe domestic or international legal systems – and in particular human rights systems without the connecting thread between fundamental principles and principles with less degree of generality, and legal rules – is affirmative.

Such a scenario should not be confused with a legal system's image where the linkage between high-level principles and concrete rules is weakened because of a dictatorship or other political formations enabling a higher degree of arbitrary and non-predictable legislation and its application. Although we can find anecdotal yet truthful evidence of how the highest courts in the former Soviet Union and China some decades ago had almost never referred to constitutional provisions, the fact remains that the constitutions were available despite being dormant. When politics or mentality changes, the potential to make use of higher-level principles available in the normative system becomes more realistic. Yet a critic might say that a situation with a dormant and non-used constitution and/or fundamental values is significantly more cynical and sinister in comparison with a situation with no constitution or articulated fundamental values at all. The second situation could be *anything goes*, and the first as *anything goes in disguise*.

A separate area of research utilising the non-coherence approach, which remains, however, distant from the current monograph, is to view the variance between the rhetoric of law and law in practice in totalitarian states. Here in our discussion, we can view images as if they existed in ideal conditions as opposed to those of the law in practice. A proponent of the latter view might say that for the practice of law it does not matter if high-level principles and some core ideas are to be found in some basic or constitutional level documents of a domestic or international legal system. Such a critic might assert that the effects on our everyday lives and common adjudication are comparable between images where there are no basic norms, or where these basic norms are dormant and distant. The critic could continue to say that the effects are also comparable if these basic norms or fundamental principles are not available at all, or if the adjudicating entity – in our case artificial intelligence or an automated decision-maker – is not capable of including them in the decision-making process. Might this not support the proposition that in practical terms the effects of artificial intelligence and automated decisions are not in any significant variance from the decisions which might be reached by human moderators or judges on similar matters. Such a proposition would hold for the majority of cases. But it is in difficult cases where normativity and the law's ideal dimension matter. The position which I have to defend is that the non-coherence between adjudication in the physical domain on the one hand, and artificial intelligence and automated decisions on the other, is manifest when the ideal dimension of law enters the scene.

When one can construe a normative image intellectually, which does not appear prima facie absurd, it is usually possible to find resemblance from physical or digital objective reality. Some examples are in order. Take Jean-Paul Sartre's autobiographic novel *The Words*[14], where in his dream the author finds himself travelling on a train towards Paris without a valid ticket. Yet he carries with him a secret of great importance for the entire nation which he needs to convey to the highest authorities. The conductor enters the wagon and Jean-Paul explains his situation. In his own thoughts, he has more right than anyone else on the train to get to Paris, despite having no ticket. Imagine the variance in responses if the conductor was a human, or if the conductor was a human-like robot. Most likely the discussion with the latter would be short and Jean-Paul would not be able to continue the journey. Yet with the human conductor one cannot exclude that higher principles would come to play and it cannot be fully excluded that the message could be delivered to Paris. Or take another abstract example, where a single mother of three is not paying income tax to the government because otherwise the children would be hungry. An automated taxation solution would keep the

[14] J.-P. Sartre, *Les Mots* (Gallimard Publishing, 1963).

discussion short and would simply refer the matter to a tax payment collector. Yet a human tax office employee might seek advice on whether the principle of the rights of the children might prevail over the state's interests in tax collection. These short examples will have to suffice here to repeat the point that there cannot be a more truly positivist decision-maker than an artificial intelligence solution. This is the triumph of the law as practice approach. As such, it stands in sharp contrast with human decision-makers, where there is at least some hope that higher principles may apply and interfere with the positivist thinking.[15]

But surely, one can construe examples to the contrary, whereby the inclusion of some general principles can lead to outcomes which seem counter to the ideas of justice and which the positive application of laws seems to allow. Exchanging individual entitlement to privacy for the promise of higher national security is a concrete example used to justify the intrusion into private spheres. The closure of the social media space in anticipation of civil unrest and the exercise of freedom to assembly is yet another example, where an automated decider would allow a gathering to proceed once all formal notifications are filed, but a diligent city official might decide otherwise and overrule what the ordinary law says. Now, leaving aside the aspects of design bias and various backdoors built into artificial intelligence solutions, basic norms and fundamental principles in judicial or quasi-judicial decision-making lead to the concern about the correctness of the solutions. This is because higher level standards can always inherently lead to multiple views, and thereby positivity and negativity become likewise inherent features of any normative system built upon ideas and principles. The more there is the inclusion of principles in adjudication, the more the outcome becomes unpredictable and challengeable from the viewpoint of correctness and truth. It is possible to assert that positivity without principles in the background minimises the possible claims for truthfulness because this property is not possible without high-level principles. A decrease in correctness is related to the weakening of positivism against principles. As such, one can conclude this discussion by the thesis of the disappearance of the claim for truth in the wider sense from artificial intelligence and automated decisions. Truthfulness is simply a category which does not make sense. This comes hand in hand with

[15] The matter of the absence of higher principles in artificial intelligence decision-making is a holistic matter, not related only to human rights. For instance, Henry Kissinger has warned that once AI is allowed to enter into the field of deciding about war, the threat of global catastrophes increases considerably due to the absence of the threshold of pain – see H. Kissinger, *Leadership: Six Studies in World Strategy* (Westminster: Penguin Press, 2022).

the increase in correctness, achievable via subsumption by AI. The variance between digital and physical realms here seems wide and starts from the conceptual level of quality measurements.

20.3 ROBUSTNESS AND AI

This theory contains the thesis of non-coherent variance between variance about general principles and their concrete application in principles of a lower degree of generality or concrete norms. In other words, if it is established that a variance of a certain degree exists between a general human rights idea; for example, how the principle of equality is understood in the digital and non-digital domains, it is usually the case that the variance between the implementation rules does not have to carry the same degree of variance. It can diminish or expand. If the initial variance regarding a high-level principle can be determined as wide, then it becomes questionable whether the variance can expand further, or whether the result of further discrepancy reaches a point where the features for comparison are transformed so deeply that the image online becomes unrecognisable, thus having almost no place in the offline human rights architecture. This proposition has to be explored regarding the principle of robustness, which appears as one of the key building blocks in rules development for AI and automated decisions.

20.3.1 *Robust AI Law*

Robustness in AI systems and law seems widely accepted as a condition sine quo non in academic discourse and policy documents. Hildebrandt takes *robust AI law* to stand for a legal system that incorporates checks and balances to resist turbulence due to unforeseen changes in the environment it constitutes and regulates.[16] Mathematics enters law in the field of AI since elsewhere Hildebrandt has noted that robust AI usually refers to computing systems that have been verified mathematically and validated by way of empirical testing.[17] To take this approach to its logical conclusion, it appears that mathematics should lead to the manifestation of principles of justice, purposiveness and legal certainty. Here robustness has the same role as

[16] See M. Hildebrandt, 'Robust AI and Robust Law (Part II: Robust Law)', COHUBICOL, 19 March 2021, www.cohubicol.com/blog/robust-ai-and-robust-law-part-ii-robust-law, accessed 21 January 2023.

[17] See M. Hildebrandt blog 'Robust AI and Robust Law (Part I: Robust AI)', COHUBICOL, 19 February 2021, www.cohubicol.com/blog/robust-ai-and-robust-law-part-i-robust-ai, accessed 21 January 2023.

balancing in the offline domain, as input elements into a proportionality test can be mathematically measured, as shown by Alexy in the weight formula.[18] A recent European Commission report generalises the academic discourse and mentions that in AI development, robustness is closely tied to explainability and making certain that *adding noise* to a given input does not change the output and should focus on minimising the impact from vulnerabilities stemming from changes in the environment.[19]

The element of robustness appears in different contexts regarding AI regulation, for instance, as one of the main building principles for developing an AI governance strategy,[20] the statement that the regulatory reform of AI should follow robust descriptions,[21] and as a tool to ensure safety in the online environment[22] and as a tool to protect the digital environment from unauthorised entries from outside.[23] Robustness in all of these aspects, to which more could be added, is seen as a key component to increase the trustworthiness of AI and its legislation.[24] And yet the statement that the element of robustness is necessary to withstand turbulences is the one which catches our attention. The rationale for this attention is simple. One does not encounter similar statements for the offline domain, that is, normative regulation exhibiting features of robustness in order to stand against turbulences from the social world. Supporters of the idea of non-coherence can notice variance in this approach since one domain necessitates normative robustness and the other does not in order to reach the common goal of stability in regulation.

The etymology of the phrase *robustness* takes us to the ancient world, where in Latin *robustus* meant a property of muscular strength or vigour. As such, it was used in connection to vulgarity, where soldiers wrote as they

[18] For the weight formula, wait and read more precisely Part V.

[19] R. Hamon, H. Junklewitz, I. Sanchez, 'Robustness and Explainability of Artificial Intelligence: From Technical to Policy Solutions', EUR 30040, Publications Office of the European Union, Luxembourg, Luxembourg, 2020, ISBN 978-92-79-14660-5 (online), doi:10.2760/57493 (online), JRC119336, respectively at 4, 18 and 1.

[20] N.-M. Aliman, L. Kester, P. Werkhoven, S. Ziesche, 'Sustainable AI Safety?' (2019) 2 *Delphi: Interdisciplinary Review of Emerging Technologies* 4, 226.

[21] C. M. Sharkey, 'AI for Retrospective Review' (2021) 8 *Belmont Law Review*, 2, 377.

[22] S. J. Shackelford, R. Dockery, 'Governing AI' (2020) *Cornell Journal of Law and Policy*, 328, DOI: http://dx.doi.org/10.2139/ssrn.3478244.

[23] H. Kim, Y. Lee, Y. Park, 'A Robust and Flexible Digital Rights Management System for Home Networks' (2010) 83 *Journal of Systems and Software*, 12, 2431–2440.

[24] European Commission High-Level Expert Group on AI, 'Ethics Guidelines for Trustworthy AI', 8 April 2019, https://digital-strategy.ec.europa.eu/en/library/ethics-guidelines-trustworthy-aip.

spoke – robust and vulgar Latin.[25] Interestingly, the terminology of robustness in the current age is sometimes used by the military, albeit not as part of the academic offline human rights vocabulary.[26] One might imagine that the soldier's task is to protect the homeland in general, and some areas or facilities in particular, and this task overshadows the weighing of various subtle interests involved. A solider needs to act first and then think of the consequences. If we take robustness as the common element of a soldier and AI, the analogy becomes clear. Robustness is a feature characterising a practice or normativity where decisions are made on the basis of limited information and where the rules for these decisions are simple. Here the end justifies the means. The less there are layers in a robust normative system or practice, the greater the efficiency of securing the goals of stability and trustworthiness. The more simple a normative system, the more one can predict its outcome, and here trust stands as a feature related to simplicity and self-evidence, and is unrelated to any moral claims. The correctness of an output achieved through a robust devise using robust normativity makes it possible to explain the output in a simplistic manner. Often this is the only explanation possible.

To understand this further, we can ask whether it is conceivable to claim the validity of a robust regulatory system and devices operating in a robust manner. Yet the claim of the validity of solutions acquired through robust devices and a robust regulatory system remains uni-layered due to the absence of arguments from the ability to criticise and/or reject. The meaning of validity changes online, and as a consequence the meaning of correctness changes as well. The variance is towards simplicity. Things which are simple are usually more easily explainable, predictable and trustworthy than things with multiple layers. The latter necessitates in law the application of various doctrines, among them balancing between rights of equal weight, and concepts for how to deal with constitutional collisions, and collisions between norms at the constitutional level and emerging new rights containing rhetoric and features of a possible constitutional status. Non-coherence between norms

[25] For context, one may look at D. Johnston (ed.), *The Cambridge Companion to Roman Law* (Cambridge: Cambridge University Press, 2015).

[26] For instance, a recent NATO Strategic Communications document and statement from a recent military report uses the expression of robustness: 'The rights granted to individuals under the *Universal Declaration on Human Rights* have since been refined, and a robust jurisprudence has developed showing how these rights interact and how they are applied'. See F. Raso, V. Mekone, 'Towards Rule of Law in the Digital Environment', prepared by the NATO Strategic Communications Centre of Excellence, date unknown, https://stratcomcoe.org/cuploads/pfiles/web_towards_rule_of_law_executive_summary_27-11.pdf, pp. 29–30, accessed 4 February 2023.

and features concerning decision-makers between the different domains, in particular automated decision-making and artificial intelligence, thus appears to be wide.

20.3.2 *Robustness of the Digital Domain* Per Se

Yet one more matter has to be taken up before the end of this chapter. It concerns the apparent inseparability of the notion of robustness from artificial intelligence and automated solutions, and the rules governing their operation. The absence of academic contestations and the uncritical acceptance of some property usually signals one of the two following scenarios. It refers either to the stage where a new human rights idea has just been introduced and fascination overshadows a critical response. Or it refers to the stage where the idea has been fully justified and stands as a completely valid property of the human rights architecture. Yet none of these scenarios hold for robustness in the digital human rights domain. Since there has been no contestation at all, it cannot be said that robustness is a valid and justified feature of the digital domain. Nor is it at the inaugural stage of introduction, where debates and criticism can be expected since it has been around in the discourse for several decades. We can term the uncritical acceptance of robustness as an intuitionistic revelation of non-coherence. What would necessitate a profound justification in the offline domain, since robustness stands at the opposite of a sophisticated and many-layered human rights normative and value system, does not appear in need of such a justification online. This also means that the level of sophistication of human rights law in the digital domain has less layers and shadows, consequently there is considerable variance from offline.

PART V

Internet Balancing Formula

21

The Internet Balancing Formula

21.1 INTRODUCTORY NOTES

The principal issue raised through non-coherence theory towards balancing conflicting rights in offline and online domains concerns justification. Can the same theoretical tools – rooted in moral philosophy, or constitutionality, or the non-positivistic concept of law – be applied to justify balancing in both domains? If yes, is there a degree of variance in the weight these tools carry, and of variance along the practice dependence/independence scale? Justifiable balancing in the offline domain claims correctness. When balancing in the online domain remains unjustified, yet dominant through discursive practice, it cannot at first sight claim correctness. Non-coherence theory lens may lead to variance in the doctrinal meaning of correctness. Perhaps what is understood as a claim to correctness in the physical world is different from the claim to correctness in the non-physical world. Variance in the meaning of correctness may consequently lead to variance in the meaning of justifiability when applied to online and offline domains. That is, what does not satisfy the conditions of correctness and justifiability under the elements inherent to offline world, may be sufficient for the online world. This variance can be translated into different degrees of rigour, or else coined as incompatibility of the elements of justifiability and correctness between the two domains.

This is the introductory background to Part V, where I will present the mathematical model for online balancing termed the Internet Balancing Formula[1]. Thereafter I will recapitulate the main points from Robert Alexy's critique of the formula and my reply by presenting a slightly revised

[1] First published in M. Susi, 'Internet Balancing Formula' (2019) 25 *European Law Journal*, Special Issue: Internet and Human Rights Law 2, 198–212.

mathematical model. The chapter continues by reflecting upon what followed the introduction of the formula. It will first address main points from objections and concurrences raised in scientific writings.

Fundamental objection against balancing in the offline domain concerns arbitrariness. Habermas formulated the core of this objection:

> True, not every right will win out over every collective good in the justifications of concrete decisions. But a right will not prevail only when the priority of a collective good over a corresponding norm can itself be justified in the light of higher norms or principles. Because norms and principles, in virtue of their deontological character, can claim to be universally binding and not just specially preferred, they possess a greater justificatory force than values. Values must be brought into a transitive order with other values from case to case. Because there are no rational standards for this, weighing takes place either arbitrarily or unreflectively, according to customary standards and hierarchies.[2]

Alexy rejects this objection through argumentation thesis,[3] which says that standards lend themselves to rational justification. This monograph has shown that the concern about arbitrariness also stands at the centre of contestations against content assessment by private entities offering online services to users. Therefore, the claim of arbitrariness can be said to apply with equal weight in both the digital and non-digital domain. From the view of non-coherence theory there is no variance between these two domains since the concern of arbitrariness is central in both. This statement is limited to abstract level. However, the responses against the arbitrariness claim are at variance, at first sight even incompatible. Earlier in this monograph, the capabilities approach was applied towards user content assessment by online. This approach says that these companies are not capable of advancing arguments for their decisions regarding remedies.[4] To put it simply, offline balancing includes the element of argumentation and online balancing does not. This objective limitation against argument-based interference into user-generated content

2 J. Habermas, *Between Facts and Norms: Contributions to a Discourse Theory of Law and Democracy*, translated by W. Rehg (Cambridge: Polity Press, 1996), p. 259. Due to the goal of this article, I will not enter into a discussion related to the matter of collective goods and values and their relationship to human rights norms.

3 R. Alexy, 'A Non-positivistic Concept of Constitutional Rights' in M. La Torre, L. Niglia, M. Susi (eds.), *The Quest for Rights: Ideal and Normative Dimensions* (Northampton, MA: Edward Elgar Publishing, 2019), p. 13.

4 See for discussion R. MacKinnon, E. Hickok, A. Bar, H.-I. Lim, 'Fostering Freedom Online: The Role of Internet Intermediaries', UNESCO Series on Internet Freedom, UNESCO, 2014, https://unesdoc.unesco.org/ark:/48223/pf0000231162, accessed 18 February 2018.

by private online entities points to incompatibility between online and offline interferences within the meaning of non-coherence theory. Recent large-scale actions by online platforms to create resemblance of argumentation does not affect the epistemic and ontological limitations,[5] it remains a mirror image of the deontological character of offline argumentative balancing.

Further elaboration of the law of balancing led Alexy to propose a mathematical weight formula, developed in 2003[6] and published in English in 2007.[7] The standard form of the Weight Formula runs as follows:

$$W_{i,j} = \frac{I_i \cdot W_i \cdot R_i}{I_j \cdot W_j \cdot R_j}$$

My impression from Alexy's writings and personal discussions with him suggest that his mathematical formula's basic idea is to minimise the norm-theoretic distinction between rules and principles. Numerical value given to principles through argumentation transforms their optimisation aspect into subsumption. The mathematical formula thus gives to balancing more determinative nature and decreases the element of arbitrariness always inseparable from proportionality. Due to the nature of legal rules, objections related to inadequacy of argumentation cannot be raised. The relation of balancing to determinate commands through mathematics can be explained through a thesis, which can be termed *argumentation insufficiency thesis*. When argumentation by itself cannot leave behind objections originating from relative absence of rationality in standards, mathematical elements can succeed in providing more clarity and foreseeability for balancing. Here mathematics has a complementary aspect to strengthen argumentation. The argumentation insufficiency thesis can be maintained towards balancing conflicting rights online but for other reasons.

The first reason is a logical consequence from the capabilities approach, as it was shown that online balancing cannot provide correlation between remedies and concrete reasons for interference. By default, online realm has argumentation deficiency.

The second reason is related to questionability of the doctrine of sameness of offline and online rights, which for the balancing landscape is translated into a challenge about the same or diversifiable abstract weight of rights to be

5 See for discussion M. K. Land, J. D. Aronson, *New Technologies for Human Rights Law and Practice* (Cambridge: Cambridge University Press, 2018).

6 R. Alexy, 'Die Gewichtsformel' in J. Jickeli, P. Kreutz, D. Reuter (eds.), *Gedächtnisschrift für Jürgen Sonnenschein* (Berlin: De Gruyter, 2003), p. 790.

7 R. Alexy, 'The Weight Formula' in J. Stelmach, B. Brożek, W. Załuski (eds.), *Frontiers of the Economic Analysis of Law* (Krakow: Jagiellonian University Press, 2007), p. 25.

protected. The monograph has reflected upon contestations towards the idea that freedom of expression and the right to privacy deserve equal protection online: some claim that freedom of expression online deserves more protection than the right to privacy, and others claim the opposite. When confronted with relativity of the abstract weight of rights to be balanced, one asks for the decisive element in setting these weights on a scale prior to balancing. Such a decisive element emerges from discursive practice and appears entirely utilitarian, as opposed to reasons of morality or constitutionality. It follows that the assignment of initial relative weight for rights to be balanced is primarily non-argumentative.

The third reason originates from the concept of internet vulnerability which dominates online argumentation-based assessment. The image of internet vulnerability reflects an ontic condition that confronts anyone who enters the digital domain.[8] Internet vulnerability realises that the traditional means of protecting one's privacy, known from the offline world, cannot be effectively realised or are considerably weakened in the digital realm. This is so because any information published on the Internet can stay online forever, and the time to react to violations of privacy is non-existent after information is published. These factors by default diminish the protection of privacy online. The internet vulnerability as an ontic condition, if accepted, will lead to a shift in the initial relationship between the conflicting rights before the balancing exercise starts; for example, the scale is set to protect privacy more if the relative weight of other factors against one another would produce an ideal equilibrium.

The fourth reason is related to the element of time as one manifestation from the capabilities approach. Within any framework of judicial balancing the courts have as long as needed to claim a correct assessment of concrete importance of conflicting rights and to establish a proper balance. Conversely on the Internet, the element of time is non-existent, as it would lead to non-effective, retrospective recognition that rights were violated and proper balance was not achieved. Effective balancing online depends on swift decisions about whether certain information published overrides someone else's concern about an intrusion into his or her private domain or other rights. Here time is a different concern from the understanding that with the passage of time the balance of interests may reverse, for example, when processing

8 Martina Gillen states that the internet vulnerability of users in cyberspace is an ontic condition, which has been downplayed but should lead to the protection of privacy. See M. Gillen, 'Human versus Inalienable Rights: Is There Still a Future for Online Protest in the Anonymous World?' (2012) 3 *European Journal for Law and Technology*, 1.

personal data.[9] The shortness of time for reasoned decision-making can easily lead ultimately to the rejection of the rationality of online balancing. Here the mathematical formula becomes central, since it allows easily established input, leading to an immediate conclusion about which of the conflicting rights in the given circumstances should prevail.

Among objections against balancing online via private entities, the concern about the transparency deficit stands out. The Council of Europe has stated that '[i]nternet service providers should put in place appropriate, clear, open and efficient procedures to respond within reasonable time limits to complaints from internet users alleging breaches of the principles included in the foregoing provisions'.[10] The United Nations '*[c]alls upon* all States to consider formulating, through transparent and inclusive processes with all stakeholders, and adopting national internet-related public policies that have the objective of universal access and enjoyment of human rights at their core'.[11] Similarly, La Rue 'encourages corporations to establish clear and unambiguous terms of service in line with international human rights norms and principles'.[12] These examples may suffice to demonstrate the concern about the arbitrariness and lack of transparency.

The current discursive practices among internet intermediaries when balancing conflicting fundamental rights work against the principle of transparency. The business model requiring transparency when balancing seems costly. The practical response has been to make at least some information about the decision-making process publicly available – not in relation to individual cases but as a matter of principle. Two examples illustrate this. The Article 29 Data Protection Working Party adopted the guidelines on 26 November 2014[13] reflecting upon the CJEU *Google* judgement.

9 G. Sartor, 'The Right to Be Forgotten: Balancing Interests in the Flux of Time' (2016) 24 *International Journal of Law and Information Technology*, 1, 72.

10 Council of Europe, Appendix to Recommendation CM/Rec(2016)1, para. 6.1, see also CM/Rec (2018)2 / Recommendation of the Committee of Ministers to Member States on the roles and responsibilities of internet intermediaries.

11 U.N. Human Rights Council, 'The Promotion, Protection and Enjoyment of Human Rights on the Internet', HRC 32nd Session, UN Doc A/HRC/32/L.20 (2016).

12 Frank La Rue, 'Report of the Special Rapporteur on the Promotion and Protection of the Right to Freedom of Opinion and Expression', HRC 17th session, UN Doc A/HRC/17/27 (2011), para. 48, see also D. Kaye, 'Report of the Special Rapporteur on the Promotion and Protection of the Right to Freedom of Opinion and Expression' UN Doc A/70/361 (2015).

13 Article 29 Data Protection Working Party, 'GUIDELINES ON THE IMPLEMENTATION OF THE COURT OF JUSTICE OF THE EUROPEAN UNION JUDGMENT ON "GOOGLE SPAIN AND INC V. AGENCIA ESPAÑOLA DE PROTECCIÓN DE DATOS (AEPD) AND MARIO COSTEJA GONZÁLEZ" C-131/12', adopted on 26 November 2014, www.dataprotection.ro/servlet/ViewDocument?id=1080, accessed 17 February 2018.

The Working Party encourages search engines to publish their own de-listing criteria and make detailed statistics available.[14] The Google Advisory Council[15] was established to formulate guidelines for the practical realisation of the right to be forgotten. Although some experts suggested that Google should provide detailed explanations of its decisions, the recommendations limit the request for transparency for making guidelines publicly available and providing anonymised statistics.[16]

The Internet Balancing Formula can become a generic instrument for overcoming the objections related to arbitrariness and the transparency deficit in private online balancing of fundamental rights. The formula overcomes the objection of arbitrariness due to reliance on one and the same standard formula in all circumstances. The objection related to transparency deficit weakens because input elements into the mathematical calculation are clear and foreseeable.

To sum up, non-coherence theory shows compatibility of images in offline and online domains concerning balancing justification. The meaning of justification and claim to correctness are at variance between the domains, as within the offline domain these concepts contain both ontological and epistemic aspects, whereas within the online domain these concepts appear entirely utilitarian. The argumentation insufficiency thesis has double meaning relative to the inherent capabilities of actors in both domains. This thesis expresses argumentation's limitations in these two domains which appear incompatible. Yet when in both domains two or more relative rights collide, one inevitably has to prevail regardless of the depth or absence of argumentation involved. This expression of the Pareto optimality opens the door to mathematical formulas. From the perspective of non-coherence theory, the process of giving mathematical value to input elements has the identical goal of raising the rationality and predictability of optimisation within the concrete legal and factual ramification. Mathematics, thus, has the clearing effect.

21.2 THE INTERNET BALANCING FORMULA

21.2.1 *Assumptions*

The Internet Balancing Formula (IBF) has to include a sufficient degree of flexibility so that its input elements and their relation to one another can be

[14] Ibid., p. 10.

[15] The Advisory Council to Google in the Right to be Forgotten, 'Report of the Advisory Council to Google on the Right to be Forgotten', 2014, http://docs.dpaq.de/8527-report_of_the_advisory_committee_to_google_on_the_right_to_be_forgotten.pdf, accessed 29 February 2018.

[16] Ibid., p. 21.

altered in response to future changes in the digital environment. The capability to respond to the changes, which may not be known today, allow us to refer to the IBF as a living instrument of fundamental rights protection.

The current assumptions are the following. First, the mathematical formula of the IBF should not enable the blocking of information which is of vital importance for the whole nation. Second, the IBF is inspired by the Weight Formula developed by Robert Alexy,[17] especially since the Weight Formula has introduced mathematics as an ordering tool to the human rights adjudication framework. Third, the input elements of the IBF are based on criteria usually identified by the courts, especially the European Court of Human Rights, for balancing conflicting rights offline, and on the additional criteria due to the ontic and epistemic considerations inseparable from the online dimension of human rights. Fourth, the IBF should be applicable to everyone; in other words, assigning concrete value to different input elements should not require any professional legal training and should be based on empirical experience.

The IBF is a quotient of the relative numerical value of two fundamental rights – the numerical value assigned as a result of input elements for the right to privacy divided by the numerical value assigned to the freedom of expression as a result of input elements. Some numerical values are on a scale from zero to one, some are on the scale from one to three, representing in the latter case the values of light (numerical value 1), moderate (numerical value 2) and intense (numerical value 3) interference. The explanation of the different scales will be provided shortly.

The current human rights global landscape has prohibited hate speech on the Internet in absolute terms, including incitements to violence and any forms of hatred. It is sufficient to note for the purposes of this book that according to this established consensus, balancing is precluded when hate speech occurs. The availability or absence of concrete criteria to establish hate speech remains outside the focus of this book. Therefore, the IBF becomes applicable after the assertion of hate speech is excluded. In other words, step one is to answer the question of whether the matter concerns hate speech. If not, then we proceed to step two.

21.2.2 *The Right to Privacy*

The following elements make up the right to privacy side of the equation.

First, the element of internet vulnerability, which has a constant numerical value of 1 – this element is represented by the capital letter 'V'. The fact that

[17] Alexy (n 7).

the capabilities of the digital realm in the future might develop towards minimising the consistent threat to privacy cannot be ruled out, so that this numerical value can transform into one of degree or be eliminated.

Second, the element of interference in privacy – there is no abstract weight, but its numerical value will depend on the intensity of the interference. A three-level scale will be used where the intensity of interference can be assessed as *light* (numerical value 1), *moderate* (numerical value 2) or *intense* (numerical value 3). The weight of the interference is therefore relative, dependent not on the subjective perception of the person who alleges or might allege a violation of privacy rights but originates from the perception of a neutral onlooker. By means of this scale, the second element of interference in the right to privacy will be determined, represented by the capital letters 'PR', while the level of intensity is represented by the small letter 'x' – designated to measure more significant elements – having the numerical value 1, 2 or 3. So far, the right to privacy side has the following mathematical formula: $V(1) + PR(x)$

Third, the element of time. This element is based on the assumption, unchallenged by the courts[18] and academia,[19] that with the passage of time the interference of privacy by some information or opinion will diminish, since the relevance of the information or opinions decreases. The influence of time upon balancing is a matter of degree, which calls for, at first sight, the arbitrary assignment of a numerical value for the years that have passed. Time will be represented by the capital letter 'T', while the level of intensity is represented by the small letter 'y' designated to measure less significant values 0.25 (passage of time more than 3 years and less than 7 years); 0.5 (passage of time more than 7 years and less than 10 years);

[18] For example, the Google judgment of the CJEU introduced the element of time in understanding 'the right', as time may change the relevance of information – CJEU – Case C-131/12 *Google Spain SL and Google Inc. v Agencia Española de Protección de Datos (AEPD) and Mario Costeja González* (13 May 2014), para. 93.

[19] Korenhof et al. have devoted an entire essay to the exploration of the element of time in the context of the right to be forgotten. They conclude by stating that '[t]aking the passing of time into consideration can help assess the information landscape at issue for the RTBF and account for the changing values of information as it ages, establishing the balance all rights must find with other interests'. See P. Korenhof, J. Ausloos, I. Szekely, M. Ambrose, G. Sarto, R. Leenes, 'Timing the Right to Be Forgotten: A Study into "Time" as a Factor in Deciding about Retention or Erasure of Data' in S. Gutwirth, R. Leenes, P. de Hert, P. (eds.), *Reforming European Data Protection Law: Law, Governance and Technology Series*, vol. 20 (Dordrecht: Springer, 2014), p. 199, DOI: https://doi.org/10.1007/978-94-017-9385-8_7.

0.75 (passage of time more than 10 years and less than 13 years); and 1 (passage of time more than 13 years). If less than 3 years have passed from the event subject to balancing, the element of time will be 0. So far, the right to privacy side has the following mathematical formula: V (1) + PR (x) + T (y)

21.2.3 *Freedom of Expression*

The following elements make up the freedom of expression side of the equation.

First, the level of public interest in the subject matter, which in the way it is published, raises someone's concern about an intrusion of privacy. The numerical value will depend on the level of public interest, which again is an objective criterion and not a subjective criterion through the eyes of the person who claims the realisation of the freedom of expression. Public interest level is related to the impact the respective information may have on the recipients.

A three-level scale will be used; the element of public interest will be represented by the capital letters 'PI', while the level of public interest is represented by the small letter 'x' – designated to measure more significant elements – having the numerical value 1, 2 or 3. Minor public interest (1) is the level of interest for local community matters or for an issue where its importance is time-sensitive, connected to a particular event. In other words, the subject matter is limited by space and/or time. Medium public interest (2) concerns matters of interest for larger communities, which may not have an immediate direct impact upon the lives of the majority. Significant public interest (3) concerns matters which are important for the entire nation, or which may have a direct effect upon the lives of the majority. For example, whether to reconstruct a community centre has a public interest level of 1; the ranking of a nation's best public universities in international rankings has a public interest level of 2, but the government proposal to introduce tuition fees in public universities instead of free education has a public interest level of 3. The level of public interest may also be '0', when, for example, the publication of information or opinions serves the goal of simply satisfying curiosity.

Objections to the Internet Balancing Formula in terms of the justifiability of the numerical values of intensity (intrusion of privacy or level of public interest) in the context of Alexy's weight formula transforms in the digital domain due to the non-availability of the element of time, which is usually associated with the possibility to articulate reasons for deciding about intensity. In the context of the weight formula, Alexy has countered objections related to intuition,[20] decisionism[21] and arbitrariness with the *argumentation thesis*, that the propositions about the intensity of interference and degrees of importance lend themselves to rational justification. Rational justification offline implies articulation but not online because of the element of time, which requires immediate reaction. Therefore, the meaning of rational justification regarding propositions about intensity and degrees of importance must be given a narrow interpretation online. This means, that the usage of the scale and numerical value to identify intensity is by itself a rational approach. The majority of neutral observers are likely to identify the level of the intensity of interference of privacy or the level of public interest on the three-level scale in the same way, given that they have the same information to start with. The Internet Balancing Formula thus assumes that the one who is making the assessment about the level of intensity belongs to this group of the majority. Even if she does not, it has to be assumed that the person's (either physical or artificial) overall approach is rational – the assessment of various situations can be described via a curve, be it platykurtic[22] or normal or any other distribution, which means that the same curve would appear in the assessment of colliding elements in the IBF. In this case the potential bias from distribution would be cancelled out because it is applied in the same way on both sides of the formula.

A separate line of research, calling perhaps for a mixed methods approach using the quantitative and qualitative methods in combination, which is not possible in this monograph, is to study whether the results of rationality in the narrow and wide sense are by and large the same in both domains. This question asks whether the assessments of the levels of intensity reached by the courts, formulated after the possibility to gain more information and take time for consideration, are comparable to those reached by human and/or artificial intelligence, which operate in the conditions of the non-availability of time. In the event of similarities, conclusions may be drawn for the process of judicial assessment. It would also allow to show the degree of variance from the perspective of non-coherence theory. The occurrence of the opposite – similarities are absent or non-significant – does not at the same time lead to

[20] R. Alexy, *A Theory of Constitutional Rights* (Oxford: Oxford University Press, 2010), pp. 82–84; see also R. Alexy, *A Theory of Legal Argumentation* (first published 1978), translated by R. Adler and N. MacCormick (Oxford: Clarendon Press, 1989), pp. 212–220.

[21] B. Schlink, 'Freiheit durch Eingriffsabwehr – Rekonstruktion der klassischen Grundrechtsfunktion' (1984) 11 *Europäische GRUNDRECHTE-Zeitschrift*, 462.

[22] Platykurtic distributions produce less extreme outliers compared with outliers found in a normal distribution.

the rejection of the IBF, since it does not claim overall correctness but correctness at the given time when assessment had to be conducted. The element of the level of public interest on the freedom of the expression side is thus represented by PI (x). It is possible to recapitulate here that correctness has different meanings within the non-coherence theory framework – one can speak of correctness within ontological meaning in the physical world, and of concrete correctness in the non-physical world defined through what is achievable within the given parameters.

The second element is whether the information concerns a public figure. The capital letters 'PF' will be used to represent this element. This is a significant element in the offline balancing of the right to privacy against the freedom of expression according to established consensus; thereby, the level of the public figure is represented by the small letter 'x' – an individual holding significant public power is given the numerical value '3'; an individual who has voluntarily entered the public domain is given the numerical value '2'; and an individual who involuntarily appears in the public domain is given the numerical value '1'. The majority of people, when asked, would be able to assess that a government minister holds significant power, that a member of parliament has voluntarily entered the public domain, and the wife of a famous football player has involuntarily entered the public domain. Case law from the European Court of Human Rights regarding the status of a public figure can serve as a source of inspiration. The IBF on the side of the freedom of expression is so far: PI (x) + PF (x)

The third element is related to how information was obtained. The rationale for this element originates from the need for differentiation in the protection of the freedom of expression online depending on the origin of the information. This element is represented by the capital letters 'OI'. Since its significance for the overall assessment is lighter, a narrower scale of 0 to 0.75 will be used, therefore the small letter 'y' is applicable. This element has a negative impact and therefore illegally obtained information is represented by '–0.75'; information obtained in a morally unacceptable yet legally acceptable way is represented by '–0.5'; and information obtained in a morally questionable way is represented by '–0.25'. The division between morally questionable and morally wrong criteria is that of degree and may change over time. The assessment regarding this division, which could be reached by the majority of the individuals in a group, represents the rational choice as a manifestation of societal values. The criterion of illegality in turn has an objective character, which does not depend on the opinion of the majority. The freedom of expression side so far is: PI (x) + PF (x)-OI (y).

21.2.4 *The Aspect of Empathy*

All the aforementioned elements in relation to the right to privacy and the freedom of expression can in principle be assessed by human or artificial intelligence. It has to be assumed that the majority of individual decisions regarding online content in the present and foreseeable future are made by artificial intelligence for major online companies. Smaller and medium online enterprises and citizen journalists make these decisions by humans. This does not mean that the outcome would be irrational. In order to retain the 'human' touch in the assessment of online content, the element of empathy will be used in the IBF. While the other elements are in principle subject to rational argumentation, the numerical value of this element of 'empathy' is the result of the moral evaluation of the colliding rights. As far as is known today, artificial intelligence is not yet capable of moral evaluation. The empathy element is a guarantee that the task of online assessment will not remain the exclusive domain of artificial intelligence. Here is an aspect of variance between the Weight Formula and the IBF since it allows duality of the factor origins of input elements. That is, when the sole factor origin for the Weight Formula is human mind, the origin for the IBF can either be the human or artificial mind, however in the latter event, human mind is retained through the empathy element.

The element of empathy is represented by the capital letter 'E', and the relative maximum weight for the whole formula is 1, with numerical values 0.25, 0.5, 0.75 and 1. The small letter 'z' is used to signify this value where the sum from both sides cannot exceed 1. This means, for example, that when the element of empathy for privacy is set at 0.25 and for freedom of expression 0.75, then the numerical value remaining from this element for privacy is 0.5.

The inclusion of empathy in the assessment of colliding online rights is not compulsory and may occur in two situations. First, when the quotient of the sum of elements of the right to privacy divided by the sum of the elements related to the freedom of expression is 1. Secondly, when the situation itself calls for distinguishing it from comparable situations for certain moral reasons, primarily when the principle of equality deserves derivation due to some specific contextual reasons which may not be connected to the collision at all.

21.2.5 *The Formula*

The previous input elements lead to the following formula:

$$\mathrm{IBF} = \frac{\mathrm{V}\ (1) + \mathrm{PR}\ (x) + \mathrm{T}\ (y) + \mathrm{E}\ (z)}{\mathrm{PI}\ (x) + \mathrm{PF}\ (x) - \mathrm{OI}\ (y) + \mathrm{E}\ (z)}$$

When the quotient is larger than 1, the right to privacy prevails and the information in questions should not be published or should be blocked.

When the quotient is smaller than 1, the situation is the opposite – the freedom of expression prevails. This result produced by the formula is not open for future argumentation, as several input elements change over time and are dependent on how something is assessed in a given context. This means, that when applied after some time due to some new need, the IBF may produce a different result.

21.2.6 *The Interest in Historical Truth*

The starting point for the application of the IBF, as explained, is after the matter of hate speech has been excluded. The application of the IBF ends at the gates of historic truth. In the other words, the IBF should not become, in principle, an instrument to block information about a matter which at the relevant time in a given society falls under the category of historic truth. What is defined as the interest in historical truth may change over time; that is, there exists a threshold that allows us to define the interest in some matter as interest in such truth. La Rue has expressed the significance of historical truth in the context of the online realm as follows: 'In the case of human rights, one of the fundamental principles to eradicate impunity is to establish the truth of human rights violations when they exist, and this is recognised as the right to truth of the victims and their families but also to society as a whole to reconstruct historical memory, to memorialise the victims of the past.'[23] The purpose of this article is not to venture into the exploration of the concept of historical truth, or its contextual dependence on concrete time and space. It suffices to note that, for the purposes of the IBF, this formula becomes non-applicable once it has been established that the matter at hand concerns historical truth. One can state, therefore, that the IBF as a mathematical formula is bordering from one side on the concept of hate speech and from the other side on the concept of historical truth.

21.3 TESTING THE INTERNET BALANCING FORMULA

In order to test the workability of the formula, the IBF is applied in two real-life cases of the European Court of Human Rights: the Delfi case[24] and the Egill Einarsson case[25]. It will also be applied to two hypothetical cases.

[23] Google Advisory Council, https://archive.google.com/advisorycouncil; La Rue (n 12), p. 31.

[24] European Court of Human Rights (ECHR) Judgement: *Delfi AS v Estonia* (2015 Grand Chamber), Application no. 64569/09.

[25] European Court of Human Rights (ECHR) Judgement: *Egill Einarsson v Iceland* (2017), Application no 24703/15.

21.3.1 *The Delfi Case*

The case concerned anonymous comments posted on Estonia's largest online news portal *Delfi* concerning an article about the destruction – by the ferry company providing a monopoly service – of an ice road leading from the mainland to the largest island. About twenty comments were insulting towards the main owner of the ferry company; a few among these were categorised as hate speech by the ECtHR. On the basis of the comments constituting hate speech, the ECtHR established that there was no violation of the freedom of expression when the online company was found to be in breach of its obligation to safeguard privacy.

This is a situation where the IBF is not applicable due to the matter of hate speech. Had there been no hate speech comments, the Court would have upheld the freedom of expression.

The IBF would indicate the following regarding comments not constituting hate speech.

From the privacy side:

- Internet vulnerability as a constant value: V = 1
- Insult in relation to business operation – minor intrusion of privacy: PR = 1
- There was no issue of time, since the comments followed immediately: T = 0
- The owner of the enterprise would not most likely merit any empathy: E = 0

From the freedom of expression side:

- The matter of the destruction of an ice road is significant for the whole state but not essential for its well-being: PI = 2
- The owner of a major enterprise is certainly a public figure: PF = 2
- The information was obtained legally: OI = 0
- And likely no empathy issue in relation to the matter from the side of expression as well: E = 0

The outcome of the IBF for the Delfi case without the matter of hate speech would be:

$$\text{IBF} = \frac{\text{V (1)} + \text{PR (1)} + \text{T (0)} + \text{E (0)} = 2}{\text{PI (2)} + \text{PF (2)} - \text{OI (0)} + \text{E (0)} = 4}$$

The IBF is 0.5, which means that freedom of expression prevails. The conclusion of the IBF is the same that the ECtHR would have reached, had there been no issue of hate speech.

21.3.2 *Egill Einarsson Case*

The matter concerned posting comments on Instagram towards Mr. Einarsson, alleging that he is guilty of rape, after he had been acquitted by the court just a few days before. Mr. Einarsson sought unsuccessfully the protection of his privacy from the Icelandic courts. These courts considered that the comments were value judgements towards an individual, who through his communication with the public at large had deliberately become a public figure. The IBF would produce the following result regarding the question of posting comments on Instagram.

From the privacy side:

- Internet vulnerability as a constant value: V = 1
- Calling someone a rapist against the judicially established facts is a major intrusion of privacy with the value: PR = 3
- There was no issue of time, since the comments followed immediately: T = 0
- Mr. Einarsson would not most likely merit any empathy: E = 0

From the side of freedom of expression:

- The public interest regarding matters of violent crimes has to be assumed. At the same time, it is significant for the whole state but not essential for its well-being: PI = 2
- Mr. Einarsson had actively communicated with the public on his own initiative; therefore, he was a public figure: PF = 2
- The information was obtained legally: OI = 0
- And likely no empathy issue in relation to the matter from the freedom of expression side means: E = 0

The outcome of the IBF for the Einarsson case is:

$$\mathrm{IBF} = \frac{\mathrm{V}\ (1) + \mathrm{PR}\ (3) + \mathrm{T}\ (0) + \mathrm{E}\ (0) = 4}{\mathrm{PI}\ (2) + \mathrm{PF}\ (2) - \mathrm{OI}\ (0) + \mathrm{E}\ (0) = 4}$$

The IBF is 1, which means that the freedom of expression and right to privacy are equally protected in the given situation. The European Court of Human Rights was not anonymous in the case: five out of seven Chamber judges voted for the finding of the infringement of the right to privacy, while the other two expressed in a dissenting opinion that the freedom of expression deserved more protection.

21.3.3 *Hypothetical Case of Fatally Ill Prime Minister Admitting the Country Will Go Bankrupt Soon*

This is a hypothetical case, where a fatally ill prime minister of country X discussed with his cabinet the imminent perspective that the government will be unable to pay out public salaries and meet other financial commitments as of next month. After making the announcement, the PM instructs the members of the cabinet to keep this information secret at least for another two weeks. During this instruction, the PM is hit by strong pain and he interrupts his instruction by mumbling '[h]ere comes the pain from the cancer again which means that I have not more than a few months to live'. The cabinet meeting is recorded. A journalist obtains against a bribe this recording and an online media enterprise considers whether to make the whole recording public. If they were to cut out the part where the PM admits to having cancer and dying soon, the public may easily think that the media is concealing something. The main editor of the media enterprise now turns to the Internet Balancing Formula for guidance.

In terms of protecting the privacy of the prime minister:

- Internet vulnerability as a constant value: V = 1
- Allowing the entire population to know that someone is dying of cancer is a major intrusion of privacy with the value: PR = 3
- There was no issue of time, since the publication of the recording would follow immediately: T = 0
- The prime minister is deeply respected by the majority in the country; he is widely seen as a person with high moral character, which could bring the empathy criterion to full: E = 1

From the freedom of expression side in relation to the publication of the recording:

- The matter of the country's possible bankruptcy is without doubt significant for the entire population and essential for its well-being: PI = 3
- The prime minister is a public figure of significant power: PF = 3
- The information was obtained illegally: OI = –0.75
- The criterion of empathy is fully used for the privacy side: E = 0

The outcome of the IBF for the hypothetical case is:

$$IBF = \frac{V\ (1) + PR\ (3) + T\ (0) + E\ (1) = 5}{PI\ (3) + PF\ (3)\ \text{-}\ OI\ (75) + E\ (0) = 5.25}$$

The IBF result is 0.95, which means that the prime minister's privacy is less protected. This would remind the attentive reader of one of the assumptions presented previously regarding the IBF – namely, this formula should not become a tool to block information which is essentially important for the entire nation.

One can see that with the passage of time the outcome may shift towards protecting privacy more. After eight years, the element of T on the privacy side would be 0.5, leading to an outcome of 5.5/5.25 = 1.05, provided all other elements remain the same. Therefore, the online company would be precluded from publishing the information, unless there is a strong argument that the interest in the prime minister's illness is an interest in historic truth.

21.3.4 *Case of Who Would Be the New Authoritarian Leader?*

In August 1991 there was a failed a political coup to overthrow Mikhail Gorbachev, the president of the Soviet Union. There was talk that plans were in place to put new figures into key positions in the Soviet republics who would be extremely loyal to the coup leaders and perhaps take repressive measures towards previous independence-minded local leaders and the intelligentsia. Mr. Arnold Rüütel was at that time one of the top leaders in Soviet Estonia. He was later also elected president in independent Estonia. It is believed that he knows who was supposed to become the new leader if the coup was to succeed. In this hypothetical case, Mr. Rüütel is giving an interview to an online media enterprise and when asked about this name, mentions Mrs. Z. This Mrs. Z. is unknown to the public, she is in her 80s and living peacefully in a small town. The main editor of the media enterprise now turns to the Internet Balancing Formula for guidance on whether to publish this name.

In terms of protecting the privacy of Mrs. Z:

- Internet vulnerability is a constant value: V = 1
- Allowing the entire population to know that someone was supposed to become the new leader of an oppressive regime is a major intrusion of privacy with the value: PR = 3
- The events referred to happened more than 25 years ago: T = 1
- The aspect of empathy cannot be assessed for Z, since she is not known at all: E = 0

From the freedom of expression side in relation to the publication of the information about Z:

- The matter is without doubt significant for the entire population: PI = 3
- Z is not a public figure yet: PF = 0
- The information was obtained legally: OI = 0
- The criterion of empathy may be irrelevant: E = 0

The outcome of the IBF for the hypothetical case is:

$$\text{IBF} = \frac{\text{V (1)} + \text{PR (3)} + \text{T (1)} + \text{E (0)} = 5}{\text{PI (3)} + \text{PF (0)} - \text{OI (0)} + \text{E (0)} = 3}$$

The outcome of the IBF for this hypothetical case is 1.67, which means that the privacy of Z clearly calls for more protection. However, if this matter is considered to concern historic truth, then the result of the IBF is not relevant.

21.4 INTERIM CONCLUSION

The Internet Balancing Formula presented in the previous section is capable of maximising the element of transparency and minimising the element of arbitrariness in private online balancing. It is therefore a tool that brings optimised order to the online dimension of conflicting fundamental rights. The formula can claim correctness in a given time–space related context. It is a rational, mathematical and living instrument.

I will now proceed to put forward the formula's critique by Professor Robert Alexy and my response and will then reflect on the points raised in subsequent academic discussion.

22

Robert Alexy's Views on the Internet Balancing Formula*

Mart Susi has proposed a mathematical formula that claims to make possible balancing in the digital dimension performed by private online companies: the Internet Balancing Formula (IBF). This balancing concerns conflicts between the freedom of expression of users of online portals and the personality right of those who are affected by what is published about them in the online portal. In terms of classical conceptions of constitutional or human rights, this is a case of the horizontal effect of these rights. But the classical or offline horizontal effect concerns a triangle with two private subjects at the bottom and the state at the top. The non-classical or online conception of this horizontal effect places a third private subject at the top of the horizontal effect triangle, the private online company. It becomes a completely private triangle. It is highly contested whether such completely private triangles are compatible with the principles of a democratic constitutional state at all, and, if they are, at which point the state has to be reintroduced in one way or another. But this question of the constitutional distribution of competences or powers shall not be our concern here. Rather, our concern is the Internet Balancing Formula as such.

Susi characterises his project as follows: 'The article will claim that the Internet Balancing Formula will increase the rational element of balancing online.'[1] This increase of rationality is possible, Susi argues, because the Internet Balancing Formula is a *mathematical formula*[2] that allows artificial intelligence to operate in online balancing. To be sure, online artificial

* These views appeared for the first time in R. Alexy, 'Mart Susi's Internet Balancing Formula' (2019) 25 *European Law Journal*, Special Issue: Internet and Human Rights Law, 2, 213–220, reprinted here with the author's permission.

1 M. Susi, 'Internet Balancing Formula' (2019) 25 *European Law Journal*, Special Issue: Internet and Human Rights Law 2, 198–212.

2 Ibid.

intelligence balancing is different in important aspects from offline human intelligence balancing. The time available for the two kinds of balancing, the *luxury of utilising time* in offline balancing and the *shortness of time* in online balancing,[3] is a fundamental source of difference. One of Susi's main theses is that this fundamental difference is not connected with the distinction between rationality and irrationality. Rather, he connects it with a distinction between 'rationality in the narrow and wide sense'.[4]

Mathematical formulas have been rare in law up to now. I have attempted to introduce *order into legal thought*[5] in the area of balancing by means of a *Weight Formula*, first published in 2002 in the postscript of *A Theory of Constitutional Rights*.[6] Susi says that his Internet Balancing Formula (IBF) 'is inspired by the Weight Formula developed by Robert Alexy'.[7] This leads to the question of how his Internet Balancing Formula is related to the Weight Formula. What is the relation between IBF and WF? That is our question. In order to analyse some aspects of this relation, I will, in a first step, present the Weight Formula. In a second step, I will then compare the Internet Balancing Formula with the Weight Formula.

22.1 THE WEIGHT FORMULA

In the postscript of *A Theory of Constitutional Rights* the Weight Formula is formulated in a rather complex way. Its standard form was developed in 2003[8] and published in English in 2007.[9] The standard form of the Weight Formula runs as follows:

$$W_{i,j} = \frac{I_i \cdot W_i \cdot R_i}{I_j \cdot W_j \cdot R_j}$$

$W_{i,j}$ represents the concrete weight of the principle P_i, say, the right to privacy, relative to the colliding principle P_j, say, freedom of expression, The weight formula defines this concrete weight as the quotient of three factors standing, so to speak, on each side of balancing. I_i and I_j are of special importance.

3 Ibid.
4 Ibid.
5 A. Barak, *The Judge in a Democracy* (Oxford: Princeton University Press, 2006), p. 173.
6 R. Alexy, *A Theory of Constitutional Rights* (Oxford: Oxford University Press, 2010).
7 Susi (n 1).
8 R. Alexy, 'Die Gewichtsformel' in J. Jickeli, P. Kreutz, D. Reuter (eds.), *Gedächtnisschrift für Jürgen Sonnenschein* (Berlin: De Gruyter, 2003), p. 790.
9 R. Alexy, 'The Weight Formula' in J. Stelmach, B. Brożek, W. Załuski (eds.), *Frontiers of the Economic Analysis of Law* (Krakow: Jagiellonian University Press, 2007), p. 25.

I_i stands for the intensity of interference with P_i. I_j represents the importance of satisfying the colliding principle P_j. I_j, too, can be understood as intensity of interference, that is, as the intensity of interference with P_j through non-interference with P_i. W_i and W_j stand for the abstract weights of the colliding principles P_i and P_j. When the abstract weights are equal, which is the case in many collisions of constitutional rights, they cancel each other out; that is, they then play no role.

I_i and I_j, and also W_i and W_j, concern the substantive dimension of balancing. R_i and R_j have a completely different character. They refer to the reliability of the empirical and normative assumptions concerning, first and foremost, the question of how intensive the interference with P_i is, and how intensive the interference with P_j would be if the interference with P_i were omitted. Over and above this, the reliability of empirical and normative assumptions can also relate to the classification of the abstract weights, that is, to W_i and W_j. The decisive point is that reliability is a factor that does not refer to the things – in our case the intensity of interference and the abstract weights. That is, it is not an ontic factor. Rather, it is a factor that refers to one's knowledge of things. That is, it is an epistemic factor. The inclusion of this epistemic factor in the weight formula is required by a second law of balancing, the epistemic law of balancing.[10]

R_i and R_j refer to normative assumptions as well as to empirical assumptions. This can be expressed by the following equation:

$$R_i = R_i^e \cdot R_i^n$$

The equation here might be called *reliability equation*. In cases in which both empirical and normative reliability are in question, R_i and R_j have to be substituted by the respective products on the right side of the reliability equation. In this way, a refined version of the weight formula[11] enters the picture:

$$W_{i,j} = \frac{I_i \cdot W_i \cdot R_i^e \cdot R_i^n}{I_j \cdot W_j \cdot R_j^e \cdot R_j^n}$$

A formula like the weight formula, which expresses a quotient of two products, is sensible only if all of the factors can be represented by numbers. This is the problem of graduation. Elsewhere,[12] I have proposed a discrete,

[10] Ibid.

[11] On this see R. Alexy, 'Formal Principles: Some Replies to Critics' (2014) 12 *International Journal of Constitutional Law*, 514.

[12] Alexy (n 6), pp. 409–410, 419; Alexy (n 9), pp. 20–26.

that is, a non-continuous triadic scale, in which geometric sequences are implemented. This scale assigns the values *light*, *moderate* and *serious* to the intensity of interference and to the abstract weights. These values are expressed by the numbers 2^0, 2^1 and 2^2, that is, by 1, 2 and 4. Where the epistemic side is concerned, that is R_i and R_j, or, in the refined version of the weight formula, R_i^e and R_i^n as well as R_j^e and R_j^n, one can work with the stages *reliable* or *certain* (r), *plausible* (p) and *not evidently false* (e), to which the numbers 2^0, 2^{-1} and 2^{-2}, that is, 1, $\frac{1}{2}$ and $\frac{1}{4}$, are to be assigned.[13] By means of these triads, most of the decisions of constitutional courts can be grasped. Where they do not suffice, that is, where one has to introduce a still more attenuated graduation, they can be extended to double-triadic scales.[14] A good deal more could be said about the Weight Formula. For the sake of a first glance at the relation between the Internet Balancing Formula and the Weight Formula, however, what has been said here ought to suffice.

It is easy to recognise that the Weight Formula is highly general[15] as well as highly abstract. It is highly general, for it refers to all collisions of all rights and all collective goods that have the character of principles. That is, the representation of the right to privacy by P_i and of freedom of expression by P_j is only a special case of the application of the Weight Formula. P_i and, with this, I_i, W_i, and R_i can refer to all other rights and collective goods. The same applies to P_j and, with this, I_j, W_j and R_j. This high generality of the Weight Formula is only possible because it is highly abstract. It says only that the concrete weight of P_i and, with this, the relation of precedence between P_i and P_j, depends on the intensity of interference, I_i and I_j, the abstract weight, W_i and W_j, and the reliability of the empirical and normative assumptions, R_i and R_j, on both sides. It says nothing about the substantive criteria of the intensity of interference, the attribution of abstract weight, or the determination of reliability of the empirical and normative assumptions on both sides. The Weight Formula only provides the scales presented, that is, the formal structure of intensity, abstract weight and reliability. The substantive classification is delegated to an argumentation that stands – as the *argumentation thesis*[16]

[13] Alexy (n 9), p. 25.

[14] Ibid., 22–23.

[15] In order to speak not only of high generality but also, in a strict sense, of highest generality, one has to conceive all forms of collisions, not only the collision between two principles. On some remarks on collisions between more than two principles, see Alexy, 'The Weight Formula' (n 9).

[16] R. Alexy, 'Proportionality and Rationality' in V. C. Jackson, M. Tushnet (eds.), *Proportionality. New Frontiers, New Challenges* (Cambridge: Cambridge University Press, 2017), p. 23.

states – in a necessary connection with the Weight Formula but takes place, in spite of this necessary connection, outside the Weight Formula.

Mart Susi's Internet Balancing Formula is, in this aspect, completely different. It is not general but highly particular, and it is not abstract but highly concrete. And it must be particular and concrete. In offline balancing the substantive dimension can and must be delegated to argumentation. Here the Weight Formula is a *form*[17] of legal argumentation. In contrast to this, rational online balancing is only possible on the basis of a solid substantive input. Susi attempts to provide precisely this with his Internet Balancing Formula.

22.2 INTERNET BALANCING FORMULA AND WEIGHT FORMULA

Susi's Internet Balancing Formula runs as follows:

$$\mathrm{IBF} = \frac{\mathrm{V(1) + PR(x) + T(y) + E(z)}}{\mathrm{PI(x) + PF(x) \text{-} OI(y) + E(z)}}$$

22.2.1 *IBF*

IBF is not only to be found here in place of $W_{i,j}$ in the Weight Formula; in addition, both expressions also stand for the same thing: the concrete weight of the right represented by the upper part of the fraction, in our case the right to privacy (P_i), relative to the right represented by the lower part of the fraction, in our case freedom of expression (P_j). This is not the only structural accordance of the two formulas. In both formulas the concrete relation of precedence depends on whether $W_{i,j}$ or IBF is greater or smaller than 1. If $W_{i,j}$ or IBF is greater than 1, then P_i precedes P_j, If $W_{i,j}$ or IBF is smaller than 1, then P_j precedes P_i.[18] But here a difference emerges. It concerns the third possible case in which $W_{i,j}$ or IBF receives the value 1, that is, the stalemate case. The existence of stalemate cases is of the utmost importance for the legitimacy of constitutional review in a democratic state. In stalemate cases the legislator has discretion in balancing.[19] The power of the constitutional court is restricted. Susi seems to avoid an analogous restriction of the competences of the private online provider by avoiding stalemates. His main instrument here is the inclusion of empathy, E(z), in his Internet Balancing Formula.[20]

[17] R. Alexy, A *Theory of Legal Argumentation* (first published 1978), translated by R. Adler and N. MacCormick (Oxford: Clarendon Press, 1989), pp. 212–220, p. 197, p. 201.

[18] Alexy (n 9), pp. 20–21; Susi (n 1), 209.

[19] Alexy (n 6), pp. 410–412.

[20] Susi (n 1).

In addition to this, he mentions *moral reasons*, primarily those referring to the *principle of equality*.[21] This point will be taken up again in the discussion of the empathy variable on the fourth place on both sides of the Internet Balancing Formula.

Up until now we have been concerned with the left side of the equations. We now proceed to the right side. Already on a first glance at the two formulas a fundamental difference on the right side becomes obvious. In the Weight Formula, all variables in the upper and lower part of the fraction are equal. In the Internet Balancing Formula only the last variable, the empathy variable, E(z), is the same in the upper and lower part. The reason for this is the particular and concrete character of the Internet Balancing Formula.

22.2.2 *V(1): Internet Vulnerability*

The upper part of the Internet Balancing Formula represents the personality right. Here, the first element is V(1). The capital letter 'V' stands for *internet vulnerability*.[22] Internet vulnerability is said to consist in the fact 'that the traditional means to protect one's privacy, known from the offline world, cannot be effectively realised or are considerably weakened in the digital realm'.[23] The ECtHR in its *Delfi* Grand Chamber judgement refers to just this when it says that 'the risk of harm posed by content and communication on the Internet to the exercise and enjoyment of human rights and freedoms, particularly the right to respect for private life, is certainly higher than that posed by the press'.[24] And the Court points this out in greater detail when it refers to 'the ease, scope and speed of the dissemination of information on the Internet, and the persistence of the information once disclosed, which may considerably aggravate the effects of unlawful speech on the Internet compared to traditional media'.[25] The question arises: what is the structure and function of internet vulnerability, that is, of V(1) in the Internet Balancing Formula, if internet vulnerability is understood in this way?

The structure of V(1) is completely different from that of all other elements of the Internet Balancing Formula. V(1) is a constant, for it expresses just one value, namely 1.[26] All other elements of the Internet Balancing Formula are

[21] Ibid.

[22] Ibid., 205.

[23] Ibid., 202.

[24] European Court of Human Rights (ECHR) Judgement: *Delfi AS v Estonia* (2015 Grand Chamber), Application no. 64569/09, para. 133.

[25] Ibid., para. 147.

[26] Susi (n 1).

variables because different values can be substituted for them. To this extent they have the same structure as the elements of the Weight Formula, which are all variables. This leads to the question of how the function of V(1) is to be understood. One aspect is apparent. The weight of the right to privacy relative to freedom of expression is enhanced. Our question is how this is to be understood in the light of the Weight Formula, which claims to explicate the basic elements of balancing and their relations in as general and abstract a way as possible. Two constructions suggest themselves. The constant V(1) can either be understood as an instrument for giving a higher abstract weight, W_i, to the right to privacy, P_i, or as an expression of an enhancement of the intensity of interference, I_i, with the right to privacy. The first alternative has to be rejected. An abstract weight can only be attributed to the right to privacy as such. If it were attributed to the right to privacy under certain conditions – in our case, communication on the Internet – it would no longer concern the abstract weight. Rather, it would concern the weight under certain conditions, that is, the concrete weight, even if the condition, namely communication on the Internet, is quite general. For this reason, only the second alternative comes into question, enhancement of the intensity of interference with the right to privacy, I_i. This implies that V(1) is a criterion for the intensity of interference. As a criterion for the intensity of interference with a principle, it is not a principle, but a rule[27] – a rule, however, that, taken alone, due to its incorporation in the Internet Balancing Formula, does not determine the result of balancing along the lines of the Internet Balancing Formula. But it provides a definitive factor in the system of factors established in a mathematical way by this formula.

This is of pivotal importance for the assessment of the differences between the Weight Formula and the Internet Balancing Formula. The Weight Formula remains completely – like its non-mathematical predecessor, the Law of Balancing[28] – in the realm of principles. The transition to the realm of rules is performed initially by the Law of Competing Principles,[29] the second of the two laws of principles theory. In contrast to this, Susi, already in his Internet Balancing Formula, includes rule elements. This is the crucial point of the difference between the two formulas. This difference becomes increasingly clear when one looks on the other elements of Susi's Internet Balancing Formula.

[27] On the distinction between rules and principles, see Alexy (n 6), pp. 47–60.

[28] Alexy (n 6), p. 102.

[29] Ibid., p. 54; on the mathematical construction of this transition see id., Alxey (n 16), pp. 26–28.

22.2.3 *PR(x): Interference into Privacy*

The second element on the side of the personality right is the 'intensity of the interference'[30] with this right. It is represented in the Internet Balancing Formula by 'PR(x)'. Susi uses a three-level scale in order to express the intensity of interference: *light*, *moderate* and *intense*.[31] This directly corresponds to the triadic scale *light*, *moderate* and *serious* used by the Weight Formula in order to determine the value of I_i.[32] There are only two differences. The first is that elements of intensity of interference are to be found in Susi's Internet Balancing Formula not only in the element of the intensity of interference expressed by PR(x) but also in other elements. I have already attempted to show that the element of internet vulnerability, V(1), includes an aspect of the intensity of interference, and I will argue that the third element on the side of the personality right, the element of time, also refers to an aspect of intensity of interference. The second difference is that Susi uses an arithmetic scale: 1, 2 and 3,[33] whereas I use a geometric one: 2^0, 2^1 and 2^2, that is, 1, 2 and 4.[34] But I shall not consider this further in the present article.

22.2.4 *T(y): Element of Time*

The third element on the side of the personality right is the *element of time*.[35] Here the main idea is 'that with the passage of time ... the relevance of information or opinions decreases'.[36] For this reason, 'with passage of time, the outcome may shift towards protecting privacy more'.[37] This corresponds to a considerable degree to an argument of the Grand Chamber of the CJEU in the *Google* judgement, which says

> that even initially lawful processing of accurate data may, in the course of time, become incompatible with the directive where those data are no longer necessary in the light of the purposes for which they were collected or processed. That is so in particular where they appear to be inadequate,

30 Susi (n 1).
31 Ibid.
32 Alexy (n 9), p. 15.
33 Susi (n 1).
34 Alexy (n 9), pp. 20–21.
35 Susi (n 1).
36 Ibid.
37 Ibid., 210.

irrelevant or no longer relevant, or excessive in the relation to those purposes and in the light of the time that has elapsed.[38]

In the Internet Balancing Formula, the element of time is represented by T (y). Susi expresses the 'shift towards protecting privacy more'[39] by means of the following five-stage scale: 0, 0.25, 0.5, 0.75 and 1. If a period of less than 3 years has passed from the event subject to balancing, time plays no role, that is to say, the value is 0.[40] A passage of time of more than 3 years and less than 7 shall receive the value 0.25; of more than 7 years and less than 10 the value 0.5; of more than 10 years and less than 13 the value 0.75; and a passage of time of more than 13 years the value 1.

Only one point is of interest here. The passing of time is, without a doubt, a relevant factor. But this is a factor that concerns an increase of the intensity of interference with the personality right. In the Weight Formula, this factor would belong to I_i.

22.2.5 *E(z): Element of Empathy*

The fourth element on the side of the personality right is the *element of empathy*,[41] represented by E(z). Susi inserts this element into his Formula 'in order to retain the "human" touch of online content assessment'.[42] In contrast to the other elements of the Internet Balancing Formula, which 'are in principle subject to rational argumentation, the numerical value of this element of "empathy"' is said to be 'the result of moral evaluation'.[43] Again, the five-stage scale 0, 0.25, 0.5, 0.75 and 1 enters the picture.[44]

The element of empathy is a problematic element. Susi himself plays down its importance. He characterises its inclusion as *not compulsory*,[45] and he adds to this that it 'may occur in two situations'.[46] Both have already been mentioned.[47] The first is the stalemate situation, that is, the situation in which IBF receives the value 1. Online balancing should take this fundamental

38 CJEU – Case C-131/12, *Google Spain SL and Google Inc. v Agencia Española de Protección de Datos (AEPD) and Mario Costeja González* (13 May 2014), para. 93.

39 Susi (n 1).

40 Ibid.

41 Ibid.

42 Ibid.

43 Ibid.

44 Ibid., 207, 209–211.

45 Ibid., 207

46 Ibid.

47 See 258.

discretionary situation as serious as offline balancing. The second is that in which 'the situation itself calls for distinguishing it from comparable situations for certain moral reasons'.[48] But moral reasons are ubiquitous in arguing about human and constitutional rights. This implies that *rational argumentation* and *moral evaluation*[49] should not be set in contraposition. The element of empathy is the only element that, like all elements of the Weight Formula, is to be found on both sides of the Internet Balancing Formula. But it is its weakest element.

22.2.6 *The Elements on the Side of Freedom of Expression*

Empathy, too, is the fourth element on the side of the colliding principle, freedom of expression. The other three elements shall be considered in connection. The reason for this is that they all concern aspects of the intensity of interference. In the short presentation of the Weight Formula, given in the previous section, I have emphasised that the importance of satisfying the colliding principle P_j, that is I_j, can be understood as intensity of interference, namely, as the intensity of interference with P_j through non-interference with P_i. My argument will be that not only all elements on the side of the personality right, except empathy, but also all elements on the side of freedom of expression, again except empathy, refer to the intensity of interference. If this should be true, the Internet Balancing Formula would be an elaboration of what I once characterised as the *core* of the Weight Formula:[50]

$$W_{i,j} = \frac{I_i}{I_j}$$

Susi's first element of the explication of I_j is public interest, PI(x). The public interest variable 'is related to the impact the respective information may have upon the recipients'.[51] As in the case of the interference with privacy, PR (x), the arithmetic scale 1, 2 and 3 is used. The number 1 stands for a minor, 2 for a medium and 3 for a significant public interest.[52] Problematic, however, is the next step, which connects these three levels with the distinction between *local community*, *larger communities* and *entire nation*.[53] To be sure, these are important criteria for the intensity of interference, but there are also other

48 Susi (n 1).
49 Ibid.
50 Alexy (n 9), p. 21.
51 Susi (n 1).
52 Ibid.
53 Ibid.

criteria for the degree of public interest. Some of them are indicated by Susi. This leads to the interesting question of the degree and the completeness of concretisation with respect to the Internet Balancing Formula. This, however, shall not be further elaborated here. In our context, only one point shall be emphasised. Public interest, PI(x), is an indispensable element of the concretisation of the intensity of interference with freedom of expression, and I fully agree with Susi when he speaks at this point of 'the numerical value of intensity'.[54]

The second element of the explication of I_j is whether the information concerns a public figure, PF(x). Again, the triadic scale 1, 2 and 3 is applied. 3 is attached to information concerning persons 'holding significant public power', 2 to a person 'who voluntarily has entered public domain' and 1 to a person 'who involuntarily appears in the public domain'.[55] These, indeed, are essential criteria for the determination of the value of I_j. This shows that the value of I_j, as well as that of I_i, can be determined by scales that concern different criteria, and that are located at a level below the elements of the Weight Formula. This can be called the *concretisation thesis*.

The third element of the explication of I_j is 'related to the way [in which] information was obtained'.[56] It is represented by OI(y). This element has a negative impact.[57] Therefore, it is connected to a scale with negative values. Illegally obtained information is represented by ¬0.75; 'information obtained in morally unacceptable yet legally acceptable way'[58] receives the value ¬0.5; and 'information obtained in morally questionable way' is represented by ¬0.25.

Susi adds to this the value 0 for information that is obtained legally.[59] This establishes a symmetry between the information OI(y), the time T(y) and the empathy scale E(z). This symmetry is interesting, for Susi stresses that the 'lighter, narrower scale of 0 to 0.75' has to be applied here.[60] This can be understood as giving a lower abstract weight to the elements of obtaining information OI(y), time T(y) and empathy E(z), in contrast to the scale 1, 2, 3 as expressing a higher abstract value. These different scales imply a reference to different abstract weights.

Much more could be said. But the points made so far ought to suffice for a first glance at the relation between the Internet Balancing Formula and the Weight Formula.

54 Ibid.
55 Ibid., 206
56 Ibid.
57 Ibid.
58 Ibid.
59 Susi (n 1), 209–211.
60 Susi (n 1).

23

Reply to Alexy Critique

My reply to Robert Alexy will focus on those aspects he devotes most attention to when analysing the IBF: whether the concept of internet vulnerability refers to the abstract weight of privacy or the intensity of interference, the concretisation thesis and the element of empathy.

23.1 INTERNET VULNERABILITY

Robert Alexy indicates that internet vulnerability in the IBF is a constant; in particular it has the value 1. As all other elements are variables, this element is different. Having noted the apparent aspect that through internet vulnerability the weight of the right to privacy relative to freedom of expression is enhanced, Alexy then proceeds to question how this is to be understood in light of the weight formula. Alexy suggests two constructions: first, that the constant V (1) can be understood as giving higher abstract weight to the right to privacy; and second, that it is an expression of an enhancement of the intensity of interference with the right to privacy.

Having rejected the option that internet vulnerability represents a higher abstract weight of privacy in relation to freedom of expression online, Alexy then adopts the second explanation – that of the intensity of interference.[1] His criticism pivots on the idea that as a constant, internet vulnerability provides a definitive factor in the system of a mathematical formula. The constant element of V brings the realm of rule elements to the IBF, which is the crucial point of difference between the two formulas.

Alexy's rejection of internet vulnerability giving higher abstract weight to the side of privacy online rests on the idea of the universality of human rights

[1] R. Alexy, 'Mart Susi's Internet Balancing Formula' (2019) 25 *European Law Journal*, Special Issue: Internet and Human Rights Law, 2, 213–220, 5.

or their independence from practice.[2] In line with this approach, the abstract weight of a particular fundamental right, once determined, becomes an absolute characteristic of this fundamental right. It is not clear from Alexy's critique whether he views the abstract weight of a fundamental right as not dependent on time and place, nor discursive practice, or whether he admits the possibility that an abstract weight may change in time. The first position would be the general absolute weight thesis and the second would be the relative absolute weight thesis. Clearly, he opposes the possibility that the abstract weight of one fundamental right may be different within one human rights system at a given moment in time, such as in human rights law and practice in the twenty-first century. I assume that, according to Alexy, the abstract weight of any fundamental right is determined outside of a specific situation of rights conflict and as such is attributable to any situation where rights collide. For balancing are of primary importance the abstract weights of rights which appear in conflict. The primary question is whether the abstract weight of any fundamental right is determined in isolation from legal, social and political contexts – as the term suggests, *in abstracto*, that is, an ideal abstract weight – or whether it is defined in constitutional and international human rights law and practice. If the first construction is correct, then conflicts may emerge between the ideal abstract weight of a fundamental right and the abstract weight attributed through human rights law. This by itself is counter to the idea of the absolute nature of any abstract weight. Should the second construction be correct, then the proposition of the absolute and unchangeable nature of the abstract weight cannot be justified due to the inevitable aspect of dynamic evolution or change in human rights law and practice.

23.2 THE PROBLEM OF ABSTRACT WEIGHT

In principle, there can be three different levels of abstract weight in positive law: fundamental rights which are absolute, fundamental rights which are relative and rights which are simply legal rights and not (yet) in the status of fundamental rights. We know from various international legal instruments

[2] For a discussion about the matter of practice dependency and practice independence of human rights, see R. Dworkin, *Law's Empire* (Cambridge, MA: Harvard University Press, 1986); R. Dworkin, *Taking Rights Seriously* (Cambridge, MA: Harvard University Press, 1977); J. Rawls, *The Law of Peoples* (Cambridge, MA: Harvard University Press, 1999); C. R. Beitz, *The Idea of Human Rights* (Oxford: Oxford University Press, 2009); J. Raz, 'Human Rights without Foundations' in S. Besson, J. Tasioulas (eds.), *The Philosophy of International Law* (Oxford: Oxford University Press, 2010).

and court practice, that freedom of expression and the right to privacy are both relatively fundamental rights.[3] This appears to lead to the conclusion that in the weight formula and the IBF – if we reject the idea of internet vulnerability as a constant (V = 1) and also reject the idea that internet vulnerability as a constant is an expression of the intensity of the interference – these two rights at all times should cancel each other out.

My non-acceptance of Robert Alexy's critique originates from the rejection of the proposition that at any given time only one abstract weight of a particular fundamental right may exist. On the contrary, there can exist multiple abstract weights of one fundamental right at any given time, and for the following reasons. The first reason concerns the source of the abstract weight of a fundamental right, that is, whether it is determined through explication or whether it originates from the ideal dimension of human rights. I have demonstrated that there are different positions in contemporary human rights law and practice regarding the relationship of freedom of expression against the right to privacy. Some suggest that the first deserves more protection; the others suggest the opposite. For the purposes of balancing, these suggestions say precisely whether the abstract weight of privacy or freedom of expression is enhanced. These suggestions are digital space specific. One may of course say that the discursive practice is wrong, and the ideal attribution of abstract weight is correct.

The second reason is related to the relativity and interdependence of the terms abstract weight and intensity of interference. Consistently intensive interference of a certain degree may turn into an abstract weight. It has to be agreed that the abstract weight of any fundamental right, leaving aside the question of whether it is determined absolutely or whether it is relative and subject to change, is an element which for the purposes of balancing two conflicting rights is predetermined before the balancing is undertaken. It is not predetermined for the individual case at hand and as such is a general category. My disagreement with Robert Alexy lies in our opposite understandings as to whether such an abstract weight represents the dominant discursive approach towards the weight of that particular right (my view), or whether it does not (Alexy's view). If to advance Alexy's proposition that internet vulnerability represents the intensity of interference in privacy, then a question emerges: what if at all situations of rights conflicts in the digital sphere the right to privacy is given higher protection by default? The concrete weight of privacy in communication on the Internet then becomes a constant, which is

[3] I take this approach as axiomatic and not in need of references.

close to or transforms into an abstract weight of privacy in the digital sphere. The question of when such a transformation occurs is a matter of the degree of the consistency of the intensity.

My third reason for disagreement concerns the general aspect of human rights development. Privacy is a rather general human right. New separate human rights may be derived from or implied by an existing well-established human right.[4] This is a process of contestation, where during a certain period of time, a new human right claim either becomes justified or rejected. Concerning privacy, take for example the right to the integrity of the body,[5] or the right to the protection of one's genetics.[6] Both of these rights are not recognised in international human rights law as independent human rights, yet both of these new rights claim an absolute nature – the bodily integrity cannot be infringed upon under any circumstances, nor can the doctor under any circumstances tell a person about his/her genetic history if the person refuses to know. Even if we agree that the abstract weight of privacy as a general human right is relative, then one has to accept that at that same moment good reasons to give specific aspects of the right to privacy higher protection by recognising their absolute nature may exist. This is another reason to assert that the abstract weight of one human right may have different levels at any given time, provided there is reasonable justification.

23.3 REVISED INTERNET BALANCING FORMULA CONTAINING THE ELEMENT OF WEIGHT

I am now prepared to review the element of internet vulnerability in the IBF. This revision is based on rejecting the understanding that privacy in digital

4 See J. Nickel, *Making Sense of Human Rights*, 2nd ed. (Singapore: Blackwell Publishing, 2007) and M. Burbergs, 'How the Right to Respect for Private and Family Life, Home and Correspondence Became the Nursery in Which New Rights Are Born: Article 8 ECHR' in E. Brems, J. Gerards (eds.), *Shaping Rights in the ECHR: The Role of the European Court of Human Rights in Determining the Scope of Human Rights* (Cambridge: Cambridge University Press, 2013), 315–329; please also follow publication by A. von Arnaud, K. von der Decken, M. Susi (eds.), *The Cambridge Handbook of New Human Rights: Recognition, Novelty and Rhetoric* (Cambridge: Cambridge University Press, 2020).

5 A. M. Viens (ed.), *The Right to Bodily Integrity* (Farnham: Ashgate, 2014).

6 See the Oviedo Convention (Council of Europe, 'Convention for the Protection of Human Rights and Dignity of the Human Being with Regard to the Application of Biology and Medicine: Convention on Human Rights and Biomedicine (ETS No. 164)', entry in force 01/12/1999'); or B. M. Knoppers, *Le génome humain: patrimoine commun de l'Humanité ?* (Montreal: Fides, 1999), p. 35; F. Francioni, 'Genetic Resources, Biotechnology and Human Rights: The International Legal Framework', in F. Francioni (ed.), *Biotechnologies and International Human Rights* (Oxford: Hart Publishing, 2007), pp. 11–12.

communication always deserves more protection than freedom of expression. Yet there are also valid arguments from those who claim the opposite – freedom of expression deserves more protection, as has been shown previously. Should the concept of internet vulnerability find consensual support, then it is possible to return this element as a constant. I therefore suggest the revised IBF, due to the input of Robert Alexy concerning the missing element of the abstract weight of the input elements, when he characterises the IBF as the core of the Weight Formula.

This revised formula introduces intensity of interference and abstract weight. The intensity of interference is noted by the capital letters 'I', where the small 'p' stands for privacy and the small 'e' stands for expression. The input elements for intensity remain the same as in the previously introduced formula for both sides, except that the element of internet vulnerability is removed from the side of privacy. The new aspect of this formula is the abstract weight given to privacy 'Wp' and freedom of expression 'We'. Should these weights be equal, based on the understanding of the sameness of rights online and offline, or on the understanding that both these rights deserve equal protection online, then the elements of weight cancel each other out. The revised formula is as follows:

$$IBF = \frac{I_p[PR\ (x) + T\ (y) + E\ (z)] + W_p}{I_e[PI\ (x) + PF\ (x)\text{-}OI\ (y) + E\ (z)] + W_e}$$

The question of the scale inevitably emerges. I propose using the scale of 0 to 2. The abstract weight of 2 is applied if either of the rights has to be recognised as an absolute right. I suggested beforehand some instances where the right to privacy can assume an absolute nature. As for freedom of expression, then certain political or social situations may lead to the need to attribute absolute weight, given these are not temporary reasons. One can imagine that in totalitarian societies this may be the case. Perhaps it is also worth considering whether the World Press Freedom Index may become a source of inspiration, so that countries characterised as having a badly deficient situation in terms of freedom of expression need to enhance this right in absolute terms.

In other instances, where the absolute nature of the rights is excluded, the approach of 'deserving more protection' leads to one of the rights being enhanced to level 1 and the other staying at level 0. The remaining matter is, how the scales are determined. Returning to the original goal of the IBF, that is, to bring order to private online balancing, then when an online platform uses the IBF, this platform has to openly state its position regarding the abstract weight of the two rights. One assumes that this position is supported by arguments and is not subject to swift changes. From the other side, such an approach does not exclude the phenomenon of forum shopping. Perhaps this is the new reality of human rights protection in the digital domain.

23.4 THE CONCRETISATION THESIS

Alexy shows that the values I_i and I_j in his Weight Formula are determined by different criteria than the input elements of the Internet Balancing Formula. The elements of the IBF are located at a level below the elements of the WF, Alexy writes. He calls this the 'concretisation thesis'.[7] The element of intensity in the Weight Formula is one of the three main input elements and is not further specified, whereas the element of intensity in the IBF consists on both sides of several input elements. I do not object to the concretisation thesis and find that it serves the goal of explaining why the IBF can serve as an ordering instrument in fundamental rights protection in the digital domain. It protects the IBF from criticism; let me draw a comparison with the Weight Formula.

The general nature of the elements of the Weight Formula has led to criticism. Poscher[8] and Somet[9] have the opinion that the balancing process depends on intuition as to the relative weight of the conflicting principles; Habermas[10] criticises the general nature of the WF using the argument of arbitrariness. Alexy's reply to all critics uses an argumentation thesis,[11] which says that all classifications underlying intensity can be based on rational argumentation. The variables of the Weight Formula represent classifications that stand in need of justification, Alexy writes. The argumentation thesis justifies these classifications and minimises the concern of arbitrariness and intuition.

This is exactly what the concretisation thesis accomplishes for the Internet Balancing Formula. It justifies the value of I on both sides because the elements which lead to the final value of I_p and I_e are known. This is different from the Weight Formula, where the absence of more concrete criteria is

7 Alexy (n 1), 1.

8 R. Poscher, 'The Principles Theory. How Many Theories and What Is Their Merit?' in M. Klatt (ed.), *Institutionalized Reason: The Jurisprudence of Robert Alexy* (Oxford: Oxford University Press, 2012), p. 241. B. Schlink, 'Freiheit durch Eingriffsabwehr – Rekonstruktion der klassischen Grundrechtsfunktion' (1984) 11 *Europäische GRUNDRECHTE-Zeitschrift* 462.

9 A. Somek, *Rechtliches Wissen* (Frankfurt: Suhrkamp, 2006), p. 135.

10 J. Habermas, *Between Facts and Norms: Contributions to a Discourse Theory of Law and Democracy*, translated by W. Rehg (Cambridge: Polity Press, 1996), p. 259.

11 R. Alexy, *A Theory of Legal Argumentation* (first published 1978), translated by R. Adler and N. MacCormick (Oxford: Clarendon Press, 1989), pp. 212–220.

compensated by the argumentation. As I have shown, argumentation and articulation is not possible in online content assessments, or to formulate it more mildly, they are possible only to a limited extent. Therefore, the concretisation thesis serves the same goal in the Internet Balancing Formula as the argumentation thesis in the Weight Formula – optimising the rational balancing of conflicting fundamental rights given the concrete legal and factual circumstances. For the purposes of non-coherence theory an image of an ellipse is visible. There is non-variance in relation to the need of balancing justification in offline and online domains alike. The thesis of argumentation deficit reveals variance due to the capabilities approach: argumentation is not possible for online balancing and is possible for offline balancing. Mathematics closes the variance and justification is achieved for both domains – for offline through the argumentation thesis and for online through the concretisation thesis.

23.5 THE ELEMENT OF EMPATHY

Alexy labels the element of empathy as the weakest element in the IBF.[12] This is because my original justification of this element was to include the aspect of morality in the balancing of conflicting rights online, but Alexy reminds me that rational argumentation and moral evaluation should not be set in contraposition.[13]

While it is certainly true that rational argumentation and moral evaluation cannot be contra-positioned, neither are they synonyms, but complementary aspects of constitutional and human rights argumentation. Here I need to return to the original idea behind the element of empathy – this is to avoid a situation where the entire online balancing of conflicting fundamental rights can be performed by artificial intelligence on the basis of algorithms. While the term itself suggests that rational argumentation entails both the aspects of rationality and argumentation, then rationality is not inherent in the term moral evaluation. Moral argumentation can be rational, yet it can also be completely irrational and yet claim correctness. Would the majority of people who face a situation of fundamental rights protection in the digital domain prefer that this can be accomplished entirely on the basis of a mathematical formula, which does not exclude the possibility that the whole operation is performed by artificial intelligence, or would they prefer that in more difficult cases human intelligence enters the stage. Intuitively it would seem that the

[12] Alexy (n 1), 7.
[13] Ibid.

majority would choose the second option. The difference between rational argumentation and moral evaluation from the perspective of explication is that the latter does not necessarily depend on justification via arguments. Something may seem *morally* preferable because it just seems so on the basis of one's consciousness, or prior unarticulated life-experience or one's perception of the prevailing morality in a society at a given time. For the purposes of the IBF, the element of empathy can be labelled the *irrationality thesis*.

Returning to one of the assumptions of the IBF – the living instrument assumption – it can be asserted, that the element of empathy may at some point in the future become unnecessary, provided that artificial intelligence becomes capable of *moral evaluation* or alternatively, the social expectations towards fundamental rights protection in the digital domain undergo some paradigmatic change, which may not be comprehensible at this given time. At the present stage in the IBF, the aspect of empathy should be applied in stalemate cases or in difficult cases.

24

The Debate

The academic debate which emerged after the first introduction of the IBF concerns either directly the formula or matters closely connected to the balancing of conflicting rights by private online portals. I will comment on selected publications, keeping in mind that the discussion is evolving and more references to the formula have appeared between the time the manuscript was delivered to the publisher and the book's publication.

24.1 THE LEGITIMACY DEFICIT

The legitimacy deficit is manifest in the discursive practices of online content assessment by private entities. Enguerrand Marique and Yseult Marique search for the source of legitimacy when private platforms set rules, monitor compliance with their own rules and finally apply sanctions.[1] Noting the unilateral character of the *contractual* horizontal relationship, they proceed to point out that online portals offer a *take it or leave it* choice without any possibility of negotiations, which in turn leaves the issue of the legitimacy of private content assessment undefined. It is suggested that new forms of legitimacy may develop based on public–private or hybrid interactions in the setting and enforcing the regulatory order of the Internet.[2] The utilitarian aspect of the non-coherence theory of digital human rights responds to the varied degrees of capability held by the two domains to provide reasons during content assessment, and leads to the observation that the normative structure of the digital domain withstands the legitimacy concerns.

[1] E. Marique, Y. Marique, 'Sanctions on Digital Platforms: Beyond the Public-Private Divide' (2019) 8 *Cambridge University Law Journal*, 2, 258–281.

[2] Ibid., 281.

Capabilities variance leads to an image of weakened or absent legitimacy of online content assessment only through the lens of the offline assessment framework; that is, when one wishes to ask the same questions and apply similar tools towards both domains. Legitimacy in the online domain may, however, originate from enforced consent, or it may have a default and undefined origin, which may lead to questioning the suitability of the legitimacy language online and its overall scope. This represents the holistic image that conceptual elements of human rights from the offline domain either cannot be transposed to the online domain *in corpore*, or that such full transposition inevitably leads to a change in meaning. In this case, a discrepancy between the appearance and meaning emerges; that is, a non-attentive observer may conclude that since the terminology remains intact between both domains it also indicates the sameness of content. This view is wrong, as has been shown on many occasions.

The stakeholder practices lead to observations by the Mariques, which are noteworthy on moral and legal philosophical levels, and validated through non-coherence theory. They note that platform operators distinguish between acceptable and problematic social behaviour, leading to a potential bias in dispute resolution processes.[3] Given the vigorous signs from practice that online portals engage various layers from the public and civil society to discuss so-called community standards, the authors conclude that the social contract online has through practice obtained different content and goals in comparison with Rousseau's ideal social contract. The goal is to reduce the distortion in public standards, the content should not bind the authority and subjects, but by excluding the authority define expectations and terms for the users (subjects). The Mariques note: 'To sustain their power, platform operators have assimilated sanctions from States' legal orders while adding a layer of their own making. This double coating has blurred the lines between public and private enforcement mechanisms.'[4] The authors write in other words about the distortion when public sanctions enter the private sphere. This is exactly the revelation of the non-coherence of public offline sphere instruments against private online instruments. When the Mariques call for a discursive framework to be established for sanctions and proportionality to address colliding rights on the modern public square,[5] the reply is that non-coherence theory constitutes such a framework.

3 Marique and Marique (n 1), 264–266.
4 Ibid., 269.
5 Ibid.

The legitimacy deficit is currently also apparent in an alternative mathematical solution with practice-affecting aspiration, proposed by a multi-country scholarly community. This simplified model by Zufall, Kimura and Peng uses elements of the privacy of information and the nature of information, and the relevance of the intrusion is affected by time.[6] The solution isolates and polarises just one element from the conflicting rights to be balanced: privacy of information is one aspect of the level of intrusion into privacy, and the nature of information is one aspect allowing us to determine the scope of the freedom of expression. The matter of algorithmic simplicity was expected and possibly characterises some or many solutions in practical use today. Measuring one element against another is characteristic of weighing and needs to be separated from balancing, which is characterised by the diversity of elements. There must exist a positive correlation between the mathematical algorithmic complexity of online balancing solutions and the legitimacy of private content assessment online. There may also exist a point where the criticism about the legitimacy deficit simply yields to an *anything goes* thesis. This thesis reflects the practical reality where issues of legitimacy and argumentation have lost their relevance.

24.2 REFLECTIONS ON THE INTERNET BALANCING FORMULA DEBATE

The dominant view of the Internet Balancing Formula (IBF) is as a concept having some role in future internet governance.

Marique and Marique identify three main issues which need to be resolved in the future regarding online platform governance.[7] The first concerns the discretion that platforms enjoy in sanctioning behaviour. The second concerns the structure of the discretion in relation to some form of control, where the authors refer explicitly to the IBF as one possible approach. The third concerns the search for legitimacy. All these issues emerge due to the incompatibility of the digital regulatory environment with the offline regulatory environment. Non-coherence theory speaks against the possibility of explaining these issues satisfactorily through rational arguments and by

6 F. Zufall, R. Kimura, L. Peng, 'A Simple Mathematical Model for the Legal Concept of Balancing of Interests' ICAIL '21: Proceedings of the Eighteenth International Conference on Artificial Intelligence and Law, June 2021, pp. 270–271, DOI: https://doi.org/10.1145/3462757.34661409.

7 Marique and Marique (n 1), 280–281.

applying instruments which are known and effectively applied in the non-digital domain. Reliance on such tools through a public–private approach includes by default an element of distortion; that is, the tools from the offline domain can be applied in the online domain with some variance. Mathematics can serve as a bridge between the two domains due to issues of discretion and its structure. In such a bridge, fundamental and operational legitimacy are interconnected in the mathematical approach towards human rights, yet independently disconnected from the regulatory environment where mathematics is applied. Mathematics is an area where non-coherence disappears; this is important for establishing the theory's scope.

In yet another article, Marique and Marique put forward four challenges in relation to the operational capabilities of the Internet Balancing Formula.[8] A replica of these observations appeared in the report submitted to the UN Internet Governance Forum held in Berlin in November 2019.[9] The first concerns the boundaries within which the formula can be applied. There is hate speech at one end and historic truth at the other end. The Mariques suggest that other values may need to be included to ensure the 'integrity of the modern public square'.[10] I reply by saying that the formula is a living instrument which can be modified in accordance with the context surrounding its application. Otherwise, the formula would remain theoretical and illusory. The abstract suggestion of other values would need to be replaced by bringing forward concrete values for further response.

The second challenge is related to the elements of empathy and internet vulnerability. This concern coincides with Alexy's response labelling empathy as the formula's weakest element. I have already replied to the criticism about empathy through the irrationality thesis. In response to Alexy, I have rejected the element of vulnerability and expressed the preparedness to return to this concept should it transpire from the discussion. Against the background of worrying information about the capacities of new artificial brains, which may soon start to determine digital landscapes, the return to the element of

[8] E. Marique, Y. Marique, 'Sanctions on Digital Platforms: Balancing Proportionality in a Modern Public Square' (2019) *Computer Law and Security Review* (issue November 2019 – forthcoming), 9, DOI: http://dx.doi.org/10.2139/ssrn.3462408.

[9] L. Belli, N. Zingales (eds.), 'Platform Values: Conflicting Rights, Artificial Intelligence and Tax Avoidance', consolidated and unedited version of the special Issue of the Computer Law and Security Review, presented at the 14th UN Internet Governance Forum, 27 November 2019, Berlin, https://cyberbrics.info/platform-values-conflicting-rights-ai-tax-avoidance, accessed 28 October 2022.

[10] Marique and Marique (n 8), 8.

vulnerability seems justified. Yet it would mean an implicit acceptance of the artificial brain's superiority. An intriguing proposition is to allow portal users a choice between two IBF versions – one containing an element of vulnerability and the other not.

The third challenge concerns the question of how collective rights and freedoms are placed against individual rights in the IBF. I reply by saying that collective rights and goods appear as an element of public interest manifest through an individual right-holder's expression. Countering collective rights against individual rights remains an abstract proposition above the concrete level of the IBF; see the concretisation thesis from the Alexy critique.

The fourth challenge concerns the difference between judicial balancing and the IBF. The argument says that the judges' conclusions are defined through discursive practice, steeped in pragmatism and incrementality. This criticism is most valuable among the many concerns raised and points to the fundamental methodological divergence of online mathematical balancing from offline judicial balancing. Previously I have replied to this concern via the argumentation insufficiency thesis and the capabilities approach. It suffices to repeat the main separating elements. The inherent absence of time in online balancing leads to the incapability of producing articulated individualised reasons, which is the core of the argumentation insufficiency thesis. The mathematical formula compensates for the insufficiency and leads to argumentation based on typologies. Empirical research may show that despite the divergence of online and offline balancing in practice, the substantive conclusions may converge. This hypothesis necessitates empirical research for validation or rejection.

Overall, the Mariques criticise the existence of too much idealism on one side, while also saying that the IBF is too practical on the other side, which blurs the image. My main praise lies with the proposition of the community of *proportionalists*,[11] who would establish public forums to share data on forms of interference and prohibited behaviours, modalities of sanctions, complaints by users and the results of the review processes. This leads by itself to an idealistic promise. They write, 'digital operators have interests to adopt moderating techniques; that is, to balance colliding values and rights with a proportionality test. However, the long-term sustainability of such a strategy relies on developing a relevant and shared justificatory framework'.[12] The IBF

[11] Ibid., 12.

[12] Marique and Marique (n 1).

is sometimes criticised for the difficulty of its application; it is said that technical support will be needed to foster the concrete use of the formula.[13] This concern can be labelled the ideal nature thesis of the IBF.

The debate I predicted about the IBF in my 2019 articles is not only related to the mathematical formula itself but contains the whole horizon of balancing in the online domain. With reference to the IBF, this discussion entails elements of experimentation and public discourse. With reference to the IBF, Douek writes:

> Unlike others, I do not wish to propose a mathematical 'internet interest-balancing formula' or tie myself to quantifiable cost-benefit analysis. Instead, I readily concede that content moderation, at least for the foreseeable future, will be messy and often wrong. But the best path forward lies in accepting and being open about this so that mistakes can be discovered and corrected, rather than merely ignored or assumed away. Experimentation is essential. The goal of acknowledging the systemic balancing inherent in content moderation is therefore not to provide a completely constraining adjudicative method, but to expose to public scrutiny the decision-making process already taking place so it can be subject to public argumentation, contestation, and disruption.[14]

I reply by saying that the mathematical formula does not exclude the discourse which Douek calls for. On the contrary, mathematics may be the only solution with a contestable structure for online balancing.

Goldman[15] has identified seven examples of the binary approach to content moderation remedies,[16] including the IBF. The IBF is also listed by others as an option when online companies are looking for solutions to balance conflicting rights.[17] Goldman alleges as a limitation the IBF's outcome – it suggests removal as the only applicable remedy.[18] This critique is justified,

[13] Ibid., 8.

[14] E. Douek, 'Governing Online Speech: From 'Posts-as-Trumps' to Proportionality and Probability' (2021) 121 *Columbia Law Review*, 3, pp. 787–788, *JSTOR*, www.jstor.org/stable/27007631.

[15] E. Goldman, 'Content Moderation Remedies' (2021) 28 *Michigan Technology Law Review*, 1, Santa Clara Univ. Legal Studies Research Paper, pp. 1–59, DOI: http://dx.doi.org/10.2139/ssrn.3810580.

[16] These include, in addition to the IBF: DMCA Online Safe Harbours, EU E-commerce directive and its progeny, the Manila Principles, Santa Clara Principles, Principles for User Generated Content Services and Graduated Response/Copyright Alert System, pp. 16–26.

[17] See doctoral thesis of M. Hiltunen, 'Cooperation, Contest, and Co-optation: Freedom of Expression and Positive Obligations in EU Social Media Content Regulation', University of Helsinki, Faculty of Law, 2020, p. 76.

[18] Goldman (n 15), pp. 20–21.

provided that we evade the element of time. It appears that the varied scope of remedies is explainable through non-coherence theory, and it also gives a more concrete reply to Goldman. The listing of effective remedies is much broader in the non-digital domain in comparison with the digital domain.

Future developments, especially when the IBF will be applied by private stakeholders, can provide valuable input for justifying my responses to various contestations as just identified.

In Lieu of the Concluding Remarks

The Trailer for the Monograph

This monograph is about the change in meaning and scope of human rights rules, principles, ideas and concepts, and the interrelationships and related actors, on moving from the physical domain into the online domain. The transposition into the digital reality can alter the meaning of well-established offline human rights to a wider or narrower extent; it can turn positivity into negativity and vice versa. The digital human rights realm has different layers of complexity in comparison with the offline realm. I have chosen to offer an image which could be seen as a *trailer*. Such trailers are used in cinematography to catch the attention of someone who is contemplating whether the movie interests them. In a similar way this academic *trailer* could catch the attention and convince the viewer to read the entire book. As in a movie trailer, the statements and thesis are not necessarily in a logical sequence and are taken sporadically from the monograph, at the same time, showing glimpses of the main topics and ideas discussed.

The offline human rights architecture is built on the premise that personal freedom and equality are absolute entitlements and not dependent on some discretionary decision. In the case of online human rights design, this premise changes as discretionary entitlement enters the arena. The aforementioned leads me to formulate the *transcendentality transposition question*. It asks whether the implicitness of human rights is determined entirely by the offline domain and is then transposed online and finds explication through online-specific practice and discourse. This is a question of underlying values and morals; however, does the online realm have a similar need for orientation in regard to what needs to be done in moral terms as the offline realm? If the implicitness of human rights online were to originate from this same online domain, it could no longer be viewed through non-coherence theory, as it would represent an entirely independent and separate paradigm of meanings and values. Yet, if implicitness was entirely or partly transposed from offline to online, a different question of the breadth of the gap between implicitness and explicitness emerges. This is a perfect question of non-coherence, as these gaps existing online and offline can be explored and compared. Since the online world is determined by technical possibilities, we can formulate the hypothesis that the gap between the implicit and explicit dimensions of human rights online are by default narrowing since these elements of implicitness which cannot be realised online are simply rejected. This will be one of the main theses this monograph will seek to respond to.

Building on an analogy with quantum mechanics, we can ask whether certain human rights exist in a shared state. This would mean, for instance, whether the right to privacy exists in a shared state with the right to freedom of expression. Or, whether the right to reputation – leaving aside the issue of whether such a self-standing right can be justified – exists in a shared state with the right of access to information. If the premise of such a shared state is correct, then it would follow that change in the scope and meaning of one right (particle in quantum mechanics) in this shared state leads to a simultaneous change in the opposite direction in the other right (particle). For human rights, this matter is related first and foremost to the relative weight of rights against one another. A new thesis can be advanced – the equilibrium of relative rights thesis – which says that for those rights existing in a shared state, when the relative weight of one right increases, the relative weight of the other right has to decrease by the respective amount.

Can dignity in the digital world be viewed as an end in itself? We quickly realise that if the answer should turn out to be negative, then the human rights digital architecture becomes completely flat. This represents the situation where there are not only no absolute human rights but everything becomes relative. This is because the basic norm itself would be relative. Here then the key notion of dignity can be measured against *competing* rights and values. But it no longer would then correspond to the place of dignity in human rights in the offline realm. In this case, the weight of dignity in the offline and online domains becomes non-coherent. This stems from the simple recognition that while dignity is a constant offline, it is relative online.

There does not appear to be any non-coherence between the idea of dignity in the online and offline spaces due to the absence of abstract definitions. Both domains rely on the intuitionistic justification of dignity. Yet, there may occur non-coherence regarding the absolute nature of dignity since the offline rights environment is multilayered, but it is not certain that the online environment is.

Doubt from a general view would allow us to say that the statement of the sameness of human rights in the digital and non-digital domains is correct and can be justified at the highest level of generality and abstractness. Here human rights in these domains are coherent, and non-coherence becomes more and more apparent in the image of digital human rights as their concreteness progresses. At one point non-coherence disappears, when human rights specific to the digital domain emerge which are not a reflection of a comparable right offline.

In reference to L. H. Hart, it appears that primary human rights rules lose more and more of their significance online in practical terms. Non-coherence theory will say that in the digital domain the link from human rights standards to primary norms becomes at least weaker in comparison with the offline domain. The thesis of the weakening of the link between primary and secondary human rights norms in the digital domain means that while human rights as values and dimensions, having the highest level of generality and abstractness, remain coherent between the digital domain and the non-digital, the human rights norms at the lower level of generality become overshadowed by secondary norms. Another way to put this would be to say that the lower-level primary human rights norms in the digital domain transform into secondary norms, which then means that they are no longer immune to adaptiveness in terms of time and necessity.

Regarding the right to privacy, the following can be said – the foundational interest is determined via our involuntary entry into the physical world. We may like or dislike what we see, or experience both feelings simultaneously. Yet the right to privacy in its ideal dimension can be viewed as a shield against the objective physical reality we did not choose to enter. The situation changes fundamentally from the digital perspective. The transformation of the right to privacy into the digital domain appears in two formats, and none of these correspond to the interest in being left alone. The first concerns the interest in another identity, which may differ to a greater or lesser degree from the physical identity. The only claim representing the interest in being left alone can be seen in the interest (in the digital domain) in leaving the physical identity behind. The other concerns modern e-solutions used by public and private entities to engage in business or public affairs. Since someone's data is recorded indefinitely, or at least for a certain period of time, the divide between the interest in being left alone and the realisability of this expectation becomes extremely wide.

The digital domain entails mechanisms which can turn this entitlement to be left alone into an absolute right. For instance, the right to be forgotten can in ideal discursive conditions eliminate all traces of someone's past. This concerns information that is legitimately in the digital domain, and yet the data subject wishes all traces of the information to disappear. A comparable situation in the offline domain remains illusory since one cannot erase human memory, although it is possible through the manipulation of written sources and photographs. This leads us, as an example, to concede that the non-coherence principle works in multiple ways – we should not only be looking at how an idea or concept from the offline domain changes online but whether the online image has a retrograding effect, which influences the original concept or idea. Yet the discourse about the details of what formats the right to privacy exactly exists and what it entails offline does not change the main conclusion, which is to note a prima facie variance in the meanings of privacy offline and online. The variance is of such a degree that it should be more appropriate to refrain from the usage of the expression of privacy in the online environment. Non-coherence becomes centre stage here, and because the digital and non-digital domains are interconnected and someone can lead parallel lives in both domains, the right to privacy has a meaning in the digital reality only as far as it enables us to realise the interest in being left alone in the non-digital reality.

The non-coherence assumption represents an element of change for the positivity or negativity associated with a human rights idea, or concept or rule offline upon transposition into another domain. There is no rule to say that what is viewed as a positive element offline increases in positivity online, and the other way around. Positivity may become negativity, and negativity, positivity. For instance, the positivity associated with anonymity offline is usually perceived as negative online. Or the other way around, displaying oneself in joyful settings in online photos seems positive, but may turn out to be negative for offline job interviews. However, non-coherence does not exclude that the scope of an offline right expands once transposed to the online domain. And should this be the case, both positivity and negativity can appear simultaneously towards one and the same right. This by itself calls into question whether the expansion of this right's scope allows us to still speak of a particular fundamental right. An alternative would be to suggest that upon transposition to online, an offline right is divided into several self-standing rights. Such a proposition needs justification from theory and practice. But should this be the case, a new challenge emerges – which of the *new* rights should continue with the offline name and how should we label the other derivate. I will explore this possibility towards the freedom of expression.

There is a shift from individual censorship towards censorship of portals or user groups, that is, from individual censorship to general censorship. There is also a tendency to censor certain topics or expressions, which as a consequence may affect not only individual sources of certain expressions or views but anyone who belongs to such a group or wishes to use those specific words to express an idea. This is because having censored an individual expression or view, the censors decide to eliminate the possibility of repetitions. The result for individual users is twofold. From one side, there is the narrowing of the freedom of expression because our ability to speak freely may be infringed not for reasons connected to us but because someone else, unknown to us, may have engaged in conversations which are deemed unsuitable for the portal. It may also happen because the public entities wish private service providers to exercise certain policies. What transpires is the weakening of the link between the individual exercising their freedom of expression vis-à-vis the censorship measures exercised in the digital domain. Here we can conclude a medium level of non-coherence. Yet, if we accept the view of the sceptics, which represents the other side of the coin, about the effectiveness of digital censorship, we could conclude a broader level of non-coherence, which lies in the discrepancy between the promise of censorship and its realisability.

Human rights online exhibit a decrease in abstractness. Separately taken this does not lead to a conclusion of non-coherence, since it reflects the ordinary multidimensional human rights architecture, where some rights are more and some less abstract. Human rights online are more concrete, hence less abstract. Yet the situation calls for a more specific examination. Speaking of their structure, at least some elements of the human rights online retain textually the same level of abstractness as offline rights. This can mean that either only the nomination, or additional features, exhibit the same image as the nomination and features offline. On the basis of the text alone, there is coherence. Then at some point secondary norms enter the scene, being presented as if they were primary norms, and they push aside the primary norms transposed from offline by entering the scene as more influential and practical, thereby highlighting the idealism of primary coherent norms online. The consequence of such a textual approach, where abstract rights are supplemented with concrete provisions, changes the nature of fundamental rights online. This is because of the decrease of universality and abstractness; at least some rights which are presented as fundamental rights online are very close to meeting or completely meeting the human right qualification criteria of abstractness and universality. We can term this phenomenon the holistic shift due to non-coherence since the overall structure of online human rights becomes less abstract and universal. The latter is due to the simple fact that online rights are what the term says – they are meant for online and consequently the circle of rights holders is narrower in comparison with human rights holders in general.

The inflation and overproduction of human rights are usually explained through the belief that human rights rhetoric and normativity are a helpful means of problem-solving. For the digital domain the reverse is correct. There is the underproduction of specific digital human rights primary norms, and the overproduction of secondary norms. We may say here that human rights rhetoric and normativity lose their promise as problem solvers in the digital domain. Here, non-coherence is clear, and it leaves open the question of whether something else has overtaken human rights functionality.

Here the discussion leads to the search for one or several common core elements for normative systems, which are independent of whatever capabilities are dominant for legal subjects in the digital and non-digital domains. In other words, even though we can accept that digital and non-digital capabilities are non-coherent, which they have to be, the question is whether there is any commonality that stands as more general over the specifics of the capabilities terminology, and therefore characterises both domains. We could explore whether the capabilities theorists have put forward any such commonalities. Now the concept of equal concern for all comes forward, viewed often as the foundational principle of ethical reasoning. This is expressed by Sen as a seminal question – *the equality of what?* My response to Sen's question is: equality in having the capability to claim equal normative authority. This would mean in translation to law that both normative paradigms determine independently what is reasonable to value. This is the basis of the respective normative constructions. Now we see that such independently existing normative systems, which are explainable through the non-coherence of value systems, can lead to normative systems of little or no variance. The similarity here would be superficial since in both systems notions like privacy and the right to disseminate information are central but their actual content differs. We can call this phenomenon the non-coherence of normative coherence.

Once we can agree that the aspect of the natality of fundamental rights, that is, fundamental rights being integral to the digital social paradigm, is lost in transfer from the non-digital domain, we see that the Frankfurt school's aspiration for general explanatory power is lost as well. The relational chain stops after digital narrative creation; that is, normativity does not follow as a logical result of internal development inside the digital domain. There is no doubt that such affordance exists in the non-digital domain's relational chain as suggested by the Frankfurt school. But it is not clear whether a digital agent has the affordance towards such external input. We can term this the thesis of doubt towards digital affordance as a fundamental right. This also reveals non-coherence, and its consequence is to question the applicability of the relational chain from discourse to narrative and from there on to normativity in the digital domain. Despite the relational chain being broken, normativity exists in and for the digital domain. If not a result of the development as proposed by the Frankfurt school, there must be other explanatory venues. The main venue among these is the concept of self-normativity.

Therefore, self-normativity assumes awareness of another normative system, and then its complete or partial rejection and full or partial replacement with another system. This assertion also applies to the digital domain with the following consequence. Self-normativity of the digital domain and digital agents means that the offline system of norms and values exists to their knowledge, and then there is the possibility to choose between their transposition or rejection, both of which can be carried out to a greater or lesser degree.

The decrease in universality and abstractness relies on the traceability to core and well-established offline human rights. Otherwise, it would not be logically possible to trace the chain of connectivity. Now, if the human rights online originate from inside the digital domain, or if the digital domain retains only a facade – such as the formal nomination of rights – but fills it with different content, we face a different paradigm which also provides new parameters to consider. Among those, abstractness and universality may not be significant. Here then we are still faced with the possibility of extensive non-coherence between the digital and non-digital domains. Such wide non-coherence shows that various theories focusing on rights development are paradigm centred; they are of little value for comprehending and explaining developments in the margins or meeting points of paradigms.

While there is no contestation – and should not be – from the side of self-made global administrative and possibly public legal norms against the legislative layer, this image does not hold for digital human rights. The absence of contestation means that self-normativity and more general legal instruments adopted by the legislature or international institutions can be viewed in some, perhaps most, legal realms as a continuum. This continuum serves the aim of enhancing legal predictability and the effectiveness of interventions. There appears no comparable continuum between self-made private rules and international or domestic legal instruments governing digital human rights. I term such an absence as the idealism abyss; that is, the idealistic nature inherent in human rights articulated by positive legal instruments is not carried uninterrupted into the self-normativity of digital agents. Perhaps the abyss is of such depth that the ideal nature of human rights in the digital domain is recreated with a different meaning of idealism through self-normativity, if at all possible. This means that the digital realm is perhaps capable of creating idealism within its own meaning.

Once the self-normativity of digital private enterprises becomes justified, the idealism abyss leads to the necessity of self-constitutionality. In this case, primary and secondary self-regulation form one logical structure. The rejection of the idealism abyss shows an image where the self-made secondary norms rely on primary- (constitutional-) level norms originating from the non-digital realm, but their content may have changed in the course of transposition. The next question now is: what happens to legitimation in such multiple networks?

The longing for universality is evident in most legal theoretical discourses and needs no repetition here. Yet the theories of digital human rights may be immune against the claim of universality for a different reason. These theories or approaches (which may not amount to the meaning of theories as we understand the word) are primarily concerned with secondary-level normativity and have no interest in totality due to the idealism abyss thesis. Non-coherence theory shows that elements of universality are absent from the transversal image of digital human rights. This is the result of the transformed nature and content of digital human rights norms and procedures in comparison with non-digital. Digital human rights theories and approaches usually have an interest in claiming universality as domain-specific and do not reach beyond the digital sphere into the non-digital, but this is not reciprocal. Human rights theories from the physical realm have the ambition of universality extending into the digital domain. Here we see that the expression of universality itself is of a non-coherent nature.

A defiant person (such a statement carrying no moral aspect), however, can continue to voice opinions in the physical realm, as difficult as this may turn out in fear of various sanctions and causing possible harm. The point here is that the physical domain does not foresee the option of finality, that is, disabling the person forever from exercising their capability to voice opinions or express views. But this is exactly what the digital domain enables.

Due to the medium level of variance, it is more accurate to say that freedom of expression online in comparison with freedom of expression offline has distinct features, among those: (i) the dual nature or scope, where in social media the scope is broad and in e-governance solutions the scope is narrow; (ii) the weakening of the link between censorship measures and individual statements and views; and (iii) due to correlation with the right to privacy, limitations to the freedom of expression because of self-restraint.

The image which opens from the digital domain about the freedom of expression shows that extreme versions are more openly exercised in comparison with the non-digital domain. This is a significant variance, and non-coherence is clearly visible. For believers, it can be said that Heaven and Hell are more open in the digital domain in contrast with the physical realm. Since we can consider that good and evil speech exist as a pair, and enhancement of one means the simultaneous enhancement of the other, it may be said that this aspect can also be applied to freedom of expression analysis offline.

A general idea may emerge, which can be termed the thesis of extremism. This means, that after transposition into a new domain, the features of a human rights idea, or characteristics of some offline traditional right, may appear within a higher spectrum than in the traditional setting. Non-coherence appears to be a condition sine qua non after any transposition of ideas, concepts and rules, at least due to the quality of dust and turbulence. Once these elements disappear, only then can the scope of non-coherence be seen in the substantive characteristics and in normativity. For instance, there was widely held scepticism after the emergence of the Internet about its resilience to any normative regulation. This was the stage of its formation. Thereafter, and notwithstanding the exact possibilities and nature of positive law in an elastic domain, the dust started to settle somewhat, and turbulence gave way to tranquility, although we may object to the idea that the process has exited the stage of turbulence. The objection originates from the appearances of close to pure forms of good and evil speech in the digital domain in communication and preventive and/or supportive policies. For instance, the design to allow only positive reflections through the function of 'likes', or the function of reporting postings which are not illegal but merely *disturbing*, is a revelation of the function that expects only good speech. And from the other side, concerns over hate speech, entrapment or deceit via digital solutions, various revenge applications, problematic adolescent usage of the Internet in general – these all exhibit features of evilness. Since such co-existence of extreme formats of speech has existed since the formation of social media platforms and internet communication channels, it may be considered one of the main specific features of freedom of speech online. Non-coherence regarding extreme formats of speech and their frequency is apparently a feature of objective and longitudinal nature.

When we can show, or have to accept, that the digital network is legitimate, constituting a variety of interconnected public and private entities, it does not necessarily follow that the normative structures which this network can produce are legitimate through the eyes of the onlooker from the non-digital space. And here an additional layer of argumentation may be needed. This would mean that network validity cannot be transposed directly to normative validity, but it has to be reflected back to the non-digital domain, and from there digital normative validity can be justified. Now, non-coherence tells us that legitimacy appears as a concept which cannot be transposed or delegated.

The main non-coherent aspect in transparency between the non-digital and digital domains lies in a simple statement that transparency towards both the Objective and Subjective sides are possible in the non-digital domain but only towards the former, the Objective, in the digital domain. Non-digital transparency is multilayered, but digital transparency is uni-layered.

It turns out that the digital transparency of someone or something is actually the result of the opposite: concealing some features, exaggerating or downplaying. Here offline transparency turns into non-transparency, which is a phenomenon of non-coherence between these two domains. Here transparency does not represent Objectivity as separate from Subjectivity but Subjectivity turned into digital Objectivity.

The previous leads to an interim conclusion. When an item to be transposed from offline to online is unclear, then the image reflected online will be further obscured. The higher the degree of the non-specificity of a human rights idea or concept offline, the more it is possible for a different domain to give the idea or concept a content with variance. This leads us to conclude that, because the meaning of transparency is vague in the offline domain, such vagueness is carried over to the digital domain with a multiplying effect.

There must exist a constant which is independent of the concrete distance between human rights concepts and ideas between the digital and non-digital domain since such distance, or the degree of variance, is relative and determined to a large extent by practice and discourse. This constant is the assumption of non-coherence, which is to say that non-coherence is an omnipresent feature characterising the comparison of human rights between paradigmatically different domains.

But in any event, the image of transparency as defined in the offline domain remains distorted online. This also means that the logic of human rights doctrinal development offline does not apply online. A distorted human rights image can only be justified through an overly simplified approach, which in turn is non-coherent with the depth of argumentation usually expected for offline human rights ideas, rules and principles.

The non-coherence between the two domains where human rights are known to exist appears in opposite directions on different layers. Expressing the following at a highly general level, which does not take into account nuances – when we can deem the physical realm to be non-transparent regarding facts and transparent regarding the process for how judicial or quasi-judicial or political decisions are taken about these facts, including some transparency about the reasons for such decisions, we see the reverse in the digital domain. This domain can provide transparency regarding facts and non-transparency regarding the process of how quasi-judicial decisions are taken about these facts, while also excluding insights into the reasons for these decisions.

Han asserts that positivity means no tolerance towards negative feelings, a lack of sensitivity towards confidentiality, proliferation and propagation instead of a search for the truth, and briefly, presenting reality in a distorted light. The supporter of this philosophical approach can quickly conclude that transparency in human rights law serves the goal of positivity enhancement. Yet non-coherence has a magnifying effect on value judgments connected with human rights ideas or principles when these are transposed from one paradigm to another. This means that the positivity associated with transparency also increases in the digital domain. Since the digital space enables close to complete transparency, and the perpetuation of the transparency through data storage and *not forgetting*, it could be said that human rights law measures in the digital domain enable as high a transparency as possible, and have to be given a *quality* label. This in turn also means that almost anything which the private domain puts forward as self-normativity, and any practice implemented to enhance transparency, would without hesitancy be viewed as positive features. Digital transparency here becomes a shield against criticisms of self-normativity and unaccountability. As such, it appears quite close to the contemporary concept of non-digital transparency, as it seems that many policy decisions and rules are justified as if being in the service of transparency.

The objections against the positivity of the transparency raised in the non-digital domain lead us likewise to a magnified image of negativity in the digital domain. In other words, a proponent of Han's assertion claiming negativity would see that such negativity grows upon transposition. Then it becomes questionable whether transparency, when dominated by negativity, corresponds any longer to the original meaning of transparency as we are used to from the traditional human rights discourse. According to the non-coherence approach, when a concept from the physical realm is transposed into the digital domain and non-coherence becomes wide, its core meaning changes. Therefore, it is already exhibiting features where the connection to its meaning before transposition is weakened to the point that one can speak of a break. The higher the degree of supposed transparency and openness in the digital domain, the stronger the immanence that many features remain hidden. In the conditions of ideal transparency, the term loses its meaning, and so it can only be defined in combination with the opposite. Complete or close to complete transparency has to mean simultaneous existence of complete or close to complete non-transparency. This is not difficult to explain, since digital transparency reflects a combination of how we wish to be seen against what we wish to hide. We can put it differently and say that since the immanent feature of complete digital transparency is positivity on the surface, there is also non-transparent negativity beyond the surface, or behind the mirror.

Building on the problem of correlation between legal certainty and argumentation, it can be said that since argumentation stands as an inherent element of certainty, at one point its scarcity makes the concept empty. In this case, an alternative concept would be more appropriate. Since the digital domain is dominated by mathematics-driven solutions, predictability seems more precisely to characterise a function in the digital domain which legal certainty performs in the non-digital domain. This concerns the possibility to foresee people's behaviour and quasi-judicial or judicial decisions as a reaction to such behaviour. The difference between legal certainty and predictability is manifold. To start with, legal certainty entails both normative and descriptive elements, whereas predictability only the latter.

Doubts can be raised whether amidst the abundant literature, decisions and policy documents such a distinction can be justified. As a sceptic of non-coherence theory and proponent of the sameness doctrine might assert, perhaps these two terms have largely overlapping meaning and which of them is chosen is not a deliberate choice so much as a matter of habit. Still, for the reader of academic literature and media postings, examining the discourse of IT law and social media communication models reveals the dominant usage of the term *predictability*, whereas the term *certainty* is almost non-existent. This is the voice from practice.

Here we can think that such a transposition leads to the appearance of justice and legal certainty with a meaning at variance. Justice achieved through online predictable content assessment is not the same justice achieved via judicial assessment following the principle of legal certainty.

The principle of legal certainty transforms into predictability upon transposition from the non-digital to the digital domain. The variance is wide; the image of legal certainty becomes heavily distorted in the digital mirror. Because predictability loses its connection to qualitative standards, it is unilayered instead of multilayered, and devoid of argumentation. The only commonality between legal certainty and predictability appears through the immunity to time thesis, and this is the main straw allowing us to speak of non-coherence since at least some common elements need to exist.

All of this demonstrates that non-coherence is to be assumed in the transposition of normative ideas and rules from one well-established normative domain to another. Here we observed a specific phenomenon of non-coherence, which is simplification and a shift towards thinness because predictability can by and large be considered legal certainty without qualitative elements, such as the ideas of justice or equality. Yet another feature of non-coherence theory is its neutrality towards the transformed images of human rights in the digital domain. This theory is not a tool for quality control or the qualitative assessment of ideas before and after transformation. It merely alerts us to the non-coherence assumption. Now, can we accept that the non-coherent image reflects a normative system where some or most elements stand outside a certain system of values. Critical questions can be asked – even if such a system were to contradict the value system of the viewer towards the distorted image. Or even if we were not able to comprehend the features of a hierarchical system which we are accustomed to term as a value system. Does wide non-coherence mean weakening a value-based normative system? There always remains the option to say that the absence of a value system is valuable by itself.

The offline model of thinking about a conflict between legal certainty and justice in the digital domain becomes arbitrary, and therefore irrational since the elements of certainty and justice are non-coherent in comparison with the original meaning of the model's elements. The question to be approached with hesitancy is that, after realising that the concept of legal certainty is at variance between the digital and non-digital domains, is there any assurance – dogmatic or practice-driven – that the idea of justice likewise does not appear at variance? Because if no such assurance can be given, all stands against relativity have fallen.

Since the terms of service are usually generally worded, and since possible negative consequences from using the digital domain remain distant, and since the perceived benefits of using the digital space are immediate as opposed to a threat of any negative consequences, and since there is a perception of arbitrariness in user content assessment in any event, a thesis of non-foreseeability by default can be advanced.

By the time this monograph is published, it is possible that new technical options via the metaverse will have vigorously emerged, where the goal of allowing people to build their own universe simultaneously carries the aspect of creating their own rules. The self-creation of rules gives someone close to absolute control of the space and foreseeability about what her own actions or those of others in the self-created room may lead to. The only unknown factor is the subjectivity of the one who creates her own rules for the metaverse space open for others to use. Such a solution does not presuppose rules and principles articulated somewhere in physical and non-physical human rights paradigms, and as such user behaviour 'at any meaningful scale is practically impossible'. Here a paradox emerges that what seems close to absolutely foreseeable for an individual user, is reflected as close to completely non-foreseeable in the image for outsiders. This prediction undoubtedly raises the concern about whether the concept of foreseeability makes any sense in the future of the digital domain.

My observations and discussions with researchers and practitioners in the field reveal the endemic absence of the specification of human rights goals from e-state strategy and practice. The new concepts of human rights by design and human rights by default, when applied to human rights protection mechanisms in vertical digital relations, are indicative of how human rights are engraved in e-state strategy and solutions as a general idea. That is, they were not part of the e-state philosophy in the first place, nor present in the initial designs. It is much easier to add a rhetorical component than to change the software since we would only then be dealing with labelling. Perhaps the expression of human-rights-washing can be introduced here. The problem originating from this caveat is the strong possibility that, when making further choices about the development of e-state principles and practical solutions, regard for human rights simply is not a relevant criterion for assessing the justifiability of the proposed measures. The main fundamental rights concern for e-statehood is whether the e-state solutions by themselves have secret doors enabling the arbitrary usage of data, which is a matter concerning the following caveat. The previous leads us to advance the hypothesis that fundamental rights are non-essential for justifying nor realising e-state solutions. Another way to formulate the same idea is to suggest that the e-state does not need fundamental rights, or even more bluntly – fundamental rights disturb the development of the e-state.

Yet there is a view from judges that business as usual continues. This is, for instance, represented by Spano when discussing the approaches of the Strasbourg Court towards user comments online. Yet it even transpires from his writing that the criteria established for offline freedom of expression assessment are not transposed unchanged to the online domain, since the element of economic interest has been added. We can call Spano's approach resistance to the idea of non-coherence. But it would be resistance to an objective dichotomy between the digital and non-digital domains. Even the Strasbourg judges would have to recognise that there is some degree of non-coherence, if just to take the elements of time and economic interest, which amounts at least to a minor transformation of the offline standards.

The question of whether the idea of proportionality as we know it from the offline domain is transposable without variance to the online domain remains under contestation. By itself such a contestation shows non-coherence, as there are important elements calling some to doubt transposability without variance as a minimum, and as a maximum whether proportionality makes sense online at all. To understand the nature of non-coherence, it is necessary to state here that contestation means an unclear reflection of an offline human right idea or concept in the online domain. Such a lack of clarity means non-coherence. Yet non-coherence is not a constant, and can change in time. The variance between human rights ideas or concepts between the two domains can fluctuate by narrowing or broadening, which is then also reflected in the non-coherence becoming wider or narrower. When the images approach one another through discourse and practice, this usually means that in both domains the respective idea or concept gives up some of its initial characteristics and adopts something from the other domain.

As a matter of fact, contestation can lead to the disappearance of non-coherence for two reasons. The first is when the digital domain absorbs entirely the meaning given to a concept or idea offline. This would be a case of transposition without variance. The sameness of rights rests on this approach. The opposite happens when it becomes obvious beyond argumentative possibilities that the meaning and function given to a human rights idea, or concept or rule in the digital domain is entirely incompatible with its offline origin. Again, not too many examples can be construed. Possibly the right to know the reasons for decisions affecting the data subject can serve as an illustration. Since the digital domain, due to the absence of the capabilities for such individual reasons, cannot furnish the data subject with reasons of a scope that is comparable with the non-digital domain, there is nothing to contest against this objective impediment.

The proposition of turning unfair normativity into a fair judicial or quasi-judicial outcome cannot be validated for the digital domain, where automated solutions or artificial intelligence are allowed to make decisions. This is because of two reasons. The first is because of a phenomenon which is primarily intuitionistic and asserts that the concept of trust in the digital domain has a blind eye towards the question of normative fairness. This is related to the objection from Radbruch's disavowal formula. Digital domain operators – automated systems and artificial intelligence – take for granted the positive features of positive or quasi-positive rules. Judges refusing to apply a legal norm which would lead to an extremely unfair outcome do so because they can exercise distrust in the law. Artificial intelligence and automated systems, on the other hand, are designed to trust the law. To put it figuratively, the degree of our trust in physical judges is related to our expectation that they are capable of distrusting the law. Likewise, our trust of automated systems and artificial intelligence is weaker because we assume that they completely trust the law.

It could be said that we cannot find a better positivist than artificial intelligence. We see here wide non-coherence between the element of trust due to capabilities. At the moment, when artificial intelligence can independently exercise disavowal and intolerability formulas, that is, articulate a reasoned understanding that a specific legal norm or rule is profoundly unfair, then the non-coherence disappears because the artificial intelligence has assumed properties comparable to human mind. Yet then we would not deal with artificial intelligence anymore, perhaps we could term such a decision-maker an artificial brain. Based on what we know at the time this monograph is being written, trust in the assessment of fairness of legal and quasi-legal rules is at wide variance between human decision-makers and artificial intelligence.

Here reference is made to the basic human rights norms which stand at the bottom of any legal structure and have their origin from outside of such a legal structure. Since the whole human rights physical realm is conditional on the existence and acceptance of some basic ideas, the question arises of how in ideal discursive conditions these basic ideas can be replaced or transformed. We have built the non-coherence theory upon the thesis that ideas, rules and concepts from the non-digital domain are transposed into the digital domain and may undergo transformation. Yet for non-coherence to make sense, at least some link to properties offline which do not transform upon transposition needs to be retained. Because if all features between digital and non-digital domains are at variance, then the point of comparison disappears. We could therefore ask whether trust in offline decision-makers also includes the hypothetical acceptance of the change in the basic norm. Or from the other perspective, that this trust entails the opposite, namely that the basic norm(s) will not be touched in judicial decision-making processes. Various views can be expressed on this matter. The non-coherence theory says that AI and automated decision-makers have no capability to challenge basic norms. This proposition excludes contestation, and as such already stands at variance from the offline domain where the matter of who can alter the basic norms and how is a valid theoretical and practical question. If they, AI and automated systems, had the capability to alter the basic norm, then the digital and non-digital domains would be completely different, despite how the words and expressions appear on the surface.

All this leads us to question whether AI solutions and automated decision-making tools can operate in a vacuum of core human rights principles. In other words, whether during the transposition of human rights–specific rules and principles with relatively high concreteness necessary to create some normative framework for AI operations, basic norms legitimising these specific rules and concrete principles were left behind. These simply were not transposed. A question of broader scope than that which is only related to the digital domain emerges. This is whether one can construe a normative system of rules and principles where there are no fundamental values specified, even if these are at the stage of contestation, or that the basic norms have not been determined.

Among specific fundamental rights, the overarching question is about the right of access to the Internet. Frequently, the matter of whether access to the Internet should be recognised as a new independent human right has been raised. There is, of course, considerable debate on the topic. In this monograph, the question is translatable to whether this right entails an aspect of having the entitlement to let go of the meaning of rights in the non-digital domain. A side effect of this entitlement is the right to dual identities and *anything goes*. I have defended these entitlements in the book. One cannot exclude that the popularity of the Internet and prediction of high fascination with Meta is partially explainable by the tiredness of just one identity.

Index

For EU product safety concerns, contact us at Calle de José Abascal, 56–1°, 28003 Madrid, Spain or eugpsr@cambridge.org.

www.ingramcontent.com/pod-product-compliance
Lightning Source LLC
LaVergne TN
LVHW011705200926
848484LV00004B/1073
* 9 7 8 1 0 0 9 4 0 7 7 0 0 *